P9-DFH-996

IN THE TIME OF THE TYRANTS

IN THE TIME OF THE TYRANTS

PANAMA: 1968–1990

R. M. KOSTER
and
GUILLERMO SÁNCHEZ

W · W · NORTON & COMPANY
NEW YORK LONDON

Printed in the United States of America.

The text of this book is composed in Times Roman,
with the display set in Futura Display.
Composition and manufacturing by the Haddon Craftsmen Inc.
Book design by Jacques Chazaud.

First Edition.

Library of Congress Cataloging in Publication Data

Koster, R. M., 1934–
In the time of the tyrants: Panama, 1968–1990 / R. M. Koster and Guillermo Sánchez.
p. cm.
1. Panama—Politics and government—1946–1981. 2. Panama—Politics and government—1981– 3. Noriega, Manuel Antonio, 1934–
4. Torrijos Herrera, Omar, 1926– 5. Corruption (in politics)—Panama. 6. Heads of state—Panama. I. Sánchez Borbón, Guillermo, 1924– . II. Title.
F1567.K67, 1990
972.8705—dc20 90–33311

ISBN 0–393–02696–5

W.W. Norton & Company, Inc., 500 Fifth Avenue, New York, N.Y. 10110
W.W. Norton & Company, Ltd., 37 Great Russell Street, London WC1B 3NU

1 2 3 4 5 6 7 8 9 0

Para Otilita que lo compartió,
y para el pueblo que lo sufrió

Coscïenza fusca
O de la propria o de l'altrui vergogna
Pur sentirà la tua parola brusca.
Ma nondimen, rimossa ogne menzogna,
Tutta tua visïon fa manifesta,
E lascia pur grattar dov´ è la rogna!

A conscience uneasy
Because of its own or someone else's shame
Might find your words harsh.
But nonetheless avoid all falsehood,
Your entire vision was manifest,
So let them scratch where it itches!
—*Paradiso*, xvii, 124–29

From the record of a Hearing to Receive Testimony on
Drugs, Law Enforcement and Foreign Policy: Panama
Wednesday, February 10, 1988

U.S. Senate
Committee on Foreign Relations
Subcommittee on Terrorism, Narcotics
and International Operations
Washington, D.C.

Testimony of Floyd Carlton Caceres, personal pilot to Generals Omar Torrijos and Manuel Noriega and convicted drug trafficker:

Senator Kerry: You know the country, you know the region, you have traveled, you have been involved in drugs and arms smuggling. You have seen friends of yours murdered and killed, and here you are wearing a hood, under federal protection. . . . What has happened in Panama?

Mr. Carlton: I will try to be brief in answering your question.

Panama's problems were the result of a military coup. Starting with General Torrijos, ties were formed with drug trafficking. . . . Starting with the military coup in 1968. . . . All the money generated by drug trafficking, kidnappings, assassinations came to banks in Panama. . . . You have corruption, drug trafficking, gun dealings, assassinations. That is the political history my country is living.

CONTENTS

ACKNOWLEDGMENTS

Many people helped us write this book, furnished us memories, documents, press clippings—far too many for us to mention by name. We are grateful to them. We owe special debts of gratitude, however, to Doña Rosario Arias de Galindo, who collected stacks and stacks of documents and old newspapers and shipped them to Guillermo Sánchez in Miami—work that exile prevented him from doing, and without which this book could not have been written—and to the Centro de Investigaciones de Derechos Humanos y Socorro Jurídico, which furnished us material developed from denunciations of human rights violations. R. M. Koster is grateful to the Florida State University, and to its president, Dr. Bernard Sliger, for sabbatical leave during January–May 1989.

NOTE

Many people who live south of the Rio Grande resent it when U.S. citizens are called "Americans," for everyone else in the hemisphere is also American, from Baffin Islanders to Patagonians. Many women resent it when a single masculine pronoun is used in a situation where "he and she," "his/hers," or something similar might be more accurate. We hereby beg everyone's pardon and announce that we mean to use the simpler, more common forms—neither in ignorance nor, surely, in arrogance but in consonance with euphony and usage.

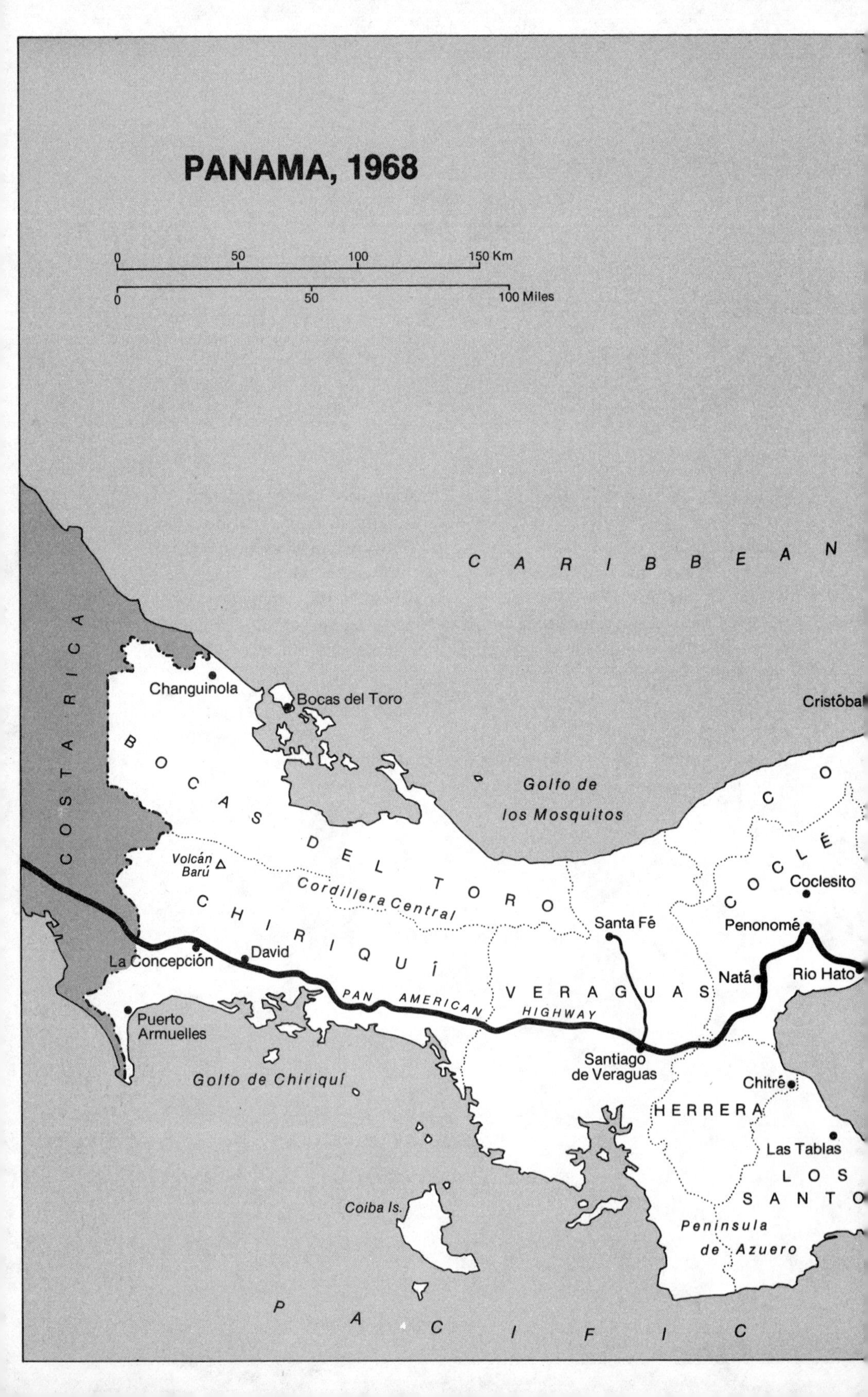
PANAMA, 1968
0
50
100
150 Km
0
50
100 Miles
C A R I B B E A N
COSTA RICA
Changuinola
Bocas del Toro
Cristóba
BOCAS DEL TORO
Golfo de
los Mosquitos
Volcán
Barú
Cordillera Central
CHIRIQUÍ
COCLÉ
Coclesito
Santa Fé
Penonomé
La Concepción
David
Natá
Rio Hato
PAN AMERICAN HIGHWAY
VERAGUAS
Puerto
Armuelles
Santiago
de Veraguas
Golfo de Chiriquí
Chitré
HERRERA
Las Tablas
LOS
SANTO
Coiba Is.
Peninsula
de Azuero
P A C I F I C

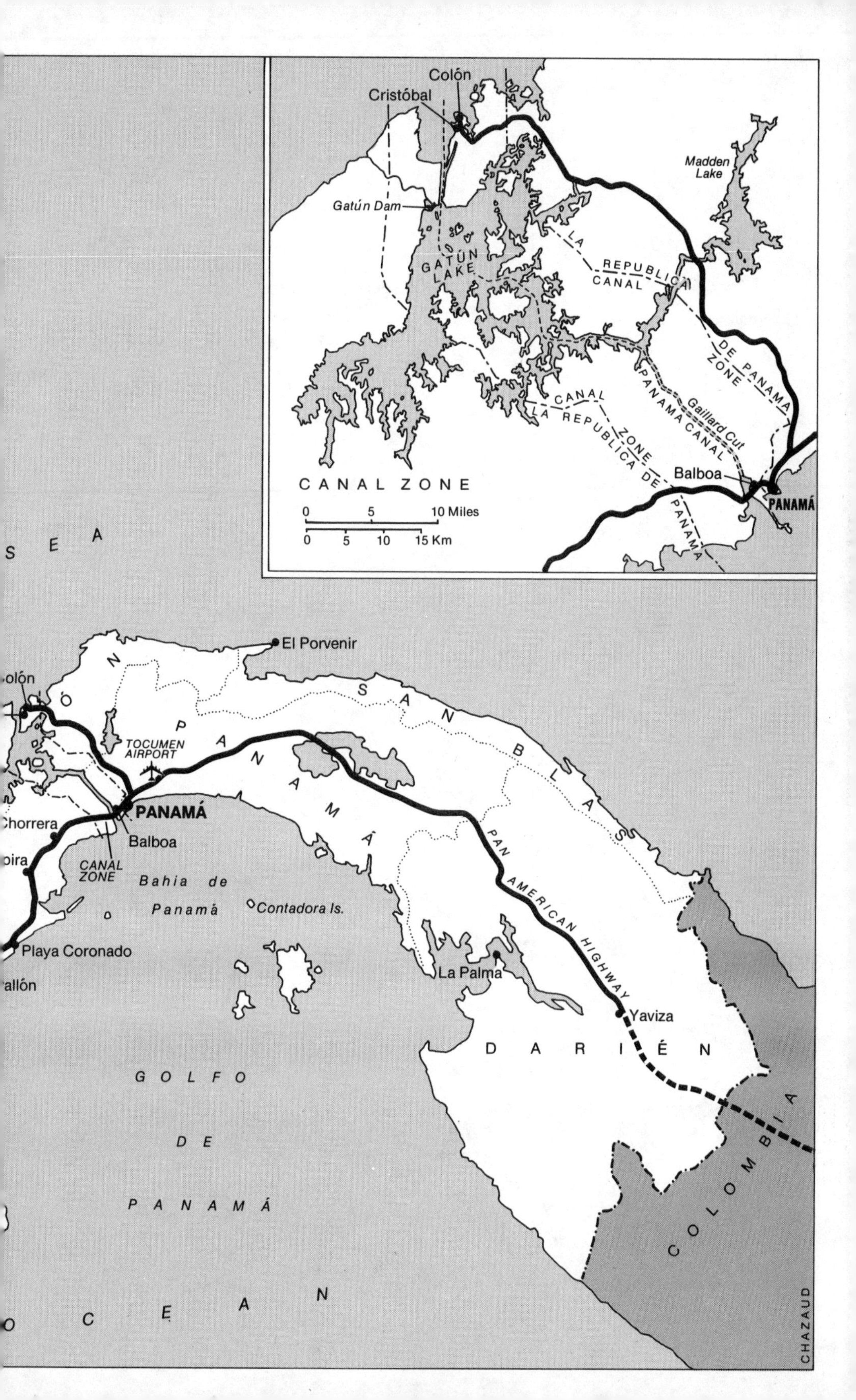
Colón
Cristóbal
Madden Lake
Gatún Dam
GATÚN LAKE
LA REPUBLICA DE PANAMA
CANAL ZONE
PANAMA CANAL
Gaillard Cut
CANAL ZONE
LA REPUBLICA DE PANAMA
Balboa
PANAMÁ
CANAL ZONE
0 5 10 Miles
0 5 10 15 Km
SEA
El Porvenir
SAN BLAS
PANAMÁ
TOCUMEN AIRPORT
PANAMÁ
Chorrera
Balboa
CANAL ZONE
Bahia de Panamá
Contadora Is.
Playa Coronado
PAN AMERICAN HIGHWAY
La Palma
Yaviza
DARIÉN
COLOMBIA
GOLFO DE PANAMÁ
OCEAN
CHAZAUD

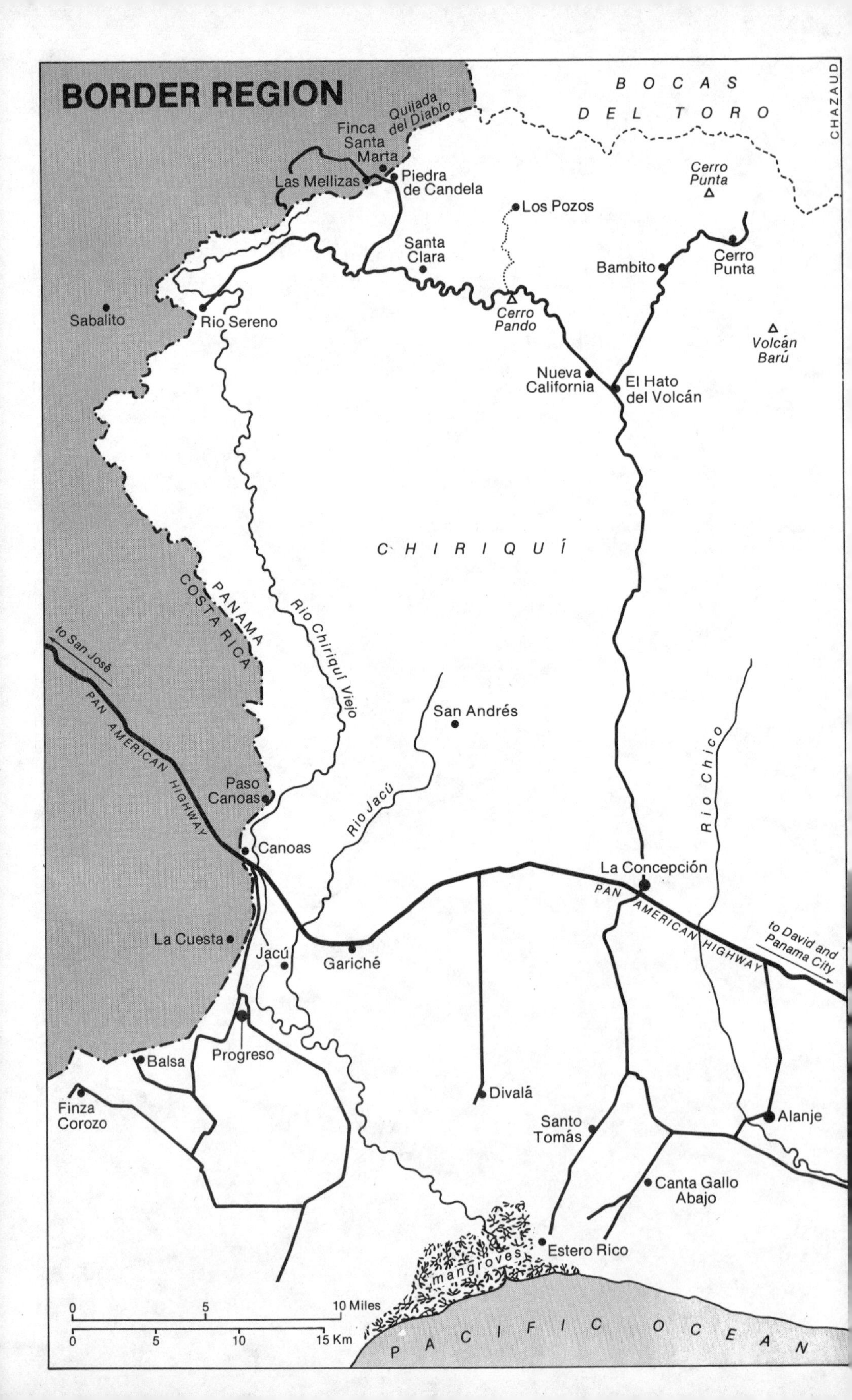
BORDER REGION
BOCAS
DEL TORO
CHAZAUD
Quijada del Diablo
Finca Santa Marta
Piedra de Candela
Las Mellizas
Los Pozos
Cerro Punta
Santa Clara
Bambito
Cerro Punta
Sabalito
Rio Sereno
Cerro Pando
Volcán Barú
Nueva California
El Hato del Volcán
CHIRIQUÍ
PANAMA
COSTA RICA
Rio Chiriquí Viejo
to San José
PAN AMERICAN HIGHWAY
San Andrés
Rio Chico
Paso Canoas
Rio Jacú
Canoas
La Concepción
PAN AMERICAN HIGHWAY
to David and Panama City
La Cuesta
Jacú
Gariché
Progreso
Balsa
Divalá
Finza Corozo
Alanje
Santo Tomás
Canta Gallo Abajo
Estero Rico
mangroves
0 5 10 Miles
0 5 10 15 Km
PACIFIC OCEAN

IN THE TIME OF THE TYRANTS

1

THE DEATH AND POSTHUMOUS VENGEANCE OF HUGO SPADAFORA

"Anything—anything can be done in this country."

—JOSEPH CONRAD, *Heart of Darkness*

On the day they were going to kill him—Friday the thirteenth of September 1985—Dr. Hugo Spadafora got up at six in the morning to do his yoga. Later, after his shower, he put on a long-sleeved striped shirt and coffee-colored trousers and had breakfast with his wife, Ariadne. Then he packed a bag, a canvas sports bag, including his diary (it was book sized, bound in vinyl, with a page for each day, the sort professionals keep for noting appointments) and some copies of the memoirs he'd published in 1980. He'd been living in San José, Costa Rica, and commuting to the contras' war in Nicaragua, but today he was going home for a visit to Panama.

He was then in his forty-sixth year and fourth revolution. At twenty-five, when other graduates of the Faculty of Medicine in Bologna, Italy, were thinking of setting up practice and getting ahead, he joined the struggle for independence in Portuguese Guinea (now Guinea-Bissau) and served two years as a *guerrillero* medic. Next came the bogus revolution in Panama proclaimed when the military seized power in October 1968. Hugo opposed it at first, treated the bullet wound of a young man wounded in a shoot-out with soldiers, for which he spent a while in prison. Later he joined, seduced by Omar Torrijos's populist rhetoric. For a time, he was vice-minister of public health. Then, in 1978, disillusioned by the corruption around him, he raised a force of volunteers and went off to Nicaragua to fight Somoza, staying on until after the fall of Managua. By 1981, he was with the contras—a restless man, operatically handsome, haunted by compassion for the downtrodden and the lust to have a cause, to be in action.

Now he was disillusioned again, and simultaneously drawn to a new adventure. Earlier in the month, he'd met with officers of the Drug Enforcement Administration (DEA) in the U.S. embassy on Calle Primera in San José to give information about contra drug dealings with Panama's current dictator, General Manuel Noriega. He'd already accused Noriega publicly of being a tyrant as well as a trafficker in drugs, and in August announced his intention to return to Panama and get back into politics. As he put it to a friend, he was "going to set off a bomb." He'd fought for freedom in two foreign countries. Now he meant to do so at home. The trip he was making that day was preparatory to a permanent relocation.

The route he chose was somewhat circuitous: light plane from San José to a rural airstrip; taxi eight miles from there to the frontier; minibus from Paso Canoa on the Panamanian side to David, the capital of Chiriquí Province; long-haul bus from David to Panama City. This was a precaution of sorts but not an effective one: he'd gone the same way several times before. And anyway, caution wasn't his method. His brother Winston remembers him at age ten, taking a dare and jumping from the bridge over Río La Villa, something no other boy in the town of Chitré would do. His life thereafter demonstrated the same attitude. He wasn't fearless. He simply didn't let fear affect his behavior. He left his house around nine. A little before noon he crossed into Panama.

Into Panama. The words have taken on a sinister resonance. Once a fortunate country, Panama had become a place of darkness. First it fell among thieves. Then it came into the clutch of an interesting monster.

General Manuel Noriega was then fifty-one, though he claimed to be five years younger. Short and stocky, tense of stance and gesture, his pudgy chin usually lifted pugnaciously, his corrugated cheeks often bulged in lewd smirks, he looked contemptibly clownish, not truly evil, a cartoon demon or a B-movie gangster, Edward G. Robinson imitating himself. But when his features slacked in rage or hatred, and a flat glassy stare froze his small eyes, he showed what he was, one of earth's most noxious inhabitants. He was a premier trafficker in drugs and weapons with a personal fortune of perhaps a billion dollars. He was absolute master of Panama, could have anything he chose done to anybody. And he was personally swinish as well as by proxy. While a lieutenant, he raped a thirteen-year-old and brutally beat up her twelve-year-old brother. He was in charge when a dissident priest, Father Héctor Gallego, was tossed to his death from a helicopter in 1971. And when the adolescent son of a prominent jeweler was caught scribbling antiregime graffiti, Noriega himself applied the electrodes to the boy's testicles and whooped with joy at each shriek and convulsion.

No one knows who his father was. His mother died a day or two after he was born. He was raised by a friend of hers, Luisa Sánchez (no kin), in a slum near the public market in Panama City. At fourteen, he was seduced by an older man. So, begin with a deep insecurity. His mother abandoned him; that she died makes no difference. And a desperate longing for love, hence his bisexuality, trying to buy love with sexual favors. Add self-loathing and the contempt of others, for while the weird code of Latin machismo extols the penetrator as manly no matter what he penetrates—woman, man, beast, melon, whatever—it reviles the penetratee without mercy. Insecurity breeds an unslakable thirst for power. Self-loathing eases the guilt power seeking brings on. Catamite and rapist in one person, each perversion balancing the other. And, finally, great strength of will and wits, or the penniless urchin scarcely survives, much less becomes the billionaire despot.

Still, he wasn't wholly disadvantaged. Like Hugo Spadafora some years after him, he attended the Instituto Nacional, Panama's best public high school. Later on, his classmates recalled his having a gift for words, and his being much less ugly than he became. He wanted to study medicine and practice psychiatry, a common ambition in the tormented, but couldn't afford it and worked as a lab assistant. Then his elder half-brother, Luis Carlos, a clerk in the Ministry of Foreign Relations, learned of a scholarship Peru was offering to its military academy. The minister, Aquilino Boyd, agreed to let Manuel Antonio have it. He was over the age limit the Peruvian army established, but that was no problem. Luis Carlos falsified a birth certificate; Boyd authenticated the falsification; young Noriega went off to Los Chorrillos.

A stern place, even by soldier's standards, as Mario Vargas Llosa, who attended it, conveys in his novel *La Ciudad y los Perros.* The Latin-American military have no real function. There follows an exaggerated emphasis on form, harsh discipline that nurtures and refines sadomasochistic tendencies. In 1960, Cadet Noriega was detained by police in Lima for raping and savagely beating a prostitute—the first sign of the Noriega the world came to know later. Also, while in Peru, he became an informant for the CIA.

On graduating, he returned to Panama and was commissioned in Panama's sole armed force, the Guardia Nacional, then somewhat between a police force and an army. In 1966, he was assigned to the Fifth Military District in Chiriquí Province when the incident with the thirteen-year-old occurred. His commanding officer, a major named Omar Torrijos, saved him. Torrijos also made him district intelligence officer, with the task of keeping an eye on the banana workers' union at United Fruit's plantations. These duties enhanced Noriega's value as a CIA "asset," and CIA connections advanced his career.

In 1968, the Guardia took power. Panama suffered invasion from within. In Chiriquí, there was resistance. Noriega pacified the province, was an enthusiastic torturer of prisoners, a conscientious terrorizer of the populace. In December 1969, he helped the rapist's friend Omar Torrijos (by then commandant of the Guardia and tyrant of Panama) survive a putsch. Torrijos made him his bagman and familiar fiend, referred appreciatively to him as *mi gangster.*

By 1972, he was in the capital, a lieutenant colonel and chief of intelligence. *Panamanian* intelligence, while working for the CIA and running errands for Fidel Castro. That's what made Noriega unique, his cynicism, his chutzpah. And his business sense, of course. He began as Torrijos's bagman but far surpassed his patron quickly enough. The Guardia general staff was a gang of extortionists, its administration little more than a squeeze, but Noriega was superthief. He had his nose in all sorts of rackets. In short, his range. Had he lived in Dante's time, the poet would have had to chop his ghost into nuggets and put one in every subpit of hell to do Noriega's versatility justice.

In 1981, Torrijos was killed in a plane crash. Command of the Guardia passed to Florencio Flórez. Who was betrayed by Rubén Paredes. Who was betrayed by Manuel Noriega. For years, Noriega had lurked like a rat in the wainscoting. In August 1983, he emerged—duped Paredes into retirement, promoted himself general, took over as commandant, renamed the Guardia Nacional the Panama Defense Forces (PDF). Then he flew off to Washington to help Bill Casey help George Shultz pick Panama's next puppet president, the fig leaf of ersatz democracy that squeamish Uncle Same absolutely required to hide the gross facts of military tyranny in its client state Panama.

The choice was a former student of Shultz's named Nicolás Barletta. His excellent English made him marketable in the United States. Meantime, his quislinghood seemed beyond question. He'd spent years as chief of economic planning dreaming up cover stories for the Guardia's looting. He lost the election in May 1984, but that was no matter. Noriega had a goon squad at hand to break up the counting procedure and fire on those who protested while uniformed soldiers watched, smiling. The body count was four dead and forty-odd wounded, but a doctored count gave Barletta a 1,700-vote victory. The president of the electoral tribunal resigned in protest, but not before the U.S. ambassador to Panama, Everett Briggs, had publicly congratulated him on the purity of the proceedings. Meanwhile, other U.S. friends of General Noriega's arranged for him to speak at the John F. Kennedy Institute at Harvard on the role of the new military in the defense of freedom in Central America—which, presumably, was to falsify elections and drop irksome priests out of helicopters.

That September, Noriega was at the height of his power. During his long tenure as chief of intelligence, he had established links to other services, many (as the CIA seems to be) states within states that follow their own agendas and pay but slender allegiance to the governments that nominally control them. He had ties to Washington and to Havana, to Israel and the PLO, and as one of the world's major criminals he was in touch with the lords of drug and arms smuggling. At all points of the ideological spectrum, in criminal and law enforcement organizations, there were powerful men who had dealt with Manuel Noriega, who owed him favors. If you were ruthless and liked to maneuver in secret, if you thought decency weakness and had contempt for human rights, Manuel Noriega was your man.

He was still on the CIA's payroll, but far from being its pawn, he could do as he cared to. The people at Langley were no match for him. The more flagrantly he betrayed them, the more secure he became, since unmasking him would be that much more of an embarrassment. And he knew things the American people were not meant to learn of. He had become the Reagan administration's accomplice in a criminal conspiracy.

We have all seen the movie where the kindly granny with the cute little lapdog is really a colonel in the KGB, where the distinguished philanthropist with the white mane and the Continental manners is in fact the Gestapo's man in Rio. We the audience know, but the hero doesn't. When Dr. Hugo Spadafora revealed details of contra drug dealing in the U.S. embassy in Costa Rica, he may have surprised the men he talked to, but at certain levels of the U.S. government his information wasn't news. Since 1983, when Congress had passed strictures against helping the contras' war in Nicaragua, U.S. support for them had proceeded illegally, with Noriega a key man in the scheme. As extra compensation, moreover, he had the gall to load cocaine on the supply planes when they flew back from Central America to Texas. U.S. authorities found out, but they could do nothing without exposing the illegal weapons airlift. After 1984, contra supply was funded in part by the cocaine barons. The U.S. government was allowing and abetting the smuggling of illegal drugs across U.S. borders in order to pursue an illegal war, so when Hugo Spadafora "revealed" what looked to him like contra drug dealings, he was just as naive as the nudnick in the movie. The difference was that his show had no happy ending. His "revelations" were liable to expose the arms airlift, the cocaine angle, the whole filthy business. The minute he opened his mouth, he was a corpse. All sorts of people needed him dead, and Manuel Noriega was delighted to oblige.

He was at the height of his power, and yet driven. A bottomless insecurity, a fearful self-loathing, a terrible envy. There are the motives for Noriega's delight to oblige. Spadafora was brave and could instill courage in others, was qualified both by talent and experience to mount and lead a *guerrilla* in Panama. Spadafora was a physician, a healer. Noriega had wished to be but missed the chance and became instead a destroyer and torturer. Spadafora was handsome. Noriega was, in the kindest term, grotesque. And Spadafora had the "daily beauty in his life" that Iago envied, the gift of health, the gift of enthusiasm, the capacity to care for things outside himself. Noriega, on the other hand . . . Noriega could have been Iago's twin.

In sum, a conquered country, a subject people, a brutal and corrupt occupying force, and a perverted tyrant with Washington's blessing, with no restraints whatsoever on the gratification of his several lusts. This was the Panama that Hugo crossed into.

He had lunch in Paso Canoa, a rabbit stew with rice and potato salad at a place called Los Mellos, a shack with tables beside it under a metal roof set up on posts, behind the bus station a few yards from the border. The owner, Iván García, remembers. More important, he remembered later that month, when Panamanian authorities were maintaining that Spadafora never crossed the border, when other witnesses were intimidated. García, whose friends call him El Guapo (Gutsy), did honor to his nickname by coming forward. Yes, Hugo was in Panama. Hugo lunched at his café. Hugo ate quickly, was in a hurry to get to the capital. He was supposed to meet his wife at the airport when she flew in from San José, but had time to give García an inscribed copy of his memoirs.

At 12:15, he got on a green-and-white Toyota Coaster model diesel minibus of the David–Frontera line, plate number 4B-52, driven by Alexis Baúles with Edwin Núñez as his assistant. A man in dark glasses got on behind him, a chunky man with Indian features and skin the color of mahogany. This was Francisco Eliécer González, a sergeant in the Defense Forces and an agent of the G-2, Panama's secret police. He had on dark trousers and a black sleeveless jersey and a cream-colored corduroy cap with little buckles on the sides. He knew some karate and had a violent nature and for these traits went by the nickname Bruce Lee.

Hugo put his bag on the rack above the bus windows and took a seat toward the front on the right-hand side. He will have looked straight at González as he leaned back, will have "made" him as G-2 the instant he saw him (all are recognizable by their inimitable loutishness), but will not have felt any anxiety. He was used to being shadowed by Noriega's goons. González sprawled in a seat on the left, one or two rows behind him. Even as he did so, the bus pulled out.

From the border to David, the Inter-American Highway runs roughly southeast, two lanes of light gray pavement unwinding in long straightaways through brush country. The land is very green at that time of the year, late in the wet season, and broken every mile or so by streams that flow southeast into the Chiriquí River: Quebrada Gapacho, Quebrada Jacú, Quebrada La Conga. The sun will have been fierce, the day hot and muggy, suffocatingly so whenever the bus stopped.

At Jacú, two miles from the border, was the first of several checkpoints set up by the PDF to control immigration. Here a guard boarded the bus to check the passengers' documents. He asked Hugo to get down, treatment normally reserved for those with improper documents but which Hugo had received on previous occasions. He went into the guard post, sat down, took a newspaper from the desk there, and began reading. González got down behind him without being asked to and paid Núñez the forty-cent fare from Paso Canoa to there as if he had reached his destination. At that, Núñez heard the guard say, "Go ahead, Hugo, it's all right." Spadafora got back on the bus. So did González. As Núñez turned to get on, he heard someone behind him in the guard post say, "The great Hugo Spadafora." When the bus started up, Núñez whispered to Baúles, "We've got Hugo Spadafora with us."

At the second checkpoint, eight miles farther on, Hugo was again asked to get down, then again allowed to continue his journey. This time González stayed put. The bus continued on another eight miles, to the town of Concepción, halting first at the outskirts, then at the bus stop beside the park, a short walk from the PDF cuartel—barracks, that is, and district headquarters. Here, as passengers were getting off, González got up and went beside Hugo and, gesturing toward the door, said, "Come with me." According to Núñez's declaration (made after El Guapo García had set him an example), Hugo looked at González with a kind of laugh, as if to say, "Who are you to be making this kind of invitation?" Then González took Hugo's bag from the rack and, saying, "Allow me," as one might to a lady or an old man, carried it off the bus. Hugo followed.

Hugo followed González past Núñez, who was at the bus door, then turned around and took his identity card out of his shirt pocket and showed it. "So you'll know who I am. I am Dr. Hugo Spadafora." Then he turned back to González, who had stopped a few paces off, and said, "Give me the bag, I'll go with you."

As Hugo and González walked toward the corner, Baúles reminded Núñez that Hugo hadn't paid. Núñez ran after him.

"Are you staying, señor?"

"I'm being detained by this member of the Defense Forces."

"Then the driver says to please pay me the fare."

Hugo paid Núñez one dollar twenty. When the bus pulled away, he and González were on the corner opposite the Montero Dental Clinic by the park in Concepción. That was the last time any civilian saw Dr. Hugo Spadafora alive.

Dr. Hugo Spadafora entered the cuartel at Concepción at one o'clock in the afternoon or thereabouts, Friday, September 13, 1985. The duty officer was Lieutenant Edgardo Jaramillo. Those with Spadafora were Francisco Eliécer González, alias Bruce Lee, and Omar Vega Miranda. Vega Miranda, too, was a PDF sergeant. He'd been on duty that day at the first checkpoint, and the likelihood is that he followed bus 4B-52 in a PDF vehicle to back González up in case of trouble. There was none. The openness of his surveillance and arrest no doubt calmed Hugo, suggested petty harassment, not anything grave. But when the door of the cuartel closed behind him, he was lost utterly, as if the waters of the deep had closed over his head.

However, he still had seven hours or so to suffer.

Hugo Spadafora was tortured in the towns of Concepción and Alanje, and near the villages of Canto Gallo, Santo Tomás, and Estero Rico, in Chiriquí Province, Republic of Panama. He was murdered in a place called Corozo, which was not even a village but an agricultural station and an outpost of the PDF.

In Concepción, probably, he was merely beaten. In Panama in the time of the tyrants, everyone taken in custody was abused, shouted at, threatened, insulted, shoved around. Hugo had an irascible nature. He will have resisted. That will have meant more blows. Not many, however. Woe to the poor fool who damaged him before his pain could be correctly inflicted and savored by people of refinement in such matters! The autopsy done on his corpse in Costa Rica found evidence of severe and prolonged beating, but he can't have got very much of it in Concepción. A poke or two in the kidney with a truncheon, a thump on the upper arm with a rifle butt, perhaps a swat on the ear with some rubber hosing, and then he was stuffed in a cell till the gourmets could gather. Which, it's likely, didn't take very long. The entertainment that followed wasn't impromptu. It seems certain that Hugo was surveilled in Costa Rica, that the PDF was informed when he left San José, if not even earlier, when he booked his passage.

In Alanje, ten miles farther along the highway, then six miles due south on a secondary road, Hugo Spadafora's suffering may have been strictly mental/emotional. Nivaldo Madriñán was in Alanje that day, major in the Defense Forces, chief of the Department of Investigations, chief torturer to successive tyrants of Panama, the most feared man in the country after Noriega. Madriñán had an acceptable reason to be there. Alanje is his birthplace, September 13 is his birthday. It can't be established for certain that he took part in what happened to Hugo Spadafora, but it's very hard to imagine his having missed it. He'd never have forgiven himself. More to the point, he'd not have forgiven the others. Hugo passed through Alanje that afternoon in a military vehicle. If Madriñán joined him and his escort, Hugo will have experienced mental/emotional suffering. He will have known then and there that he would be tortured.

Canto Gallo and Santo Tomás and Estero Rico are tiny villages quite close to the shore. They took Hugo Spadafora from one to another, like a band of carousers dragging the bridegroom from tavern to tavern on the last night of his bachelorhood. The land there is in rice, low fields, and, toward the sea, clutches of mangrove from which the tracks emerge as from tunnels onto lovely, long, white-sand beaches breakered softly by the unsoilable Pacific. According to the campesinos of the region, they took Hugo down to the beaches far from the houses, no doubt so that his howling wouldn't be heard. A beach party, then, a movable fiesta, with a fresh salt breeze and warm sunlight, and the lapsing beat of gentle surf.

Who were they, these revelers? According to Winston Spadafora, Major Luis Córdoba presided. He may well have been seconded by Nivaldo Madriñán. Which is not to suggest even for an instant that Major Madriñán ceded pride of place as a dispenser of torment to anyone, but merely that, like every gallant officer of the Panama Defense Forces, he had a keen regard for martial etiquette. Chiriquí, after all, was Córdoba's province. Captain Mario del Cid was on hand, the commandant of the penal colony on Coiba Island, as fearsome a place as any on the planet. He flew over specially to join the fun. And a lieutenant named Arturo Marquínez, and a sergeant Venero Morales, and a man named Castillo and perhaps others. And General Manuel Antonio Noriega. He was physically in Paris but present in spirit. And by telephone also, according to the National Security Agency. His communications hookup included an open satellite line—it cost $5,000 a day—and that afternoon (or evening if you were in Paris) the National Security Agency monitored a satellite conversation between Major Luis Córdoba and General Manuel Noriega, part of which went as follows:

Cordoba: We have the rabid dog.

Noriega: And what does one do with a dog that has rabies?

A chilling exchange, one must say. Dr. Spadafora likened to a rabid beast, when actually he was a healthy human. Indicative of his status in the eyes of his captors. And ominous also. Suggestive that they meant to resolve the conflict between what he actually was and how they viewed him by relieving him of his health and humanity. Chilling and ominous, and more so than you probably suppose. Manuel Noriega, the former laboratory assistant, had something quite specific in mind when he devised the speech code he was using with Luis Córdoba. Untreated rabies is invariably fatal, but "in many cases the reaction to the vaccine is almost as severe as the disease itself." What one does, therefore—or at least did in Panama (Guillermo Sánchez, too, was once a lab assistant)—with a dog suspected of having rabies (supposing it had bitten someone) was to cut the dog's head off so that a pathologist might examine brain tissue for a definitive diagnosis.

But what did they do first with Dr. Hugo Spadafora? They jabbed sharp objects under his fingernails, the blade of a knife or bamboo slivers, something like that. Probably that was first, that was the hors d'oeuvre, though they will have been beating him all the while, and vilifying him and shouting threats and insults, and playing with him obscenely and laughing at him, making fun of his pain. That was probably first because, though the pain is exquisite (as anyone knows who's done it by mistake, jabbed something sharp under a fingernail), there's no sense of being mutilated. Run a sharp thing under a nail, and it hurts very badly, but you know it will heal up and you'll be all right. True horror is in being permanently damaged, busted up, ruined, wrecked for good. So the fingernail business was probably just foreplay.

Did they question him? No doubt they did. Not because he had secrets they wanted but to give what they were doing a semblance of sanity. No doubt they asked him what he told the DEA, whom he met with, what they looked like, and so forth, and no doubt sooner or later he told them. But none of it mattered. They tortured him to calm Noriega's envy and because they enjoyed torturing people.

At one point they stripped him naked. With appropriate tweaks and pinches, one supposes, degrading little pokes and prods and feels. Then someone took a sharp knife and made two careful, deep, symmetrical cuts, on the inside of each of his legs, from just above the knee to the mid-thigh. The point here was to disable his thigh muscles so that he couldn't close his legs and thus disturb the pleasure they meant to take of him. Of everything about Hugo Spadafora's suffering, these cuts are what trouble one most. They argue that his ordeal was nothing special, that many others suffered similarly at the hands of Panama's tyrants. The fellow who made those cuts was no novice. He had theoretical knowledge and hands-on experience. Without them, someone would have had to hold Hugo's legs, a tiresome thing in Panama's climate. And there's the added torment, the hideous helplessness, the shame of lying there splayed, naked to one's enemies. Perhaps the expertise expressed in those cuts was what so many U.S. officials were referring to—Ambassador Briggs, Southern Command C-in-C General John Galvin—when they praised the PDF's "professionalism."

Otherwise, proceedings followed tradition. The autopsy found Spadafora's testicles monstrously swollen, the result (it seems) of prolonged bastinado. And something was jammed up his rectum, a pole of some sort. The autopsy found his rectum massively damaged. The act is commonplace, expressive of what seems a widespread pathology. Rioting inmates at the New Mexico State Prison used a broomstick on one of the guards a few years back. Nicolai Yezhof, architect of Stalin's bloodiest purge, was wont during a troublesome interrogation to smash the leg off a chair and use that. The act is supremely degrading. The region is richly nerved, so pain is considerable. Injury to the prostate gland provides the horror of permanent sexual impairment. And it must make cowardly perverts feel brave and manly. The mind's eye sees them grin, and one knows instantly why the concept of hell was devised. There ought to be a place for those tormentors.

Well, for Dr. Hugo Spadafora the world became an endless howl. Was a phone patch done from a vehicle radio so that his howling could be savored in Paris? There's no evidence one way or another, but one has to think yes, yes that seems likely. Why pay $5,000 a day for a fancy hookup if not to savor your enemy's howls? The mind's ear hears those howls and an answering chortle. The mind's eye, helpless, watches the tormentors, till winded by effort and pleasure they flop down on the sand beside the obscenity they are making out of a brave and cultured human being, panting, chuckling as they prod it with sticks. Then they heave themselves up and drag it to the vehicle, dump it inside, and go off amid wan smiles to another spot for another round of fun.

When they were finished, spent if you like, they broke two of his ribs. This must have had some ritual meaning for them. Dr. Mauro Zúñiga got the same. Then, like honest craftsmen, they signed their work, used a needle and indelible ink to tattoo "F-8" on Hugo Spadafora's shoulder. And the sun went down as on any other evening. And the stars came out, and maybe the moon also. We could look that up, find out if the moon shone that night, and if so, if it was full or half or quarter, but enough's enough. There's a limit to the shame and rage one can deal with.

But, readers, before we leave this part of our story, please permit us a word in advice, a thing we learned the hard way. We hope and suppose that your countries are civilized, but Panama, too, was a civilized country once. Don't assume your spotless land can't be taken over, or that no nasty tyrant will ever harm you. That's what people in Panama thought, and look what happened.

Between seven and eight on the evening of Friday the thirteenth of September 1985, Dr. Hugo Spadafora was brought by military vehicle to the PDF outpost at Corozo, less than a mile from the Costa Rican border. He was very badly battered but still alive. He was placed on the cement floor of the barracks. The cook in the detachment sat down astraddle his chest and plunged a butcher knife into his throat. Dr. Spadafora made a spasmodic movement. At that, the cook hurriedly sawed off his head amid sprays of blood and horripilant gurgles.

Hugo Spadafora's head was buried in the yard in front of the barracks. His headless body was put in a U.S. Mail bag—how obtained we don't know—and loaded on the vehicle that brought it. Convoyed by another vehicle, the body was driven into Costa Rica. The border in that region runs along a road. Crossing back and forth is no problem. At a place called El Roblito, the body was dumped in a ravine. On their way back, the soldiers stopped at a banana-packing station called Balsa and washed both vehicles.

At Corozo, soldiers heated water and scrubbed the floor. Then they got drunk. Another drinking party took place on Coiba Island, in an area called Playa Hermosa, away from the penal colony where, seven years earlier, the volunteer force raised by Dr. Hugo Spadafora had received training before going off to fight tyranny in Nicaragua. A plane carrying Captain del Cid and other persons landed at the strip there, and a great celebration was held that went on until the high hours before dawn.

On Monday, September 16, a yellow dog began whining and scraping nervously near the spot where Hugo Spadafora's head was buried. Soldiers killed it with rifle fire. That night, they dug up Hugo's head and took it we don't know where.

On the evening of Saturday the fourteenth of September 1985, Guillermo Sánchez Borbón was in the newsroom of *La Prensa,* an independent daily established in 1980. Part of the price exacted from Omar Torrijos for Senate ratification of the Canal treaties—and the part that hurt him most to pay—was that he allow a little free speech in Panama, for instance, a newspaper independent of his tyranny. In the five years since *La Prensa*'s founding, it had had its offices wrecked by goons with crowbars, its staff beaten up, its publisher forced into exile, and its whole operation closed down from time to time. In short, it must have been doing something right. Sánchez's column was its most popular feature.

To begin with, the column was often funny. Sánchez had learned from Chaplin how funny dictators can be, and from Mandelstam's widow how much they hate being made fun of. Besides, he was a born-again Marxist: an apostate of Karl, an apostle of Groucho.

Also, his column was informative. Everyone knew that if Sánchez received authentic information, he would put it in the paper. So he got things like a Xerox copy of a canceled check in five figures drawn on the social security fund and payable to a party backing Nicky Barletta. And the news that a certain colonel had gold-plated fixtures in his bathroom—which by poetic license was transformed into a solid-gold toilet seat. On doctor's orders, Sànchez had stopped writing poetry years before, but his license was still valid. Sources supplied information, the dictatorship comedy. The columns more or less wrote themselves.

Sánchez was under no illusions. The dictatorship was funny only when viewed from oblique angles. To regard it head-on, as one was often forced to, to come upon (as R. M. Koster had, one otherwise pleasant morning, at a normally placid corner in the residential quarter where he and Sánchez lived) seven soldiers beating one boy with hoses, leaning avidly over him as he writhed on the sidewalk, jostling each other to get their blows in, would have strained even Groucho's sense of humor. And of course Sánchez got threats. And was beaten up, waylaid by hoodlums, and knocked to the pavement and bloodied—hardly a feat with a bookish, plumpish, sixtyish gentleman. But he rarely knew who his sources were and so was at little risk of betraying them. He had no wife, no children, no money—nothing he could be cowed by the threat of losing. As for his life, it was in used condition. He supposed he wouldn't mind parting with it much. And finally, he was having an excellent time. It was depressing to watch the whole world heap praise on the cowardly perverts who tyrannized Panama, and what they did often moved him to shame and fury, but he liked what he was doing and knew it was right.

At seven in the evening, then, on Saturday the fourteenth of September 1985, Sánchez's phone rang in the newsroom of *La Prensa.* It was one of Hugo Spadafora's sisters. Hugo had left San José the previous morning and still hadn't arrived. Sánchez had scarcely hung up when the phone rang again. Hugo's father, Dom Carmelo, was downstairs, accompanied by several members of the family. They were worried, but not overly. They supposed Hugo was being held in communicado. They and Sánchez decided the best thing to do was to make the news public. Franklin Bósquez, the city editor, composed a short notice: Dr. Hugo Spadafora was missing; his family was concerned. No comment was made, nor any theory ventured as to what might have happened.

The next night, when he came in, Sánchez was handed a hysterical communiqué issued by Colonel Julio Ow Young, chief of the G-2 since Noriega's ascension to commandant. To speak of missing persons, it blustered, and to feel concern over rash speculations made by *La Prensa* for political purposes, was to seek to defame the armed forces. And it went on to urge investigation of the "crime" of having published word that Hugo Spadafora had disappeared. Sánchez knew then that something terrible had happened. Ow Young's communiqué was a confession. The next day, Monday the sixteenth, TV Channel 6 in San José broadcast the news that a headless corpse found at El Roblito two days earlier had been identified as that of Dr. Hugo Spadafora.

That night, Sánchez received a great many calls—people giving information, others requesting it, still others merely trying to ease their grief. He learned of Hugo's having lunched at Los Mellos, of his having ridden on bus 4B-52, of his having been arrested by Bruce Lee González, all of which was in his column the next morning. After ten-thirty or so, the calls subsided. Then, around eleven, the phone rang again. A voice whispered, "Corozo." Before Sánchez could ask what that meant—the word itself means a kind of palm tree—the line went dead. The incident was repeated three nights running. Meanwhile, with the dictatorship trying to hold the untenable thesis that the crime had been done in Costa Rica, Sánchez learned more details and published them, and went on to speculate that, as Spadafora had been last seen alive outside the cuartel in Concepción, inside the cuartel was where he had been murdered.

On the fourth night, the night this last speculation was published, the voice did not break off after whispering, "Corozo." "Corozo," it went on, "is a technical station and military outpost. Don't get mixed up. They didn't kill Hugo Spadafora in the lockup at Concepción; they killed him in Corozo."

Sánchez waited, hoping to hear the same from some other source. Finally, he used a method he had for dealing with stuff that smelled true but lacked confirmation: he assumed a schoolmaster's tone and assigned homework. "For homework, write one sheet on what happened at Corozo." Something like that appeared in his column on September 24. That night the mystery voice called again. The name, it said, had caused panic among Hugo's murderers.

With all this, the *procurador* of the nation—roughly the same as attorney general in the United States—was going on radio every day begging Sánchez to give him more leads. As if he wanted any! As if he couldn't have given Bruce Lee González a grilling if he even half cared to make an investigation! He was a large, soft, doughy man named Calvo, nicknamed Mamellena—"Fill-me-up," after a large, soft, doughy variety of pastry. He did not in the least want to know more about the murder, but pretending he did was a way to rattle cages. On the twenty-fifth, Sánchez's column recommended that he retrace Hugo's route as Sánchez had been given it by two terrified campesinos brought to the phone by someone calling from Chiriquí—Concepción–Alanje–et cetera, the stations of the cross in Hugo's cavalry—with a warning to take care on the beach at Estero Rico, and a hope that he might finish the trip alive, and best wishes for heart-to-heart chats with the natives, and the suggestion that, for dessert, he eat a *corozo.*

The U.S. embassy, for its part, swallowed hard at the murder, then put out the tale that it had been ordered by PDF Chief of Staff Roberto Díaz, next in line to Noriega, the colonel of the gold-plated bathroom fixtures. Despite his penchant for conspicuous consumption, Díaz was supposed to be a leftist, so the disinformation had a double prong: protect Washington's favorite and wound an unpalatable potential successor. The only drawback was that no one believed it. Noriega's apologists knew he ran the country, whether he was on its soil or not. Insiders among them were, besides, aware that Díaz had been shocked by the murder and terrified by the direction Noriega was taking, that he'd tried to put a palace coup together, and that, all the way from Paris, Noriega had quashed it. As for Noriega's opponents . . .

In those days, Koster and Sánchez were in the habit of lunching two or three times a month with a man from the embassy—let's call him Phil—who may or may not have been the CIA station chief. On the twenty-fifth, the three were at Windows, a swank restaurant atop the Bank of Boston Building, owned by one of Noriega's gun- and drug-running protégés. In due course, Phil floated the U.S. line. With a certain embarrassment, for he was a clever man, a wit and a linguist, and no less an ironist than the others at the table. Díaz, he said, may have done Spadafora's murder. Why? To discredit Noriega. To Phil's personal credit, he took the reaction manfully. Both his companions began to hoot wildly:

Discredit your aunt Eulalia! Noriega didn't need anyone to discredit him! He did a terrific job all by himself!

Meanwhile, the country too was reacting. With horror, as well might any country, but Panama felt a special repugnance. Its first hero, Balboa, discoverer of the Pacific, had been unjustly beheaded in

1519, an atrocity that Panamanians learn in grade school to abhor and that stands in chilling contrast to most of Panama's subsequent history. Till 1968, the land never knew tyranny. Till Noriega, Panama's tyrants practiced restraint, murdered only those they felt they had to, and went about it as discretely as they could. Now, it seemed, a recessive gene for demonic cruelty was reasserting itself, changing Panama's character utterly. The old confidence that Panama was different, would never be like its tormented neighbors—that trust was fading. Everywhere there was a sense of foreboding, even among those who from greed or cowardice or love of ease deceived themselves about the regime that ruled them, endowing it with spurious virtues.

Hugo Spadafora had been a hero to many, especially to those who, like him, were fooled by Torrijos, who believed in Panama's "revolution." Even those who thought Hugo wrongheaded admired his courage and idealism. No details of his torture were given out, but the photo of his headless corpse lying naked and tagged on a mortuary table sickened everyone who saw it. And filled all with terror, a reaction that Noriega surely intended. Killing Hugo wasn't just amusement. It had its political purpose, intimidation. If that could be done to Hugo Spadafora, no one who opposed Noriega was safe. But, more than terror, the crime brought disgust and anger. Noriega was schooling his countrymen in toughness, and though their graduation was still some years off, from all parts of the republic voices joined those of Hugo's family in calling for the creation of a special commission to investigate the crime and bring its authors to justice.

Hugo's family. What an example they set. With dignity, with calm, with faith in the future, above all with imagination they voiced their call: Justice for Hugo. There, one feels, was the difference between the murdered man and his murderer, a family whose love and support reached beyond death, the difference between health and sickness, decency and evil, civilization and barbarism. The family is still Panama's basic social unit. Despite the upheaval wrought by years of tyranny, Panama has still not reached the stage where the solitary individual is forced to seek substitutes in political movements or business corporations or secular religions foisted by the state. In the aftermath of what might easily have been a devastating tragedy, the hideous slaughter of its most gifted member, the Spadafora family showed how sound and resilient the institution of the family can be.

And what a service they did their countrymen, furnishing them means of expression where, hitherto, most had been mute. They began on the twenty-third with a day-long fast outside the United Nations office in Panama City. On the twenty-fourth, they formally petitioned the puppet legislature to vote the special commission into existence, and Winston began a hunger strike that lasted nineteen days and ended only with the archbishop's intercession. And there were masses and marches, events that thousands participated in. The human chain, for instance, forged in the capital on October 25, from the papal nunciature (where Guido and Carmenza Spadafora had chained themselves) to the presidential palace. It stretched three miles through all kinds of neighborhoods, along palm-lined Avenida Balboa by the bay, in and out of narrow streets in the old city, and people of all classes joined it, calling out to others to join also. No police were about. None were needed. In all the afternoon, there was no incident, only thousands of Panamanians, serious and yet light-hearted, joining hands together for justice. And, in December, the 300-kilometer walk from Chitré, where Hugo was born, to Panama City. It began on the sixteenth, with the family and certain friends, but when they reached the Canal, on Christmas Eve, their number had grown to over a thousand, and thirty thousand more came out to meet them, packing the Bridge of the Americas and its approaches.

Long before Christmas, the country's reaction, animated by the Spadafora family's campaign, had produced decisive political consequences. Toward the end of September, with the cry for justice rising, Colonel Díaz decided, not without reason, that since the murder had happened while he was in charge, he might end up being blamed for it. He suggested that Noriega arrest Córdoba. When Noriega, who was still outside Panama, refused, Díaz urged him at least to arrest some sergeants and privates, the ones who'd actually cut Hugo's head off. Later on, they might be spirited from the country, but their arrest would at least ease the pressure. All this was gone into very gingerly, with no hint that Díaz thought Noriega was involved. Again Noriega refused, and at that Díaz began, very gingerly indeed, to put a coup together. He approached Lieutenant Colonels Marcos Justine and Elías Castillo and ordered two companies of the "2000" Battalion from Fuerte Cimarrón, east of the capital, to PDF headquarters.

Almost at once Noriega called him. What were all the troop movements about? In case of street demonstrations, Díaz improvised, scared stiff at his boss's transatlantic omniscience. And when Justine and Castillo developed cold feet, Díaz panicked and built himself a scapegoat. He called two dozen or so civilian politicians, starting with the puppet vice-president Eric Delvalle, and told them Nicky Barletta was using the Spadafora case in an attempt to dump General Noriega.

Events gave the story much credibility. On September 24, Barletta had flown to New York to give a speech at the UN. While he was there, a journalist asked him about the special investigating commission the Spadaforas were demanding, and Barletta said he meant to name one. The crime's grossness, it seems, exceeded his quislinghood's limits, or hearing so many people call him Señor Presidente bemused him into thinking he had power. Whatever the case, his rebellion couldn't be countenanced. Noriega had returned to Panama. Within hours of his remark, Barletta was summoned home also. When his plane pulled up at the gate at Torrijos Airport on the morning of Friday, September 27, ground personnel noticed "F-8" scrawled on one of its windows. Barletta was escorted directly to PDF headquarters and closeted with Noriega and Díaz. In the fourteen hours that followed, they forced him by threat to resign the office they had given him by fraud eleven months earlier.

Vice-President Delvalle made no objection. He put on the trappings of office just stripped from Barletta as avidly as ever a dog lapped vomit, nor was any dog ever more reverent toward its master. As soon as he was sworn in as puppet president, Delvalle went *on foot* the half mile from the palace to PDF headquarters, grinning houndishly all the way, to fawn publicly on Manuel Noriega, and for thirty months thereafter he grinned and fawned—begged, retrieved, rolled over, heeled on cue—as the ring of evil tightened on his country and his countrymen were ever more harshly oppressed, till at length he was no longer useful and Noriega thrust him out as he had Barletta.

Hugo Spadafora was taking vengeance, however, though no one noticed at the time. So long as Noriega remained Washington's favorite, he might as well have been in Eden. But Barletta the fig leaf was also the forbidden fruit. Of every tree, Noriega might freely eat—murder whom he cared to, torture to his heart's ease—but he must not touch Nicky. George Shultz and Bill Casey had picked him. The United States of America had lied grossly in the matter of his supposed election. So when Noriega tossed Nicky out, he began to fall from grace with Washington.

Unfortunately, this was not always clear to Noriega. On December 17, he received a visit from Admiral John Poindexter, President

Reagan's national security adviser, who asked him to consider the possibility of restoring Barletta to office and thought it would be useful for him to send certain officers abroad—presumably, Córdoba, Madriñán, and del Cid—until the furor over Spadafora subsided. Simultaneously, a meeting was going on in the Executive Office Building, next door to the White House, between Mr. Constantine Menges, a member of the National Security Council Staff, and three representatives of the Panamanian government, lobbyists whom Noriega had hired to help bridge the rift between him and Washington, and Menges was reading them the riot act. Noriega would have to make changes in the Defense Forces. For starters, he had to replace the officers involved in the murder of Hugo Spadafora. He had, besides, to stop dealing with the Cubans. And he had to hold free elections at once, or recount the 1984 votes and install Arnulfo Arias, the actual victor (and, incidentally, the president deposed in 1968 when the military seized power). In short, there were two distinct U.S. positions. It was as if the United States had two different governments.

Which, in fact, it did. One government, the insiders, knew about the arms airlift and the Medellín connection and, no doubt, all manner of other unsavory dealings in which Noriega was its accomplice, and hence refrained from jumping on him too heavily, lest he be unavailable next time, lest (perish the thought!) he blab. The other government saw him as, purely and simply, an SOB, and not necessarily Uncle Sam's, either, what with dealing with Castro and purging Barletta the fig leaf. Small wonder Noriega was confused! Nor could he be blamed for paying scant attention to the U.S. officials who treated him harshly and for heeding instead those who used kid gloves. This sending of two different signals, the inevitable consequence of a policy designed primarily to dodge the Congress and deceive the American people, continued for at least two years and was the principal cause of the United States's inability to secure its national interest with regard to getting Noriega out of Panama and restoring the isthmus to friendly hands.

But no matter what signals were sent him, Noriega's fall from grace was never reversed. Like participants in a marriage going sour, he and Washington kissed and made up a number of times, but neither really meant it, and each reconciliation was briefer then the one before, till in the end both parties simply stopped trying. So on Friday, September 27, 1985, Manuel Noriega's easy days were over. He still had years to strut and bluster, but never again was it going to be much fun.

That same day every G-2 agent received Sánchez's picture and orders to arrest him dead or alive. He was getting close to the truth. The evening before, he'd told Koster, "If they find me without my head, look for it in Noriega's desk drawer." On his way home from lunch, a neighbor stopped him on the corner. The G-2 were waiting in his apartment. At that moment a taxi came by, and Sánchez stopped it. That afternoon he took refuge with the papal nuncio.

The nuncio, Monseñor José Sebastián Laboa, was a Spanish Basque Sánchez's age—that is, about sixty—who had been in Panama nearly a year. A day or two after taking his post, on the urging of a Panamanian layman (a man recommended by previous Vatican legates), he had said some kind words about General Noriega, whom the layman had described as a man of peace. The next morning in *La Prensa,* he received both barrels of Sánchez's scorn, complete with wordplay on his surname: "Boa Lauds Viper," or "Boa to Rattler: 'I Love You,' "—that sort of thing. By noon, churchmen in Panama had apprised him of Noriega's true nature, and that evening he went to *La Prensa* to tell Sánchez he'd made a mistake and had no hard feelings. From then on, the two were friendly. On September 27, after the Venezuelan ambassador was unable because of illness to take a call, Sánchez asked his niece to contact Laboa. It was traditional for Latin-American countries to grant the hunted refuge in their embassies. Would the Vatican do likewise? "¡Por supuesto!" replied Monseñor Laboa, and Guillermo Sánchez thus became the first (but not last) of Laboa's such guests.

The *nunciatura* was on the corner of Avenida Balboa and Via Italia, at the edge of Panama City's Punta Paitilla sector, a two-story building with an ample front garden, the whole enclosed by a high wall. The ground floor had the embassy's offices, a large reception room, a dining room, the pantry and kitchen, and quarters for the nuns who ran Laboa's household. Above were the nuncio's rooms and other bedrooms, one occupied by the nuncio's deputy, a library-study, and a broad terrace. The furnishings downstairs were rich but formal—elegant, heavy, stiff, Spanish colonial. Everything above was simple and Spartan, the rooms almost empty, therefore wide and airy. Sánchez's room was on the building's east side. His window showed only high rises and a sliver of street. The terrace, however, on which he could stroll after dark, gave on Via Italia, and from the library he could see the city and the hazy green cordillera beyond it.

Sánchez's bed was hard, but that helped his lumbago. He could not write his column, but he had never made a fetish of work. When guests came, he was obliged to stay in his room, for no one but his niece knew where he was hiding, but when they left, Laboa brought him the new rumors. By then, Sánchez was a great connoisseur of the genre, what with all the anonymous tips he received, and could tell a rumor's provenance and reliability without the slightest pause for reflection, the way a great hitter can distinguish pitches by picking up the spin on the ball. He was often forced to spoil Laboa's pleasure over what seemed to the priest a juicy tidbit, sighing that it was surely a plant from Havana, or a fabrication designed by the CIA, but Laboa never complained at these disabusings, or grew stingy in relating new tales. And the *nunciatura*'s austerity stopped at mealtime. LaBoa's housekeeper, Madre Angelina, had lived most of her life in Panama but had never lost her native touch for pasta.

Madre Angelina was some years older than Laboa and Sánchez, small and round and lively, with an Italian's love of conspiracy and intrigue. She delighted in helping Sánchez hide out, would have delighted in it under almost any circumstances, but took a special pleasure in that his only "crime" was telling the truth and his persecutor Manuel Noriega. She knew Noriega of old and hated him genially, having been attached to the Chiriquí diocese when Noriega was commanding in the province. "Oh, that Pineapple Face!" she would exclaim on recounting one of his villainies to Sánchez, bunching her fingers together and shaking them in the air below her chin. Then she'd collect herself, recall her religion, and heap her protégé's plate with more lasagna.

Sánchez stayed two weeks and gained twelve pounds. Morning and afternoon, he read Saint Augustine, first the *Confessions,* then *The City of God,* works he'd been yearning for years to reread without ever finding the necessary leisure. When representatives of the Inter-American Press Association worked out his emergence from hiding, obtaining guarantees from Chief of Staff Díaz that he wouldn't be taken without due process of law, he wasn't exactly sad to leave, but if, when he dies, he's allowed to design his own paradise, it will be a great deal like the *nunciatura.*

With Sánchez in hiding, out of touch with his sources, and his column absent from the paper, the Spadafora case dropped somewhat from public view. The government forbade all mention of it in the media it controlled, which included all television stations, and on October 11, the seventeenth anniversary of the military's taking power, organized a march "for peace and against sedition," and of "apology to the Defense Forces." Yes, you read correctly. Apology to the murderers. Peace, though they were waging war on the people.

From that day, anyone who spoke against Noriega and his uniformed goons was branded as "seditious." In their minds, they and Panama were coterminous. The march had a good turnout. Public employees were ordered to take part, on pain of being fired, and roll was taken before the thing started. The murder case, however, would not go away.

Before taking refuge with the nuncio, Sánchez had received a document with a wealth of detail about the crime, essentially the story told above in these pages. It was vouched for by a person of great moral authority, but Sánchez preferred to wait for some confirmation before publishing its contents. These he copied at once; then he burned the original. In normal circumstances, he would have turned the document over to the authorities, but circumstances in Panama weren't normal, and hadn't been for years. Far from wishing to establish the truth, the authorities knew it only too well and wished to hide it.

Two months went by. Sánchez spent half of the first in Laboa's care. Thereafter he was back at *La Prensa,* but nothing new about the murder surfaced. The torrents of November came, the great downpours that precede Panama's dry season. The national holidays came and went with sullen high school students refusing to parade past Delvalle, turning their backs on the reviewing stand, and the puppet minister of education, Manuel Solís Palma, spitefully ordering them expelled en masse. Finally, on November 25, Sánchez received confirmation of the documents contents and no longer had need or right to keep the terrible story to himself. He put it in his column the next day, first pruning details and certain touches that seemed liable to betray his source's identity—which Sánchez still doesn't know—to someone familiar with the PDF. In the years since he wrote that column, he has received other confirmations. The surest, however, came almost at once. The Defense Forces took the packing plant at Balsa apart piece by piece and carried it away. Then they leveled the ground with bulldozers. It was as if the place had never existed.

On December 18, Sánchez was called before a prosecutor and questioned for several hours. The whole thing turned on Balsa and Corozo. What the Ministry of Justice wished to know was who had told Sánchez about those places. Sánchez had no trouble guessing why and was happy he could say truthfully he didn't know, and that he'd burned the document's original. That same afternoon Mamellena Calvo declared the case officially closed. The investigation, he said, couldn't continue, because no one knew who had murdered Hugo Spadafora.

Nineteen eighty-six was officially declared the "Year of Peace—Security without War," by order of General of Forces Manuel Noriega. All over Panama, signs with that slogan blossomed, often embossed with a ring of five stars, the general's insignia, and little white doves flapping bravely zenithward. Sánchez stopped calling Noriega "Bokassa" and referred to him instead as "the Peace Pigeon" and went on writing about Spadafora's murder and other abuses. And on February 7, the Fourth Superior Court in Chiriquí formally absolved, declared free of guilt all members of the Defense Forces whom Sánchez and others had cited as having taken part in Spadafora's arrest—the very men whose interrogation by an independent tribunal could unravel the tangle and lead to the crime's material and intellectual authors. On the eighteenth, Sánchez was brought before another prosecutor, Ana Belfon, a person entirely Noriega's instrument, and told to his horror that he was being sued for calumny by Omar Vega Miranda and two others.

Sánchez's horror needs some explaining to people who reside in civilized countries. Since Noriega's ascension to command, Panama had enacted a new calumny law that, if not unique, was at least unusual. Anyone accused in a civil suit could be put behind bars for five years of preventive detention. Five years on an accusation, no trial required. As it happened, the columns mentioned by Sánchez's accusers in their suit were those of September 11, 13, 17, and 21, 1985. When the first two appeared, Hugo Spadafora was alive and well in Costa Rica. The third made no mention of Sánchez's accusers. The fourth was imaginary. September 21, 1985, was a Saturday, and on Saturdays Sánchez's column did not appear. That would have been enough to have the action thrown out, but Sánchez was living in Panama in the time of the tyrants. As soon as he signed his deposition, he went directly to La Modelo Prison.

Oh, La Modelo! Who could see you and ever forget? Even from the outside, the place is depressing, fortresslike, a city block square, with twenty-foot walls and little turrets with gun slots. And inside . . .

Galleries like zoo pavilions run the whole length and breadth of the prison. In them are penned hundreds and hundreds of men reduced to the minimum human expression in filth, in stench, in misery, in despair. Sánchez was put in the basement with the most wretched, a plumpish, bookish gentleman of sixty-one, holding his trousers up with one hand (for his belt had been taken), holding the other out a little in front of him, peering with bifocals through the gloom.

As soon as he entered, eight or ten men surrounded him. Then one of them came closer, stuck his face almost against Sánchez's, and studied him with an ethnologist's care. When satisfied, he asked whom Sánchez had murdered. Everyone in the cell had murdered someone.

At that, a man who'd been reading a newspaper lifted his gaze and said, "He's Sánchez Borbón. He writes 'En Pocas Palabras.' I read it whenever I get the chance."

Sánchez saw that the paper he had was that day's *La Prensa,* but seeing it, hearing his column referred to in educated and intelligent tones, only heightened the unrealness of the gallery, of its pale yellow bulb burning high up near the ceiling, of the thin light that seeped from a window almost that high.

"He's in for political reasons," the reader continued. "He gives it to the government, to Noriega especially."

Then another, a black man with finely sculpted features, began questioning Sánchez—not with hostile intent, it seemed, just curiosity. For what political cause was he in prison? What attacks? What particular cases?

"For none in particular," Sánchez answered, "for all in general." But then a man who'd come in from a neighboring cell and seated himself on the floor near the questioner looked up at Sánchez with great interest and malignity.

"Maybe for the Spadafora case," he sneered.

That satisfied the black man, who got up and went out, but the sneerer continued, "You killed Spadafora, didn't you?"

"Certainly not!" said Sánchez, but for some reason this enraged the sneerer.

"Tell the truth! You killed him! Did you or didn't you? Don't lie to me! I don't like being lied to!"

"You know very well who killed him," broke in the reader. "The Defense Forces killed him. This man is a journalist."

All the while, the ethnologist had kept gazing at Sánchez, and saying from time to time, "What a sweet mouth you have."

Then another came up, a man in a cap, and began explaining his extraordinary sexual gifts, which were mainly going to waste now with his caging. Another offered Sánchez the services of his personal catamite, and grew furious when Sánchez refused the offer. Across the aisle was La Galera de los Locos (the Gallery of the Madmen)—

as if Sánchez's cellmates didn't qualify—where crazies sang and begged and shouted insults. Ceaselessly. Other prisoners taunted them to see their lunacies, or had them commit perversions for a piece of bread or cigarette in reward.

A bearded man saluted Sánchez and told him his story. He'd spent seven and a half years on Coiba Island, for though everyone agreed he was crazy, and thus not responsible for the murder he'd done, the state mental hospital refused to take him, on the ground that his madness exceeded the place's norms. Then a man who lay reclined in an improvised hammock related the hellish existence in La Modelo, and went on, with the others agreeing, that Coiba was better, for though you had to work hard every day, at least you felt like a man, like a human being. In the labor of clearing ground, of planting and harvesting, inmates regained their dignity a little. There was always the risk of being shot "while escaping," or of abuse by the guards, who were all sadists, but it was better than the slow agony of the galleries.

Then the ethnologist swore he would rape Sánchez as soon as night fell. "Not you, me," protested the man with the cap. A furious squabble ensued between the two, and was joined by the man whose catamite Sánchez had refused. Just as quickly, the squabble then subsided, and the question was resolved by the flip of a coin. The ethnologist won, and thereby considered he could dispose as he wished with Sánchez, after the requisite softening up, but then the bearded man leaned in and warned him, "Whoever messes with the old guy dies."

The beard drew Sánchez apart, told him not to worry. He showed Sánchez a knife he had under his sleeve. "Later we'll go upstairs," he said to Sánchez, as if assuring Sánchez that there he'd be safe, but behind him the newspaper reader was making faces warning Sánchez not to believe a word.

Sánchez stood there blinking, disoriented. A guard came in and beat on the bars with his nightstick, his face contorted in rage and pallid in madness beyond anything Sánchez had seen among the prisoners. "What'll you do if they rape you?" the guard screamed at Sánchez. Sánchez looked at him in silence. The guard went out.

Then Sánchez's self-styled protector, whom Sánchez didn't know whether to trust or not (but who, he learned later, was used by the prison guards for their filthiest errands), rummaged in a corner of his cell and in his pockets, and at once there appeared four or five little straws and a small paper plate and on it a mound of cocaine, which his cellmates partook of in quick snorts. It was the first time Sánchez had witnessed that sort of ritual. Later he learned what it signified in La Modelo. It was a preparation for a gang rape.

The ethnologist snorted and smiled and shook himself doglike. Then he looked up and screamed that it soon would be dark. He made as if to rush at Sánchez but was held back by the asylum's reject and stood raging in his grasp screaming threats and obscenities. Across the aisle, the madmen squeaked and threw excrement. Oh, La Modelo!

Meanwhile, a campaign was being waged on Sánchez's behalf. Radio Mundial and other independent stations organized a network throughout the country to mobilize calls for his release, and friends were calling people of influence outside Panama. Monseñor Laboa called the Vatican. Koster, who had been active for twenty years in Democratic party politics in the United States suddenly found out why and called everyone he knew in Washington. He also called Phil at the embassy, where calls were coming in from senators and congressmen he'd already called and from others called by the publisher of *La Prensa,* Roberto Eisenmann, in exile in Boston. Phil called Ambassador Briggs in his limo on the way to visit puppet President Delvalle. So even as the ethnologist raged at Sánchez, Delvalle and the rest of Panama's government was being harried from all sides to let him go. It happened, then, that bail was agreed to and Sánchez put at liberty just before sundown.

A crowd had seen him to the prosecutor's that morning. A larger crowd was at the prison when he emerged. It was still quite light, much lighter than in the basement of La Modelo, and there were, besides, TV cameras, so Sánchez emerged blinking, more or less blind, and was startled by the shouts and applause of the people. But right away he began to distinguish the faces of friends and relations, and with that emotion took over, and his eyes grew very wet, and his voice broke, and fielding as best he could the questions flung at him by reporters, he made his way through embraces and handclasps to his lawyer's car.

Here, too, Hugo Spadafora was taking revenge. The United States had decided to signal its cooling ardor by changing ambassadors. Now Noriega's creatures had jailed Guillermo Sánchez and provoked the campaign noted above on the eve of the new man's confirmation hearing in the U.S. Senate. Such things are usually brief and boring, with one or two senators present just for form's sake, one or two aides, the candidate, and his family. Not so in the case of Mr.

Arthur Davis. The room was packed with reporters and TV crews. Every member of the subcommittee showed up. And each pleased himself by asking the ambassador designate whether he believed in democracy and freedom of speech and human rights and civilian control of the military. On taking his post, Mr. Davis demonstrated very clearly that he did, in fact, hold such values, but his confirmation hearing put the United States on record as having them as the basis of its policy toward Panama—something that still wasn't true but that had hardly been hinted at before. Noriega's discomfort was accelerated a little.

* * *

Guillermo Sánchez went on writing his column. In July, though, he was sued for calumny again. Panamanian justice disallowed bail in the case of a second accusation. It was one thing, Sánchez decided, to risk one's life; another to end it in the Gallery of the Madmen. He went into exile.

Six agents of the G-2 saw him off at the airport. And brought a special well-wisher with them. As Sánchez was being seen through emigration, a pair of arms seized him from behind and mad laughter hooted. It was his false protector from La Modelo, the man who, when Sánchez had been raped by all who cared to, would have put a knife in his heart. Crime of passion, the regime's newspapers would have called it, just another falling-out among perverts.

Sánchez didn't stop trembling till the plane was airborne.

2

THE COUP D'ETAT

In October 1968, the Republic of Panama was, by reasonable criteria, a lucky country. Admittedly, it was neither large nor rich in resources nor accustomed to (much less adept at) bullying its neighbors. Unlike the Argentine and the Texan, the Panamanian did not claim prestige on the basis of birthplace. He would have been smiled at or met with a blank stare. Few people thought of Panama beyond its borders, and most of those knew it only for the Canal and were liable to suppose it a U.S. possession. For the rest, its name, unlike "La France" conjured no *gloire,* unlike "Deutschland" no dreams of *über alles,* but rather warm-weather headgear and bananas. And yet, when one reasoned things out, the country was lucky.

To begin with, it was at peace, and had been for most of its history. There, where it counted most, Panama was different from its neighbors. It had known pirate raids in the sixteenth and seventeenth centuries, culminating in Henry Morgan's famous sack of the capital in 1671. While a province of Colombia, it experienced *guerrillas.* There was a border scuffle with Costa Rica in 1921, and one with U.S. police and soldiers in and near the Canal Zone in 1964, but the record hardly made Panama out as bloodthirsty. The Iberian obsessions with death and cruelty never took root there. Panama's social processes were characterized by a gentleness, a respect for life and its fragility, that set it apart and seemed a talisman against collective woe. Independence from Spain was won without bloodshed. Independence from Colombia cost but a single life. Internal squabbles rarely came to violence, and when they did, it was usually on a small scale and relieved by a lightness that drained the terror from it. When a dissident student claimed to have been tortured, it turned out that he'd been made to swallow a roach—unpleasant, but hardly torture as Panama came to know it. When a dissident politician imported a force of invaders, the leader leaped from the boat that had brought them draped picturesquely in bullet bandoliers, missed the dinghy he was jumping into, and sank like a stone, and the rest surrendered without further casualty. Two-thirds of our terrible century had come and gone, yet its customary horrors had bypassed Panama—no wars, no massacres, no institutionalized cruelties. That alone would have made it a lucky country.

And Panama was prosperous. A canny ruling class of merchants knew how to exploit Panama's geographical position so that trade flourished. They used the dollar instead of a vulnerable national currency. They devised a system of government that kept graft within bounds and restrained the state from botching the economy. That economy was growing briskly, at 8 percent yearly, almost three times as fast as the population. Investment was up, unemployment down. And wealth was more evenly distributed than anywhere else in Latin America. There, too, Panama was different. The richest group in the country was no more than a *haute bourgeoisie* by Chilean or Guatemalan standards, while the fearful squalor and ingrained despair common to most of the region were not proper to Panama. Unlike most of its neighbors, Panama had a large and growing middle class. The mood of the country was buoyant: things were pretty good and getting better.

Panama had a good measure of social justice. Infant mortality was too high, especially in the hinterland. At sixty-two years, life expectancy was too low. But the water was clean, thanks to efficient sanitation, and the dysentery and fevers once epidemic were things of the past. Land reform had been put through before landlessness had become a political problem, and with it programs of technical assistance, without which land reform is only a cruel joke. Literacy was higher and educational opportunity better than anywhere else in the region. A public university had been founded in 1936 and brought to good standards by scholar-refugees from Hitler's Europe and Franco's Spain. And priorities were sensibly ordered. Panama spent a higher percentage of its national product on education than did any other country in the hemisphere, the United States included.

Educational opportunity meant social mobility. The middle class could be reached in one generation from the lowest point on the social spectrum. Manuel Noriega, then a lieutenant, was proof of it. Even the top class, called *rabiblancos*—"white tails," after the palely tail-plumed local songbird, by virtue of their mainly Caucasian extraction—had traditionally been willing to admit a talented outsider, to marry a daughter to him and endorse his application to the Club Union, thereby renewing the blood and co-opting a potential adversary.

Panama was cosmopolitan. The hinterland was mainly mestizo—that is, mixed Amerindian and Iberian—but the transit zone of Colón and Panama, one of the world's great trade routes, had all the races and nearly all ethnic stocks. The chief strains were Amerindian, Spanish, and African, some of the latter Spanish-speaking and Catholic, a large minority English-speaking Protestants, descendants of Jamaicans and Barbadians who immigrated during the Canal construction era. All the nations of Europe were represented—the French, especially, for there had been significant settlement during Ferdinand de Lesseps's 1880s to build a canal attempt, and the Greeks, with their mercantile and seafaring heritage. There were Sephardim, Ashkenazim, and Middle Eastern Jews, Hindus and Sikhs, one of the largest Chinese colonies in Latin America, North and South Americans, and, of course, mixes and blends of them all. Most, too, had contributed something—music, language, cuisine—to the lively life-style of the capital. Panama was no parochial backwater but open to the world culturally as well as economically and geographically.

Panama was democratic and ostensibly stable. It had seen its times of electoral fraud and of turbulence—the monstrous ballot-box stuffing of 1936, the period in 1949 when four presidents held office in three months—but now the country seemed to have outgrown them. The three presidents immediately past had been chosen freely and fairly and had served out their constitutional terms. Widespread fraud in the election just concluded had been unmasked on television, for all to see, and then the false count rectified and credentials delivered to legitimate winners, president and vice-presidents, deputies to the National Assembly. Once and for all, or so it seemed, Panama could put political vices behind it and proceed maturely in liberty and order.

And Panama was a free country. Publications of every viewpoint circulated; two TV and many radio stations broadcast—all without censorship. No one was in jail for political reasons. No one was denied basic human rights. No one feared for his life or his livelihood because of his opinions or loyalties. How different from so many places!

None of this is to say that Panama was asleep. Indeed, there was an issue that engaged the passions of most citizens, that of the country's relations with the United States, particularly as these touched on national sovereignty. Sixty-five years before, in the mood of the moment, the United States had imposed a treaty on Panama whereby the latter, in return for U.S. protection and indirect benefits of having the Canal built on its territory, ceded de facto sovereignty over its most valuable real estate, a ten-by-fifty-mile strip stretching from the Atlantic port of Colón to Panama City on the Pacific. A perpetuity clause established that the agreement would remain legally valid till the Last Judgment or the collapse of the universe, whichever came later, and the United States made itself at home, creating not just the Canal but houses, commissary stores, schools, hospitals, theaters, bowling alleys, baseball fields, clubs, and cemeteries for a host of expressly imported Americans, everything from airfields to a zoo, and a governmental apparatus and two pay scales for U.S. and non–U.S. workers, and conspicuously a number of military bases.

However sensible and stylish this arrangement may have been in 1903—and Panamanians protested it from the outset—it was neither by the mid-1960s. The Canal's importance had diminished; Panama had progressed. The foreign enclave in its midst acquired the aspect of a malignant tumor, stunting the country's growth and obsessing the people, while the benefits to the United States of de facto sovereignty nowhere compensated the cost that might be expected from the disaffection it bred in Panama. All this became clear in January 1964, when bungling by U.S. officials in the matter of how and where flags would be flown precipitated four days of rioting, in which twenty-one Panamanians and four Americans perished and over five hundred on both sides were wounded.

In December of the same year, however, the presidents of the two countries jointly declared their attention to redo the treaty. Every Panamanian wanted a new one. Later on, when drafts were presented, there was much disagreement over what it should say, but in October 1968 none of that was on the table. The issue was, therefore, one that united Panamanians, a source of social cohesion, another reason why the country was lucky.

But here, this says it all: the police wore no firearms. They didn't have to; Panama was a good place. Not for tourists, particularly, though some tourists came. Not for drug and weapons dealers as it became later, not for vacationing terrorists and practicing sadists. Panama was a civilized country where (it was said with some truth) Carnival was the only thing taken seriously.

That Carnival, by the way, was something to witness, something (if you were lucky) to take part in. Not opulent and snooty like New Orleans's Mardi Gras, not a jet-set must like Carnival in Rio, but a very serious thing, *una cosa muy seria,* where everyone in the country proceeded flat out at the serious business of having a good time. *Comparsas?* Every rung on the social ladder had *comparsas*—the Viking ship, with boys in horned helmets and girls in metal brassieres, that rowed atop a truck into the Club Union, or the pirate band in purple *bombachas* of cheapest rayon that paraded down the Avenida Central. *Alegría?* The *alegría* of the capital was rivaled only by that of the interior: Penonomé, where Carnival was aquatic, where the floats actually floated on the Río Coclé; Las Tablas, where Calle Arriba and Calle Abajo (High and Low streets) competed in costumes, in dancing, in drinking as well as in the loveliness of queens and princesses. Two months later, in April, the middle and upper classes celebrated more weddings than in all other months combined. Nine months later, in November, obstetricians worked overtime, delivering bumper crops of seven-month babies. And the *toldos,* the public dance halls under tents, where relays of bands throbbed from dusk to daybreak. And the *carne en palito* sizzling fragrantly on braziers long after midnight. And the flowers, the strewn confetti, the orgiastic surge of massed dancers on their way to "bury the fish" at dawn on Ash Wednesday:

> *Panameño, Panameño, Panameño vida mía,*
> *Yo quiero que tú me llevas al tambor de la alegría!*

Panamanians, visitors found, were courteous and kind, relaxed and friendly, eager to be liked, hardly ever arrogant or pushy. *Alegría.* The word means mirth and merriment and joy. The concept suggests smiling faces, music and dancing, love of life, easygoing laughter. Panama had it. And kept it long into the tyranny. Panama's *alegría* was the last thing to go. Panama was a lucky country.

Three clouds, however, hung on the horizon. Three flaws, coming together, were about to reverse Panama's fortune. One had to do with an institution, one with an individual, one with the people in general.

In the first place, that Panama was civilized wasn't all luck. An act of conspicuous wisdom early in its history prevented its being poisoned by the chief blight of Latin America, the one thing more than all others combined that accounts for the barbarity that plagues the region. This is, of course, militarism, the domination of national life by a parasitic caste dedicated to violence.

At the time of Panama's independence from Colombia—November 1903—the commander of the garrison, Esteban Huertas, joined with the separatists from conviction reinforced by a bribe. In reward, he and his troops became Panama's army. General Huertas was short like Napoleon and one-armed like Lord Nelson. Otherwise, he resembled these commanders only in ambition. In November 1904, he tried to seize power. The president of Panama called the U.S. ambassador. The ambassador summoned troops from the Canal Zone. The attempt was quashed. Huertas was given a stipend for study abroad (which he spent, it seems, in Parisian brothels). The army was disarmed and disbanded. "In the interest of preserving a stable political climate," a Panamanian historian notes. And an American political scientist observes, "From the standpoint of the United States, the existence of an army presented a potential challenge to U.S. military power." How sensible everyone was back in those days! Panama jogged along nicely with a police force until generalized foolishness took over.

The police were an outfit of no particular discipline but respectful to citizens. Apart from arresting the odd thief and drunkard, their main task seemed to be chasing children who played in the streets. Membership constituted no sinecure, conferred no prestige. No young Panamanian of talent and ambition thought half a minute of joining unless he had no prospect whatsoever of a career in business or one of the professions.

Such a person was José Antonio Remón Cantera (1908–1955, president of Panama from 1952 to 1955), a burly, energetic man nicknamed Chichi (Baby Face) in regard of the tiny features bunched together as if for warmth in the center of his many-chinned, richly jowled visage. The sixth child of a profligate who reduced his widow to taking in sewing and his brood to the estate of poor relations, Remón suffered all his life from an acute and suppurating status deficiency whose chief symptom was hyperactive ambition. The only higher education he found was via scholarship at Mexico's military academy. He graduated third in his class (1931), the first native-born Panamanian to receive military schooling, but the only job he found was in the police.

Remón joined, having no choice, but in disdain of cophood affected the bearing of a Latin-style soldier. He was rude in dress and gesture, crude in taste, high-handed, foulmouthed, and quick-tempered, a terror to subordinates, a consumer in bulk of alcohol and female flesh. These traits showed in clearest relief when he was president. He was the first such to go about jacketless in the loose and flowing *guayabera* shirt, a wonderfully apt garment for Panama's climate but still Remón's term beneath a president's dignity. He was the only president to go carousing with cronies in the cabarets on Fifth of May Plaza—the Happyland, where Juan Perón met his second wife, Isabel; the Louisiana and Kelly's Ritz, where soldiers from the Canal Zone whooped in English and artistes made deals with drinkers for horizontal diversions after the last show. And when two aspirants to a government contract tried extortion, fixed him up with a girl from Costa Rica, then showed him the pictures they'd taken of him in rut, he forestalled their pitch by guffawing loudly and saying he'd take two of this one and three of that. To top things off, he died by violence, machine-gunned to death in his box at the racetrack on January 2, 1955.

Remón's personal militarization was mirrored in the institution he joined, partly because of his efforts, partly because of events. In January 1931, a few months before Remón returned to Panama, a revolution of sorts took place, the coming to power by coup d'état of a new generation imbued with nationalist and populist ideas, intent on modernizing the country and recovering sovereignty in the Canal Zone. These ideas and aims suggested the need for something like an army, as did the ease with which Panama's new leaders had slipped into the presidential palace and grabbed power. Meanwhile, a change in U.S. policy had put an end to direct incursions by U.S. troops as Washington's way to arbitrate power on the isthmus. The U.S. ambassador retained the last word, but the Policía Nacional had taken over as chief purveyor of violence, or the threat of it, when one or the other was needed to keep a president in power or enable his protégé to steal an election. So presidents spent more money on the police. And once Remón had established the precedent, other young Panamanians began taking advantage of scholarships offered by Panama's neighbors for study at their military academies, and to follow such study with joining the police. These developments nudged the police down the path to militarization and toward a place in Panamanian society similar to that occupied by the military in other countries of Latin America.

What place exactly? In the 1940s and later, almost all Panamanian cadets were graduated in El Salvador, Nicaragua, Peru, or Venezuela, countries where the military was either in de facto power or the base of support for a military man who suppressed civil liberties. These countries, besides, were rigidly stratified socially, deficient in democratic institutions and educational opportunity. The military was the sole means of social mobility for a disadvantaged young man, the one way out of the circle of misery, provided he tore himself from society and accepted the status of privileged pariah that went with being a career soldier. The members of these armies, the officers who taught in the academies, spoke often of patriotism, but they meant no such thing as normal people know it. Their *patria* was the military itself, and the military dominated the life of the country, not as one element among others that had gained pride of place, but as a thing apart, above the nation.

The Policía Nacional was still three decades from that position when Remón became commandant in 1947. He meant to make it a base for personal power, a thing not managed before and one a man of less forceful personality would likely have failed at. His first aim was firm control of the organization, and for this he needed the officers who'd come up through the ranks, of whom there were many more than academy graduates. He cultivated these men, and at no hardship either: he was as crude in taste and manners as they were. On the other hand, if the police were to be his springboard to power—and it was the only springboard he could lay hands on—it had to have more prestige. So he pressed its militarization, in part by raising fewer enlisted men to officer rank. Remón's simultaneous pursuit of these somewhat opposite policies had a lot to do with forming the character of the emerging Panamanian military, with making it at once populist and elitist.

Other harbingers of the future were meddling in politics and corruption. When calvary units smashed a protest march in December 1947—students and leftists objected to renewal of a wartime bases treaty with the United States—the action owed more to Remón's anticommunist and pro–U.S. sentiments than to orders from his civilian superiors. So partisan were the police in the 1948 election that Domingo Díaz owed Remón the presidency—a debt the commandant collected in benefits for himself and his officers, increased funds for the institution, and greater political belligerency for both. Meanwhile, the police ran prostitution—a lucrative business, given Panama's status as a garrison and maritime crossroads—and an illegal traffic in weapons that grossed $60,000 a month during the ten years

(1948–58) of civil strife in Colombia—a pittance by Noriegan standards but not bad for those days, not bad for starters. Which monkeyshines almost provoked a comeuppance, almost got militarism nipped in the bud, when, at the end of 1949, Daniel Chanis, a distinguished physician and Díaz's vice-president, who'd taken over when Díaz died, called Remón to the palace and summarily dismissed him for abusing his office. Remón asked leave to go to headquarters to communicate the presidential order himself, giving his word of honor that he would obey it. Chanis very foolishly agreed, whereupon Remón withdrew and returned with troops and threw Dr. Chanis out of office.

This action, which ended in a recount of the 1948 ballots and a reversal of the fraud pulled in that year, was the closest thing to a military coup in Panama's history yet not at all like those in other countries. Its objective was limited: removal of an obstacle to the commandant's ambitions. Remón never dreamed of seizing power, much less of bringing the police in with him to the detriment of other institutions, and when he sought the presidency three years later, he did so by traditional methods, taking the trouble to form a party and win an election. Once president, he besoldiered himself at last—retroactively, as it were, since before taking office he resigned his commission. He had the police renamed Guardia Nacional and restructured along military lines. To him, it was rather like a grown man's engineering his parents' wedding. For the rest of the country, it was a foolish mistake. Still, its consequences need not have been tragic but for an extremely foolish decision by those who governed the United States of America.

Traditional U.S. policy toward Latin America, applied in varying strengths throughout the region, in proportion to how patiently a country would hold still for it, was for the maintenance of client states responsive to U.S. influence and subservient to the business interests of U.S. entrepreneurs and firms. The instrument of this policy on the ground was the ruling elite of each country—that is to say, the people who owned it—who were bound to the United States by shared economic values, those associated with laissez-faire capitalism. In the wake of World War II, however, the societies of Latin America began to collapse and the owner class to lose its grip on power, under the pressure of rising popular aspirations to social justice, economic equity, political participation, and (in countries like Cuba, Nicaragua, and Panama) effective national independence. The resulting instability threatened the client-state system and seemed to make Latin America vulnerable to revolutionary Marxism, which in those days was seen as spreading like a disease from a reservoir of contagion in the Soviet Union. In response, the United States decided to change its instrument, more or less to divorce the monied elites and embrace instead the military establishments.

Two separate rationales informed this decision—one by and for realists or cynics, the other of an idealistic cast. In the first, the Latin-American military, bound by gratitude to the United States for cash lavished on them, and by greed for yet more cash to come, would defend U.S. interests—shore up the client-state system, immunize their countries against revolution—by forcible repression or the threat of it, masked with cosmetic daubs of reform. In the second, they would go about promoting social justice, hawking democracy and fairness, so as to foster the emergence of independent viable states and stable societies, bound to the United States by shared political values, in which revolution was rendered unnecessary by the willingness and ability of government to meet the people's aspirations. These two approaches coexisted from the 1950s into the 1980s, emphasis varying from one to the other according to country and to which political party held the White House. In both, the military were Uncle Sam's chosen people and the beneficiary of U.S. largesse.

The decision to make the Latin-American military Uncle Sam's instrument owed a good deal to the relative ease with which funds could be extracted from Congress for defense purposes. And cash was why the Latins went along. When Panama changed Policía to Guardia, for instance, the latter became eligible to receive aid under the Mutual Security Act of 1951. One can understand (if not excuse) the Latins. People are so often blinded by money. But how ostensibly sane Americans ever imagined that any good could come, to themselves or their neighbors, of their pampering the Latin-American military is beyond the power of reason to deduce. Americans have taken care not to pamper their own military, not to let it put on airs and so forth, though the U.S. military serve an honorable function and are as decent as any other segment of society, qualifications lacking in Latin America.

In Latin America, the military are at best drones, at worst cancers. When one asks what function they serve, traditional responses don't apply. Defend the state? Protect life and property? Maintain order? Not in the slightest. They threaten the state when they do not consume it, abuse the citizenry, and waste its substance, and their idea of order is caprice for themselves and for everyone else a deathlike rigidity. Their only legitimate function (and the claim is slender) lies in the realm of public relations. Now and then, here and there, more or less, they lend an illusion of courage and virility to societies that lack more constructive values, though the illusion tends to retard true progress, and in practice the courage often turns out to be bravado, the virility cruelty.

In Latin America, a military career offers no honor, no glory. Insofar as the military actually fight, they do so almost invariably against fellow countrymen who have taken up arms to combat military tyranny. Mainly they degrade unarmed civilians in the riskless wholesaling of terror and pain. The profession of arms, which like love and religion can be a path to loyalty and abnegation, becomes a cul-de-sac, an obscene parody. Soldiering loses its connotation of stoic virtue and comes instead to signal sloth and ease, the chance to preen in resplendent self-importance, to lord it over those who do actual work, and, at the end of the rainbow, to display greed and savagery in bullying one's country. And if, despite these negative incentives, a decent fellow now and then joins up, he is soon enough brutalized and corrupted.

By what prodigies of self-deception did responsible Americans come to imagine that bullies would be dependable agents? They'd take the money, of course, no problem there. They'd kill and maim, too, so long as it didn't get dangerous, didn't go beyond butchering peasants, torturing prisoners, raping nuns. But why on earth should they defend U.S. interests? It wasn't that (as with the owner class) their interests and the United States's coincided, or that (as in the old days) the United States could compel its clients' obedience by the fact or threat of sending in marines. And whose pipe dream was it that extortionists would turn into philosopher-kings dispensing equity and social justice? When the military take power in Latin America, the best that one can hope for is that they'll bleed the land white and then drop off like leeches, letting the civilians back into office at least long enough to restore the economy. Encourage them to change institutions, and you get what happened in Panama, perpetual despotism at increasing degrees of squalor. If the United States had taken the money it spent on the uniformed gorilocrats of Latin America, and filled 747s with twenties and fifties, and flown over the continent shoveling cash out the doors, more good would have come from the taxpayers' sacrifice, more benefit to the United States and its neighbors.

As for Panama, it had no real military, so its good neighbor to the north came and supplied one. Imagine a luckless community where all but one or two people have a foul ailment, and along comes a mad millionaire and offers one of the healthy folks money and injects the deadly virus into him. Panama had no military caste, so the United States began to grow one on the formula Toys plus Training yields Esprit de Corps and Elitism. You say Panama should have turned down the money? We say Dr. Frankenstein shouldn't go round making monsters. Whoever it was in Washington who decided to give the Guardia Nacional guns and bullets ought to have been submitted to psychiatric evaluation and, if found sane, shot for treason. The Guardia weren't going to storm the Kremlin or drive Fidel Castro from Cuba. There were only two groups those guns and bullets could hurt: the people of Panama, with whom the United States enjoyed friendly relations, and the American serviceman who might have to be committed in battle to put their Uncle Sam's monster in its place.

In 1968, then, the Panamanian Guardia Nacional was well along the road to being a full-fledged Latin-American army. Its force of 5,000 men and 465 officers, its $3 million a year from the United States on top of its budget allocation, made it overawing in a country of 1.5 million peaceful citizens, for it had a monopoly on the means of violence and no external enemies to worry about, no "war on its horizon" such as all armies should have, lest "sooner or later they fall on their own nation." As an institution, it played a political hand, most recently in attempting to influence the outcome of the year's election, and it saw itself as unjustly put upon by politicians who had no regard for its forms and traditions yet were forever asking it to clean up its messes and reap unpopularity thereby. The pride of its troops was buoyed by modern weapons and efficient training by U.S. instructors, while the tiny minds of its officers were crammed with intoxicating ideas. That civilians were no good at governing, being both dishonest and "too complicated"—that is, addicted to intricate analysis. That governing was, in fact, simple: you gave orders and saw to it that they were followed. That the Guardia had a historic mission to rescue Panama's honor and secure its future. In short, a band of armed barbarians was loose in the country, drunk on resentment and visionary dreams. That was one cloud on Panama's horizon.

Another had to do with the president who took office on October 1. This was Arnulfo Arias, the most interesting figure of Panama's republican history and its salient political personality during six decades.

General Huertas's sexology stipend wasn't the only scholarship given out in the early days of Panama's independence. Another, for study at Cambridge, went to a young mestizo named Harmodio Arias, who'd come to the capital barefoot and sold newspapers and somehow made it through school impressing his teachers. He returned a doctor of laws, joined a top firm, married into the *rabiblanco* Guardia family, made money, established himself as a jurist, founded a newspaper empire, and served a term (1932–36) as president, along the way paying for his younger brother's education in the United States. Arnulfo earned an M.D. at Harvard and seems to have been a talented physician but soon developed a stronger interest in politics. In 1930, he joined a group called Acción Comunal and within a year led it in overthrowing the government.

Acción Comunal was founded in 1923, a year after Mussolini took power in Italy, the year of the Munich beer hall putsch. Like Ku Klux Klansmen, its members wore sheets to meetings. Its line was ethnocentric and xenophobic. As may be supposed, it was radical and rightist. By 1931, however, its mystique had become relaxed enough to embody the resentment of young politicos toward the monopoly enjoyed by Panama's Liberal party, as well as unrest engendered by the worldwide financial crisis that was hitting mercantile Panama especially hard. That Arnulfo joined showed that the outfit meant business. That Harmodio sympathized showed it had practical possibilities. The plan was to take power, install a new generation, and modernize Panama.

On New Year's Day, 1930, President Florencio Arosemena entertained at the palace, an ornate, three-story building fronting the bay in the old part of Panama City. Arnulfo Arias was one of the guests. At one point, he left the party and went about unlocking windows on the ground floor. The coup was on for the following night. At show time, though, Acción Comunal got stage fright. Dr. Arias restored morale—his prescription was rum, in some versions of the story—and led the way to the palace, machine gun in hand. Four corpses later, Arosemena was out and Harmodio installed as provisional president. After two weeks, he stepped down in favor of Arosemena's vice-president, but by then a point had been made and a deal cut. In 1932, Harmodio Arias became constitutional president of the republic, whereupon he disbanded Acción Comunal, put through just enough reform to satisfy the as yet unawakened masses, and governed so as to calm the ruling elite, into which he was by then fully assimilated. His term, in fact, was the calmest in Panama's history at least partly because his brother was out of the country.

Arnulfo was ambassador to France, ambassador to Italy. Visited Germany, visited Russia. He was scheduled to run for president in 1940—the constitution prohibited a president's blood relation from succeeding him directly—and when he came home in 1938 he brought ideas with him. He took the Partido Revolutionario Nacional, which Harmodio had formed (it was neither revolutionary nor very nationalistic), and made it over into a mass movement of the Facist/Nazi stamp fanatically devoted to El Caudillo. The last was Arnulfo's title for himself, the Spanish equivalent of Il Duce or Der Führer. His program attracted the dispossessed—urban masses, mestizo peasantry—young technocrats eager to get on with the modernization Harmodio had promised but not pressed, and just about everyone with a chip on his shoulder, for Arnulfo meant to turn things upside down, end *rabiblanco* privilege and curb foreign influence and purify the so-called Panamanian race.

His greatest asset was himself. Panama has known no one like him, before or since, and there have been few men on the planet during this century more adept at transforming disparate individuals into a cohesive, frenzied crowd. Slender, handsome, vigorous, magnetic, eyes flashing demonically from a stern frown, voice clarioning mumbo jumbo in the familiar accents of the Panamanian countryside, Arnulfo didn't ask for votes but demanded them, didn't cater to the public but abused and insulted it, yet wherever he went people thronged to hear him; the more harshly he scolded, the louder they roared. Nor did he leave the outcome entirely to popularity but sent goon squads into the streets and so harried the partisans of his opponent that the latter abandoned the race, leaving him the sole candidate. He took office amid great popular enthusiasm and not a little apprehension on the part of the *rabiblancos,* of sober elements of the community, of observers in the Canal Zone and the United States.

Arnulfo Arias put through land reform and instituted a progressive income tax and established a system of social security that served Panama well for four decades, until Omar Torrijos and company wrecked it. He gave the vote to women and settled a sticky border dispute with Costa Rica. No Panamanian president did so many things the country needed so quickly, but his method was so spasmodic, his other measures so ill considered (not to say insane), that when he was stripped of his office a little more than a year after he'd assumed it, most Panamanians heaved a sigh of relief. He went after the country like Don Juan pursuing a virgin, and the country threw itself into his arms, but then he kept demanding new favors, each more outrageous than the last, till what had passed for seduction looked like rape.

Arnulfo put through a new constitution that lengthened his term to six years and gave him all kinds of special powers—put it through by plebiscite and saw to it that the right people voted, though the law stipulated a more deliberate method. He exacted political "contributions" from government employees on pain of their being fired. He ran slot-machine and protection rackets, ordered teachers and market workers to wear uniforms, and put controls on the press so his abuses wouldn't be carped at. In the name of independence, he issued a currency that had no backing. The swindle flopped in a few days, so few people lost money, but in the name of nationalism he adopted racial policies that damaged many. Chinese, Jewish, and East Indian storekeepers were baited and forced to sell cheap to Arnulfo's favorites. Foreign businesses and factories were expropriated. And forty thousand Panamanians of West Indian descent were menaced with loss of Panamanian citizenship.

Nonetheless, and in a fashion that became characteristic of him, he also took steps to remove himself from office. Then and thereafter, power deranged him. It was as if he craved restraint but could not fully govern his own actions and therefore set about to procure his own downfall—like the killer who sends the police clues and leads, who begs to be stopped before he kills again. In 1941, with the Battle of the Atlantic raging and the United States, while formally neutral, virtually allied with Great Britain, Franklin Roosevelt asked Arnulfo to authorize the arming of Panamanian flag vessels, then as now a significant portion of the world's merchant fleet. Arnulfo refused. This was in line with his Axis sympathies and with his nationalism, if not with the realities of geography and power, but then, having provoked the United States to ire, he committed a lunacy. He became enthralled with a Cuban woman—some have said she was a U.S. agent—and decided to pay her a visit, this despite a constitutional provision prohibiting the president from leaving the country without the assembly's permission. In those days, Panama City's airport was in the Canal Zone. Despite dark glasses and false papers, Arnulfo was recognized. How he hoped not to be is beyond explanation. In any case, Canal Zone authorities informed the U.S. ambassador, who informed the minister of justice, Ricardo de la Guardia, going on to say that if he cared to take power, the United States would recognize him. It is a long-standing peculiarity of Panama that everyone not only wants to be president but considers himself the best person for the job. De la Guardia got a ruling from the Supreme Court removing Arnulfo, forced the vice-president's resignation, and took over, rescinding Arnulfo's noxious measures but leaving his progressive ones in place.

Arnulfo went into exile. From Argentina, he sent emissaries to regroup his party. Then he returned and took personal charge of its reconstruction. It stopped being a Fascist/Nazi mass movement but was no less devoted, and it had a new name, Panameñista (Panamanianist). In 1948, he ran again for election, and won hands down, but was denied victory. *Rabiblanco* pressure, backed up by Colonel Remón and the police, persuaded the electoral tribunal to declare enough of Arnulfo's votes invalid to give the presidency to his opponent. A year later, though, when Remón dumped Dr. Chanis for presuming to fire him, he and Arnulfo cut a deal. The 1948 ballots were exhumed and recounted. Lo and behold, Arnulfo had won after all.

But hadn't mellowed. Out of power, he was measured and enlightened. No one, it seemed, understood Panama so well, had pondered its problems so deeply, knew so clearly what its future required. No one could lead it so wisely, or represent it to the world with such dignity. But when he was president . . . He threatened to shut down opposition newspapers and to deprive unions of their statutory rights. He had critics imprisoned, and set up his own paramilitary force, called the Boinas Negras (Black Berets), to give Remón something to think about. His usual expression was a manic grin that gave him the look of the Joker in *Batman.* His wild statements made sober folk doubt his sanity. His own brother Harmodio opposed him. But he still radiated charm, hypnotized the masses, and had no enemies these days in Washington, not with the Cold War in progress, not with his anticommunist background. Who knows how long he might have stayed in power if he'd only gone about things circumspectly, if he hadn't been programmed to self-destruct. One evening in May 1951, he went on radio and, with no groundwork laid, no foreplay whatsoever, announced that he meant to dissolve the National Assembly, suspend the Supreme Court, and abolish the constitution. And strengthen the president's powers. And, oh yes, make his term six years.

The next morning, the middle class was in the streets. Fifteen thousand businessmen, professionals, and their wives gathered at police headquarters shouting for Remón to remove Arnulfo. Remón moved, but even with the palace besieged, Arnulfo refused to surrender. Two officers of the Presidential Guard were shot dead, one of them, perhaps, by the president in person. Finally, after two days of chaos, Arnulfo left the palace vowing to return. He was formally impeached, stripped for life of his rights to vote and hold office, and jailed for ten months. Then he went to his coffee farm in Chiriquí, apparently into permanent retirement, but Panama hadn't seen the last of him, not by a long shot.

The machinery of the Partido Panameñista all but rusted away, yet many Panamanians remained loyal to Arnulfo. In 1960, the Liberal candidate, Roberto Chiari, courted these by vowing to restore Arnulfo's rights. No one blamed him for making the promise. No one dreamed he would keep it. But Chiari's first act as president was to rehabilitate Arnulfo politically. Arnulfo said he hadn't requested it, that he was out of politics forever, but four years later he turned on his benefactor, accused Chiari of incompetence and false nationalism, and ran for president again. And lost. Honestly, it seems, for the first time, but he was a political player again and remained one till his death twenty-four years later.

Meanwhile, the mercantile elite that had run Panama since 1903 on the principles of weak government, a strong private sector, and no hitting low, no driving an opponent to permanent rancor, was losing its will to tussle with the country's problems and its willingness to drop social barriers and admit new blood and its sense of having a mandate to direct things. Meanwhile, too, the world kept getting harder to figure out, what with the United States (the center of Panama's world) talking now of a firm hand and resisting the communists, now of giving the people this, that, and the other. Politicians stopped believing their own slogans, even when they brayed them most fervently. Panama's political system was coming unstuck. It happened, then, in the fall of 1967, with elections scheduled for May 1 the following year, that a group of influential politicos—a disparate lot whose only point in common was that they all had opposed Arnulfo Arias—made a pilgrimage to Chiriquí to ask Arnulfo Arias to run for president.

Some were chieftains of small parties that had been in the coalition formed by Chiari's successor as president, Marcos Robles, and that now, with his term nearly over, and his handpicked successor, David Samudio, an evident loser, decided to bolt. These included the president of the Partido Republicano, to which the incumbent vice-president, Max Delvalle, belonged. Others were members of the party

Remón had founded and that hadn't won an election for more than a decade. And there was Harmodio's son Gilberto. His presence signaled a family rapprochement. And the least expected of all possible pilgrims, the former ambassador to the UN George W. Westerman, principal leader of Panama's West Indian community, a man whose citizenship Arnulfo had threatened to rescind in 1941. All wanted Arnulfo Arias to save the republic and (in passing) lead them back to the troughs of power. And why not? Wasn't he Panama's foremost politician? The past was over and done with. Arnulfo was pushing seventy and had been out of office for sixteen years. Surely he was calm by now. In any case, Arnulfo obliged them. The *liberales* put up David Samudio. A sprightly election campaign ensued.

Robles, like most of his predecessors (and not a few presidents of the United States), used his office to help his anointed heir. The difference was that he did it more boldly than usual, to the point where one day, in the course of a passionate intervention in the National Assembly, Dr. Carlos Ivan Zúñiga suggested he might be impeached. From then on, it became the opposition's practice to threaten Robles with impeachment—not that anyone meant to go through with it (for the dangers were clear), but so as to keep his meddling somewhat within limits.

Besides Arnulfo and Samudio, however, there was a third candidate, Dr. Antonio González Revilla, an eminent surgeon but a political rookie. His party, the Christian Democrats, was still in its infancy. Its only claim to people's attention was that its lone deputy had the democratic but not very Christian name Moisés Cohen, and since it hadn't come close enough to power to abuse it, its adherents (in the manner of old maids) were very keen to note the sins of others and deplore the great lack of purity in the world. One fine day, then, Dr. González took to the airwaves and announced that he was offering a bill of impeachment against President Robles. Sure enough, the thing was presented, and the opposition deputies, a majority now with the previous fall's defections and prisoners of their own rhetoric, had no choice but to pass it. The trial was held, Robles was stripped of his office, and his vice-president, Max Delvalle, named in his place. But as Delvalle no longer belonged to the government coalition, the Supreme Court declared the bill unconstitutional and Delvalle's elevation void. With the legislative and the judicial branches thus deadlocked as to who should lead the executive, only force—the Guardia, that is—could decide the conflict.

Now there was no question where the Guardia stood. The Guardia and Arnulfo were mortal enemies. Biological enemies, for one had the masses, the other the means of repression, and each had already drawn blood, Arnulfo in contesting the Guardia's monoply on the instruments of violence, the Guardia in blasting Arnulfo from the palace. And besides, there was a personal feud between Arnulfo and Guardia Commandant Brigadier General Bolívar Vallarino that went back to 1951, when Arnulfo had called Vallarino a traitor, and Vallarino had called Arnulfo a fascist. So when Arnulfo's ally Max Delvalle went to the assembly with his partisans to receive the sash of office, Guardia troops (commanded by a lieutenant colonel named Omar Torrijos) intercepted them in Fifth of May Plaza and dispersed them with tear gas. Robles continued as president, and the Guardia mobilized its resources to give the election to Samudio. Voters were harassed and intimidated, talliers dragged from voting tables and jailed, ballot boxes made off with at gunpoint. But with the election stolen, Vallarino got scared. The *arnulfistas* refused to go tamely. They went into the streets, and battles between them and Samudio's supporters seemed likely to precipitate civil war. So Vallarino made a deal with Arnulfo. He would recognize Arnulfo's victory and retire in October. Arnulfo would appoint new commandants according to the Guardia's seniority list.

When the terms of the pact were made public, the officers of the Guardia were enraged. In loyalty to their commander, to protect their institution, they had stolen the election from Arnulfo, earning Arnulfo's eternal hatred. Now Vallarino had made a separate peace and undone the theft, leaving them at El Caudillo's mercy. There was talk of a preemptive coup—from officers, even from President Robles, who advocated his own overthrow as a means of preventing Arnulfo's taking office. The talk centered on, and stopped with, a major named Boris Martínez, the brightest and most competent man in the Guardia, and one of the few who were clean of taints of corruption. Martínez declined. Arnulfo might still keep his part of the bargain to respect the Guardia's structure and its officers as professionals. The seed had been planted, however. Panama inched that much closer to the edge.

That, then, was the second cloud on Panama's horizon: a president who represented the will of the people but not its best judgment, a volatile man with a history of allergy to power, the merest whiff of which unplugged his reason and goosed him into a manic dance.

And, finally, the last cloud, one that presaged the storm ahead more than the two others. The people of Panama didn't know their good fortune. Or, guessing it, they thought it would never run out.

For the most part, they didn't realize their country was lucky. After all, it was neither large nor rich in resources, nor in the least adept at bullying its neighbors. They looked at countries that were—the United States, for example—and saw wealth and power, triumph and pride. It didn't matter that the United States was fighting its fourth major war of the century, a war that was rending it almost to pieces, or that it had its share of domestic problems, its quota of pain, its allotment of despair. Panamanians looked and felt envious.

They looked at Panama and saw what was wrong: poverty, graft, foreign occupation. That the poverty might get worse didn't occur to them, or that the graft they saw then would soon seem honesty's image. As for occupation, the real thing was coming, brutal and rapacious, complete with quislings and camp followers, by an army whose personnel were native to the country but whose purposes were foreign to the people's well-being. All that was off in the future, and so beyond most people's imagining. Oh yes, of course, they were better off than other Central Americans, better off than Africans, better off than most Asians. They had peace, but that didn't seem much; they'd always had it. And freedom, but they had no sense of its worth. Modest prosperity, some social justice, what of it? What about poverty? What about graft? What about the circus they'd been watching, combinations and recombinations, deals made and unmade, an impeachment voted and then rescinded, an election stolen and given back? They looked at Panama and felt ashamed and outraged, said things couldn't go on the way they were going.

Like food to the French, drink to the Swedes, love to the Italians, and fratricide to the Irish, politics was their national obsession. Everyone was involved, playing or rooting. Avidly, but with no great concern for the outcome. It was only a game. The rule was no hitting low. Nothing very terrible could happen. No one dreamed (much less allowed the dream to inform his action) that a minor bend in the rules was about to change everything, that bit by bit the pleasant game could turn deadly. Arnulfo and Robles, Drs. Zúñiga and González Revilla, General Vallarino, Major Martínez—all look, in hindsight, like figures in a *danse macabre.* Or perhaps that's too solemn. In hindsight, Panama looks like Chaplin in *The Gold Rush,* strutting purposefully along, not realizing he's on the lip of a chasm.

Panama was different, that's what one heard. Then and later: Panama wasn't like other countries. Its people weren't violent. Its soil wasn't fertile for dictatorship. And it all was quite true. Everything that happened happened uniquely, *à la panamanienne.* But the country still got wrecked. In its own fashion, yes, but wrecked nonetheless. And the attitude of the people contributed greatly. It was as if they were scared they'd miss the twentieth century and not collect their due share of its horrors, as if they craved to live in interesting times.

* * *

In the days before he took office, Arnulfo began to give ominous signs of unbalance, the mixed arrogance and lunacy that had already toppled him twice in the past. Five months earlier, Panama had seen the attempt at vote fraud crumble, and the people's choices recognized as victors, in a spectacle that suggested political maturity. Now the president-elect went about openly despoiling deputies of their legitimately won credentials and passing these out to mediocrities who would vote tamely according to his orders. Nor were his targets always opponents like Moisés Torrijos, Lieutenant Colonel Omar's elder brother. With insane impartiality, he also dumped members of his own coalition. And in a move whose effects could only be to infuriate officers and lessen his chances for working with them smoothly, he named as his aide-de-camp—that is, his official liaison with the Guardia—a man, Luis Carlos Duque, who though a graduate of Chile's police academy had never been a policeman or a soldier, who hadn't lived in Panama for twenty years, and who was not personally acquainted with a single one of the Guardia's more than five thousand officers, noncoms, and privates.

Nor did the symptoms ease with his swearing-in. Marcos Robles, the outgoing president, didn't attend it. He left for Coral Gables on September 30. Perhaps it was this indignity that caused him to appoint his barber, a man named Vernaza, chief of the National Department of Investigations. The act was not entirely empty of logic. As one who had held a razor to Arnulfo's throat every morning for thirty years and never slit it—a temptation not all Panamanians could have resisted—Vernaza was at least worthy of trust. But as he had no other qualification, his appointment was an affront to everyone concerned with public order, to the country as whole. Meanwhile, Arnulfo made it plain that he would take revenge on the officers who had participated in the vote swindle by posting them as attachés in backwater countries, a form of exile that may have been merited but that instantly made him a number of desperate enemies.

One can argue that Arnulfo had no choice but to purge these

officers before they purged him, that appointing Vernaza and Duque made no difference, that the business of the deputies was beside the point, that the Guardia meant to move against him anyway. And one need not argue at all regarding results. Nothing Arnulfo did or might have done can justify the coup d'état and the years of tyranny that followed. Nonetheless, Arnulfo has much to answer for. His actions were clearly provocative. Worse, they were ineffective. They infuriated the Guardia officers without really hurting them, even engendered some foolish sympathy for them. Then, having broken the spirit of his pact with Vallarino, he proceeded to break the letter. On October 9, Colonel José Pinilla, the next senior officer on the Guardia's list, came to the palace on Arnulfo's summons, expecting a general's star and the post of first commandant. What he got was the boot. "You've served the fatherland," Arnulfo told him. "Go home." Pinilla was due to retire in December anyway, but Arnulfo had to show who was boss.

On the night of October 10, a company from Greece presented *King Oedipus.* In Greek, but that was no drawback. The actors were excellent, and most of the audience knew the plot. Besides, there was a kind of prologue to remind them that Sophocles is a modern poet, that the theme of *hybris* is never out of date. The house lights dimmed, then suddenly came back on. In strode the president of the republic with half the members of his cabinet in tow. The resulting ovation shook the building. Arnulfo took it as his natural right, as haughtily as Oedipus at the play's opening, though he'd already been deposed twice and was destined to be so again in twenty-four hours. "He's either sure of himself or unconscious," a member of that audience remembers thinking. Actually, he was both.

Let us, then, leave Arnulfo gloating—he had only a day to do so before departing the scene for ten years—and pick up the trail of Major Boris Martínez, who'd come to his career entirely by accident, then pursued it somewhat unorthodoxly. A classmate of Noriega's at the Instituto Nacional, and like Noriega both poor and a would-be physician, he qualified via grades for a medical scholarship offered by Mexico. But in that particular year, 1952, grades didn't count. The scholarship had been promised to the son of one of President Remón's buddies. In consolation, Remón wangled another, this one in engineering to his alma mater, which Martínez accepted with good grace. Except that when he got to Mexico, it turned out to be for military studies, though maybe, later on, he might transfer to the engineering school, and so on. The transfer never materialized. Martínez graduated, returned to Panama, found no good job, and joined the Guardia as a sublieutenant.

He would have better suited a better army. He was a stern young man, un-Panamanian in his seriousness, uncompromising in his idealism. Assigned to street patrol in the capital, he soon noticed a complex and lucrative symbiosis between the Guardia and the purveyors of vice. He refused to take part: would not take bribes, would not defer to bribers, despite admonitions from his superiors. Had he sprouted wings, he could not have stood out more clearly from others in uniform, and his odd honesty, which in the end ruined him, would surely have blighted his career had he not also shown exceptional brilliance and energy, along with efficiency, loyalty, and personal magnetism. He made his chiefs look good, helped his peers get out of scrapes, and despite his sternness was popular with the soldiers, so the benefits of accepting him outweighed the sense of moral inferiority one felt in his presence. Although five or ten officers outranked him, in 1968 he was the Guardia's true commander. No one would try any big thing without him. Few hesitated to follow where he led.

That fall, Martínez commanded in Chiriquí Province. He had not involved himself in many electoral monkeyshines and thus was not among those scheduled for "exile," though Arnulfo did program his transfer to Herrera, no doubt as part of the show-who's-boss operation. Herrera was a less important province, but since Martínez would once again be in command, the posting was, on paper at least, no demotion. Martínez prepared to accept it without chafing, sent his belongings to Chitré, the province's capital, and arranged his mind for an extended stay, perhaps until after the 1972 elections.

We come, then, to Friday, October 11, 1968. In the United States (which was having perhaps the worst year of its history, a year that began with the *Pueblo* incident and the Tet offensive, and ended with the election of Richard Nixon), *Apollo 7* lifted off successfully. In Panama, a coup d'état was about to do likewise. That morning, Major Boris Martínez was in Panama City to attend the ceremony in which Vallarino gave way to Lieutenant Colonel Bolívar Urrutia, Arnulfo's choice as commandant of the Guardia and its ranking officer after Pinilla's summary dismissal.

Martínez's first stop was La Comandancia (Guardia headquarters), a four-story fortress across from La Modelo Prison guarded by an alabaster effigy of Remón. There he heard that Luis Carlos Duque, Arnulfo's aide-de-camp, had visited the cuartel at Tocumen Airport and had been insolent to the duty officer, Sublieutenant

Leonidas Macías. This may not sound too terrible in English. However, Latins in general and Panamanians in particular are, by Anglo-Saxon standards, very sensitive to insults, real or imagined. Besides, persons in uniform claim a monopoly on insolence and feel the tiniest slight by a civilian—which was what the Guardia considered Duque—as if it were a heavy blow. As for Panamanian officers, their remarkable touchiness, put beside their complete unconcern for the feelings of others, deserves the attention of neurological researchers.

The next thing Martínez learned of was the transfers. These had been known via rumor for a few days, but it was somehow worse to see them published in that morning's newspaper with no prior notification to headquarters, much less consultation with the Guardia command. And of course there was Arnulfo's contemptuous breaking of the pact he'd so recently made with Vallarino, his needless affront to Colonel Pinilla, his evident intention to wreck the Guardia Nacional as an institution and geld its officers as military professionals. The pleas "Do something!" rained on Martínez.

Martínez went next to the cuartel at Panamá Viejo, where the change of command was to be celebrated and where the mood was, if anything, more tense. This was also where the decision to strike was taken, the most cinematic of possible locations, overlooking the bay, where long low breakers rolled in softly, amid the ruins of Old Panama, sacked and burned by Morgan's pirates in 1671. There Martínez ran into his closest friend in the Guardia, Lieutenant Colonel Omar Torrijos.

The two could scarcely have been more different in temperament, though there seems to have been a true comradeship between them, of the sort between Don Quixote and Sancho Panza, or (better perhaps) Prince Hal and Falstaff. Torrijos, who at thirty-nine was four years Martínez's elder, chose a career in the Guardia for the excellent reason that he couldn't do better. A middle child in the large family of a provincial schoolteacher, he was neither very bright nor at all industrious, and had been obliged to leave the Instituto, and lucky to get through a provincial high school and El Salvador's military academy. On the other hand, he was easygoing and likable, acceptably fond of whisky and women, unencumbered by excess idealism or integrity. He adapted well to soldiering Panamanian style and floated upward.

Not without occasional problems, however, which Martínez had a way of helping him through. For instance, there was the time he got howling drunk in a cantina named Lo Dudo (I Doubt It) and accused

Vallarino of having murdered Remón. He was reported, but Martínez was the one dispatched to arrest him and first sent a friend to get him out of there, then took his time arriving on the scene. And in 1959, during the Guardia's first counterinsurgency ruckus, Martínez saved Torrijos again. Inspired by Fidel Castro and armed with a few shotguns, a group of university students took to the hills in Veraguas Province. A company was sent after them with Torrijos commanding and Martínez as his exec. At the first sign of action, Omar Torrijos bolted, got shotgun pellets in the buttocks—somewhat a red badge, but not of courage. His career, at least, suffered no damage. Martínez managed things till the students surrendered and told no tales till after Torrijos betrayed him.

Now Torrijos was in trouble again. He'd been in the election fraud up to his armpits, going around with a bag full of money buying up precinct captains, so he was slated to be banished. To El Salvador of all places! He'd tried to negotiate, and Arnulfo's minister of government had been rude to him. He'd asked for $5,000 to compensate for the bribes he wouldn't collect, and all he got was a paltry $2,500. There he was at the change-of-command celebration, already drunk though the party had just started, begging with tears in his eyes for Martínez to help him, to use his influence to have the transfer rescinded, or at least to get him a little more cash.

Martínez had other things on his mind. His own future, that of the Guardia, Panama's also. He was faced with the chance of a lifetime. Should he take it? Could he let it go by? He told Torrijos to act like a man and turned back to the party. With that, up came Juan David Morgan, Vallarino's son-in-law and a rising young lawyer, to press him about leading a coup d'état. Sometime in the next half hour, Martínez decided that was what he would do.

He collected his brother-in-law, Captain Humberto Jiménez, who was in charge of the Guardia armory, and went in Jiménez's car to Tocumen Airport. He assured himself that the cuartel there would rally to him and picked up the support of Major Federico Boyd, who commanded the cavalry squadron and who offered to take and hold La Comandancia. With these points taken care of, he flew back to David, but first he had another chat with Torrijos, who had followed him out to the airport in the car of one of his buddies, the Colón contractor Demetrio "Jimmy" Lakas. In response to another tearful plea for help, Martínez told Torrijos not to worry, to go home and say nothing to anyone, all would be well. He didn't say what he was up to. For one thing, Torrijos was drunk. For another, he couldn't be counted on, drunk or sober. And Lakas was a notorious blabbermouth who would spray word of the coup all over Panama.

Which, as things went, wouldn't have mattered. By the time Martínez left the capital, it was seething with coup rumors, most of them accurate. Nonetheless, Arnulfo was taken by surprise. He and his advisers zombied toward the abyss, taking no heed, noticing nothing, drunk on power and self-importance. Guillermo Sánchez remembers mentioning the possibility of a coup to a mid-level *arnulfista* as the two were riding in the latter's car. "Let them try it!" the man blustered, lifting his jacket from the seat beside him to show the tommy gun resting underneath. The next time Sánchez saw him, both were prisoners. Not in La Modelo, which was overflowing, but in a holding pen in La Comandancia. The man hadn't fired a shot. Later he became a pillar of the dictatorship.

In Chiriquí, meanwhile, Boris Martínez was busy. Not overly, however; a plan already existed. It was called Plan A. U.S. Army counterintelligence had designed it as a means of reversing a communist seizure of power. That Panama's communists might even dream of such an adventure would have thoroughly amused anyone who knew them, but no doubt such plans were drawn for all the world's countries and distributed to their respective armed forces, whether or not they were actually threatened. How many coups d'état were thereby facilitated, and how much human freedom and dignity crushed, would make an interesting subject for investigation. In any case, the plan was there, and provided for seizing communications and so on, for whatever one does on such occasions. When Martínez arrived at his cuartel in David, he first secured the cooperation of his own officers—including Lieutenant Manuel Noriega, who as intelligence officer would implement the plan in Chiriquí. Then he called round the country, lining up other adherents.

Almost to a man, the key officers were joined. Major Armando Contreras pledged the garrison in Colón. Majors Ramos and Sanjur the cuarteles at Santiago and Panamá Viejo. Major Rodrigo García at La Modelo argued a little, then agreed when he judged that the coup was a sure thing. Ozores, commander in Chitré, declared himself neutral, which was all Martínez really needed from him. Only Major Bolívar Rodríguez, commanding the Presidential Guard, was opposed. Like every other Guardia officer, he had taken an oath to defend the constitution. The odd thing was, he took it seriously. On getting his answer, Martínez called one of his subordinates, a Lieutenant Correa, with whom he was personally friendly, recruited him for the coup, and told him to hold Rodríguez in his office but not to harm him. At 4:30 in the afternoon, Plan A began to go into effect with the closing of Panama's border with Costa Rica.

Just before 5:00 P.M., Costa Rica's President Trejos Fernández placed a call to Arnulfo Arias in Panama. Arnulfo either wouldn't or couldn't take it, so Trejos called Hildebrando Nicosia, Arnulfo's closest adviser for twenty years and now his minister of the presidency, a post corresponding to White House chief of staff. What was happening in Panama, asked Trejos, that had caused the border to be sealed and, according to Costa Rica's Guardia Civil, the wholesale arrest of *arnulfistas* in Chiriquí Province? Nicosia's response still seems incredible. He didn't press Trejos Fernández for details. He said, "Nothing, everything's normal," and after some courtesies hung up the phone. Nor is there any indication that he told Arnulfo about the call!

Could something have been done at that late hour? No one can say. That something could have been tried goes without saying. A speech to the nation over TV and radio would have been heard in eight of Panama's nine provinces. A call to defend democracy might have been answered. There were officers who believed in it, and the troops, like most lower-class Panamanians, were *arnulfistas* almost to a man. But nothing was tried, because no one in the government would open his eyes to see what was happening, even when, like Nicosia, he had his face dunked in it. The whole country had been talking of a coup, was talking of it even as it was in progress, but hardly anyone took it at all seriously. After all, Panama was the only state in Latin America that had never had a military takeover. Even Costa Rica had had one in the 1910s, but Panama didn't know what one was. The gay and confident Panama that was going to die that night wasn't, it seems, really of this world. The very traits that made it a good place were what doomed it.

By 7:30, Plan A was in effect throughout Chiriquí, with all radio stations linked on a single hookup and an announcer coming on every few minutes advising listeners of a special message to follow. As Martínez was about to go on the air, the background music struck him as familiar, and he asked Lieutenant Noriega if he knew it. Noriega did; he'd chosen it himself. It was the "Horst Wessel Lied," the Nazi anthem. Thus appropriately introduced, and with Noriegan *Galgenhumor* in the reference to Arnulfo's early flirtation with fascism and Noriega's own barbarities to come, Martínez proclaimed the government's overthrow and martial law. Then, with every soldier he could spare and all the weapons they could lay their hands on, he left by plane for Panama City. He had to take command at Guardia headquarters before his friend Omar Torrijos wrecked everything.

Torrijos was in the Canal Zone that evening, at the home of Efraín Angueira, a forty-eight-year-old native of Puerto Rico serving with U.S. Army counterintelligence and assigned as liaison with the Guardia Nacional. And perhaps Torrijos's control agent also, for it was U.S. intelligence policy to have Guardia officers on the clandestine payroll as a lever for manipulating their actions, while Torrijos was richly equipped for finkhood by his chronic booze and cash-flow problems. At any rate, he was there and he was drunk, along with the Guardia majors Neco Bernal and Pili Silvera and the ubiquitous Demetrio Lakas, when word of the coup reached them. Lakas dragged Torrijos partway to sobriety with applications of cold water and hot coffee, and the four Panamanians set off for Guardia headquarters, a five-minute drive from Angueira's house on Fort Amador. It was then about eight o'clock in the evening.

They stopped first at La Modelo, perhaps to get a sense of the situation. Which was as follows: Martínez had Chiriquí, as he'd finished proclaiming. Boyd had headquarters. Jiménez had Colonel Urrutia locked in a cell. The Presidential Guard was with the coup makers, and there was no resistance from any quarter, but Arnulfo hadn't been located yet. With Vallarino and Pinilla in retirement, Urrutia under arrest, and his deputy, Lieutenant Colonel Aristides Hassán (longtime chief of the transit bureau), no more than a traffic cop and not present anyway, Torrijos was in line to take command. With that established, the four began walking the short, downhill block to headquarters, but after a few steps Torrijos panicked, wanted to bolt back to the Canal Zone.

"¡Hijo de puta!" squealed Lakas. He yanked a pistol from under his *guayabera* and stuck it in Torrijos's ribs. With his left hand, he seized Torrijos's shoulder and pulled him toward headquarters. He didn't put the pistol back till they got there.

There's a clip for your highlight reel! The burly Lakas . . . Not the full pachydermic burliness he achieved during his long puppet presidency, the heavy bulge of throat and chest and forearm, the skowish thrust of gut, the breadth of rump, but a solidity and force not to be gibed at when animated by sugarplum visions of pelf . . . The burly Lakas shoves Torrijos toward power, and Torrijos—the future strongman!—lets himself be shoved, pasty-faced, disheveled, nerves begging for a drink, because he fears the man at his side more than the destiny around the corner. But Torrijos's funk may not have been wholly a defect. That he could be fearful and irresolute—cowardly, if you like—we know not just from his conduct on coup night but from similar behavior in Veraguas in 1959 and in Mexico in 1969 on the occasion (see chapter 3) of the attempt to overthrow him. But the actions he was to take in a few minutes, in which he was joined by certain of his colleagues, suggest not only fright for his own skin but a healthy trepidation for Panama also. Perhaps one gives them credit they don't merit, but it may be that Torrijos and some other officers—Sanjur for one, Silvera for another—sensed they were smashing something fine and irreparable, a dream country (Cambodia and Lebanon were two others) whose existence on planet Earth in the twentieth century was amazing if not miraculous. They weren't up to quitting the coup, much less to opposing it, but they seem to have tried to stop it from going too far.

At headquarters—where excitement and confusion reigned, with reports coming in and orders being issued and Martínez phoning every few minutes—Torrijos and others began to talk about having Arnulfo's vice-president take over, a *rabiblanco* politician called Raúl Arango. Someone advised Martínez, or perhaps consulted him. Either way, his reaction was clear. He ordered Torrijos to do nothing till he got there. "If you put 'Lul' [Arango] in power, I'll shoot the lot of you! I'm on my way!"

Martínez has since held that installing Arango or any other civilian would have brought violence, that the people would not have borne dumping their idol Arnulfo as part of just another politicians' game, that the only way to make the coup stick was for it to be the end of that sort of foolishness, for the Guardia to correct abuses and hold elections and turn the country over to the winners. But it was Martínez himself, more than any other person in Panama, who required an idealistic aim. He, not the situation, demanded it. He needed something more lofty in the way of a purpose than protecting the Guardia's structure from tampering and a few of its officers from four years without bribes. He couldn't live with breaking his oath for that, or because his comrades' appeals flattered his ego. His moral rigidity wouldn't permit it. He'd taken a risk, and now, evidently, he'd won, and the payoff couldn't be cheap like the May vote fraud. That was why he piled 120 soldiers into three civilian DC-3s for a wild takeoff (during which his own overloaded aircraft nearly crashed) and a night flight to the capital. Panama would have been better off if he'd been less priggish.

Or less ambitious. The difference between him and Torrijos, Sanjur, and Silvera may have merely been that the latter lacked ambition. Whatever the case, they didn't obey his order but went right ahead and offered the presidency to Arango. He turned them down, and his wife gave their envoy, Sanjur, a piece of her mind. (There's another picture: Major Sanjur—slight, handsome, prematurely gray—slinks toward the door, while Señora Arango, carrying the weight of middle age and righteous anger, pelts his hunched shoulders with insults.) Next, they tried to form a junta of "notables" but found no one who qualified willing to serve. They preferred civilian rule, and if possible a whiff of constitutionality, to military dictatorship. Martínez would have none of it, and might have undone a deal with bullets had Torrijos and company managed to put one together.

Once at headquarters, Martínez imposed his will. No more rummaging for civilian politicians. The Guardia itself would run Panama. To begin with, he gave orders to arrest all officers who sympathized with Arnulfo or believed in preserving constitutional procedures. So it went with Bolívar Rodríguez and others. Next, he asked for Colonels Pinilla and Urrutia, sent a car to fetch the former from his home, went himself to the latter's cell and released him. Then and there, he persuaded Urrutia to codirect a two-person junta. Pinilla would be its president, Urrutia its . . . Martínez cast about for a title and came up with the unfortunate choice of "member" (in Spanish, *miembro*)—unfortunate because the word is a popular euphemism, in Panama as elsewhere, for the principal male instrument of generation, so that during the junta's fourteen-month existence Urrutia's title gave rise to innumerable jokes, all of them salacious, and thus caused its wearer endless embarrassment.

In forming the junta, Martínez symbolically reconsecrated the Guardia seniority list that Arnulfo had profaned, and publicly rehabilitated the slighted Pinilla. Next, still upholding seniority, he designated Hassán the Guardia's commandant, though true command clearly reposed with him. How he lost it to Torrijos, we shall see presently. For now, it may be observed that his punctilio is altogether characteristic of garrison as opposed to combat soldiers and perhaps indicative of overly rigid toilet training in childhood. Above all, one notes its selectivity. How reverent Martínez was of military propriety, how unfailing in his genuflections to it! How odd, then, and how sad for his country, that his fastidiousness did not extend to Panama's constitution, or to the oath he'd sworn to defend it!

Panama's civilians had, meanwhile, been spending an ordinary evening until, in this way or that, they learned of the coup. At eight-thirty or thereabouts, Guillermo Sánchez Borbón was at his regular table on the sidewalk outside the Café Boulevard, in his regular seat facing out across Avenida Balboa toward the palm trees, the parapet, and the bay, toward the shrimp boats lying at mooring three hundred yards out, shimmered in the lights of the palace on a point of land off to the right, toward the pinpoint running lights of merchant vessels lying at anchor in the roadstead of the Canal. He, his nephew David, and three friends were drinking coffee or *chicha* or maybe beer, discussing, ach! he doesn't remember, when up ran Floyd Britton, leader of the minuscule pro-China fraction of Panama's minuscule collection of practicing communists. Out of breath and saying that the Guardia was taking power, that Chiriquí had already fallen, that the rest of the country was liable to go any minute, though he was going to try to arrange some resistance. That's where and how and from whom Sánchez heard of the coup, and also the last he saw of his friend Britton. Both were imprisoned, but Britton went to the penal colony on Coiba Island and was murdered there on Omar Torrijos's orders.

A few blocks off, a reception was in progress at the home of J. J. Espino, newly appointed comptroller of the republic. The house bulged with distinguished figures of the government, the president and first lady included, not one of whom had the least inkling that power was being pulled from under them. A bit before nine, Arnulfo and his wife, Mireya, excused themselves. Rodrigo Sánchez Borbón, Guillermo's brother, who'd just been elected to the assembly, stayed on, chatting with the minister of education, Rubén Arosemena. Suddenly, a relative of Arosemena's burst in, in bedroom slippers. Arosemena began to upbraid him for his poor manners when the other interrupted. A coup was on, the Guardia was taking power! That was where and when and from whom most of the government learned, but the waiters at the Boulevard had known for at least half an hour.

From Espino's, Dr. Arias and his señora went to the Teatro Lux, on Avenida Perú and Calle 34. R. M. Koster and his señora were there that night also. They heard the bustle just as the show was starting, turned round and saw the presidential pair. The movie that night was a western called *Firecreek*—with James Stewart and Henry Fonda—an execrable turkey despite its stars, with a convoluted plot and no action to speak of. Arnulfo, at least, didn't have to sit through it. A few minutes after the feature started, his bodyguards turned on the car radio and thereby discovered that a straightforward plot with plenty of action was going on that very night in Panama. One of them entered the theater, sat down behind Arnulfo, and whispered something to him. Arnulfo remained seated for a minute or two, then turned to Mireya. "Let's go," he said, adding, when she asked why, "I'm tired." Mireya, dropped off at her house, did not learn of the coup for another two hours.

Let us now follow Dr. Arnulfo Arias on his last ride through Panama City for ten years. From the house where he dropped off Mireya, he went to a residence he kept on Avenida Balboa and Calle 33, but scarcely stopped, for one of his bodyguards noticed that the soldiers who should have been on guard there were nowhere about. They had, in fact, been recalled, and a few minutes later troops surrounded the house and began blazing away at it with rifles and tommy guns, firing hundreds of rounds that terrified some but not all of the occupants. These were the aged mother of Arnulfo's first wife and a pair of her relatives. The latter disconnected the old lady's hearing aid when the truckloads of soldiers arrived, and she slept soundly through the whole incident.

Arnulfo headed next for the palace and the supposed protection of the Presidential Guard. At high speed, as may be imagined, along Avenida Balboa, past the Café Boulevard, where patrons were still sitting placidly and conversing! The government was being toppled and a military dictatorship installed, but that was no reason to wreck a pleasant evening. This was Panama; there was nothing to get worked up about, though the café did empty out a few minutes later when troops began blasting Arnulfo's house two blocks off. Well, he at least was excited, he and his bodyguards and his driver, speeding through streets that looked perfectly normal, up Calle 18 to Avenida Central, down Central, past Plaza Santa Ana, into the oldest part of the capital, built after Morgan had burned the original city, with sea walls so massive that when the king of Spain got the bill for them, he went to the west window of Escorial and asked his ministers why they weren't visible. But before they reached the cathedral, they saw the square beyond it full of soldiers. Hope of reaching the palace ran out at once.

Right! Arnulfo ordered, and right the car turned, down Calle 8, which is barely wide enough for one-way traffic, especially since there are always cars parked on the right-hand sidewalk with their right fenders almost scraping the buildings. Down cobblestoned Calle 8, one short block to Avenida A. Which is narrow too at that corner, though it broadens at the next if one turns right. Which

Arnulfo's car did with appropriate screech of tires and fishtailing, past the Church of San José, insignificant from without but housing the great Golden Altar, a relic of when Panama was the richest city on earth, saved from Morgan when the citizens painted it black and hauled it off to an island in the bay. Off Arnulfo sped, back away from the palace, off the point of land it sits on, for his idea now was to get to headquarters, where someone loyal to his oath might be in charge, but near headquarters the way was blocked by soldiers in battle dress, and with that Arnulfo opted for escape. Which was as well. Besides firing on his home, the Guardia occupied his properties in Chiriquí Province, shot his dog and burned the warehouse on his coffee farm, shot cattle on his ranch, and burned the house, and wrecked three tractors—depredations that foreshadowed what the country was in for. They might have murdered Arnulfo had they caught him, but he had his driver turn up a side street parallel to the one Lakas had shoved Torrijos down an hour or so earlier, then left along Transversal 1 and drove to Avenida 4 de Julio and into the Canal Zone, where the United States was sovereign.

Thus ended the third administration of Dr. Arnulfo Arias, ten days, eleven hours, and forty-some minutes after it began. His partisans, and those of democracy in Panama, consoled themselves with the bitter wine of its having established a new world's record for brevity, but even that small comfort proved transitory. A short time later, the president of an African republic was deposed and arrested by soldiers during his inaugural ceremony, immediately after being sworn in.

3

THE BRIEF TIME OF BORIS MARTÍNEZ

"A man should not be too wise," goes a Norse proverb, "lest he know his own fate in advance." Few in Panama supposed when the coup occurred that they were fated to live under a dictatorship, much less one that would last for over two decades. Over and again, Panamanians had heard and repeated a phrase so well known that it has been attributed to a number of the country's early statesmen: "Panama is not fertile soil for dictatorship." Most Panamanians, in fact, took the coup lightly. Arnulfo Arias had been thrown out of office. Nothing new there. The only surprise was that it had happened so quickly. *Pues bien,* he'd begun his craziness sooner than usual, but it wasn't as if something serious had happened. In a day or two, there'd be a new president, and everything would go back to normal.

Many politicians were among the deluded. David Samudio, the candidate thrashed by Arnulfo, fell all over himself rushing to Guardia headquarters in the goofy belief that he would be handed power. Carlos and Fernando Eleta trotted behind him. They owned a TV station, and Fernando fancied himself presidential. And there were others. Even those who understood the younger officers and who'd had nightmares of their ruling the country were caught off balance. Able as its politicos were at electoral flimflam, they had nothing in their repertoire of stunts and maneuvers that equipped them to confront the events at hand.

There was no way to be sure what was occurring. Had Arnulfo

been killed in the fusillade on his house? Was he under arrest, was he in hiding? Guillermo Sánchez remembers spending the night of October 11–12 in the home of his brother José María, until recently ambassador to Colombia. No Panamanian stations were on the air. Channel 8 in the Canal one showed movie after movie. From time to time, the bottom of the screen lit up with a warning for U.S. personnel to avoid Panama—"due to political developments"—but the same was shown during any trifling demonstration. Not a word about the coup d'état. Sometime before midnight, the phone rang. Radio Caracol in Bogotá was calling José María. For news, but the caller ended up giving, not getting. Through him, the brothers learned that Arnulfo had taken refuge in the Zone.

Late at night, those who had radios turned on began picking up a scratchy, faint signal that identified itself as Radio Clandestina. The announcer correctly named the coup's principal authors, Martínez and Boyd, and in an agitated voice called on people to go into the streets and declare a general strike, "to finish once and for all with this corrupt militarism." At length, those who stayed awake all night or rose at daybreak heard the first communiqué of the country's new masters broadcast over a few radio stations that came back on the air under Guardia vigilance. "Guardia officers," it said, "have decided to act with high patriotism to install in the republic a provisional government that will clear the way for a return to the democratic order disturbed by ambitious and misguided politicians."

At 7:40, stations announced that constitutional guarantees had been suspended, that freedom of assembly, expression, and so on no longer existed. The only daily available was *El Mundo,* a paper owned by David Samudio, the losing candidate in the recent election and, till his own disillusionment with them, slavishly supportive of the coup makers. At 1:00 P.M., what were called provisional statutes were issued over the signatures of Colonels Pinilla and Urrutia, president and member of what was called the Provisional Junta of Government. Designed to put people at ease, the statutes said little: existing laws were in effect; international obligations would be honored. Free transit supposedly existed on all streets and highways, but those who moved about in the capital found soldiers in combat rig at important intersections stopping cars and pedestrians, making people identify themselves, subjecting individuals to search and arrest.

For R. M. Koster, who stayed home, the twelfth was more or less a normal Saturday. As was usual, friends came by after lunch to play chess. One, an *arnulfista,* suffered a few jokes at his expense, but not even he was outraged by the coup. Arnulfo, he felt, had been asking for trouble. And no one feared the extinction of freedom or the Guardia's staying permanently in power. Guillermo Sánchez, on the other hand, saw what was on the horizon with terrible clarity, even glimpsed his own imprisonment and exile. He noted the city's calm, but also the worry on people's faces. Some of it, no doubt, was his own concern projected, but he visited many neighborhoods that day, saw many sorts besides middle-class people; and the lower class, besides being strong for Arnulfo, knew the Guardia Nacional better than anyone. Ignorant, brutal, corrupt: that was the Guardia. They were trouble enough without being in power.

For Sánchez that day, time moved to the rhythms of infancy. Minutes dragged. Hours were endless. In the morning, he drove around with a friend who worked at *La Hora,* owned by the heirs of Arnulfo's brother Harmodio but soon to be taken over by the dictatorship along with the Arias family's three other dailies. A copy of the paper lay on the car seat, headlines screaming condemnation of the Guardia—one of a very few copies that saw the light, because moments after the editorial staff left the paper, soldiers arrived to confiscate the edition and, in passing, knock the typographers about. Later, Sánchez ran into a friend, Renato Pereira, and received another of the day's shocks. The day before, Pereira had been one of Arnulf's luminaries, all swollen with the pomp of being in power, but overnight he seemed to have experienced a conversion of the sort that came to Saint Paul on the road to Damascus. The day before, Pereira's eyes had been dark, but now he saw clearly, and Arnulfo's policies, which he'd tortured language to justify, now showed themselves ill advised, no, absolute madness! Sánchez, who'd never cared much for Arnulfo's policies but who valued democracy and civil liberties, had meant to sound Pereira out on the chances of organizing some sort of resistance to the coup, but now he saw he'd be better off looking elsewhere. Pereira was not out of power long. He floated upward with the dictatorship and became one of Noriega's closest advisers.

Arnulfo, meanwhile, was in the Canal Zone living at the home of a relative married to an American and maintaining a headquarters in an empty house put at his disposal by the United States. Almost as soon as he arrived there, he began to be joined by partisans, members of his government or of the National Assembly, who like him were seeking both refuge and a way back to power—an entourage that at its flood numbered nearly two hundred and included three puppet presidents-to-be, Aristides Royo, Jorge Illueca, and Manuel Solís Palma, the first a creature of the tyrant Omar Torrijos, the last two of the tyrant Manuel Noriega. Here, in a sort of internal exile, Arnulfo presided at spectral cabinet meetings and issued phantom decrees. At 5:00 P.M. on the twelfth, a message from him was read over Radio Clandestina in which he assured the country that he was taking all necessary measures to ensure peace and public order. What these were wasn't specified, but ten minutes later the Guardia declared a curfew from 9:00 at night till 5:30 in the morning, and that measure was strictly enforced.

Besides keeping order, the Guardia was collecting accomplices. This was a very sad thing for the country, for had civilians refused to collaborate, had no one trouped down to headquarters to put himself at the Guardia's orders, military rule would not have lasted a week. Exactly how many Guardia officers it would have taken in those days to change a light bulb has never been reliably computed, but the lot were surely not up to running the country. Nor were they the sort (even assuming them competent) to spend hours at their desks, day after day, doing the actual work of administration. They would have howled for mercy and scuttled back to their cuarteles, but for the availability of quislings.

Continued availability, for as a class the Guardia's tools lacked hardihood. There were some whose willingness to grovel was virtually limitless. Eric Delvalle is an example. He was pleased to replace Barletta in the wake of Dr. Spadafora's murder, having pledged to quash the investigation and begun his term with a pilgrimage on foot from the palace to Guardia headquarters to preen his subservience to Noriega. He remained pleased to serve through the worst part of the repression in 1987. Most of these cat's-paws wore out quickly, however. Others could always be found, though, to replace them, driven by ambition or simply by greed. It was a sad thing. By Saturday night, barely twenty-four hours after Martínez's proclamation, a civilian cabinet had been recruited.

Some of its members, it seems, had honest motives—were able, that is, to deceive themselves about the character of the man they were serving and about the nature of that service itself, which was to fool the people about the Guardia's purposes. For instance, there was Carlos López Guevara, a law professor, who took the post of foreign minister. Dr. López had supported Arnulfo Arias, had worked hard to get him elected and even harder to have the election stand up in the face of the wholesale fraud that was attempted. Later on, he felt outraged (and, it seems, personally betrayed) when Arnulfo began passing out seats in the assembly as if they were so many loaves and fishes that he himself had miraculously multiplied. Dr. López expected the Guardia to end such abuses. That was why he took a place in the cabinet, and his presence went a long way toward making Guardia rule respectable.

Dr. López Guevara was short, and because of his shortness held himself very erect, with his shoulders squared and his chin canted alertly. He had a little mustache and a sheepskin from Harvard. His sincerity was patent. The government he belonged to would show "democratic and Christian attitudes toward the republic." So he said in a televised speech on October 20. Before he gave that speech, though, on the morning of October 14, less than twenty-four hours after he was sworn in as a minister, troops brutally suppressed a peaceful protest march by students of the National University, hosing many to the pavement, chasing others into the Social Security Administration Hospital across the street from the university campus, discharging tear gas inside the hospital, distributing discomfort quite democratically, but displaying a clearly un-Christian attitude, yet Dr. López gave the speech and continued to serve. He resigned in January, along with four of his colleagues, over the junta's failure to restore effective constitutional guarantees, but reentered the government later and served in one post or another for a number of years while troops continued to suppress protest, until his son was badly beaten as a result. With that, Dr. López Guevara left the military government once and for all.

That was a marvel of God, wondrous to witness! Not the son's beating, the father's enlightenment. Despite his Harvard degree, Dr. López was stupid. He believed the government worthy of his service, although troops in its employ beat citizens for peaceably seeking their rights as human beings. But God healed Dr. López's wits. When his own son was beaten, Dr. Lopez at last got the point.

The swearing-in was held at noon on Sunday. Junta and cabinet, all took an oath, though to exactly what no one seems to remember. Not the constitution, that much is certain. Nonetheless, an oath was sworn, and a squalid concurrence of bootlickers gathered in witness. More, it was shown on TV, and it was worth watching. There was pudgy President of the Junta Pinilla drawn up to his full five feet with his arms pressed to his sides in rigid attention, and there beside him, slouched at parade rest with his elbows poking out bonily, loomed Urrutia the Member, though he was bowlegged from twenty years in the cavalry squadron. The peak of Pinilla's kepi . . . You know how high the peaks of kepis are in all the armies of Latin America, to the point where they defeat their purpose and emphasize the wearer's shortness instead of making him look taller. Well, the peak of Pinilla's kepi rose forever yet never reached the height of Urrutia's shoulder, while Urrutia wore no kepi at all, no doubt lest its peak soar out of the picture. One thought of Mutt and Jeff, then (by unconscious association of comic strips and the title El Miembro) of the pornographic comics of adolescence, in which a diminutive character was wont to sport a giant member. A thousand jokes were making the rounds by nightfall, and if Panama bore dictatorship for twenty years, it may be because the dictatorship was so ridiculous and the people so richly blessed with the gift of laughter.

Visual buffoonery was followed by verbal. Dr. Juan Materno Vásquez, the new minister of the presidency, attempted to dress the coup makers' sordid motives in a robe of patriotism and high ideals. Materno, a Colón lawyer, was one of a number of leftist intellectuals who followed the Guardia into power, and one of Panama's most durable quislings. He was very vain of his command of language, though in fact he was more the pedant than the poet, invariably choosing academic correctness over idiomatic vigor and ease of expression. The effect of his foppish verbs and prissy syntax, taken with the enforced solemnity of his features and the quivering of his pendulous nether lip, was to score in boldface all the lies he was telling. Had people known they'd be hearing him for years to come, it would have taken something from his performance, but it was very funny at the time. In retrospect, however, one phrase is chilling. The new regime, Materno promised, would bring "revolution without dictatorship." The reference here was to how the Guardia meant to justify what was, after all, the naked theft of power, and indeed, within a short time, a bogus revolution was initiated, with bogus beneficiaries and bogus victims, and brayed about at great length by Materno and others. Meanwhile, though, a real revolution was in progress, one that transferred political power to the military as an institution and economic power to the ranking officers as individuals.

The swearing-in purged the shock effect of the coup. It also served notice that the Guardia didn't mean to leave power quickly. Opposition began to gather the next day, as the protest march at the university illustrates. Already, however, a circumstance existed that was to characterize Panama at critical moments in the future and greatly comfort successive tyrants: there was one dictatorship and any number of oppositions to it.

To begin with, there was Arnulfo. He wanted power back and

supported the general strike his followers called for, but he seems to have based his hopes on the United States and to have overestimated the U.S. commitment to him and democracy as fully as he'd underestimated the Guardia. Radio Clandestina, which at some point began calling itself Radio Rebelde, favored Arnulfo's return and broadcast his messages but wasn't controlled or even guided by him and served mainly as an echo chamber for the fantasies of its two principals, Gaspar Suárez and Alonso Pinzón. These two wander coupled through nearly three decades of Panama's history, beginning as *arnulfistas,* ending as pawns of Noriega, dreaming always of violence, sowing it whenever possible. Suárez, a former Guardia officer and commander of the paramilitary Boinas Negras, passed his time at the microphone directing imaginary troops in imaginary operations. Pinzón's grip on reality was scarcely firmer. It appears that opposition to the coup would have been more effective had Radio Clandestina/Rebelde never gone on the air.

Meanwhile, by Friday the eighteenth, the "Popular Front against the Dictatorship" had been formed "to take all means of civil resistance for a return of constitutional order with civil liberties," beginning with the strike that was supposed to start at dawn on Monday. The list of participating organizations is impressive, so much so (there were more than thirty) that one wonders how the Guardia kept power, till one notes that no business groups were among them and that their unity was superficial. It is doubful, for instance, that the medical and bar associations were very firmly behind that portion of the Front's manifesto declaring opposition to "oligarchy" and "imperialism." These were leftist code words for the *rabiblancos* and the United States, while many of Panama's physicians and lawyers were either *rabiblancos* or pro–United States or both. And how comfortable together were the (communist) Labor Federation of the Workers of the Republic and the (anticommunist) Isthmian Federation of Christian Workers? The Front was for a "democratic solution," but as to what this might mean there were as many opinions as there were groups under the Front's ad hoc umbrella, if not as there were individuals in the groups, while the absence of any reference to Arnulfo shows how deeply the Front was split from the other main base of resistance to the dictatorship, the claimant with a constitutional case and a large following.

The Union of University Students, which entered the Front when the latter agreed to oppose the "oligarchy" and "imperialism", used its fly sheet *Voz Universitaria* to print a message of support from a student league based in Havana, annoying groups on the Front's right and lending credibility to attacks in *El Mundo* that dismissed the Front as no more than a bunch of communists. The Christian Democrats, for their part, abjured both the Front and Arnulfo and set up a clandestine information service that published bulletins from something called the National Resistance Movement. The residents of San Miguelito, a working-class suburb of Panama City, formed their own resistance committee and issued their own lengthy manifesto and made their own nonnegotiable demands, and there may have been other groups equally militant, equally independent, and equally useless that merciful time has swept under oblivion's rug.

Spanish has no word for "teamwork," because the thing is so rare where Spanish is spoken. Military discipline enforces unity. The coexistence of these two circumstances probably has much to do with the prevalence of military regimes in Spanish America and General Franco's long tyranny in Spain itself. It certainly was important in Panama. That the opposition was fragmented gave the dictatorship the political equivalent of interior lines of communication in warfare. The dictatorship could shift resources to meet separate threats. In 1968, many more Panamanians opposed the dictatorship than supported it. Opponents, though, were also opposing each other, or at least could not bring their force to bear on one point, so the dictatorship was always superior locally.

The officers who had stolen power, however, did not at first appreciate their good fortune and spent a very anxious week. Their first fear was of a rising by *arnulfistas,* and they were glad that Arnulfo took refuge in the Canal Zone rather than in some populous lower-class neighborhood, where love of him and hatred of them was intense. Next, they feared a general strike, and began to take steps to prevent such before it was organized. These ended up involving them in some duplicity. They persuaded a past president of the chamber of commerce with the wonderfully capitalistic name Henry Ford to take a post in the cabinet, and got a business-as-usual communiqué from the chamber, by promising implacable sternness toward communism. At the same time, they attempted to curb the strike efforts of workers and students by making a pact with Panama's communists.

We mean Panama's Moscow-line communists, the Partido del Pueblo (PDP, People's party). These had always opposed Arnulfo, so some basis for an alliance existed. Besides, in the past election, the PDP had supported certain candidates for deputy who seemed to be receptive to the cause, including Moisés Torrijos, Omar's elder brother, who'd toured the Soviet Union with an officially sponsored journalists' group and then spoken well of his hosts in a couple of columns. To a Latin-American communist of the era, that was enough to make a person "progressive," though adult Panamanians ought to have known that Monchi Torrijos would take anyone's freebie and give fair value in hogwash in return. In any case, with Monchi as go-between, the coup makers arranged a tryst with the PDP. Neither side sent top people, but a brief romp as bedfellows ensued. The Guardia agreed to tolerate the Partido; the Partido agreed to sabotage the strike.

Certain PDP members didn't keep discipline. José Tuñón, for instance, and José Carrillo, a labor and student leader respectively. Both were arrested. Tuñón died in prison as a result of ill treatment and being denied medical care. Carrillo had his kidneys destroyed in repeated beatings, and for the rest of his life (which was much shortened) had to have dialysis three times a week. Those who kept the pact got a few weeks' indulgence. Then they too were imprisoned and tormented. On the other hand, their efforts to wreck the strike weren't very efficient. The strike failed, but not because of the communists.

The Beijing liners were used even more harshly. To begin with, they'd backed Arnulfo. Besides, they were high-profile agitators, hence useful victims when it came to persuading businessmen that the coup deserved their support. All who could be caught were locked up. Special treatment, though, was reserved for the sect's two chief leaders, Floyd Britton and Alvaro Menéndez Franco. Both had been part of the student *guerrilla* in 1959 in Veraguas Province when Omar Torrijos disgraced himself. They were arrested the night of the coup and held in La Modelo till early in November 1969. Then they were sent to Coiba Island.

What else were the Guardia officers doing? They were dissolving the assembly and firing the electoral tribunal and banning all political parties. And forbidding bail for those charged with chiseling the government. And, oh yes, cutting out superfluous government jobs. This was Boris Martínez trying to establish a republic of virtue in one of the last spots on earth where one might take root. Forbidding bail was, in its way, as terrible as Robespierre's guillotine. It petrified every politician in the country, for who was there who'd ever held office who couldn't be accused of lining his pockets? With bail abolished, a charge equaled a conviction, for trial could be infinitely delayed. Observe:

On Monday after the coup, Panama's most respected newspaper, *La Estrella,* carried a scornful notice advising its readers that it had been barred from appearing on Saturday and Sunday, and now was being censored, by order of the Guardia Nacional. This tone changed, however, a few days later with the arrest of its owner, Tomás Altamirano Duque (who had held office under Marcos Robles as a member of the directing board of the Social Security Administration), on a charge of having collected commissions for approving loans. He was never tried, however. In February 1969, Torrijos ousted Martínez, and Torrijos cared much less about how Duque might have harmed Panama than about how Duque might help him. Five months in La Modelo had meantime so purged Duque of anti-Guardia prejudice that he and Torrijos quickly reached an accord. He was released and took a plum post in the government, so that the phrase "From Prison to Glory" (used in advertising the film *Papillon*) was for a time applied to him. Thenceforward he served faithfully in every puppet regime brought forth by the tyrants, and his newspaper praised them unflaggingly, no matter how disgusting their abuses.

The part about cutting superfluous jobs—department heads were to say which jobs weren't needed, and those who didn't report would be summarily canned—was aimed at an institution called La Botella, beloved from the Rio Grande to Patagonia and especially so in Panama. La Botella—literally, "The Bottle"—means that if you're in power you get to create special posts whose incumbents have nothing to do but show up for their paychecks, and portion these out to deserving folks of your choice, typically to your wife's unemployable brothers and young ladies of affectionate disposition. Boris Martínez was against it. That was Martínez, all right: taking all the fun out of public service. No wonder he didn't last long.

There were, besides, populist measures, such as freezing the prices of basic commodities and legalizing the land tenure of squatters. And secret talks with U.S. representatives about getting Arnulfo out of the Canal Zone. And Martínez and Torrijos promoted themselves to colonel, with Martínez jumping a rank. And protest was suppressed and the people intimidated. Homes were raided with a great show of horrific weapons. Supporters of Arnulfo, or of the Popular Front against the Dictatorship, were beaten and abused in front of their families, and taken off to prison as if they were criminals. This repression proved effective, enough for the regime to make a show of confidence on the eve of the strike by setting the curfew hour back to midnight.

On the same day, Sunday, October 20, another TV display was provided. First off was Materno Vásquez, who in the manner of Moses to the children of Israel delivered a decalogue he'd received from on high, ten "Postulates of the Revolution without Dictatorship and of Liberty with Order." Shorn of verbal posies, they were as follows:

1. Administrative cleanup and repudiation of communism.
2. Eradication of corruption.
3. Eradication of nepotism.
4. Establishment of a new scale of values, with appointment on the basis of ability and honesty.
5. Limitation of the size of the bureaucracy.
6. Impartial administration of justice.
7. Use of state resources for the benefit of the many, not the few.
8. Removal of the Guardia from politics.
9. Identification of the junta's ideals and action with the Guardia.
10. Free and fair elections.

This brief anthology of reformist clichés is all Martínez bequeathed to the science of politics. The aims mentioned in it were already being cynically betrayed and were destined to be mocked a thousandfold in the course of two decades of tyranny. Point 9 excepted, of course. Let's be fair. The ideals and action of the provisional junta were at all times identified with the Guardia Nacional. The ideals were greed and brutality, the action such as to produce a despotism tempered by stupidity and sloth.

Having read the postulates, Materno discoursed on them. Other ministers followed him before the camera, including López Guevara, as has been mentioned. On the whole, the program achieved its purpose, which was to diminish support for the strike. That Materno was a black man may have helped make the junta and its supposed aims somewhat more credible to the urban masses of Colón and the capital. López Guevara's sincerity may have helped the middle class suspend its disbelief of the Guardia's. Mainly, though, the postulates and the speeches were instruments through which people who craved to believe might delude themselves.

Great stores of the will to believe were required. Scarcely an adult in Panama was without firsthand knowledge of Guardia cupidity. The first thing R. M. Koster was told when he got to the country was to keep a five-dollar bill clipped to his driver's license as an infallible specific against traffic tickets. The Guardia motto, "Todo por la patria" ("All for country") was everywhere parodied in popular speech as "Todo por la plata" ("Everything for money"). Anyone who knew the Guardia knew that Gabriel's trumpet would sound before it adhered to the postulates that touched on corruption and nepotism, on honesty and ability. Then there were postulates 8 and 10. The Guardia, surely, had no need to seek power in order to remove itself from politics, while the immediate effect of its "revolution" was to overturn the results of a free and fair election held only five months before. Still, everyone knew that the Guardia was in power, and meant to remain there at least for a time. Most everyone, therefore, wished to believe it benign. Only a few suspected the depth of the iniquity into which the Guardia might sink once it was master of the country. Had Panamanians known, they'd have fought for their freedom, "not with spears only, but with axes too."

Yet another obstacle to such resistance, and a priceless favor to the coup makers, was provided by the Panamanian Catholic church. The country's archbishop, the Most Reverend Tomás Clavel Méndez, had taken a firm stand for democracy following the May election, arguing eloquently and effectively for respecting the suffrage and the will of the people. Clavel was in Rome when the coup occurred, and was in the process of resigning his office for reasons that had nothing to do with Panamanian politics. In his absence, the next-highest church official in the country, Monseñor Marcos McGrath, bishop of Veraguas, directed himself to the faithful on October 19, in a message that seemed to excuse the Guardia's action. The current situation, he said, was the result of an accumulation of social, political, and economic immorality. Even the church was guilty in not presenting the evangelical message forcefully enough. Because, he went on, of the resulting "lack of Christian conscience, the country is now living moments of anxiety which, in the midst of pain, are an invitation for radical change in every man who wants to remain faithful to the message of the Lord."

Though addressed to McGrath's parishioners in Santiago, the statement appeared on the front page of *La Estrella* on the second day of the strike, October 22, and was taken as the church's official position. Indeed, it became such, for the church never denied a word of it. It left the regime overjoyed, its opponents deflated. It did not simply hint that the Guardia might have a case. It suggested that the coup was made in heaven! What other radical change had occurred lately? More, it implied repudiation of Archbishop Clavel's posture. It closed with a plea for Christian behavior, with prayers for peace and justice, and so on and so forth, but by then the damage had been done. It had given people cause to do nothing, to accept events, to wonder if they might not be for the best.

McGrath was the youngest of four sons born in the Canal Zone to an American couple who came to the isthmus during Canal construction and stayed on to work for the Canal once it was complete. He stood six feet four and was earnestly good-looking—a "manly man," in short, like Chaucer's monk, who looked entirely virile in a cassock without ceasing for an instant to look priestly. His mind, besides, was quick. He was good at languages. His voice could be both vibrant and surprisingly gentle according to the matter of his sermon, and he had, along with all the social graces, a knack for politics, a feel for the things of this world of the sort that enabled two of his brothers to become extremely successful as businessmen. Early on, these qualities won him the patronage of Francis Cardinal Spellman of New York, and his career in the church was correspondingly brilliant. He was a monsignor and a bishop while still under forty. He was certain, it seemed, to be a cardinal soon. Then the 1964 clash between Panamanians and Americans along the Canal Zone border cruelly ambushed his ambitions. From then on, it would never be meet for Panama's first cardinal to be a gringo.

McGrath did what he could in remedy. He took up Panamanian citizenship—his right, since the Canal Zone, no matter who ran it, never ceased to be Panamanian soil. He virtually ceased speaking English in public. He changed his Christian names in practice (and perhaps in law also) from Mark Gregory to Marcos Gregorio. A wish to be fully Panamanian and ambition, if ambition animated the wish, may account for his sermon of October 19 and for his comportment during the time of the tyrants.

In January 1969, McGrath succeeded Clavel as archbishop of Panama. For twenty years, he kept the same mealymouthed tone, even when one of his priests was horribly murdered. He never actually endorsed the dictatorship, but he never excoriated it either. One might say, in Christian charity, that he erred in judgment, that he believed the coup makers to be patriots, that later on, when it was clear that they meant the country no good, he judged discretion the better part of valor, or thought it wise to turn the other cheek, lest by challenging the dictatorship he precipitate violence. Whatever his reasons, however, Panama deserved better. The church in Panama wandered from its own values, betraying itself and those who looked to it for guidance.

So did the United States of America. Like the church, the United States is a thing of this world that is dedicated to transcendent values, that was founded so that they might flourish on this planet. These values—freedom, democracy, rule of law, and so forth—are the reason why the United States exists, yet (sadly) from time to time they appear an encumbrance to the mortal men and women who make U.S. policy. So was it with regard to the dictatorship in Panama.

The United States did not instigate the coup, or support it, or even know of it till it was in progress. On the evening of October 11, 1968, both the U.S. ambassador to Panama, Charles Adair, and the governor of the Canal Zone, Walter Leber, were in Washington—hardly where they'd have been had they possessed the least inkling of what was afoot, and Martínez himself didn't make up his mind till that morning. Adair and Leber were en route back to their posts at 2:00 A.M. on the twelfth. Later that day, Secretary of State Dean Rusk expressed "deep concern" over the coup and announced that U.S. relations with Panama had been automatically severed with the overthrow of the legitimate government. One can argue that responsible officials ought to have known that when the United States began to pamper the Guardia it would be only a matter of time till the Guardia seized power, yet Washington was clearly surprised and to a point shocked by the Guardia's action.

The treatment first shown Arnulfo bears this out. He was given asylum and quite a bit more—a place to use as his headquarters and leave to meet with his partisans, who were also allowed to shelter and move about freely under the flag and protection of the United States. He was given, in short, a base of operations. This immediate response by the United States reflected American traditions and values, respect for the will of the people, and a healthy coldness toward those who sought by violence to annul it.

But then, after two or three days, everything changed. Governor Leber and his subordinates began to show unease at Arnulfo's presence. The democratically elected, constitutionally sworn, and unlawfully deposed leader of a nation with which the United States had friendly relations ceased to be welcome and became a frightful embarrassment, a roach in the salad, a smear of something unwholesome on the rug. The government of the United States had mulled the coup over, and its "deep concern" gave way to a "sigh of relief."

This relief may be explained quickly. Like most hugely popular leaders, Arnulfo was something of a prima donna and wonderfully independent in his actions. That is to say, he was hard to push around. Now this leader the people adored had been replaced by a group with no popular following, a group respected by none and reviled by many, men whom no Panamanian had chosen, all of whom were supposed to feel grateful toward the United States, some of whom were in the pay of U.S. intelligence. Mortal men and (perhaps) women in Washington, and especially in the Department of Defense, knew that Arnulfo was difficult to manipulate, judged that the Guardia would be a great deal more tractable, and decided that having the Guardia in power in Panama was better for the United States.

They might have been right had they served a different country, one with no treasury of moral power, or one unsure of its day-to-day survival. But since they served a great nation, with noble traditions and excellent hopes for the future, it's a pity they didn't take a longer view. It would have been better for the United States had democracy continued in Panama. Even generals and admirals can see that today. It's a pity the United States had no one twenty years ago who knew Napoleon's views on the relation between material and moral power, for they would have counseled fidelity to U.S. values.

On Thursday, October 17, Hubert H. Humphrey, who knew what the United States was about, promised in a campaign speech to review military policy so as to make it harder for "predatory colonels" to strangle democracy in Latin America. That same day, the U.S. government's sigh of relief at the advent of colonelocracy in Panama was given substance in an order issued by Governor Leber. Panamanians seeking political asylum in the Canal Zone were to present themselves for formal internment, at which time they would give up any weapons they bore and from which time they would be "prohibited from engaging in political activity of any sort." Those not wishing to be interned were to leave at once. Among the first of these was José D. Bazán, constitutional second vice-president of Panama. The Guardia had been given advance notice of Leber's order and had all streets leading from the Canal Zone covered. Bazán was taken straight to La Modelo.

Getting Arnulfo out took a bit longer. Martínez and company were especially anxious to have him off the isthmus by the time the strike started. Canal Zone authorities subjected Arnulfo to extreme pressure along the lines that his presence would lead to bloodshed and that he could do more from Washington toward getting reinstated, through the United Nations and the Organization of American States. Neither the stick nor the carrot seems very persuasive from the vantage of twenty years on, but both probably did to an Arnulfo forced to watch the Guardia persecuting Panamanians while he himself was being stripped of his followers. Besides, he must have seen that if he did not leave of his own volition, the United States would forcibly remove him, and that would have been devastating to his pride. He flew to Washington in a U.S. Air Force plane on Monday evening, October 21, some twelve hours after the strike began. On November 12, a week after the election of Richard Nixon, the United States formally recognized the junta headed by Colonel Pinilla.

The United States, then, did not invent the dictatorship in Panama. All the United States did was make it possible and then stand by, as it were, with arms crossed. And then support it materially and morally. And then pretend it wasn't a dictatorship at all. And go on and on, year after year, until it had betrayed itself thoroughly, and had cruelly betrayed those who looked to it for guidance. And in the end the United States paid dearly for wandering from its values with regard to Panama. Shared values, it turns out, are safer guides in choosing playmates than supposed gratitude or vulnerability to being pushed around. In the long run, it turns out, the United States had nothing to gain and a great deal to lose from Panama's being run by thieves and sadists. How sad it was and is and will remain that the sometime Last Best Hope for Mankind made not a peep, lifted not a finger, at the snuffing out of freedom in a country it had midwifed into existence!

But for Arnulfo's departure, the strike might have worked. Admittedly, its inception was shaky. On Monday morning, no more than half the bus drivers stayed out. In San Miguelito, barricades were set up, and buses that operated there were stoned, but most businesses in the capital were open. On the main streets, long lines of vehicles proceeded single file, each driver seeking the track of the one ahead of him to avoid tacks strewn in the thousands by strike makers. Much of this traffic, however, consisted of people seeking provisions for a long siege. By Monday afternoon, it was greatly diminished, and on Tuesday the strike seemed to gather momentum. At noon, though, came the news that Arnulfo had left the country. Demoralized and furious, people resolved to sacrifice no further. On Wednesday, the country was back at work.

The new regime had withstood counterattack. Those directing it now set about entrenching power. They still faced resistance. Guerrilla activity, urban and rural, flared and smoldered for over a year. But a decisive sector, if not a majority, was resigned to having the Guardia run things awhile. Many were sincerely fed up with politics, which seemed to them little more than fraud and calumny and a scramble for pelf. They were glad for a rest from all that and naively swallowed the pledge of a cleanup, or supposed the new crowd couldn't be worse than the old. Others judged there was nothing they could do anyway and strove to disregard their own common sense, and to disremember the lessons of history. They told each other that, anyway, it was still Panama, that nothing really bad was going to happen, that if it did it would happen to communists anyway, or to *arnulfistas* or others who looked for trouble, or anyway not people like themselves. And for years this delusion was tenable, partly because the regime used a certain restraint, largely because it controlled communication. The harm to all came in small increments, each of them bearable, or was of the sort whose effects are felt only long afterward. The harm too great or blatant to be ignored fell only on "other people," that mysterious breed whose welfare seems unimportant and against whom every tyranny always strikes first.

Panamanians put on a normality whose aspect convinced them and those outside the country that no true discontent existed. Nonetheless, the garment was flimsy. One night toward the end of October, Guillermo Sánchez was watching a movie at the Presidente, a first-run theater that drew an upper- and middle-class audience. During the show, there was a power failure, not an uncommon occurrence, nor one that could be blamed on the government, since in those days electricity was supplied by a private concern. Two minutes, three minutes went by. Then, suddenly, unexpectedly, pandemonium: whistles, hoots, and, above all, abuse of the Guardia, shouts of "¡Hijos de puta!" of "¡Gorilas de mierda!" as men and even some women took advantage of the darkness to vent the hate and anger they were stuffed with. The din persisted and grew, then ceased abruptly, like a radio whose plug has been kicked out, the instant the screen lit up again. Spectators glanced about exchanging malicious smiles and grins of complicity. Then the incident was over. Discontent was pushed down again, not just below the level of overt expression, below the level of consciousness itself.

One sector's discontent wasn't repressed. Panama's students didn't delude themselves, or go gently into dictatorship's night.

They'd marched on October 14. They marched on November 3 also, and again on December 12, inspiring teachers to march with them. These protests were suppressed of course. With blows and arrests and (on December 2) bullets. And, as if to affirm tyranny's compact with ignorance, with the closing of educational facilities. Troops raided the Instituto Nacional, where Martínez and most of the other coup makers had studied. It was closed down indefinitely, and forty students were arrested and eighty-two teachers fired from their jobs. The university was occupied in the dead of night. Doors were smashed in and laboratories wrecked and offices looted. The university was autonomous and inviolable, but Dr. Materno Vásquez found "juridical" pretexts for its occupation and closure, though without that free university, established freely by a democratic government, he would never have been a lawyer or anything else.

Free speech went the way of free education. The Arias papers, closed on October 12, were stolen by the regime—their names and logos along with their plant and facilities—and reemerged as organs of the dictatorship. *El Mundo* disappeared quickly enough. When David Samudio finally realized that the coup had not been organized for his benefit, *El Mundo* began to carp a little, and was duly assigned a censor, and in a tardy display of dignity refused to accept one and stopped publishing instead. The gelding of *La Estrella* has been detailed. Broadcasting was also brought under control. Foreign periodicals were screened and offending issues confiscated. The country, in short, was insulated against truth to the limit of the regime's capacity.

The jails were full of political prisoners. The entire leadership of the Partido del Pueblo. The entire Movimiento Universitario Revolucionario (the Maoist group), leaders and followers too. All the national and provincial hierarchy of Arnulfo's Partido Panameñista, all its officers, all its principal militants. Much of Arnulfo's government, including Second Vice-President of the Republic José D. Bazán. All these went to prison, along with everyone who'd ever annoyed anyone in the Guardia, who'd taken a girlfriend away from this or that sergeant, or made a pass at this or that corporal's wife, or shown disrespect toward or looked the wrong way at a private. In the cell Guillermo Sánchez was put in was a chap, a cantina brawler, who'd been inside since before the election, who was finishing his time, and who the day he was released was rearrested, and put back in the same cell, for looking the wrong way at a Guardia private directing traffic two blocks from the jail.

Sánchez was jailed in simple political vengeance. Earlier in the year, when the Guardia combined with Samudio in an attempt to steal the election, Omar Torrijos was entrusted with stealing three provinces, among them Bocas del Toro, on Panama's north coast, where United Fruit has its big banana plantations. Torrijos turned the theft over to Captain Juan Meléndez, and Meléndez did his level best. Days before the polls opened, he had everyone he could think of under lock and key—all the party reps for Arnulfo's coalition, all the precinct captains, all the delegates to all the voting tables. The chief figure, though, was Rodrigo Sánchez Borbón, Guillermo's elder brother, former deputy, former governor of the province, and now a candidate for deputy again for the Partido Republicano, which was running no candidate of its own for president but backing Arnulfo.

The Partido Republicano merits a paragraph. Its chieftains were Max Delvalle, Marcel Penso, and Jose D. Bazán. The first two were the richest men in Panama, scions of Sephardic families of great renown and antiquity. The third was the closest thing to Richard J. Daley ever produced in Panama, a man with an unfailing electoral machine—this in Panama's second city, Colón, where the majority of the population is of West Indian origin. Nationally the party had no platform but was a federation of separate organizations each of which did and said what was required to win in its particular locality. Delvalle and Penso, as may be imagined, were conservatives. Rodrigo Sánchez, who had the Guaymí Indians and the banana workers, was a socialist, but his stance in the province was to the left of the communists. It was said that the Republicano was the party of the minorities: Indians, blacks, and Jewish millionaires.

Rodrigo Sánchez, then, was the main man in Bocas, and Guillermo, his younger brother, was his campaign manager. Meléndez put them both under house arrest, and rounded up their Guaymí activists two days before the election and shipped them by plane to Panama City and left them at the airport without money or shoes, and when Rodrigo broke house arrest later that day, Meléndez had him captured and marooned on a desert island in the gulf. None of it worked, though. Rodrigo took 90 percent of the votes in his race for deputy and carried the province for Arnulfo just as firmly. So ballot boxes were stolen and protesters fired on and nine of them wounded, and Rodrigo was put in prison, and Guillermo and nine others were crammed into a one-man cell for three days, but though eighteen of the thirty-eight ballot boxes were emptied out and stuffed with Samudio votes, the count still came out wrong, and the banana workers went out, promising that not one banana would be picked until Rodrigo Sánchez had his deputy's credentials, and Meléndez knew he was beaten and threw in the sponge. He was howled at by Torrijos, and both blamed Guillermo—unjustly, since the humiliation had been administered by the people of the province, while if an individual had to be singled out, it ought to have been Rodrigo; but that was how things were, Guillermo got blamed. So when, after the coup, Meléndez's hachetman, Sergeant Villamil, ran into Guillermo in a cantina in Panama City, Villamil, using Meléndez's authority, had him put in jail—not in La Modelo, a needle wouldn't have fit there, but in a communal cell in Guardia headquarters.

There were over a hundred prisoners in that lockup. Many were politicals like Sánchez, but the majority were ordinary jailbirds. An *arnulfista* gave him a strip of cardboard to sleep on, for the cement floor was cold as well as hard, and Sanchez was having an attack of lumbago (which, oddly enough, his stay in prison cured). The criminals had a hierarchy as rigid as the Holy Roman church's, and in the morning Sánchez was taken before the "bishop," who gave audiences in a corner of the cell, and submitted to a minute catechism. Which, evidently, he passed, for orders were issued not to steal his money or his cardboard, and arrangements made with a guard for him to buy toilet gear and coffee and a sweet roll every morning. That night a man was put in making great hubbub about his innocence, and how he earned his bread by the sweat of his brow, whereupon His Grace switched on a flashlight, aimed it at the fellow's face, then thundered, "Shit! Mau-Mau again! Thief, you never worked in your strumpet life! Shut up and let people sleep!" And all night long drunks were brought in and put in a smaller cell farther down the corridor. To a man, they yelled, "¡Viva Arnulfo!" as they streeled by, provoking loud cheers from Sánchez's cell, and furtive glances of amusement from the guards, for all of them were closet *arnulfistas.*

Meanwhile, Rodrigo negotiated with Meléndez: how long would his brother have to languish in prison to cleanse the stain he'd given the captain's honor? After much importuning, Meléndez agreed to order Guillermo's release on condition that he leave the country. As this seemed harsh, Rodrigo approached Torrijos—and found that Torrijos not only upheld his subordinate but had reason of his own to enforce the sanction. The banana company, he said, was tired of Guillermo's agitating its workers, and he, Torrijos, wanted the company happy. So Guillermo Sánchez went wandering in exile—Mexico, Guatemala, Costa Rica, the first of two terms of exile that he suffered, learning as Dante had (and so many others!) "how salt other people's bread tastes, and how hard a road it is to go up and down on other people's stairs."

"So are the sons of men snared in an evil time when it falleth suddenly upon them." As preachers have anciently warned, life is unfair. But what makes writing fact (as compared to fiction) unnerving is that life is also often unrealistic, and in poor taste. After Torrijos ousted Boris Martínez, Juan Meléndez plotted to oust Torrijos. Sergeant Villamil betrayed the plan. Torrijos sent Meléndez into exile, an odd, unrealistic exile during which he received his captain's pay. And years later, after both he and Sánchez had been allowed to come home, Meléndez, most unrealistically, experienced a religious conversion and joined an evangelical sect. More, one night, in an exhibition of kitsch that even Dostoyevsky would have retched at, he called Sánchez up and addressed him as brother and babbled about loving God and one's neighbor. Sánchez assumed he was joking but mentioned the incident to a person who knew Meléndez and was flabbergasted to learn that Meléndez was in earnest, that he'd seen the light, that he spent his nights reading the Bible and his days distributing pious tracts door-to-door—Juan Meléndez, of all people on earth!—and that his dream, frustrated by the humorless Guardia general staff, was to return to Bocas del Toro and kneel before the multitude and beg pardon for the outrages he had committed so long ago when he commanded there.

With Villamil life took its time but dealt more fittingly, yet in the end not fittingly enough. In reward for betraying Meléndez, he was made a lieutenant and assigned to the newly created G-2, as an agent of which he took part in a notable murder. Rubén Miró, who'd been accused and acquitted of killing General José Remón, the father of militarism in Panama, went out to get some ice cubes on a New Year's Eve, 1969, and was found the next day with over fifty bullets in his body and his penis, cigarlike, in the side of his mouth, the latter touch Villamil's signature. In June 1987, early in the crisis preceding the dictatorship's final phase, Villamil, by then a captain, saw a crowd of demonstrators coming down his street one evening and ran out, pistol in hand, to teach them a lesson. A soldier took him for the crowd's leader and drilled him through the head—better late than never—but the lout lived. Decent, useful people have died of bee bites, but Villamil, drilled in the noodle, survived!

Hundreds were jailed and hundreds were forced into exile, and meanwhile a duumvirate had taken over. Not Pinilla and his member. Everyone knew they were a pair of jerks. Boris Martínez and Omar Torrijos gave the orders, presided at cabinet sessions, met with groups from all sectors of the country, though of the two Martínez did the talking, while Torrijos leaned back and rolled his eyes upward and listened. They reorganized the Guardia along straight military lines, with a general staff that Martínez became chief of. Torrijos became commandant, with Aristides Hassán going into retirement. This at a ceremony on December 5 in the cuartel at Tocumen, and Martínez became a full colonel, and the majors who were in command on October 11 became lieutenant colonels, and the captains who were commanding all became majors.

At six the next afternoon, the two colonels entertained local bankers in the presidential suite of El Panamá. This was the swankiest hotel in the country, designed by Edward Durell Stone and named building of the year worldwide in 1956—tall and white on a hill above the bay and the city, and the presidential suite was on the top floor. Again Torrijos listened and Martínez talked. And won the bankers over to a man. They wanted to know if and when there'd be elections, and whether (as rumor had it) guerrillas were active in Chiriquí Province, and if they might nudge interest rates up a little, and Martínez was frank and forthcoming about these concerns. His "dearest wish," he said, and that of his colleagues, was to have elections in 1970, but first they had to save the country, or their sacrifice would be vain. There were no guerrillas, he said, anywhere in the country. As for interest rates, the bankers had his promise that an authorization to raise them would be put out soon.

Well, one for three is good in baseball. Interest rates went up, no question there. But Martínez was pumping gas in Miami long before any elections were held, and twenty years later there still hadn't been free ones. As for guerrillas . . .

In the highlands of Chiriquí around Cerro Punta, the immediate response of some to the coup was to start fighting. An hour or so before midnight on October 12, a group of about ten men armed with .22 rifles and light shotguns ambushed a Guardia patrol truck near the village of Nueva California. Without stopping it or wounding anyone inside but getting the Guardia's attention. At 4:00 A.M.: nearly a hundred *guardias* reinforced the detachment at Volcán, and at dawn on the thirteenth they went into action, burning the homes of known *arnulfistas* and making numerous arrests. They did not catch the ambushers. These went up onto the flanks of Cerro Pando and then over the border into Costa Rica. Later that day, one of those arrested, a man with the odd nickname Cariñito (Dearie) was killed by members of the Guardia Nacional in the cuartel at Piedra Candela, the first political prisoner murdered during the dictatorship.

Other opponents of the coup made their way across the border, among them Rafael Franceshi, a director of the Partido Panameñista, and Enrique Moreno, once one of Arnulfo's bodyguards. And were welcomed by Costa Ricans, who had known military tyranny and had gone through a civil war to get rid of it. Besides, Arnulfo had a good friend, and his partisans a powerful protector, in Dr. Rafael Calderón Guardia, former President of Costa Rica and key supporter of the current president, José Joaquín Trejos. Initially, Costa Rican authorities not only gave exiles from Panama a safe haven but identified with those who favored resistance and made no objection to their mounting operations from Costa Rican territory. Arnulfo sent Franceshi some money. He and Moreno bought weapons—a Thompson and three other submachine guns, two Garands and two Mausers and a carbine, a .45-caliber pistol and twelve .22s. On November 22, a band of thirty guerrillas crossed into Panama.

In front went Ariosto González. He was from a place called Los Pozos and a natural leader, well known and liked throughout the border region and at home on all its trails and mountains. He and Manuel Díaz and Titico Quintero were *comandantes.* Also present was Hugo Alberto Casanova, who'd been in the car with Arnulfo on the wild ride through Panama City to the Canal Zone, and José Sabin and his son, also called José, who was killed on the border nine days later, and five who'd been at the Nueva California ambush. There were, besides, three Costa Ricans (including the famous Osito Solano, famous first, in his youth, as a soccer player, then as a famous fighter in the 1948 civil war) and a Uruguayan named Walter Sardiñas.

Sardiñas was an idealist and an adventurer of the rash-bold Che Guevara sort, born a few years too soon for the Tupamaros, so he, like Che, went north in search of a cause. He never expected to find one in Panama, but he ended up linked to three of its tyrants. Two days after Boris Martínez took power, Sardiñas led the first effective resistance, a shootout in the Calidonia quarter of Panama City in which three *guardias* died. In 1970, he was murdered in Costa Rica on a contract let by Omar Torrijos and so blessed by the spineless Costa Rican authorities that the murderers posed for a photograph with the corpse! They blasted Sardiñas through the door of the furnished room where he lay too sick to get up, but before Torrijos had him murdered he fought in Chiriquí Province against troops commanded by Manuel Noriega.

González took them up onto a ridge just inside Panama called Quijada del Diablo. The name translates as Devil's Jawbone, and the feature is rugged—steep, scarred by ravines, thickly jungled. The top is above 6,000 feet in elevation, and anyone up there can not only see both oceans but look right down into Piedra Candela—a dozen or so frame houses and shacks clustered on both sides of the border. Food came from just about everyone in the vicinity, and help in the form of money from as far away as Concepción and David. Enrique Moreno, in Costa Rica, undertook to supply munitions and weapons.

On November 28, there arrived in camp an American named Kimball who'd been recruited by *arnulfistas* in Bugaba. He'd served in the U.S. Army and had seen action in Southeast Asia. He gave the group some training, and on November 30 he directed an ambush—or tried to, at least, for in the end his directions weren't followed.

The Guardia ran a daily patrol of about fifty men from Piedra Candela to a border marker at the base of Quijada del Diablo on a farm that belonged to some Catholic fathers. The plan was to hit them at the top of their climb, just below the farm. Sixteen took part, including Solano and another Costa Rican, who'd picked up the nickname Culebra (Snake) for the ease with which he maneuvered in the jungle. They left camp at 3:00 A.M. and were in positions picked by Kimball by 6:30, but no patrol showed. Around nine, they heard machine-gun fire from the farm, almost certainly practice fire. The Guardia was already there, had probably gone up the evening before and bivouacked, but anyway was between them and their base. Withdrawal was in order, but on the way, as they were crossing the farm along a wooded ridge opposite the farmhouse, the point man, whose name was Onofre Quintero, spotted some *guardias* below them. Kimball's directions were not to shoot and to keep withdrawing. The shots they'd heard before had come from above. Going after those below would get them caught between two groups. Quintero, though, with his enemies in his sights, couldn't resist. He opened fire, beginning an exchange that lasted two hours. Twelve *guardias* were killed and others hit. One *guerrillero,* a man with the bellicose name Fidel Guerra, took cover behind the arched roots of a fig tree and was burned on the belly by a bullet that spent its force burrowing through wood and dropped into his shirt. When the shooting stopped, the *guerrilleros* dispersed in small groups along different trails. All returned to camp that afternoon.

Put baldly thus, the thing sounds fantastic. A handful of poorly armed amateurs—only two had seen warfare, and only one had ever worn a uniform—had engaged a superior force of well-equipped, trained troops on unfavorable ground, and had not only hurt them badly but got away clean, not a drop of blood lost, just a burn on the belly! However, they wanted to fight and the Guardia didn't. And had surprise on their side, and were on home ground, and the Guardia's training didn't come up to the circumstances. Those below, in the open, against whom the guerrillas' first fire was directed, did not fire back but simply bolted, bolted and ran—the ones, in any case, who were able to do so. They ran all the way to Mellizas, in Costa Rica, three kilometers off as the crow flies and only God knows how far on the panicky, roundabout scamper they must have taken. There they asked where they were and how they could get back to Panama, and were very distressed, especially the wounded. The ones who couldn't run lay where they fell, either dead at once or soon put out of misery. Their comrades showed no concern for them. Those higher up on the ridge fired their weapons and had the guerrillas properly pinned down, but their aim was poor, and they didn't use their advantage of high ground and numbers to maneuver down and engage at close quarters.

This was the first action between guerrillas and the Guardia. It speaks volumes about the latter's morale but cannot have done very much to improve it. Indeed, this and other encounters like it explain the sovereign fear of guerrillas held by Panama's successive tyrants and seen clearest in Noriega's fear of Dr. Hugo Spadafora. Oddly, however, it left the guerrillas shaken and cost them heavier casualties than they had inflicted. The three Costa Ricans declared it madness to fight the Guardia armed as they were. They left camp that evening. So did Kimball. He, too, cited the group's weapons, though he may have had unexpressed misgivings about its discipline. Others left also, but the telling loss was the experience possessed by Solano and Kimball.

Solano continued to befriend those who fought the Guardia. Guillermo Sánchez, whose wanderings in exile did not bring him to Costa Rica until after the guerrillas had disbanded, remembers Solano's attentions to former combatants, mostly peasants who lived in great hardship and whom Solano treated with moving tenderness. And he saved the life of Manuel Solís Palma in the spring of 1969, when Solís came to Costa Rica to take charge of provisioning the guerrillas. Omar Torrijos sent a gangster called Orejita (Little Ear) Ruiz to kill him, but Solano found out and intercepted Ruiz, catching up with him on a street in San José convoyed by two policemen whom the politicians Torrijos was bribing had assigned as guides. "I know you're here to murder Solís Palma," Solano told him. "There's a plane for Panama at five this afternoon. If you don't take it, at six I will kill you." Everyone in Costa Rica knew Osito Solano. The two cops told Orejita that Osito meant business, and Orejita was on the five o'clock plane. Torrijos then decided to take care of Solís Palma through political pressure, had him arrested and held incommunicado for more than a week, and then put over the border into Nicaragua—unbathed, unshaved, and barefoot, for the Costa Ricans, in their servility, threw in these amenities, but Solís Palma had more dignity and less shame at that moment than when, nineteen years later, splendidly arrayed but wasted in spirit, he became Manuel Noriega's puppet president.

Kimball would have done better to stay in the mountains. He was taken the next morning near Bambito, a town between Volcán and Cerro Punta, and died under torture, or was killed when of no further use or amusement. In August 1969, an American named David Godino was arrested in David and held in the cuartel overnight before being sent to the capital and released. Other prisoners told him about Kimball—his name, that he'd served in Vietnam, that he was held for four or five months in solitary confinement and tortured frequently and then heard no more of. The last other prisoners knew of him was that his captors had him strung up by the neck with his hands cuffed behind him and his toes just touching the floor. It was in connection with Kimball's death that Guillermo Sánchez, then in Costa Rica, first heard the name Manuel Noriega.

Noriega, Noriega. His name tolls through all the time of the tyrants. His first mission after the coup, a day or so after, was to take a squad up to a place in that region called Río Sereno and bring down a pair of U.S. Peace Corps volunteers, Susan and John Freivalds, who the Guardia thought might be helping the *guerrilleros.* The Freivalds, then in their twenties, remember the trip. It took two days to go twenty miles, for the roads were washed out. En route, Lieutenant Noriega requisitioned a horse and let Mrs. Freivalds ride it, but the gesture was less gentlemanly than it appears. He had her carry the squad's automatic rifle and wear a green Guardia cap. If there were snipers about, she'd draw their fire. Military rule was scarcely begun when he began to play a key role. With Martínez heading the Guardia general staff and running the country, command in Chiriquí devolved on Captain Aristóteles García, who was promoted to major on December 5. A few months later, García was implicated in a plot and sent into exile, whereupon Noriega became commander. In the interim, he'd been busy stifling dissent. By the morning of Kimball's capture, December 1, there were already over four hundred men being held in the cuartel at David. Many, like Kimball, were tortured. In the countryside, a systematic campaign of repression was waged. Peasants were beaten, were staked out naked for days under the high sun, were murdered out of hand, had their poor ranchos burned to the ground and their families put outside at the height of the rains. Manuel Noriega was teaching Chiricanos not to help the guerrillas.

Such efforts invariably accompany operations against guerrillas, even when they are conducted by men and armed forces with pretensions to honor. It is difficult to bring guerrillas to battle and expensive to hunt them in their lairs. The best strategy is to hit their supply lines, forgetting (if the thought is unpleasant) that these are maintained by noncombatants. There is, too, a morale factor. Fighting guerrillas is frustrating, and there is no enemy that troops hate more, for their hatred of guerrillas is compounded by envy. Guerrillas are free, a lot freer than soldiers, and on home ground, and full of purpose, and figures of romance, and . . . Everything troops would like to be but aren't. In order to keep their chins up, troops need an object on which to vent their frustration and hate, and the civilian populace is available. The people of Chiriquí Province would have suffered no matter who directed the repression. They were especially unlucky that the person in charge was Manuel Noriega.

Or put it that Martínez and Torrijos chose wisely. They knew exactly what they were getting. Both had had Noriega as a subaltern, and his career in sadism antedated the coup. On one occasion, while a sublieutenant under Torrijos, Noriega came drunk into the lockup in David carrying a two-by-four and, laughing wildly, battered at the prisoners, broke heads and limbs while men scrambled and squealed like rats to get out of his way. And Martínez, for his part, told an interviewer that Noriega, while in his command, had prisoners buggered with a *tolete,* the hardwood billy club *guardias* carry while on street patrol, though it's unclear whether he wielded the implement personally or just watched. Indeed, it says much about Torrijos, Martínez, and the Guardia Nacional that this conduct was known and Noriega left free to pursue it, instead of being court-martialed and punished. Perhaps all felt that his skills might someday come in handy—as if ramming objects up men's rectums were a useful ability for a soldier to cultivate, like knowing how to run a machine or speak a foreign language. And of course, unfortunately, it is. If you want to seize power and set up a tyranny, Noriega's skills (or, if you like, his pathologies) are precisely the thing, and if the system engineered by Martínez and established by Torrijos were installed in Switzerland or Denmark, a Noriega would surely emerge there, and in twenty years he would be in full power.

And the man's style, his morbid humor . . . The bishop of David assigned a nun to visit the prisoners in Noriega's cuartel—Mother Angelina, originally from Italy, though she lived more than half her life in Panama. Sometimes political prisoners gave her little notes, messages to their families that they were all right, or that they needed soap or suchlike. One day, as she was leaving, she was arrested and searched on Noriega's orders. The messages were found and confiscated. The next day, when she entered the collective cell, she found all the men naked, fifty men and not a handkerchief to the whole lot, covering themselves with their hands when they saw her. No messages, of course, nowhere to hide them, and a fine joke as well, on the prisoners, on Mother Angelina, on the church, on religion in general, on chastity, modesty, courtesy, and decency, a joke enjoyable in conception, design, execution, and contemplation. There are so many ways to cause human beings discomfort, and Manuel Noriega, it seems, knows every one.

Noriega battered Chiriquí Province, put fear of death into the townspeople, and so terrorized the campesinos that hundreds left homes and land and fled across the border into Costa Rica. Aid to the guerrillas dried up. In the first days of December, over a hundred young men arrived on Quijada del Diablo to join the guerrillas, but most had to be sent home; there was nothing to feed them.

Aid from Costa Rica was curtailed also. A systematic bribery effort turned officials there from friends to persecutors of Panamanian insurgents and exiles. The main figures were Omar Torrijos and one of his drinking companions, Frank Marshall Jiménez, a deputy to the Costa Rican assembly and leader of a far-right movement called Costa Rica Libre. More than cash, they used whisky from the Colón Free Zone, which they smuggled by the truckload over the border to take advantage of Costa Rica's high import duties and the Costa Ricans' taste for scotch. Later, when priggish Boris Martínez was out of the picture, it was Marshall who gave Torrijos the idea of forming a corporation and doing contraband on a businesslike basis. The result was Transit, S.A., the Guardia Nacional's first criminal enterprise, in which top officers held shares and made fortunes, but first contraband was used to win influence in Costa Rica. The very night of the clash above Piedra Candela, a Guardia force was allowed to cross the border and kidnap Enrique Moreno, the key man in the guerrillas' supply lines.

The kidnappers included Orejita Ruiz and Sergeant Villamil, the Guardia's top thugs at that time. Since Moreno put up a struggle, Ruiz shot him twice, once through each thigh, with his .38, then proceeded to steal his watch and all his money. By dawn on Sunday, December 1, Moreno was in the cuartel at David, but it was Tuesday afternoon before he had food or medical attention. He was kept outdoors in a patio, handcuffed, leashed round the neck like a beast, entirely naked. There he lay, under sun and rain, in his own blood and excrement, kicked and beaten with hoses during interrogation, till the scandal raised in Costa Rica over the manner of his capture resulted in his receiving more humane treatment—a year in La Modelo and then exile. With his removal from Costa Rica, contact was broken between the guerrillas on Quijada del Diablo and Rafael Franceshi in San José.

At these events, Ariosto González decided to move camp back from the border to near Los Pozos, to the farm of a man named Cruz Mojica who'd been with the resistance from the first, providing food and information and shelter. The band left Quijada del Diablo before dawn on December 6 and reached Mojica's at nightfall over back trails; they found the house burned down, and horses, cows, and dogs and chickens slaughtered, and where the patio of the house had been they found a fresh grave. Sardiñas and Onofre Quintero dug there, and less than two feet down found Cruz Mojica with bayonet wounds in his face and all parts of his body.

The guerrillas stayed there that night and in the morning split into two groups, one under Onofre Quintero going to Tisingal, on the flanks of Cerro Pando, and the other, under González, making camp near Los Pozos. Both groups were together in Los Pozos from December 24 till January 1, then met again on January 6. By then, only ten were left, with nine weapons between them. The question was whether to attack or disband the outfit. They decided to attack Piedra Candela, where thirty *guardias* were stationed.

In those days, the cuartel at Piedra Candela was a large shack facing the dirt road that forms the border. The attack was set for Thursday, January 9, a holiday in Panama commemorating the sovereignty riots in the Canal Zone in 1964. By 6:00 A.M. the guerrillas were in position, those with .22s and shotguns behind the cuartel to give diversionary fire, those with heavier weapons in front, across the road on Costa Rican territory, ready to open up through the doorway and windows when the *guardias* went to defend their rear. Two other men had joined up on the eighth, so the guerrilla force numbered twelve men.

The attack went in at seven-thirty. By nine return fire had all but ceased, and Ariosto González was about to call for those still alive to surrender, when a large number of Costa Rican rural police came on the scene firing their weapons, clearly on the side of their Panamanian colleagues. At that, the guerrillas dispersed, most into Costa Rica.

Fifteen *guardias* were killed that morning. One guerrilla died also, Ramón Mojica Santamaría, a relative of the man murdered at Los Pozos. The Guardia stripped his body and hacked it in pieces and took photographs and had leaflets made up. These bore the legend "So die, without God or country, those who betray the people," and were dropped by plane all over the frontier region.

Guerrilla activity continued in Chiriquí until October 1969. New fighters joined. Other ambushes were conducted. Few in or outside Panama heard of them, though, and that was a pity. Panamanians would have had cause for pride and might have been ashamed or inspired to greater resistance. The world would not have swallowed the lies put out about Panama's "benevolent" dictatorship, and in passing would have had something worth watching, a genuinely democratic insurgency made up of small landholders fighting to restore a legitimate government, clean of ideology and lust for power. And that, one suspects, was the problem. Workaday journalists couldn't make copy from it. Guerrillas were supposed to be revolutionaries, dispossessed peasants led by engagé intellectuals in a struggle to overturn an exploitive order, etc., etc., blah, blah, or hard-eyed terrorists trained in Cuba and directed from Moscow, blah, blah, etc. No cliché fit the fighters in Chiriquí Province. For the world to learn of them would have required imagination from writers and readers alike.

Why few in Panama heard is a different story. The regime moved heaven and earth to keep people from hearing, for the guerrillas couldn't be dealt with like other opponents, characterized as "oligarchs" or "corrupt politicians," or tagged with some other discrediting label and so dismissed. They were, quite simply, free humans who wished to stay free, and that sort of thing must be stopped if one means to have tyranny, and not allowed to taint others by its example. Besides, the guerrillas showed up the Guardia, proved that far from being soldiers it was a rabble in uniform, very nasty to the unarmed and the handcuffed but not to be overly feared if one stood up to it. There were never, perhaps, more than a hundred in the field at any one time, but the guerrillas had Panama's tyrants quaking, haunted them then and thereafter with nightmare visions of a nation in arms come down from the Chiriquí highlands to sweep their forces aside and put them in prison, to put them against a wall and take their lives. Besides, guerrilla activity attested to and dramatized the regime's chief problems, its illegitimacy and its lack of support, for as if in concert with the guerrillas, five cabinet members resigned on January 8, 1969, the day before the fight at Piedra Candela.

These were the very men whose good repute and sincerity had given the coup a tincture of respectability at a time when such was badly needed to calm the populace and coax the United States toward recognition. They included Dr. Lopez Guevara and Sr. Ford. Their complaint was that the military decided important matters without consulting them and was abusing citizens' rights, both of which procedures they might well have predicted had they heeded history's lessons or their own common sense.

The resignations shook the colonels briefly. Torrijos announced that the five had been fired for conflicts of interest and for being "out of tune" with the revolution. No accurate news was permitted about the matter, certainly not the ministers' letter of resignation, and the foreign papers that mentioned it were seized from their distributors and garbaged. It soon was clear, though, that the ministers wouldn't be missed. As the *Miami Herald* suggested, their resigning was "a blow to the [regime's] prestige," but, now that it had firm power, prestige was unnecessary. In the end, the ministers' exit proved a blessing. It made way for the right sort of person and by accident forced the adoption of guidelines for recruiting civilian collaborationists that served diverse tyrants year in and year out. Henceforward only sycophants were selected. These came in two models: nonentities who in just times would not have dreamed of ever reaching high office and who, on being raised to it, would love the tyrant with all their heart and soul, and the Guardia as themselves; and capable persons with double portions of greed and ambition to make up for their total lack of scruple.

The prototype of the first was Modesto Justiniani. He was lame and blamed the prejudice of others for his lack of advancement, rather than the mediocrity that actually caused it, thereby accumulating a store of resentment that years in power could not suffice to discharge. In the ordinary course of events, he might have ended his career in bureaucracy as an official of second rank in one department or another. Now he replaced Eduardo Morgan, a partner in the country's leading law firm, as minister of government and justice. He was scrapingly servile to everyone in uniform, despotic to subordinates, arbitrary to the general public, and merciless to the poor souls whose consignment to prison or exile he slavered to endorse. And over the years a whole class was formed in his image, men and women endowed by the dictatorship with undeservedly high salaries and toothsome perquisites, who were the dictatorship's faithful spaniels. Not a single minister ever resigned again—not in protest anyway, not unless his resignation was requested.

Among the second sort were some notable rogues, planet-class liars, thieves that Ali Baba would have blushed to behold. Their portraits will be attempted at appropriate stages in this history.

A third problem for the regime had to do with its internal harmony—third to surface (since it was born illegitimate and without support) but first to be solved. Here a word is required on the dynamics of power during the tyranny.

Most departures from political legitimacy are responses to problems of overcomplication. All have the effect of simplifying things drastically. The coup in Panama was no exception. It pruned off everything in the political thicket, leaving the Guardia at once the state and the only constituency whose support mattered. Some civilian institutions were retained. Others were confected. All were mere decoration empty of vibrancy. Certain civilians were given highly paid posts and lofty titles, and were suffered to give themselves airs of importance, but all were disposable, there to be chewed and spat out. Gaudy achievements and aims were megaphoned to the four points of the compass by figures of the regime and apologists for it, benefits to the nation that the new order had brought or meant to deliver. All this was falsehood. What one had was government of, by, and for the Guardia.

All meaningful politics was Guardia politics and took place within a group of officers whose composition and size were not defined formally but which usually included the general staff and the main troop commanders and never numbered more than a dozen or so. Whoever controlled this group, or enjoyed its approval, controlled the Guardia by military discipline, which is based on fear of death in every army, and on fear of death by torture in armies that promote men like Noriega. And whoever controlled the Guardia controlled Panama, border to border, coast to coast, by force.

As for the workers and peasants, the students and teachers, the government clerks and those in the private sector, the doctors, the lawyers, the merchants, the bankers, the businessmen—all these could be useful, here and there, in looting the country, in making it hold still for forcible rape, and thus, now and then, were accorded trinkets and baubles, but none counted an eyelash in determining who had power and who didn't. The relationship between the people of Panama and the Guardia is clearly expressed in the Arab proverb "The dogs bark, but the caravan moves on." One may whip a dog when it barks or feed it rump steak, but the dog is not politically significant. All this was clear early on, and then was lost sight of when the system was purring smoothly and didn't have to show what made it function, force based on fear of death. It became clear again on the morning of Monday, July 27, 1987, with the egregious spectacle of a commando assault on a private dwelling, preceded by softening-up from flying gunships, in the Altos del Golf sector of Panama City.

Power, in short, was held narrowly during the tyranny, even during the phase of consolidation. The essential regime was composed of a dozen or so men, and no factor was so important politically as this group's internal harmony. It was decisive in mounting the coup and bringing it off: all key officers were in tune with each other. Yet, even while the coup was being consummated, discord began, and Martínez had to hurl himself and his troops to the capital to stop colleagues from giving power back to civilians. This discord seems momentary, for the thought of relinquishing power never again enters an officer's mind, but it sprang from a fundamental divergence of purpose, a disagreement over what the coup was for, a profound difference of character and values.

It may be that Martínez made the coup from vanity, found it irresistibly seductive that brother officers and prominent civilians should look to him for leadership and urge him to act, but when he did act he could not have a frivolous purpose. His vanity did not allow it. He refused to countenance a return to the *status quo ante* Arnulfo and set out instead to make Panama over. "New values," says postulate 4 of the "Revolution without Dictatorship and of Liberty with Order." And where were these new values to come from? From Boris Martínez, of course, who was serious to the point of being without humor, straightforward past the point of tactlessness, Calvinistically addicted to work and disdainful of pleasure, and above all else incorruptibly honest.

So, Down with nepotism! Down with La Botella! No bail for vipers accused of bilking the state! The U.S. ambassador called on Martínez to ask the release of a certain viper. No! said Martínez, the viper stays in jail. The ambassador called again and proposed convening Canal treaty negotiations. No! said Martínez again. The government he led had not been elected, thus lacked the representativity to negotiate something so important to the republic—as if Mr. Adair didn't know this, as if such moralizing (though just) wasn't insulting. And when Martínez found Mr. Efraín Angueira of U.S. Army intelligence—Angueira of the well-stocked bar and bill-stuffed wallet, of the duty-free appliances from the PX—yakking with Torrijos and other officers in the lounge at headquarters, Martínez drove him forth as brusquely and self-righteously as Jesus of Nazareth drove the money changers from the temple, and warned him if he came back he'd go to La Modelo.

Now, Martínez's values were sometimes pretended to by Guardia officers, but heaven knows they were not widely practiced. Torrijos, for instance. All he'd wanted was not to be sent to El Salvador, to go on enjoying his bribes and his booze and his bimbos. That he became Martínez's silent partner in power was because Martínez wanted it that way. Part was comradeship, part was that Torrijos was useful, had political skills and connections that Martínez lacked and (as the "*buen muchacho*" and "good ol' boy") was on easy terms with other Guardia officers, who respected Martínez but didn't much care for him.

By January, these officers were about fed up with Martínez, as Martínez should have known and carefully considered. At his lead, they had taken a big step, overthrown a popular president and seized power, thereby involving themselves in still other actions, and these were consequential also, such as locking up a great number of their fellow countrymen and exiling almost as many and torturing a few hundred and murdering others, not to dwell on burning people's homes and killing their livestock and beating them in front of their families—all in a few months—and when you do things like that, you can make enemies. In fact, they'd made many, and some of them had guns and were shooting back. Not many, thank God! but they had killed *guardias.* The uniform wasn't bulletproof. Having power didn't make you invulnerable. And one thing those officers knew was that they hadn't done all that and made all those enemies just to starve with Boris Martínez on the barren heights of Probity and Clean Government!

They'd thrown out to keep him from gelding the Guardia. Some also felt like being Panama's masters. By the time the dust had settled, all liked the idea. Maybe they weren't too clear on what that could mean, how big big shots could be when they got to make the rules up as they went on, when a dozen or so men had all the power, but once they had it they began to get hints. Twelve years later, Martínez remembered "incredible offers" that he resisted. Resisted, too, on behalf of his colleagues. That would have been enough, but he didn't stop there. He treated his colleagues rudely, flung their dishonesty in their faces—as if it were something to be ashamed of! Everyone always nibbled a bit at the till. Everyone but him, he was the oddball! Not just in the Guardia, in Panama too. Wanted to stop La Botella, can you believe it! That's what you say when other people have power. When you have it, what's it for if not to get your girlfriend a job? One where she doesn't work, so you can drop by in the day if you get a few minutes, so when you drop by at night she isn't exhausted and can concentrate on helping you relax. If she's got no job, you have to give her money, and that's not fair to your wife, not fair to your children. And with your wife's brother a job's even more important. If you can't get him a job, you may have to support him, but get him a job and, by God! your wife will respect you, and stop nagging you about your girlfriend.

Jimmy Lakes knew what he was doing when he shoved his pal Torrijos into power. Torrijos may not have known, but Lakas knew. Lakas was a businessman, he'd worked for a living. He was solving all his problems, putting himself on easy street for life, and it can't have taken too long to explain it, what you could do if you ran an entire country with no one looking over your shoulder to check, with everyone else out in front standing in line. But Boris Martínez said, No! You mustn't do that! No, no, no, no, no, you must be honest! When they'd never been honest before, not in their lives. Now they were supposed to start being honest when they were the law, the law and the prophets too! It's a tribute to Boris Martínez, to the toughness he projected and must have possessed, that he lasted as long as he did, almost four months.

The United States wanted Martínez out also, and colluded in his ouster if not connived in it. Martínez was too independent, an attitude Washington found tiresome in Latin leaders, even those with wide popular mandates, and didn't feel bound to put up with from a colonel who'd just stolen power using weapons paid for by the American taxpayer. On general principles, Washington wanted him out, and look what you got if you got someone better: the right kind of colonel could do the right kind of Canal deal, and then make sure the Panamanians bought it. It was already becoming clear that so broad and deep a gulf existed between Panamanian treaty aspirations and what a U.S. Senate might ratify that getting a treaty at all might be impossible if both countries went at it democratically. It would certainly be a lot easier if someone who'd play ball were in charge in Panama, and in this (one assumes) Angueira would vouch for Torrijos.

Torrijos. His mythographers make him out a colossus, and it's just possible he was enough of one to take the lead in defenestrating Martínez, but remembering him on coup night it's easier to see him as a poor henpecked devil being implacably nagged from all sides at once. By Jimmy Lakas and other civilian buddies, by his equally larcenous comrades in arms, by Efraín Angueira and several leashes of gringos: *Do something about Boris Martínez!* A scary thought, a thought to make him shudder, for Boris Martínez was mean, not to be dumped on without great trepidation. But fear was also nagging him to do something, his own fear and the fears of others. Fear was a motive along with greed. Something had to be done about Boris, so a deal could be cut with the United States so the United States would help against the guerrillas and all the other enemies the Guardia had made—so the United States would help the Guardia stay in power, for even then, early in 1969, there was no other hope for those at the top. Too many Panamanians had been jailed and exiled and tortured and murdered for those at the top to get off if the Guardia left power. Poor Torrijos: nagged from all sides at once and from inside too.

Reverberations of the turmoil within the regime seeped out to the rest of the country. And were leaked out too, once they'd been properly processed, for at some point Torrijos gave in to the naggers (or, if you like the colossus myth, won colleagues over), and a plot against Martínez was put together. The leaks were made to furnish justification. What seeped was the friction between him and Torrijos. Panamanians knew a showdown between them was coming. They were betting on Boris because he was tougher and brighter, but rooting for Omar because what was leaked was the supposed cause of the friction: Omar was moderate, Boris radical; Boris wanted more, Omar less, revolution. This happened to be true but was beside the point. Omar and pals wanted a license to steal and Washington's help in never having to pay for it, while Washington wanted a ball-playing strongman, and Boris was an obstacle to these wants' fulfillment. There was the real story, and had Panamanians known it, they'd have put their money on Omar.

Martínez claims he suspected nothing, and one believes him. He cannot have failed to notice the strain between himself and Torrijos but seems to have put it down to legitimate political differences that could be worked out. "He was my friend," Martínez says plaintively. "I helped him, I put him where he was. I never suspected him." And if this sounds incongruous in a man who, four months before, had toppled a government, it may have been supported by other reasoning. Martínez knew himself to be brave, energetic, and clever. He knew Torrijos to be cowardly, lazy, and only moderately intelligent. "How," he may have wondered, assuming suspicion did nip at him once or twice, "is Omar Torrijos going to betray *me?*" Quite easily, events answer, as they rack up yet another example of arrogance chastised.

A pretext, an immediate cause, was required. Not for the country, for the troops. They appreciated Martínez's qualities and might not have stomached his being chucked out for no reason. On February 21, Martínez supplied the makings of one in a radio talk about land reform. Few heard the talk itself, in which Martínez proposed distributing untilled land and other similarly mild measures, but everyone soon heard about it. Radical, that's what it was! Communistic! Variations on this theme were sung by a chorus of tame journalists, then taken up by professional anticommunists with appropriate head shaking and tongue clucking. Later the mythographers echoed them, so that now even scholarly works make Martínez's "radicalism" the reason for his fall and mention the land reform speech, though without quoting it. Once the speech had been given and heard about, the only thing left to do was pick the day.

On February 23, 1969, Colonel Boris Martínez arrived at Guardia headquarters at six in the morning. He went to the rooms he had there and took a shower. While he was dressing, he received a call from Demetrio Lakas—just to say hello, said Lakas, but probably to ascertain if Martínez had come in. From his rooms, Martínez went to the mess and had breakfast with Lieutenant Colonels Federico Boyd and Humberto Ramos, and his brother-in-law Major Humberto Jiménez. While they were eating, Lieutenant Colonel Juan Bernal came in, visibly nervous, and told Martínez that Colonel Torrijos needed to speak with him urgently. Martínez got up at once and left the mess.

Waiting for him, pistols in hand, behind the door of Torrijos's office were Lieutenant Colonels Ramiro Silvera and Nentzen-Franco. Both pistol-whipped Martínez on the back of his head, dropping him to the floor, stunned but still conscious. They cuffed his hands behind him and covered his mouth with heavy green plastic baling tape. Torrijos watched, standing behind his desk, his eyes bulged wide and sweat beading his cheeks.

Martínez was locked in a nearby room with a sentinel. The same ambush was pulled on Boyd and Ramos. At about ten-thirty the three, still handcuffed and muzzled, were put in a patrol wagon and driven to Tocumen Airport and put aboard a DC-3 along with Jiménez, for whom cuffs and tape were not, evidently, thought necessary. The tape was to keep the officers from ordering lower ranks to release them. Neither it nor the handcuffs were removed until the plane was on final approach to Miami.

Miami, Florida, U.S.A. Where, as travelers will have remarked, foreign visitors do not drop in as the whim takes them but are required to have and show visas and other documents, where foreign regimes cannot just deposit undesirables. That Martínez and the three others were allowed entry proves that the United States colluded in their expulsion, as does the offer made to Martínez by Panama's ambassador to the United States, Roberto Alemán (who was at the airport waiting to receive him) of a spot on the Inter-American Defense Board, for such appointments require consent *(agrément)* from the United States. Martínez refused it flatly, turned his back on Alemán, and left the airport. He had twenty dollars in his pocket. With his departure, the Panamanian dictatorship was no longer troubled by impulses toward honesty or the Guardia by pretensions to honor.

4

EARLY IN THE TIME OF OMAR TORRIJOS

A little before seven in the evening on Saturday, December 13, 1969, Brigadier General Omar Torrijos, Commander in Chief of the Panamanian National Guard and Maximum Leader of the Revolution without Dictatorship and of Liberty with Order, got on board a Pan American Airways 707 at Tocumen International Airport in Panama. With him were the engineer Demetrio Lakas, director of the Social Security Administration, Lieutenant Colonel Rubén D. Paredes of the Guardia general staff, and Sergeant Luis García, cupbearer, convoy, and dogsbody. A mare named Quimera, property of the brothers Carlos and Fernando Eleta, was running the next afternoon in Mexico City, and the four meant to cheer her to the winner's circle. In short, the Maximum Leader was taking a break. A break he could do with, one he could claim he deserved. More than nine months had passed since he'd betrayed his benefactor Boris Martínez and taken over as Panama's tyrant, the most active months of his hitherto torpid existence. They had, besides, brought cause for satisfaction.

The countryside was calm; there was that to begin with. Guerrilla bands had dispersed; that danger was over. One reason was help from the United States, the first instance of which came on January 31, when the Guardia learned of a plan by university students to dynamite the hydroelectric facility at La Yeguada in Coclé Province. Troops were airlifted to the region in U.S. helicopters from the Canal Zone and surprised the five saboteurs in a coffee grove near the village of Quije. One *guardia* was killed and two wounded in the ensuing battle, as against three guerrillas killed and two captured. The two, one of them a woman named Dora Moreno, were taken to the village and tortured awhile, then machine-gunned for the instruction of the locals.

By then, Richard Nixon was in the White House. One of his first acts as president was to dispatch Nelson Rockefeller on a tour of Latin America to find facts on which to base hemispheric policy, but since his report described the Latin-American military as "the essential force for constructive social change" in the region, he cannot have been in very close touch with reality. An occurrence while he was in Panama supports that view. Rockefeller counseled Omar Torrijos not to hold elections, which was like advising Dracula not to go sunbathing.

U.S. help for the Guardia included photo reconnaissance as well as the loan of helicopters and crews. And specialized training at installations in the Canal Zone. And uniforms and boots and other supplies. All of which seemed odd to Jerry L. Dodson, U.S. consul in David, in view of the way the Guardia treated Americans. Americans were harassed when they tried to cross the border. Americans were jailed for no cause at all and denied access to their government's representatives. Two hitchhikers were held for four months without charges and might never have been released had not Dodson learned of their plight in a smuggled message. Then there was the case of Everett Kimball. His mother wrote Dodson letter after letter. The Guardia refused to answer questions about him, but in May Dodson heard from a prisoner that he was dead and had to report that to his mother.

Worst of all, in Dodson's view, the U.S. embassy showed no concern whatsoever. Dodson had personal knowledge of thirty or forty cases of Guardia mistreatment of U.S. citizens between December 1968 and June 1969, yet Ambassador Adair made not a peep of protest. No one at the embassy cared any more about the welfare of Americans (except, of course, for those who were rich or well known) than about the welfare of Panamanians. The United States fed the Guardia equipment. The Guardia did as it pleased. When Dodson pressed matters, he was told that U.S. policy was to support the Guardia, "the one force for stability in the country."

On June 5, 1969, Dodson resigned from the Foreign Service to protest this policy, which he found "contrary to the best interests of the United States" as well as being "inconsistent with [U.S.] national principles." Dodson was only twenty-six. He believed in things like democracy and freedom and the government's standing up for its citizens. Had he known that Lieutenant Manuel Noriega had been working for the U.S. government as long as he had, or that the CIA may have okayed Kimball's murder, he wouldn't have cared much for that either.

But young as he was, Mr. Dodson was right. Messrs. Nixon and Rockefeller weren't. Also Messrs. Kissinger et al. The policy was against U.S. interests. The policy was stupid; so were those who made it. What one needed were more Dodsons and fewer Kissingers. No Kissingers at all, thank you very much, if the best they could come up with by way of policy made the United States betray its citizens and its heritage. How cowardly to let scum abuse your countrymen when you are the main means of their staying in power! How sad for the poor wretches starving on ridges, for the peasants forced into exile with nothing but the rags on their backs, having to face not only the Guardia's cruelty but American high-tech as well, all because they had the unpardonable presumption to believe in democracy and freedom!

Credit for clearing guerrillas from Chiriquí Province went officially to Manuel Noriega, who in February was promoted to captain and put in command of the Guardia's best rifle company. His troops' main activity consisted of terror strikes against the populace, but they did manage to kill Ariosto González. He had a friend in Los Pozos called Miranda. Noriega had the man's wife arrested, and in this way got him to send word to González that he had a sum of money for him from the Partido Panameñista. González suspected a trap, but his people were desperate. He went down from Cerro Pando to get the money. Fifty or sixty *guardias* were waiting for him. Their first shots missed, and González took refuge in a canebrake. The *guardias* fired into it until the cane was threshed to the ground. Then two were daring enough to go in. They found Ariosto González's body shot almost to pieces. The guerrillas never had another leader of his mettle. By October, the last of them was gone from the Chiriquí highlands. Noriega was promoted to major and put in command of the province. There he might have stayed for years in obscurity, had Omar Torrijos not gone on his Mexico fling.

The repression in Chiriquí, and the business of tyranny in general, was greatly facilitated by the dictatorship's monopoly on the means of communication. *La Estrella* was suitably docile, what with its owner, Tomás Altamirano Duque, ensconced in the cabinet as director of the National Institute of Culture, while retaining vivid memories of La Modelo. Milder variations on this theme of carrot and stick kept the electronic media in line. Meanwhile, the Guardia general staff had acquired its own press empire, the one built by Arnulfo's brother Harmodio: the afternoon *Panamá-América,* its English-language edition the *Panama American,* and the tabloids *Critica* and *La Hora.* All four were shut down on the night of the coup. Then, by a spurious suit and illegal court orders, Harmodio's heirs were despoiled of ownership. Then the despoilers were themselves despoiled, very likely with good compensation. The judge who arranged the swindle went on the Supreme Court, and the papers reopened under Guardia auspices. Once possessed of these excellent tribunes, Torrijos and company, after the school of Joe Stalin, set about falsifying the past and the present and prejudicing the future as much as they could, painting all Panama's history until their advent as an uninterrupted pageant of evil and woe, reporting the people of Panama orgasmic with delight to be ruled by them, and vilifying all who suggested otherwise.

Few lies were needed about business, however. Business was good. Post coup uncertainty, along with Martínez's purge of public employees, had slowed things down for a little, but now the economy, which had been strong anyway, was jogging along very nicely, and (best of all) Torrijos could take some of the credit. Purely by chance, but luck's more useful than wisdom. Back in 1967, major street improvements had been programmed in the capital, and plans drawn up, and financing obtained. Then the Liberals' coalition crumbled, and the 1968 campaign got under way, and the project was shelved till a new government took office. With the coup, the Guardia inherited it—blueprints, bonds, the whole affair. And got it going at once, to the gape-mouthed approval of citizens, few of whom knew the whole story. "These guys don't fool around like politicians. These guys come in, and paf! they get things done!"

Similarly, in 1966 Panama had been chosen as host of the 1970 Central American and Caribbean Games. Land had been acquired, facilities designed—a stadium, an arena, a pool, and so forth. Loans had been subscribed and money deposited. All Torrijos had to do was break ground and cut ribbons, make speeches, sip champagne, and smile for the cameras. And slap on modish, propagandistic labels: Revolution Stadium, New Panama Arena.

More, Arnulfo had brought in as economic adviser a clever, well-connected Israeli named Schlomo Glicksberg. His contract was with the Panamanian nation. He had no qualm fulfilling it, though the government that had drawn it no longer existed. Right away he proved his worth by persuading the Chiriquí Land Company, the subsidiary of United Brands that grew and picked and shipped Panama's bananas, to tide the coup makers over with a quick million. A few months later he served as go-between in procuring a $30 million loan from Goldman Sachs—a huge sum in that day for a country like Panama. To buy heavy equipment for the Ministry of Public Works, and yes, equipment was purchased, bulldozers, graders, excavators. They were paraded on the coup's first anniversary like tanks and missile launchers in Red Square. But first a sizable chunk was peeled off for insiders, the start of a great tradition in skimming from development loans.

There was no one, after all, to complain about it, no one in the world to answer to. Money bills were no longer debated. The National Assembly had been dissolved. Where the money went no longer mattered. The state's finances were a state secret. During the tyranny of Omar Torrijos, the Republic of Panama acquired the highest per capita national debt in the world and the world's worst ratio of debt to revenue. Neither, one feels, was easy to attain. There were, by then, well over a hundred countries in the world, most of them run by thieves and many by maniacs. Achieving both simultaneously demanded total contempt by those in authority for the nation they pretended to serve, plus the criminal collusion of international bankers, who must have hauled in whopping kickbacks for so cynically sandbagging their institutions, especially as the debt grew larger and larger, and revenue smaller, and lending to Panama devilish to justify. Meanwhile the lot of the common man grew harder, but insiders prospered beyond their greediest fancies. The true revolution was under way. Political power had been transferred to the Guardia Nacional as an institution. Now economic power was being transferred to Guardia big shots and their civilian hangers-on as individuals. Skimming from development loans was one method. Looting the state was another. There's a story—apocryphal perhaps, but if so *ben trovato*—about Jimmy Lakas, Torrijos's crony and junketmate and first puppet president, who set the tone for civilian collaborators of the Guardia with regard to the feathering of nests. Lakas, the story goes, was on an elevator with a bunch of people, around 1985, after he'd left the government, and a little old lady glares and bites her lip and finally blurts, "Señor Lakas, you stole ten million dollars!" and Lakas smiles indulgently, and shakes his head. "Not at all, señora, I stole twenty."

And businesses were muscled in on. Selling duty-free liquor was a good business, dockside in Cristobal, at the Atlantic terminus of the Canal where cruise ships stopped, and at Tocumen Airport, an important air junction, where many passengers had to change planes. So one day the people in that business were told to pack up their inventories and get out. That business had just become the monopoly of a company owned by Guardia big shots. And illegal enterprises were founded. Large-scale trafficking in drugs by regime insiders didn't begin, it seems, till 1970, though Floyd Carlton, one of Torrijos's pilots, testified before the U.S. Senate that Torrijos got in contact with drug lords as soon as he took over. Transit, S.A., was in business, however, smuggling liquor and taking a protection cut on everything that moved through the Colón Free Zone, and before long the whole country would be up for sale. To hear some of his speeches, Omar Torrijos thought little of capitalism, but plenty of businessmen thrived during his reign, especially those with Guardia connections. Boris the Clean was gone. Long live Omar the Corrupt!

Meanwhile, the fake revolution had got under way, the program of falsehood and bribery that produced that notable phantom Omar the Compassionate, Protector of the Poor, Shield of the Downtrodden. Chief stage manager of this ongoing illusion was a lawyer named Rómulo Escobar, one of the cleverest men in Panama, with an unblinking eye for the main chance. He'd been one of Arnulfo's most fervent supporters, yet he had more to do with perpetuating the Guardia's tyranny than any number of colonels, majors, and captains. It was he who pointed out to Omar Torrijos that the Guardia could not hope to stay long in power without at least a façade of political backing and a hint of political philosophy. Then he told him how the simulacra of both might be fashioned by the pretense of a demarche to the left.

Escobar shared the Maximum Leader's addiction to whisky, but he could stir an audience drunk or sober, could spout graceful cadenzas of Marxist theory and jargon while actually believing in nothing at all. Like Juan Materno, he was driven by resentment. As a youth, he'd been expelled from the communist party for the crime of having more talent than its leaders, and the souring the experience wrought in his character condemned him to accumulate still further slights. He had many times sought appointment as a law professor, but each time his prospective colleagues voted him down for his complete lack of scruples, or simply for his rudeness and bad humor. Torrijos, who liked to humiliate intellectuals, rewarded Escobar's services by making him rector of the National University, but first he made him minister of labor, and the bogus revolution got under way.

In April 1969, Escobar called for the formation of a single national labor federation, supposedly to give the toiling masses more power. On May Day, Torrijos flew west to banana country, and addressed the workers, and proclaimed his solidarity with their struggle. Shortly thereafter, he appointed student activists to the Institute of Agrarian Reform. And so on. Leftward, ho! But it was a con. The point of the single federation was to give the state (that is, the Guardia) control of the workers, enabling the regime to buy labor leaders wholesale. The banana workers' true champions were in jail or in exile—that's what the fruit company got for the quick million it gave the coup makers in 1968—and the way was open for Torrijos's hacks to take control of the banana workers' union. As for the students, their movement too was scheduled for corruption. Some student leaders were put on the government payroll. Others were simply handed cash.

Here's what Torrijos's May Day speech was worth: In October 1963, while Torrijos commanded in the province, a banana workers' organizer named Rodolfo Aguilar was murdered in Chiriquí. In those days, such events were uncommon and frowned on. An investigation was held. Two members of Torrijos's command, a Captain Barroso and our friend Orejita Ruiz, then a private, were arraigned. Another, it seems likely, ought to have been, for the victim was found with burns all over his body and other symptoms of torture that constituted a signature of sorts. Sure enough, at the trial, Lieutenant Manuel Noriega, who was in attendance, lost all control of his nerves and began to squall like a man possessed, making all kinds of threats and insults, so that Judge Candanedo had to have him forcibly thrust from the courtroom. Barroso and Ruiz were convicted and sentenced to prison, but one of the first acts of the Revolution without Dictatorship and of Liberty with Order was to annul the sentences and set the murderers free—an act unlikely to inspire *guardias* of any rank with respect for the persons and lives of civilians. Barroso seems to have had the good sense, if not the decency, to creep back under the rock he had emerged from, for nothing more is heard about or of him. Torrijos knew Orejita's worth, however. Torrijos assigned Orejita to his personal escort and gave him many filthy errands to run. As for Noriega, he made Judge Candanedo's life impossible, so that the man was obliged to leave the province.

The bogus revolution was endlessly useful. It lamed the workers' and students' organizations, corrupted their leaders, drugged the rest with lies. It gave the regime a whiff of moral purpose, lent an appearance of ideological grounding to what was in essence the drunken marauding of brigands. And what returns it brought later! In enabling Torrijos to pose as the people's general, its sleepless defender against the "exploiters" (the same "oligarchs" and "lackeys of Wall Street" who prospered so wonderfully during his reign), it allowed him to pose as an enemy of the United States also. Torrijos was going to play clever, bold Jack-in-the-beanstalk while Uncle Sam grimaced and growled, "Fee, fie, foe, fum!" and get all kinds of political benefit from the masquerade—in Panama, in Europe, in the Third World, and (pricelessly!) among liberals in the United States.

But who had helped him become Panama's tyrant, colluding in (if not conniving at) Boris's ouster? Who'd helped his troops wipe out democratic insurgents? Who'd turned a blind eye when his troops "mistreated" American citizens? And who was going to lavish AID funds on him and urge the banks to lend him more, even as he blustered against the *yanquis?* El Coloso del Norte, that's who, his gentle, mild, indulgent Tío Sam, who'd bought him drinks and given him a shoulder to cry on when he was just a washed-up major, one of a kennel of finks run by the "liaison officer" Efraín Angueira. And he never forgot which side of the bread had the butter. When the United States needed a favor, Torrijos came running. So let's have those hats off for the fake revolution. It was only breath and saliva, that and a bribe here and there, a chat now and then with Castro or Qaddafi, but look at the return Torrijos got on it!

The spectral leap leftward could not be convincing, however, until a slight contradiction was resolved. All Panama's serious leftists were in La Modelo, eating swill and being eaten by vermin, if not getting their kidneys kicked in by the guards. So on November 3 Torrijos had gotten them out, five weeks before his trip to the track in Mexico.

Not all had the same destination. Years later, when the fake revolution was at its apogee and Torrijos's entourage stuffed with communists, he confessed to an American visitor that there were some he couldn't deal with. He meant there were some he couldn't con or buy, but these, as it happened, were in the minority. The Moscow liners of the Partido del Pueblo were, in the main, an easygoing sort who liked the romance of thinking themselves revolutionaries, and the sense of moral cleanliness that goes with feeling one is for the downtrodden, but they didn't care to pay much for those in hardship. They were always willing to deal and with anyone, for they could always devise an argument for the deal's being tactically useful in their supposed struggle. That was the sort who joined the PDP, or in any case who lasted in it, for Moscow accepted Panama's being in the U.S. sphere of influence and made sure its party there harbored no hotheads who might cause the motherland trouble with Washington.

Then there was the Maoist faction, the Movimiento de Unidad Revolucionaria (MUR, Revolutionary Unity Movement), impatient, violent, passionate, uncompromising. They were a tiny band and prized their tininess as an emblem of their purity. They made no deals, certainly not with the Guardia. They could be killed, of course, and sometimes broken, but they could not be bought.

This was more than just an annoyance to Omar Torrijos. The comportment of the extreme left threatened his mode of governing and his self-esteem, for he was both corrupt and a corrupter. Besides, the MUR members still at large were making an urban *guerrilla* against him, setting off petards and shooting *guardias* and even robbing a bank or two. Floyd Britton directed their raids from La Modelo.

Britton was of West Indian descent and very dark skinned, tall and muscular and energetic. He was a violent man yet intensely likable, amiable and polite in his treatment of others, with an inner joyfulness that transcended hardship. People were drawn to him, even those who hated what he stood for. If no guards in La Modelo shared his politics, some will have been won by his personality. Either way, he managed to communicate with his followers, and that was infuriating. Besides, Torrijos had borne him and Alvaro Menéndez a grudge since the student *guerrilla* in 1959. So on November 3, 1969, the sixty-sixth anniversary of Panama's independence from Colombia, La Modelo Prison was emptied of communists. Those of the PDP were sent in exile to Chile. Floyd Britton and Alvaro Menéndez and five other members of the MUR were sent to the penal colony on Coiba Island.

Coiba is ten miles wide and thirty miles long, mountainous and thickly jungled. It lies less than forty miles off the southern coast of Veraguas but might as well be on the far side of the moon as far as prisoners there are concerned. A launch from the mainland makes two trips a month, and light planes land there in emergencies, but prisoners are cut off from the world entirely. There is a central camp and nine others, some accessible only by water. No one escapes, for the seas there are full of sharks—unless one calls it escape when a prisoner runs off into the jungle to die of snakebite or starvation. The penal colony was established in 1912, but no political prisoners had ever been sent there until November 4, 1969, when the seven members of the MUR arrived.

A gala welcome was laid on for the two guests of honor, a terrible beating administered by seven G-2 agents before some three hundred prisoners in the plaza between the church and the cuartel in the main camp. Britton and Menéndez tried to stand up to it but were hurled against the church wall, then clubbed and punched and karate chopped, and when on the ground kicked. The most violent attacker, who addressed himself only to Britton, was a tall, ruddy-faced man named Fernández. "You're ugly, Britton!" he shouted over and over. "What are you doing with a white wife?" Later on, Britton told Menéndez that Fernández was his wife's brother.

After that, Britton was singled out for beating, was beaten daily or more often, at the guards' whim. It was clear they'd been told his survival was not required. "Return not requested" was what was put on the orders of those sent to Nazi death camps. A similar sign had been affixed to Britton. At one point, he was handcuffed, and the cuffs tied to a horse's tail, and the horse whipped round and round the plaza. On another occasion, his companions were brought for a look at him after a beating session. He lay huddled in a corner of the hut gasping heavily, his eyes monstrously bulged from blows to his head. "This is how we deal with communists," the guard said proudly.

Under these beatings, Britton deteriorated rapidly, particularly because of damage to his kidneys. He had great difficulty urinating. He passed large quantities of blood. No doctor was on the island, and none was sent for. On the twelfth or thereabouts, the seven political prisoners were sent to different camps. On the twenty-ninth, they were returned to central to receive attention from a medical team sent out from the mainland. All but Britton. When the six were together, they noted his absence, and a short while later a trusty called Roque came and said Britton was dead. A decision, evidently, was taken that in no way was the medical team to see him. Later Roque told Menéndez that Floyd Britton had died delirious, and that at the end he weighed hardly a hundred pounds.

Two weeks later, the Maximum Leader went on his junket. And why not? Everything was a sea of milk in Panama. The Guardia was in power, and he was firmly in command.

Well, perhaps not that firmly. At five in the morning on Monday, December 15, after an expensive day at the races and an exhausting night on the town, the Maximum Leader was roused by the telephone. Alejandro Remón, Panamanian ambassador to Mexico, gave him a number to call, urgently, in Panama. Torrijos called; Colonel Bolívar Urrutia answered. From him and, moments later, from Colonel José Pinilla, president of the junta, Torrijos learned that he was no longer Guardia commandant. He would be taken care of financially. His family would be sent to him on the next plane. But he was not to return to his country.

Putschmeister was Colonel Amado Sanjur—slim, prematurely gray, impeccably military after the style of French *paras* (he affected camouflage battle dress, sleeves tightly rolled), but more the politician than the soldier with good contacts among the civilian power brokers who'd flourished before the 1968 coup. We saw him last that same night, being pelted with insults by Vice-President Raúl Arango's wife for trying to get Arango to take over. Sanjur's views hadn't changed. He considered dictatorship bad for the Guardia. He was, besides, alarmed by Torrijos's turn left, and by his nascent cult as a populist leader. He moved the moment Torrijos was out of the country and encountered no resistance to speak of. By Sunday afternoon, December 14, he had the general staff and the junta behind him. Escobar and Materno Vásquez were in La Modelo, along with three officers loyal to Torrijos, Manuel Araúz, Florencio Flórez, and Ricardo García. International telephone service was cut, and Colonel Pinilla had agreed to resign from the junta in favor of a civilian so that elections might be held in six months. Then Sanjur made his first mistake, and it was sufficient.

Colonel Ramiro Silvera was the Guardia's ranking officer after Torrijos and emblematic of the institution. He was torpid, vain, headstrong, venal, and stupid. He spent the weekend of December 13–14 in the countryside, beginning in Ocú, in Herrera Province, and drinking his way leisurely back to his beach house at Playa Corona, sixty miles west of the capital. There he was Sunday afternoon, nursing a hangover, when a messenger reached him. Sanjur, who'd had no qualm at unseating a general, now felt bound by military protocol to ask his senior, Silvera, to take command.

Silvera released the officers Sanjur had jailed, reopened international communications, and quickly persuaded Pinilla not to resign or say anything foolish about holding elections, nothing with a firm timetable, for example. The first act announced that the putsch makers weren't in earnest. It and the second invited a counterputsch. The third assured they would have no support from the people, for if the dictatorship by the Guardia was going to continue, if no more was going to happen than when Torrijos ousted Boris Martínez, why should the people care one way or another? There followed two all-night meetings, one at the palace where Pinilla, Urrutia, and Sanjur brought civilian functionaries on board, the other at Guardia headquarters presided at by Silvera and attended by officers. Then came the call to Remón and the call from Torrijos. Then those in Panama got wearily to tying loose ends, while in Mexico Jimmy Lakas and Rubén Paredes were prodding Torrijos onto the pages of legend.

What Torrijos ended up doing was rent a plane and fly home and regain power—the stuff of legend, no question there. That he had to be prodded to do it is incidental, as is the help he had from potent allies, and the help he had from imbecile adversaries. Mythology itself has poltroon heroes who make it on the moxie of others and undeserved favor from on high—for instance, Jason, in equal parts wimpish and pimpish, carried by his shipmates, then by his girlfriend, but the Lad of the Golden Fleece to anyone asking, as if to prove that glory can come without merit. Under pressure, Torrijos was ever irresolute, and think of the wringer his feelings were put through that morning! Shock, disbelief, anxiety, anger, resentment. Self-blame: he'd got himself hoodwinked like Boris Martínez. Self-pity: with Martínez there'd been a complaint, but he, Omar, was a river of loot to his colleagues. Nakedness, shame, the sense of crowds jeering at him. Relief: he was getting off easy; he had killed people. Resignation: thank God it was over; at least he was safe. He was willing to take his pension and slink to the wings, but first he slunk to where his companions were sleeping for a little shared victimhood and commiseration—a weak man who would not have harmed anyone if Lakas hadn't pushed him and Martínez pulled him and others nagged and nattered him to power.

But Lakas wasn't relieved, not for an instant. Lakas had only begun to get rich. Paredes wasn't resigned. He was destined to be tyrant of Panama. He didn't mean to live without ambition in the hungry land of might-have-been. They didn't commiserate, they prodded: yelled at Torrijos, told him to be a man. Lakas, it seems, threatened to shoot him outright if he refused to lead them back to pelf and power. One imagines the bearlike Lakas bellowing fury and quickly supposes Torrijos more fearful of him than of any fate he might encounter in Panama. And besides, they propped him up, told him they were with him—as, of course, they were, he being their meal ticket. The upshot was he agreed to return. Then the question was how. They couldn't take Pan Am and get off at the airport like ordinary passengers, and to top things off the Eletas' mare had lost, and they had only a few hundred dollars among them. It would also be nice to be welcomed, not shot, when they got there.

Ambassador Remón got them an airplane. Emilia Arosemena, the embassy secretary, agreed to write a check to pay the rental. The efforts of both were rewarded. He got the consulate in New York City and she the embassy he vacated. While they were earning these plums, Torrijos was on the phone recruiting supporters, with no worse luck than Sanjur had had two days before. Guardia officers were loyal to whoever was asking, a posture Silvera had made possible by freeing those who'd refused to join the putsch. And Torrijos could not have sounded out anyone, and would have faced a very chancy return, but for Silvera's obtuseness in reopening international phone service.

Among those who pledged their loyalty was the one officer whose help was crucial. This was Major Manuel Noriega, commanding the Fifth Military District, Chiriquí Province, and thus in control of the airport at David, the closest in Panama to Mexico and the only viable place for Torrijos to land. And why not, you ask, why shouldn't Noriega be loyal? Hadn't Torrijos saved him twice when he was a lieutenant, and shown him trust and advancement since? Well, that same day Noriega's brother Luis Carlos accepted the post of minister of labor from the officers who were throwing Torrijos out! They, too, supposed they had Noriega with them. He was, then, well positioned with both parties, a thing that became a trademark with him, and able, in fact, to determine the winner. Why he chose Torrijos had little or nothing to do with how Torrijos had treated him but was a matter of the policy of the United States.

Which seems to have been based on Matthew 6:3—"Let not thy left hand know what thy right hand doeth." Sanjur moved against Torrijos with the advice and consent of U.S. intelligence as represented by Efraín Angueira and a man named Armando Parada, his superior, who lived in Panama but was attached to Southern Command in the Canal Zone. *Military* intelligence. The CIA wasn't informed and wasn't amused. The Pentagon and its agents on the isthmus took Torrijos's leftist rhetoric at face value and gave the putsch their blessing if they didn't provoke it. Subtler minds at Langley knew Torrijos for an opportunist and his "revolution" for a forgery. Far from being alarmed when he turned pinkish, they judged the color good camouflage. Silvera might be as corrupt and thus as cooperative, but Torrijos was a known quality, and the less he looked like Washington's choice, the more useful he was.

Agency rivalry no doubt played a part also, along with the vanity and ambitions of individuals. That rivalry must now concern us for a moment.

U.S. spookkeepers notoriously feud with each other, but none more bitterly and intensely than CIA and army intelligence (CIC). In 1957, therefore, with a view toward making their mutual hostility somewhat less harmful to the national interest, a demarcation line was drawn between the "turfs" of the two outfits. The U.S. Army might spy on other armed forces, but civilian targets belonged to the CIA.

In Panama, this had an amusing consequence that illustrates the way things worked in practice. A young man was serving with military intelligence who happened to be sole heir to a notable fortune. He was dating the daughter of a government bigwig and receiving many attentions from her parents as eligible bachelors often do—dinners at home, weekends in the country. His motives were entirely recreational, but he heard some interesting things from the girl's father, and as a good soldier reported them to his superiors. How much the information enhanced U.S. national security may not have been easy to measure even then, but it certainly enabled the military intelligence group's colonel to upstage the CIA station chief more than once, and when the latter found out how this had happened, he claimed the bigwig as his legitimate prey. The heir was summarily ordered to break off the romance and a CIA operative assigned to begin one. The girl, it seems, took it all in stride, but her father was inconsolable at losing so grand a potential son-in-law. The CIA's man never set foot in his house, much less gathered any pearls of intelligence from him. The station chief, though, was no longer upstaged by the colonel, so from his vantage the tale had a happy ending.

How, then, did Manuel Noriega, a serving officer of an armed force, the Guardia Nacional, come to be on the CIA's payroll? The likelihood is that it was a case of his being assigned in Chiriquí Province, far from the army's ambit in the Canal Zone, and that as intelligence officer of the Fifth Military District, Noriega had to do with monitoring the activities of the left-leaning banana workers' union, a prime CIA target, given that the plantations were owned and run by a subsidiary of the United Fruit Company. Finally, there are persistent rumors that while still a student at the Instituto Nacional, that is to say in 1952 or before, Noriega offered to provide the CIA information concerning his left-leaning classmates. Whether he was actually vetted and recruited them is beyond the authors' capacity to determine, but if he did make the approach, his name would have been put on file and his whereabouts checked now and then, just in case he might become useful, and useful is certainly what he became.

After the 1968 coup, and especially after the passing of Boris Martínez, CIA operatives more or less supplanted those of army intelligence in dealings between Torrijos and U.S. spookdom. In approving the putsch, the army's men were, in a sense, regaining power in Panama.

There were, of course, some good reasons for wanting Torrijos chucked out. His involvement in drug trafficking seems to have begun about this time. And truly subtle minds (such as, one rushes to grant, do not commonly associate themselves with intelligence work during peacetime) might have judged that if one were to have the Guardia in power, it might be good procedure to boot the top goon out every six months or so, as insurance against his growing uppity—that is, lest he start aspiring above his station.

In any case, there was a U.S. intelligence outfit on each side of Sanjur's putsch against Torrijos, and the CIA came out winning—that is, convinced decision makers in Washington that the U.S. national interest lay with Torrijos. His return to command of the Guardia was, besides, feasible on account of a well-placed "asset," Major Manuel Noriega. So it was that Noriega, who had fixed things so that he'd prosper no matter who won, sided with Torrijos and allowed him to land and provided a base for his return to power.

Besides officers in Panama, Torrijos spoke with Colonel Rodrigo García, who was visiting academy classmates in El Salvador, and with Sidar Cisneros Leyva, confidential adviser to General Anastasio Somoza, dictator of Nicaragua, assuring himself of a welcome in two spots along his route. Like García, Torrijos was a graduate of El Salvador's military academy and had many friends among the country's armed forces. Somoza had received him in Managua earlier that year, and he was personally friendly with Cisneros Leyva. But allowing him to proceed across their borders, allowing him to refuel his plane on their soil, constituted intervention by both countries in the internal affairs of Panama, something the leadership of neither would have dreamed of in that year of grace, 1969, without first checking carefully with Washington. Washington, evidently, gave its okay—that is, its left hand undid on Monday what its right hand had done the day before.

Torrijos, Lakas, and Paredes took off from Mexico City at 10:45 that morning, local time, delayed by fog an hour and a half. The plane was a single-engined air taxi, the pilot a Mexican named Luis Posada, the cover story that Torrijos's father was dying, hence Torrijos couldn't wait for Pan Am that night. At the end of the first leg, in Tapachula, on the frontier with Guatemala, Torrijos felt faint. In his account, he says the problem was altitude. It may also have been hangover or funk. In any case, he lay down under a tree and sucked at a lemon while Posada refueled the plane and Lakas bribed the authorities to overlook Posada's lack of a passport, and when these formalities had been seen to, he was ready to proceed with his feat.

In San Salvador, they dropped Lakas—he continued on to Panama the next day—and were joined by Colonel García and the most famous flyer in Central America. This was Red Grey, a onetime U.S. Army Air Corps fighter pilot and as of July that year, at age fifty-one, the ace of the Salvadoran air force in the so-called Soccer War with Honduras. In between, Grey had lived in Chiriquí, Panama, flying for local airlines and the banana company, and had been helped out in hard times by Omar Torrijos. Now he offered his services, and they were welcome. David Airport had no landing lights, was officially closed to traffic after dark. Posada, being a Mexican, might have risked a night landing, but neither he nor any other newcomer pilot would have been a favorite to succeed. Grey, on the other hand, had been in and out of that field a thousand times, day and night, drunk and sober, in all weathers.

Next stop was Las Mercedes, home base of the Nicaraguan air force, eight miles east of Managua. Somoza and Cisneros were waiting when Torrijos touched down. The two dictators talked for a time apart from the others. The final leg of the flight proceeded in Somoza's personal twin-engine Aero Commander, with Grey at the controls and Posada beside him and an escort of three Nicaraguan air force jets. Torrijos took leave of Cisneros with these words: "Somoza has been like a father, I'll never forget it."

Grey raised David Airport Tower ten miles out. In English. He was a legitimate gringo soldier of fortune with no Spanish despite two decades in Latin America. The field had been occupied by Noriega's troops for eight hours, and its personnel held more or less prisoner while the major played his usual double game, waiting to welcome Torrijos while assuring Silvera in the capital that not even Torrijos's orderly, Sergeant Luis García, would enter Panama via Chiriquí. The technician on duty, who had Lieutenant Luis del Cid standing over him, answered Grey nervously and requested information regarding Grey's passengers, and there followed some radiophonic fencing. Then Del Cid took the mike. Torrijos recognized his voice and identified himself. There were clouds over the airport, but Grey brought the Aero Commander down through them with no hesitation. Truck headlamps lit the end of the runway. Torrijos was on the ground at 1:15 A.M., Panama time, December 16, twelve and a half hours after leaving Mexico City. By that evening, he was in charge at Guardia headquarters after a triumphant progress by road from David to the capital.

Thereafter, December 16 was celebrated as Loyalty Day, and much was made of the supposed mystic bonds between Torrijos, the Guardia, and the nation. The whole episode, though, is best seen as a gloss on Shakespeare (*King Lear,* act 4, scene 6, line 161): "A dog's obey'd in office." Whoever had rank in the Guardia could exercise it. The Guardia was loyal to whoever was there. The same officers who shed no tears, much less blood, at Torrijos's "destitution from command" (the phrase is Sanjur's) spared no expense of breath and saliva cheering his return, and were followed robotically by their soldiers and the horde of civilian bootlickers who marched in the Guardia's train after it took power. As for the nation, it didn't care who prevailed. One uniformed thief was the same as another.

The long flight, the tiny plane, the night landing, and so forth were eagerly seized upon by sycophant mythmakers and transformed into a gaseous chanson de geste. Risks were grotesquely inflated, trivial incidents sung in epic tones, to the point where even Torrijistas were relieved when, years later (Torrijos was dead and he tyrant of Panama) Paredes put things somewhat in perspective by revealing that he and Torrijos had high blood pressure, and were taking diuretic medication, and thus spent much of the flight relieving themselves into a tin can and passing it from one to the other. In this and all other versions, however, the stop in Nicaragua was sternly suppressed, along with the Aero Commander and everything that touched on Tachito Somoza, who was already widely known and justly loathed as a greater pig than his infamous namesake and father. Panamanians, who had their faces smeared in reality daily, knew that Torrijos and he were companions in swinehood, both tyrants, both murderers, both thieves, but it was not meet that the world should make the connection.

The fantasy of an intrepid Torrijos was never widely subscribed to by Panamanians. It sold well abroad, though. With its companion phantom the caring Torrijos, it lent his regime a needed whiff of legitimacy. The men who forked out the loans and raked in the kick-backs knew perfectly well who was getting the money, and that their banks would likely not see it again, but they couldn't very well say so in public. "Loaned that goon in Panama fifty million this morning. Point and a half for me, why else would I do it? Biggest bunch of thugs you ever heard of. Going to pick the place clean before they're finished, and God help the poor bastards who have to live there?" No, that was no good, pretense was needed. The man was brave as a lion, the people loved him. The country was forging ahead under sound leadership, and wise bankers were making that wonderful progress possible.

The men who ran the United States knew Omar Torrijos, and believed that a tyrant was easier to deal with than a government that represented the people and respected their rights. But Richard Nixon couldn't admit (as FDR had of Somoza *père*) that a protégé of the United States was an SOB. Times had changed, and so had American presidents. Pretense now was required. The geste of Torrijos's return therefore came in handy.

There were, besides the mushy minded who had to con themselves before they conned others. Nelson Rockefeller and *Time* magazine babbled about the "new" Latin-American military, which like that other figment the "new" Nixon were somehow supposed to be benign. The Latin-American military were, of course, exactly the same as always—ignorant, brutal, corrupt, malign as sarcoma—except they now kept strings of bedoctored flunkies and could, if pressed, prate some modish slogans, "structural change," "social transformation," and so forth. *Time* and Rockefeller may not have been lying outright. They may, instead, have been autobamboozled through ingestion of fantasies like those about Torrijos. Felipe González of Spain would also adore him. Carlos Andrés Pérez of Venezuela was soon to be fawning abjectly at his feet. And Hamilton Jordan would flutter to him over and over, would swoop to Torrijos's beach house at Farallón like a sparrow to horse droppings. All the myths of Torrijos played well abroad. The return to power was one of the most popular.

The putsch and its aftermath also gave Torrijos a chance to rearrange things politically, to make things more stable. Pinilla and Urrutia he simply sent home. He installed Demetrio Lakas as junta president, and as member a lawyer named Arturo Sucre, who'd been in the short-lived cabinet picked by Silvera. In all this, he showed intelligence, and that being stripped of command had taught him something. A stupid man would have gobbled the mythmakers' fancies and goofily believed himself loved—by the Guardia, by the people, in short a true hero. A stupid man would have indulged a taste for vengeance. The putsch, though, had taught Torrijos that the Guardia was, essentially, fickle. Success rarely teaches anything useful. Intelligent people learn to learn from setbacks.

Torrijos refrained from taking revenge on Pinilla and Urrutia and thus refrained from making himself hated in the Guardia. He was, besides, bright enough to realize that the people did not love anyone in uniform. The people wanted civilians in power. Which couldn't be, for he and the others meant to continue the tyranny, if only because ending it would be dangerous for them. At least, though, he could give the people some pretense, the political equivalent of Vaseline. The state's ceremonial figureheads could be civilians. That would salve the people's sores a little. Sucre's appointment was a gesture toward the right and Torrijos's way of showing he had no animus against the sectors that distrusted him most deeply and had greeted the putsch with most enthusiasm, the *rabiblancos,* the business community, and the chiefs of the outlawed political parties.

Some firmness had to be shown, though, someone had to be punished. Silvera and Sanjur went to La Modelo, along with Lieutenant Colonel Luis Nentzen-Franco, who had also been prominent in the failed putsch. They were not, it seems, particularly mistreated, and some six months later, at 1:30 in the morning on June 8, 1970, the three escaped. Since they took refuge in the Canal Zone and were granted asylum, despite Panama's efforts to have them turned over, and since they later went to the United States, it appears that their Uncle Sam was making amends for the awful mess they'd gotten themselves into while acting with the advice and consent of U.S. Army intelligence. By that time, Angueira and Parada were long gone from the isthmus.

Escobar and Materno were put back into the cabinet. Glicksberg and his fellow economist Nicky Barletta were kept on despite their conspicuous glee at a party celebrating Silvera's ascension to commandant. One begins to see Torrijos's mature style of ruling. He arranged about him disparate persons and bunches—cronies, advisers, confidential agents—representing different constituencies and efforts, none of whom had much access to any other, each of whom thought himself the general's favorite, all of whom he played off one against the other: leftist intellectuals, businessmen operators, technocrats (bedoctored or otherwise), dealers in this or that sort of contraband, drinking-buddies-cum-weekly-flyers-in of fresh whores from Miami. Each bunch saw a different Omar Torrijos. Torrijoses came in abundant variety. There were always enough to go around.

Foremost, of course, among the tyrant's associates were the top officers of the Guardia. If there was an authentic Torrijos, they saw him. From 1970 on, they were convinced that they would do best with Omar. With them, it seems, he dealt fairly and honestly. Each got his generous slice of the country to feed on and grow fat.

Some officers who'd joined the putsch were purged in its aftermath, along with some who were lukewarm to it and some like Ricardo García who'd opposed it but whom, for some reason, Omar Torrijos disliked. His favorites, meanwhile, were promoted and given key commands or staff positions. Rodrigo García became second commandant. Paredes prospered. As for Manuel Noriega, he was destined for truly great things.

A text underscored by the putsch against Omar Torrijos was one he'd heard Rómulo Escobar preaching for months, one he'd already begun translating into action: something to stand for, someone to back him up. Without these, or at least their lifelike appearance, he'd have great trouble keeping power or getting much reward from its possession. Since losing power might mean paying for his crimes, he occupied himself with their acquisition.

His political creed, what he'd best pretend to believe in, was dictated by fashion and circumstance. The mode in Third World leaders was nationalist-populist. Panama had its special issue, the Canal Zone. So Torrijos was for sovereignty and social justice, against the gringos and the oligarchs. How he handled the first will be looked at in the next chapter. With the second, he had a problem—or would have, had he cared at all for truth. Panama's oligarchy—and it was rapacious!—was composed of the top Guardia officers and their clustered infestations of civilian parasites. Its leader was Omar Torrijos. He got round this rub, however, with two falsehoods: he pretended the *rabiblancos* were oligarchs, and he pretended to oppose them.

As for support, he sought it widely, and got it from some very different sources, including Washington, Moscow, and Havana, Menachem Begin and Muammar Qaddafi. His firmest support in Panama came from elites, the rich and the Guardia, but in the wake of the putsch he established three bases. One he built, and one he bought, and one he more or less bluffed into existence.

The base he built might be considered bought also. It was the closest thing he had to a true following, and it served him and succeeding tyrants well so long as it wasn't tested too severely. It consisted of state employees, bureaucrats mainly. Where Boris Martínez had wished to limit bureaucracy, Omar Torrijos made it swell grotesquely so as to create a class dependent on him, a mass with something of a stake in prolonging his tyranny and whose livelihoods he could lop whenever he pleased. The program was scarcely original and took no great art to accomplish, merely contempt for the nation's long-term interests. Growth proceeded mainly by cell division and was financed like a Ponzi scheme or chain letter, with new money borrowed to pay the lenders of old.

All government bureaus expanded, and new ones were born, and entities split, and split-offs split in turn. The Ministry of Planning swam off from the Ministry of the Presidency and spawned all manner of lesser departments. The Ministry (singular) of Labor and Health became the Ministries (plural) of Health and Labor. Agriculture split from Agriculture and Commerce, then split into Agriculture and Agricultural Development. The autonomous Institute of Culture and Sports emerged fully grown from Omar Torrijos's brow as a toothsome plum with which to bribe Tomás Altamirano Duque, and within a year sports and culture each had its own institute, and budget and staff and office space and equipment, and brothers-in-law and girlfriends with *botellas.*

The private company that provided telephone and electric service was nationalized at a stiff cost to the state, then caused to divide amoeba-ishly into two institutes. State corporations were created for every purpose, and some were created for no purpose at all, wall-to-wall *botellas* from president to porter. There was a State Corporation for the Development of the [Costa Rican] Border Region of Alanje and Barú, and a State Corporation for the Development or Eastern Chiriquí Province, and so on east to the border with Colombia. Cities were chopped and provinces sliced into districts, and each was equipped with a mayor and a council, and a staff of folks to make work for one another, and brothers-in-law, of course, and also girlfriends to stop by for their paychecks every fortnight. Elevation to mayor or councilman was by appointment. No elections were held, not even fake ones, till 1972.

Meanwhile, reform decrees were issued in sheaves, supposedly to address needs of the people but in fact to justify the state's tumorous growth. And also to swell the sums that the state managed. For example, the decree reforming the Social Security Administration provided for that state entity to assume the risks hitherto borne by private companies in insuring workers against on-the-job injury—and, of course, to collect the premiums also. The point here was simple, and also applied to the nationalization of electric and telephone service, and to every other aspect of the state's expansion: the more money that came into the state's custody, the more that could be skimmed or scooped or siphoned, or drained or dredged or otherwise detached for the transfer to the bulging accounts and pockets of top Guardia officers and the civilian parasites' parasites who fed off them.

The decrees, besides, had propaganda value, not so much for what they said or accomplished but just by being issued, for the suggestion they gave that the government cared. A few did some good for a while. For a while, reform of the health services, for example, had some meaning in terms of lives lengthened and pain eased. The slogan "Salud igual para todos" ("Equal health for all") seemed for a time to reflect a sincere desire to raise the standards of health care for poor people. The desire faded soon, though, if it ever existed. The idea of equality became a pretext for putting thousands of people into the health care system on the Social Security Administration who had never had quotas docked from their salaries and matched by payments from their employers, so that the budget for public health might be cut and funds detatched for transfer, et cetera. So the social security system became overloaded. The Social Security Administration Hospital, once Panama's pride, had sick people bedded down in the corridors, and doctors trying to treat them on the basis of what medicines might be in stock, and nurses resterilizing disposable hypodermic needles, and emergency room patients holding their own intravenous fluid bottles because there were no stands and no money to buy them. Equality was achieved all right, but at lower standards.

Those reforms that were not mere camouflage to begin with, or poorly thought out, or botched in execution, were thus perverted from their original purposes into new ways to loot the state and cheat the people. Little of lasting use was achieved. In 1968, Avenida Perú in Panama City was a two-way thoroughfare, and a program of street reform instituted by General Torrijos made it one-way running east, and the measure greatly eased traffic congestion. Other than that, however, there was nothing. That was the dictatorship's one discernible plus.

Few saw that back then, though. Few suspected the depth of Torrijos and company's cynicism. In the first months of 1970, when the reform decrees came thick and fast, there was a palpable feeling in

Panama of work being done at high speed for the good of the country, and in those months, founded on nothing really (if not on the actual betrayal of the people), Torrijos amassed a store of goodwill on which he traded successfully for years.

Surely he had the goodwill of those tens of thousands who went to work in the new or expanded departments, often at good pay for doing little. And if some were ingrates and brooded upon the regime's abuses—the curbs on free expression, the way men in uniform shoved civilians around—at least they knew their nice jobs could be snatched in a twinkling, and kept their misgivings to themselves, and showed up to applaud when they were told to. Thus he built (and/or bought) a base to help him keep power, and (as it were, in one motion, with elegance, with grace) enlarged the pools of cash that one might steal from to help make power's possession rewarding.

Nor did he neglect his family while dispensing state employment and power's rewards. Brother Moisés was ambassador to Argentina, then held a post in the foreign ministry which enabled him to traffic in heroin (five kilos a week, by the general's own estimate), and then was ambassador to Spain. Brother Hugo was head of the national casinos and invented an infallible system for blackjack. The maximum bet was supposed to be $200, but Hugo played up to $10,000 a card, and might play five or six hands at once, and when he lost he simply kept doubling his bet, and played on until he'd won what he cared to that session. Brother Marden was head of the national post office. Sisters Berta, Joya, and Aurea all had posts in the government, and so did sisters-in-law Flor and Susana, and brother-in-law Marcelino, and too many cousins to list without being tiresome.

The base of support Torrijos bought outright was the Partido del Pueblo (PDP), the Moscow- and Havana-line communist party. First, though, he had to deal with the Peking liners, for with the murder of Floyd Britton these intensified their opposition to the dictatorship. The chief figures now were Britton's younger brother Federico, and a youth with the nom de guerre Cocaleca (the word signifies a kind of beetle, and also a dance step based on the beetle's locomotion), and four brothers named González Santizo. Their most colorful caper was a heist of the casino at El Panamá Hotel, using a car that a sympathizer had bought from an officer of the U.S. embassy and that still bore diplomatic plates. After that, the group was pitilessly hunted down.

The car was traced to its new owner, and his house was raided. Three of the four González Santizo brothers were caught and killed there. Encarnación González, the brothers' father, was arrested for the crime of having such sons, and was thrown from a helicopter. Then Cocaleca was wounded in the leg and eye and captured, and after months in prison he was broken. Later he worked for the G-2. It was at this time, early in 1970, that a young doctor named Hugo Spadafora was called to treat a wounded member and paid for it with a term in La Modelo, the first appearance of one of the chief actors in the drama of Panama's tyranny.

The guerrillas were killed or captured, or fled abroad. Federico Britton received asylum in the Mexican embassy and lived for many years outside Panama but returned in the 1980s. Alvaro Menéndez Franco was brought from Coiba to La Modelo after Floyd Britton's death caused a scandal. He ended up making peace with the dictatorship and backing his friend's murderer, Omar Torrijos.

The last González Santizo brother lives in Sweden. In the late 1970s, when the new Canal-treaty package was about to be submitted for ratification to the U.S. Senate, Torrijos visited Stockholm for a meeting with Olaf Palme. He met as well with Panamanian exiles and had the unspeakably bad taste to ask after González Santizo's father. "Dead," the young man replied. "The Guardia threw him out of a helicopter." There was no way, of course, that Torrijos could have forgotten. Nor was there any way that the man could have been thus murdered without Torrijos's approval. It is hard to say which action was slimier: ordering the murder or later pretending innocence of it.

Matchmaking between Torrijos and the Partido del Pueblo occupied most of 1970. It may even have been in progress in November 1969, when PDP leaders, along with other leftists, were released from La Modelo and exiled to Chile. After the putsch in December, and in any case by March 1970, when the celebration of a world youth congress in Santiago forced the PDP to put out a clear party line, Panamanians under communist discipline spoke openly of the correctness of working with the dictatorship, given its "anti-oligarchic" character. The adjective, of course, had a code meaning and signified imaginary opposition to an imaginary oligarchy, since the only true oligarchs were the Guardia and its principal hangers-on. One of the go-betweens was a lawyer named Rafael González, once a partner in Harmodio Arias's firm and a man with an odd political trajectory. In his youth, he'd been vaguely a leftist but not a communist. In the early 1950s, he won a fellowship for postgraduate study at Harvard and had no trouble getting a U.S. visa. But there, in the barren gloom of the bourgeois midnight, with Joe McCarthy's bloodhounds in full cry, in the least propitious region of the space-time continuum, he saw the Marxist-Leninist light and was converted. On his return, his friends found him transformed. As the firmness of his faith could scarcely be doubted, he was a credible envoy to the PDP.

The other intermediary was the far more obscure Conrado Gutiérrez, a third- or fourth-rank figure in the Federación de Estudiantes de Panama (FEP, Panama Students' Federation) whom Torrijos picked, why no one knows, to reorganize the student movement as an ally of the Guardia—in plain terms, to corrupt it. Gutiérrez was the sluice through which money poured, hundreds of thousands of dollars during his brief term of service. As by enchantment, he leaped from misery to affluence: three homes, including a high-rise penthouse; three or four fancy cars, one of which he managed to wreck in 1972 or thereabouts, killing himself in the process. In 1970, he was a principal bridge between the Guardia and the communists, negotiating the return from exile of the PDP politburo, minus one or two comrades who were willing to present baboonishly for Khrushchev or Castro but drew the line at Omar Torrijos.

Most accepted. Those who refused found their hard lot instantly worsened. Salvador Allende had been inaugurated six weeks before. Panama's communists had their Chilean comrades lobby with the state against the renegades. These suffered suspicion and surveillance and harassment, persecution that culminated in January 1972, with the expulsion from Chile of all Panamanians who, for not wishing to embrace Omar Torrijos, found themselves still there in exile. Most were at the brink of starvation to start with, working as pick and shovel day laborers, living in shantytowns of the sort that shame all the big towns of Latin America, the ant-heap clusters of hovels that the Chileans call *cayampas,* that is to say, "funguses." Now they were put under arrest and over the border, shoved penniless into Peru. The Peruvians, though, had their own military dictatorship composed, of the same species of reptile as that in Panama. They could hardly pamper the ingrates who'd refused the bounty of Omar the Compassionate. So the exiles were shunted off on a tortuous pilgrimage around South America, till the Danes, of all people, came to their aid and gave them a haven. There, in Denmark, they had to bear capitalist horrors, bourgeois torments such as happily had been expunged by the enlightened rulers of Chile, Peru, and Panama, but at least they could get their breath; at least they knew where they would sleep tomorrow.

Well, then, Torrijos bought the Partido del Pueblo with what Martínez and he had taken from it: the rights of its members to live freely in their own country, to express their convictions, to work toward translating these into reality. Tossed in, so to speak, as sweetener was a monopoly on political action. For the next nine years, the PDP was the only party suffered to operate anywhere on Panamanian soil. And here's a great advantage for a tyrant: he can buy human beings with their own belongings, and/or those of others, and at those prices bargains abound. What, then, did Torrijos get through the transaction?

The Partido del Pueblo had never had much of a following. It was not going to mobilize masses of people in support of or opposition to anything. On the other hand, it had some suasion with labor and more with the students. It was useful, therefore, in keeping these sectors tame. What the Guardia worried about as threats to its power were a general strike and street demonstrations. Labor was the key to the first. In Panama, only students did the latter—those at public high schools in the capital and Colón, and to an extent those at the National University—until the anti-Noriega clashes of 1987. The pact with the PDP, then, was something of an insurance policy.

Torrijos also got a modest rent-a-crowd service. No huge throngs such as he later on gathered by marching public employees to the meeting place in lockstep and dragooning peasants from the countryside, but if one wanted a hundred-odd people with placards, or youths hurling insults and the occasional rock, the PDP could turn them out on short notice. Sometimes when Torrijos wanted to do something, he first had a mob of that sort stomp about and demand it. What the PDP did best, though, was make up slogans. The function may not seem important at first glance, unless the glance pierces the mind of a Guardia officer, and until one reflects that tyrants need catchy lies badly. Not for use on the people, whom no amount or quality of rhetoric can befuddle from the truth of their oppression, but to keep up their own morale and that of their cohorts, and to fool those looking on from without. The PDP sloganed in a wide range of banalities. Romantic-chivalric: the 1968 coup, a vulgar theft of power, became *la gesta octubrina*—the October geste or daring deed or exploit. Bucolic: the system of administration, a corrupt bungle, was described as *la yunta pueblo-gobierno*—the yoke or harness in which people and government pulled together. Socialist-realist: the Guardia, at best bribe takers, at worst murderers, was referred to as *el brazo armado del pueblo*—the people's weapon (or weaponed) arm.

In those days, too, one began to hear the word *proceso,* as in *proceso de cambios revolucionarios* ("process of revolutionary changes"). This was not a PDP coinage but was imported from Peru, where uniformed goons had seized power a few weeks before their counterparts did in Panama—snuffing free expression, pacting with the communists, buying intellectuals wholesale (thereby acquiring all manner of verbal trinkets), bathing themselves in fake-populist drivel, and toweling off with the national flag—but they at least murdered and exiled few of their countrymen and had shame enough to creep back to their barracks after scarcely ten years of glutting, before their poor country was utterly wasted.

In the early 1970s, Peru's dictatorship seemed to be functioning well, provided one viewed it from a distance, so in putting together what amounted to an ad campaign for Panama's tyranny, the PDP did a good deal of straight cribbing. Including this gem: a decree prepared by the Ministry of Education, where most of the PDP's government posts were located, mandated the teaching of Quechua, a native Peruvian dialect, in regions inhabited by Panamanian Indians. A Peruvian law had been Xeroxed into effect without having even been read by its supposed authors. There's slavish aping. One might as well have prescribed courses in Kurdish. As for the term *proceso,* the Argentine generals later picked it up and adopted it despite its leftist parentage. It was, after all, an excellent euphemism for what happened in all three countries: the armed forces waged war against their own countries and countrymen.

Finally, the PDP was the kind of mongrel that will cringe at the least show of backbone by an adversary but whose yelp is exceedingly shrill and annoying. Panamanians are, as a nation, polite and good-natured, respectful almost to a fault of the feelings of others. A Panamanian will not say no if you ask him a favor. He may not do the favor, but in regard of your feelings he will not disappoint you by declining. Yet just as one now and then finds a Frenchman who likes to put others at their ease instead of making them feel inferior, some few Panamanians are vicious, venomous, vituperative—*merde* souled, in brief—and the PDP was a magnet for them. One thinks of Secundino Torres Gudiño, ample-paunched sometime commentator on Radio Nacional—Torres Gudiño of the false smile, the coprophagous grin, for whom no slander was too farfetched or disgusting, so long as its victim lacked means of retaliation. About him (and his brethren in slime throughout the party), Torrijos may well have reasoned, as Lyndon Johnson did about J. Edgar Hoover, that it was "better to have him inside the tent pissing out than outside pissing in."

But the PDP was the meagerest part of the bargain. Along with it, Torrijos got a broad inventory of benefits, services, and opportunities provided by its parent and sister organizations, the Soviet Union and the Republic of Cuba.

The pact led, for example, to the reestablishment of diplomatic relations between Panama and Cuba, suspended after the advent of Fidel Castro, and this, in turn, brought many tasty tidbits. Radio Havana, which many Panamanians listened to and which had correctly labeled the Guardia hoodlums, now promoted its general staff to progressives and patriots and spoke wonders of the *proceso.* So Torrijos's monopoly on communication was strengthened, and the people of Panama were further isolated, more deeply alone, that much less able to offer resistance.

In long decades of tyranny, such as Panama suffered, the great temptation is to give in to the tyrant, to accept him in one's heart just as one is forced by fear to pretend acceptance in one's overt statements. This undid many, from Alvaro Menéndez to Manuel Solís Palma, for in the struggle against that temptation what one most needs are friends who will ratify one's perceptions—in this case, that Torrijos was a clownish swindler and his rule a cruel joke. Panamanians found none. The United States had supported the dictatorship almost from its inception, and now, with the pact, so did the Soviet Union. The allies of each followed tamely. The only things the East and West agreed on was that Panamanians should not have freedom, and that the tyranny they underwent should be called a blessing.

Cuba undertook not to install a *guerrilla* in Panama, or to countenance one, should it arise spontaneously. Cuba eased Panama's entry into an association of loose Soviet satellites that insulted language by calling itself "nonaligned"—a maneuver that brought Torrijos much political benefit, though not until the late 1970s. But let's talk about things that count, let's talk about money. Cuba used its connection with Panama to get round the U.S. trade embargo. Panama was the bypass through which U.S. goods and technology flowed to Cuba and farther east, and through which Cuban products reached U.S. markets and earned dollars—a big boost for Castro and company but not an eleemosynary activity on the part of the progressive patriots of the Guardia general staff. They gorged themselves on that trade. Even years later they clung and fed.

Cuba's mission to Panama numbered over a hundred, including

representatives of the Dirección General de Intelligencia. They had a safe house on a large plot of ground in the pleasant residential quarter of Coco del Mar, which sometimes at night emitted hideous screams. Perhaps they were teaching Noriega new techniques. Or he was teaching them. Or they were jollying through a torturer's jam session. In any case, with the pact, the dictatorship acquired the services of the Soviet bloc's worldwide spy and goon network.

There were, besides, the Marxist-Leninist faith, with its sacred books and prophets and saints and martyrs, and the Marxist-Leninist church, with its prayers and its dogma, its pope in Moscow and bishops around the globe, its ecclesiastics and exorcists and lay preachers—an immense and highly efficient apparatus for producing and propagating mumbo jumbo. To consume it, there were the Marxist-Leninist faithful, and millions more not yet actually converts, but sympathetic, willing to hold still and listen. There were hosts of near-morons chanting rosaries of buzzwords and two gifted but (at best) confused artists who composed fictions about a figment they called Torrijos and presented these as works of fact.

These were Graham Greene and Gabriel García Márquez. Both, as was their right, were on the left. Both despised the United States of America. Both, in their confusion, believed Torrijos's fake revolution authentic and supposed him a painful thorn in Uncle Sam's paw. Greene, who knew but a very few words of Spanish, was brought to Panama at the people's expense and filled like a sausage with foolishness by José de Jesús Martínez—to the point where he saw Torrijos as a Graham Greene character. In short, Greene took the precaution of fooling himself before going on to fool others in an influential piece in the *New York Review of Books.* García Márquez, a better artist than Greene, composed a fine condemnation of despotism *(El Otoño del Patriarca),* then extolled it in the person of Omar Torrijos in a piece called "Cruce de Mula con Tigre." Delusion or mendacity? It's hard to say.

Whatever their motives, Greene and García Márquez were most useful to Torrijos in making him palatable to intellectuals in the English- and Spanish-speaking worlds. Torrijos had them, and a cloud of humbugs of inferior talents, all toiling at the looms of falsehood. The upshot was he became a celebrity, a world figure, a hero even. Who says you can't make a silk purse from a sow's ear?

But how much, you ask, did this pact with the red Satan cost him, how much did it cost in trouble for him from Washington? Nothing. Zero. Washington gave its blessing. Richard Nixon was in the Oval

Office. Henry Kissinger was down in the White House basement directing the National Security Council staff. This pair could rise above principle. They certainly didn't balk at ideology. What they wanted in Panama was stability. The best guarantors of that besides Omar and his mandrills were Fidel Castro and Leonid Brezhnev. The pact constituted their admission and acceptance that Panama was in the U.S. sphere of influence and not to be (in their clumsy word) "disbalanced."

Washington also wanted, though somewhat down the road, to restructure its treaty relations with Panama. There was, however, little leeway for boat rocking or wave making between what Panama wanted and what a U.S. Senate might ratify. The pact ensured communist support—or, better perhaps, an absence of communist carping—for whatever treaty emerged from negotiations.

But let's talk about something important, let's talk about money. What better gauge is there of satisfaction or pique? So little did Washington mind Torrijos's pact with the PDP and its godfathers that in the early 1970s the United States poured aid funds into Panama at the highest per capita rate in all the world. "In 1972, for example, the loans and grants figure . . . was $52 million, or nearly $35 for each of the country's 1.5 million inhabitants."

Yes, indeed, the PDP was a bargain. Next to nothing forked out for it, yet with it he got help from both God and Mammon. There he was at the start of 1971, smiled on by Lenin the Father and Castro the Son and Marx the Holy Ghost, while the capitalists shoved money at him.

5

THE MARTYRDOM OF HÉCTOR GALLEGO

The third horse of Torrijos's troika was largely a figment, but that didn't mean it wasn't sturdy and spirited, and at least as useful as the other two. This was the *campesinado,* the peasantry—not homesteaders such as fought on Quijada del Diablo, Ariosto González, Onofre Quintero and company (whom Stalin would have called kulaks), but slash-and-burn subsistence farmers at the outer margin of Panamanian life. They were physically real, of course, laughed and wept, loved and suffered, but they lived dispersed on the land in tiny hamlets sometimes a day on foot from road or town, had no class coherence, were illiterate, and seldom saw money, so that even if someone commanded their total loyalty, there was little of practical use he could put it to, in an election, say, or a strike or a boycott, or a coup d'état or a putsch or an insurrection.

Politically, that is to say, they didn't exist, which meant, in turn, that they could be invented: defined more or less as one pleased and claimed as a following. This Torrijos did, to his great benefit.

Who launched him on this course? The United States, that's who. Its crazed response to threat in Latin America was the doctrine of national security, whereby the region's military would stabilize their respective societies, by dictatorship and state terror if need be, and keep their countries pure of Soviet influence—this though communism's sole triumph, the revolution in Cuba, came in reaction to military dictatorship. The doctrine called for two sorts of effort to use as stick and carrot with campesinos: counterinsurgency and civic action, the latter being certain forms of rural assistance paid for by the United States and delivered by the local military, who were encouraged (as if that were needed!) to take the credit. Omar Torrijos was one of the first Panamanian officers to be initiated into these mysteries, in a year-long course at the School of the Americas, on Fort Gulick, in the Canal Zone. But listen to a voice of experience, to Jack Hood Vaughn, U.S. ambassador to Panama in the wake of the January 1964 sovereignty riots and later assistant secretary of state for inter-American affairs, director of the Peace Corps, and an actor in and observer of Latin America in a variety of nongovernmental capacities. Vaughn's acquaintance with Torrijos lasted seventeen years, comprised more than fifty serious meetings, and included a view of the tyrant-to-be at civic action four years before the Guardia took power, when Torrijos was commanding in Chiriquí Province.

"He [Torrijos] was specializing in his big political initiative then, which was to be seen as the savior, the benefactor, the caring leader. He would round up doctors and dentists and take them in a caravan, and they would go out overnight, two full days of pulling teeth and physical examinations and all sorts of feeding programs with the CARE people. He invited me to witness this, and I went up and spent a day with them."

Vaughn has a souvenir of the visit, a group photo snapped against a frondy background with Major Torrijos in the center, beaming charismatically, as he was wont later on to do from posters and postage stamps. Vaughn is on Torrijos's right, very slim, somewhat sunburned, and looking (with his clipped hair, open shirt, and khaki trousers) more the marine platoon leader he'd been twenty years before in the South Pacific than the plenipotentiary of a world power. On Torrijos's left are village headmen, behind him the doctors and dentists, and there in the back, stolid, expressionless, Sublieutenant Manuel Noriega.

"Torrijos made five, six, seven speeches that day. Of all the military men I met in Latin America—and I met a lot of them—he was the most impressive speaker. I don't mean haranguing a multitude. Talking to fifty campesinos, a village. He didn't condescend, and yet he reached them, but I don't think the fire in his eye was the fire of compassion, to the betterment of the Panamanian people, because he screwed them up pretty badly. I don't know any of the military who cared at all. In that *acción cívica* they were there for other purposes. They were not out there to cure the rural sick in Chiriquí, believe me. I never sensed any compassion.

"Civic action did more to put the military in power than anything else we ever did. It was a concerted effort to get the troops out of the barracks, building roads and public showers, and suddenly the colonel or major in charge—for the first time in their lives, they were applauded by civilians. What an aphrodisiac that is! And we did it all over Latin America. We gave a lot of civic action money to Torrijos and company, and we put them in business."

Why did it have to be them? one wonders sadly. Why not the hairdressers, why not the public accountants? Any group given all that money, equipment, and training could have "stabilized" Panamanian society, and couldn't have run the country worse than the Guardia did, while any group but the Guardia could have been sent packing if, like the Guardia, it proved malignant. If American policymakers had to be stupid, why couldn't they have picked a less damaging tool? Nor was their stupidity evident only in hindsight. As early as April 1969, the Rand Corporation, not what most would call a radical outfit, issued this warning: "United States preconceptions about the seriousness of the Communist threat and about the subsequent need for counter-insurgency and civic action for the Latin American military are producing undesired results. Paradoxically, U.S. policies appear simultaneously to encourage authoritarian regimes and to antagonize the military who lead them." But the United States put Torrijos and company in business, and he kept at civic action till the day he died. In fact, at the moment he died, he was on his way to a place called Coclesito to visit his favorite flock of pet campesinos.

He kept them for show, you understand, for display only, so as to have a claim to legitimacy. Every politician has to represent someone, has to have a group he's supposed to be taking care of, unless he wants to admit he's a despot or a fraud. Whom could Torrijos display? Himself and his family? His drinking pals, Jimmy Lakas and the rest? His cotyrants on the Guardia general staff? The others with connections who were stealing fortunes? The bureaucrats he created meaningless posts for? The *rabiblancos* who thrived while the money flowed? The guardias whom he let extort bribes and push people around? No, none of the regime's beneficiaries was respectable, so he flashed the campesinos as his constituents.

—Okay, Torrijos, who do you represent?

—Panama. The people of Panama.

—Come on, come on, who do you mean by "the people"?

—The campesinos, that's who, that's who I mean!

Which wasn't true, but who would prove him a liar? Someone, but wait, we'll get to him in a minute.

First of all, the campesinos came cheap. They were subsistence farmers, not city dwellers. TV hadn't made them aware of all that they lacked. They could be satisfied partly with grants of state land. Panama had plenty of unused state land. There was no need to bother with expropriation. In general, the unowned land wasn't too fertile, but that didn't matter; it didn't have to be. Its parceling could still be gaudily megaphoned, so many thousand hectares in such and such provinces. And the gringos were high on helping campesinos, so gringo money would pay a lot of the bill.

Campesinos, too, made excellent pets. As good as guinea pigs for experimenting on. Slash-and-burn agriculture depletes the soil, which in the tropics is low in fertility anyway. Dispersion, meanwhile, makes delivery of state services difficult. A school and a hospital can't be put outside each hovel. Torrijos's communists, however, had a formulaic solution to these problems, straight from the horse's mouth of all earthly wisdom, that they were more than eager to try out. This was to concentrate campesinos on collectives and have them farm in a mechanized way.

These settlements were called *asentamientos* and were much crowed about as the way to bring campesinos into national life. All told, Torrijos established more than two hundred at a cost of almost a million dollars each. The one at Coclesito was the most lavish. They didn't work, but that was no matter, not so long as the state controlled communications, and even later, when for a while there was free expression, the *asentamientos'* failure didn't embarrass. Their designers simply refused to acknowledge reality and called their critics "agents of imperialism," or "tools of the oligarchy," or "enemies of the people." In the end nothing was left, except for a spectral association, a grouping of ghosts, a confederation of vanished *asentamientos.* With, to be sure, a flesh-and-bone board of directors, drawing palpable salaries from the state, or Panama's communists might have their faith shaken. Your Gorbachev's a rare bird in the world of self-deception that Marxists inhabit. It's hard to admit one's life has been for nothing—work and privation and struggle, prison and exile, all for naught because one picked the wrong cause. How hard to die knowing one's lived vainly!

"I've plowed the sea!" gasped Simón Bolívar, between terrible fits of coughing, burning with a fever nothing could ease. And also, repeating words heard in his childhood, "I have preached in the desert!" And he died, of consumption and sorrow.

The *asentamientos* were no more than a welfare scheme for the fraction of Panama's peasants on them, costly, and hypocritical also, but they looked nice enough, especially from a distance. The mechanization that was supposed to make them viable economically made them debt-heavy instead. It devalued the campesinos' labor, made them dependent on government technicians, in short, turned them to pets. But excellent pets, friendly and, above all, photogenic. Torrijos couldn't be photographed with them too often.

Adopting the campesinos as his supposed following brought Torrijos two other significant benefits: a mystique or ideology that he found useful, and an imaginary Torrijos he liked pretending to be. In Panama, as it were by geography's mandate, and more so since the building of the Canal, power, wealth, and with them social distinction have concentrated in the transit zone's cities, particularly the capital of the republic. Population, too, has tended to flow there, for whatever the defects of Panama City, life outside it in what Panamanians call "the interior" is, by comparison, nasty, brutish, and short, at least as it involves agricultural labor. The last thing Panamanians want is to be campesinos. On the other hand, the further removed from the soil they become, the more attractive the life that it offers appears to them, simple (so they suppose) and innocent, stern perhaps but, therefore, innately noble. Which is merely to say that Panamanians are as vulnerable as anyone else to the sly charm of Rousseauian romantic twaddle.

Torrijos's publicists played to this vulnerability. The interior, so went the line, was the true Panama, the campesino the true Panamanian. Praise was sung of campesino virtues—honesty, that is to say, and hard work—and pearls strewn of campesino wisdom, so that, by association, Torrijos and company might forget that they were corrupt and lazy, might forgive themselves for having scant education, even turn the stigma to a mark of distinction. Torrijos himself aped campesino pith and simplicity in a number of catchy, quotable phrases that did much to propagate his fake populist message.

On the sincerity of his patriotic commitment: "What I want for my children is what I want for my country."

On the need for Panama to steer its own course apart from that of either superpower: "A Panamanian aspirin for a Panamanian headache."

On the identification of his personal ambitions with the aspirations of his countrymen: "I don't want to enter history, I just want to enter the Canal Zone."

Fake populism and fake rural orientation. The Torrijos regime was nothing if not elitist. Meanwhile, its center of gravity was in the capital, for its only mass of constituents was the bureaucracy. The mystique of the campesino gave Torrijos's fake revolution a fake beneficiary, and in passing masked very real gerrymandering when Torrijos formalized his very real tyranny. For instance, the Bella Vista district of Panama City, with over fifteen thousand electors, gets the same representation—that is, one vote—as rural districts with under one hundred. Torrijos may not have done much for the campesinos, but they certainly did a lot for him. The campesinos' richest gift to Torrijos may have been the chance to play a role he enjoyed, to be a person he liked, a figure he respected: in Vaughn's words, the savior, the benefactor, the caring leader. "One man in his time plays many parts," says Shakespeare, then goes on to mention seven in a series, each proper to a certain time of life. There were at least that many Omar Torrijoses, and all were current during his time as a tyrant, 1969–81. They didn't succeed one another; they alternated, came onstage and went off according to circumstance, depending on who was around.

Something like that may, of course, be said of everyone. People seem different to different companions. But with Torrijos one notes dramatic variations. As, for instance, between the Torrijos Hamilton Jordan got mellow drunk with and the Torrijos who captivated Graham Greene. The first was a "good ol' boy," Panama model, easygoing, not entirely unprincipled, but no one's zealot, a corner cutter, a pragmatic guy, and always ready to help out a good buddy, Uncle Sam, say, take a decomposing Shah off his hands, for example. The second was a committed revolutionary, suitable for inclusion in any of Greene's novels. This latter Torrijos, like Greene himself, viewed the United States with contempt and loathing as the source of most contemporary suffering. Jordan could never have boozed with this fellow. This isn't to say that Torrijos fooled Greene or fooled Jordan. The surpassing likelihood is that he fooled both, or furnished each the means to fool himself.

Some people get bored being merely one person, or don't like the person they are and pretend to be others, or are actually several persons sharing one body, or are no one in particular, fluid that is, whose personalities take the shape of the vessel, the hopes or desires or fantasies of whom they're with. One sort of successful whore, for instance, becomes the person (or thing) the client desires that evening, whoever the client, whatever evening it is—or, at the least, a convincing facsimile. So most everyone could have his own Torrijos, including the greed-driven cutthroats of the Guardia general staff, who were satisfied he was as cynical as they were, and whom he kept working smoothly together by practicing an honesty he showed few others: each got his due chunk of the loot. One supposes he found this role to his liking.

He certainly loved playing the caring leader. In the early 1970s, he spent most of his weekends helicoptering to campesino villages. Later on, his favorite place was Coclesito, and he had an airstrip constructed there. He would drop from the sky like a proper divinity to hear and answer prayers and speak his word. He was a great listener, with the politician's gift of appearing interested, of actually being interested most of the time. People interested Omar Torrijos, as they tend to interest good politicians, as insects interest good entomologists. The small boons campesinos asked were easily granted—after all, the fellow was a tyrant—but nonetheless seemed to give him a feeling of power. His speeches, as Jack Vaughn noted, were impressive, but more so, one feels, to guests he felt like impressing than to their putative audience.

This pose, at times, took on a Nazarene tincture, as though he saw himself as Savior with a capital *S*—as when he denominated as his chosen people "the Indian, the peasant, the poor, the one who's anemic, the one who walks bent over," or when he spoke of rank and hierarchy, his jargon for the distinction letter and spirit, as here in a supposed speech to soldiers reported by José de Jesús Martínez:

"Rank is given by decree. Hierarchy is won by exemplary acts.

"The man who has rank says, 'Go.' The man who has hierarchy says, 'Follow me.'

"Reason confers rank. Need confers hierarchy.

"And in Panama, hunger has the maximum hierarchy."

Or as, supposedly, he said of himself, his rank was brigadier general, his hierarchy general of the poor.

No question, he loved the role, and he played it effectively, convincing those who wished to believe. That's all an actor can do, all an actor needs to do usually. A fake shouldn't be asked to compete with authenticity. Only a sadist and spoilsport would do that. It was only human of Omar Torrijos to feel unfairly used, threatened, and furious when he realized the caring leader, the very character he was playing at being, was present in flesh and blood, showing him up, and right there in his native Veraguas too. Weekend miming can't measure up to full-time truth. Poor Torrijos had no choice in the matter. There was nothing he could do but have the truth murdered.

* * *

On the night they were going to "disappear" him, Wednesday, June 9, 1971, Father Héctor Gallego went to bed early. He meant to rise at four and travel to Santiago for an 8:00 A.M. meeting with his bishop. He was staying on the outskirts of town with a campesino named Jacinto Peña.

He was in his thirty-fourth year and fifth in the priesthood, the son of campesinos from Antioquia, in Colombia. From boyhood, he'd wished to serve God by serving others, an odd child who worried about other children's hunger, who pressed his father to give what he could to those needier. The only time, his parents said, that he displeased them was when he volunteered to serve in Panama rather than take a placid post near home. He was a slender man who looked half his age, with thick horn-rim glasses and delicate long fingers: parish priest in Santa Fe, Veraguas.

Veraguas. Panama was a lucky country. Veraguas was its unlucky province. On its Atlantic coast, in February 1503, Columbus established what he intended to be a permanent settlement, the first such by Europeans on the mainland of the Western Hemisphere. It lasted two months, and most of the colonists perished. In 1537, the Spanish crown made Veraguas a dukedom—but only to furnish Columbus's grandson a title and get a cheap settlement of a lawsuit he'd filed. Gold was found in 1558, but by 1589 the vein had run out and the mines were abandoned. Thereafter Veraguas slipped into deserved obscurity. In 1736, Fray Pedro Morcillo, the bishop of Panama, found that its inhabitants "live mostly in the bush . . . and are very poor people . . . isolated and feeble at work." So, more or less, they were two centuries later, though their poverty came chiefly from that of the soil, and their feebleness from the rigor of the climate, endemic fevers, and chronic anemia. Veraguas had Panama's lowest per capita income, highest incidence of illiteracy, and sole examples of latifundia (one of Latin America's sources of social injustice)—large tracts of uncultivated land in private hands. It had, besides, a sort of aristocracy (though the phrase "petty tyrants" perhaps describes them more clearly), political chieftains and their relations somewhat the mirror image of the *rabiblancos,* in that their base was agriculture not commerce, their outlook xenophobic not cosmopolitan, their politics reactionary not progressive.

The first breath of change came in the mid-1930s with the establishment in Santiago, the provincial capital, of a normal school on European models. It soon became a center of culture, and also of political unrest. To it in 1948, with the end of the Costa Rican civil war, came a refugee from the losing side, Carlos Luis Sáenz, a first-rate teacher, a gifted poet, and a dedicated communist. From then to the time of our story, even after Sáenz returned to Costa Rica, Veraguas was a bastion of the Partido del Pueblo and the main focus of class struggle in Panama. Accordingly, the Catholic church committed its best resources to the province, priests dedicated to achieving economic and social justice within the framework of Christianity.

Veraguas: towns with a church and a clutch of adobe houses, and beyond them the cane-walled ranchos of the campesinos who work land ruined by erosion that scarcely bears and in no way repays their efforts to cultivate it. From Santiago, on the Pan-American Highway, a road climbs north into the cordillera, closed to all but four-wheel-drive vehicles most of the year. Santa Fe is where the road ends, just below the continental divide, in a forest that gets ten feet of rainfall yearly—rains yet more abundant than elsewhere in the province, foliage yet more lush, land yet more eroded and impoverished. In 1968, when Gallego came there, the town had six hundred people, four stores, and a school. Ten thousand campesinos lived around and beyond it in scattered hamlets reachable over jungle trails, as mired in serfdom as ever muzhiks were in Gogol's Russia. They couldn't get their produce to the large towns, hence had to sell for a pittance to Santa Fe storekeepers, to whom they were eternally in debt. They had no worth to themselves, therefore no dignity, but lived condemned in a cycle of want and dependence. Nor was there any hope of release for their children, who were needed for work on the land, thus could not go to school, even if they lived near enough to reach it—"a reality," in Gallego's words, "of subject people, who for a loan of ten dollars must pay back twenty, and if they don't, then they go to jail."

Gallego set about to change this reality. The townspeople, he discovered, did not want it changed, particularly Don Alvaro Vernaza, owner of the town's largest store and political satrap, first cousin, of the then-major Omar Torrijos. Gallego turned to the campesinos. They accepted him. He was, it seems, an immensely likable person, but acceptance was mainly a matter of how he behaved.

He worked alongside the campesinos, and just as hard as they did, with machete or bush hook. He took no fees for baptisms, weddings, or funerals, but lived on the dollar a day he got from the diocese. He ate rice and beans and dressed simply, slept in a tiny rancho of bamboo and palm alongside the larger shack of the same materials that (since there was no church) served for masses and meetings.

He began by visiting his parishioners. It took a month. There were sixty hamlets in the region, including seven around Río Luis that took more than a day to reach on foot through the forest. Later on, when the campesinos were aware of the unity required to put what he was teaching them into practice, he created centers accessible in under two hours from a number of hamlets. At these, he met with hamlet representatives monthly.

But figure the cost of those meetings in will and effort! The ground is mountainous and thickly jungled. The trails are choked with mud most of the year. And overgrown with vines, and mazed with creepers. One has to cut one's way most of the time. Rain comes down as if from upturned barrels. Then heat lifts wraiths of steam from the spongy earth. Three hours to El Cedro, crossing two rivers. Six hours to Pescara, six to Gatu. What Gallego meant to do (and, amazingly, accomplished!) was to organize the campesinos in a cooperative, but first he organized them in Christian communities. The church had thought of cooperatives before him, just as Torrijos and the communists thought of them after, but Gallego made the thought live through his example, and because he worked from life, not from a theory. Before organizing came education, but before that he presented his credentials: limitless effort, limitless will; zero privilege, total commitment.

He set up Bible study groups where the campesinos, mainly illiterate but not stupid, analyzed texts and related them to their lives. From these emerged men he called responsables, men to depend on, leaders thrust up, as it were, by the hamlets themselves. At first there were thirty, later on fifty, of these. Gallego met with them monthly for a day and a half, to plan and review work programs once things were organized, but at first for a course that he described as follows:

"It was, above all, a course in motivation, a Christian sharing with certain motivational themes based on biblical texts and directed toward planting an idea of change, an idea of liberation, an idea of recognizing one's own values, and an idea too that to live a Christian life we have to organize, we have to experience and feel what community is in every place where communities are."

To feel what community is and, therefore, to organize; to organize and, therefore, to know one's values; to know one's own values and, thus, achieve liberation through change. What sort of change? Here is Gallego again:

"When a campesino becomes aware of economic domination, he

also becomes aware that to cause a change, for a new society to be born, he can't keep contributing to the system of domination."

A caring leader, in short, *and* a revolutionary: as utterly true and authentic in both capacities as General Omar Torrijos was false.

Two years of this authenticity, this will and effort, this patient teaching by word and example, paid off in a self-sustaining cooperative with a store that granted credit on decent terms and a secondhand four-wheel-drive station wagon. And paid off, on the townspeople's side, in resentment and malice. The campesino's helplessness and squalor was essential to their sense of worth and importance. Construction materials for a new church were made off with. Campesinos were insulted and harassed. Gallego was slandered. In November 1969, he wrote a parish bulletin that was prophetic:

> "If the world hates you, know that it hated me first."
>
> I read this verse in the Gospel of Saint John 15:18, and it did not catch my attention. I had read it and heard it so many times!
>
> I kept on reading, and in the next chapter I found another similar verse: "The hour is coming when whoever kills you will think he is offering a service to God" (John 16:2).
>
> This seemed to me a repetition of the same idea, and I opened the New Testament to the Acts of the Apostles, chapter 6, verse 8, and following, where it speaks of Stephen as a strong man whom his enemies cannot stand up to, because he speaks with wisdom the Holy Spirit gave him.
>
> "Then THEY PAID SOME to say they had heard him speak blasphemous words against Moses and God, and in the end they had him stoned to death."
>
> And I thought of:
>
> John the Baptist
> The martyrs of all eras
> The Kennedys
> Martin Luther King and so many other men who valiantly denounced sinful situations.
>
> These men have to be persecuted, calumniated, and killed because their attitude conflicts with an unjust world.
>
> Then I understood what Christ meant in the Gospel of Saint John, for all those who pay attention to His words. I understood that when a person or a community is hated for faith, it is a good SIGN. It is a sign that LIGHT is illuminating the darkness.

In June 1970, during celebrations regarding the town's patron saint, townspeople "dragged the statue of Saint Peter out of Gallego's church-hut and beat the priest because he and the peasants had wanted a celebration based on prayer and solidarity instead of the drunken brawls that had greeted religious processions in the past. It was the townspeople's saint, and they were not going to share him with any 'dirty peasants or that communist priest' Héctor Gallego."

This incident was followed by others. In May 1968, shortly after Gallego came to Santa Fe and just before the national elections, Torrijos's cousin Alvaro Vernaza had sought support for David Samudio against Arnulfo Arias by giving the town an old electrical generator from his sugar plantation, and some campesinos who resented the bribe had damaged the machine. The damage was less than ten dollars, but now, two years later, in July 1970, Vernaza accused Gallego of the "crime." Don Alvaro's store was making a lot less money now that the campesinos had one of their own, nor was he much of a political boss any longer, so he accused Gallego of vandalism and had him locked up in Santiago.

Gallego was in the cuartel only a few days, but hundreds of campesinos gathered to support him. Those of the hamlet of Vuelto Largo wrote the bishop of Veraguas, Monseñor Vásquez Pinto, asking him to intervene in the case. Gallego, they wrote, "showed us how to find ourselves. We didn't know what participation was, and now we know. There are strange people in town who say they don't want to see campesinos at mass on Sundays, and that those of us in Christian communities are communists. We beg you not to let Padre Héctor leave us."

Vásquez Pinto did intervene. The charge against Gallego was dropped. But when he accompanied Gallego back to Santa Fe, Vernaza tried to run him over, then whipped him with a metal cable. Student volunteers who worked with Gallego during their vacation, January to March 1971, were arrested as guerrillas and held for a time and mistreated. Then, in May 1971, campesinos in the hamlet of Cerro successfully stood up for a woman, Juana González, when a townsman named Ruiz who had government connections tried to have her house torn down. A confrontation occurred. Gallego was threatened. On the night of the twenty-second, his rancho was burned down around him, and he was lucky to get out alive.

"If the world hates you . . ."

By this time, Héctor Gallego was probably doomed. He was simply too effective at the business of helping campesinos find dignity. Here is how he defined the situation a day or two after the first attempt on his life:

The most interesting thing about this struggle to defend Señora Juana's house isn't the response of her community but of all the communities around Santa Fe. As such it represents the struggle and the attitude of a movement that won't permit itself to be exploited any longer. The campesinos are seeing things more clearly every day and are taking firmer stances. They are in the right, and they are resolved. This incident has helped to strengthen the movement much more in its conscience, in its daily ability . . . to stand up to anything, to the bosses, to the authorities, to whatever.

Gallego's accomplishment and attitude doomed him. Now he drew up his death warrant in a letter to General Torrijos himself. The general had plans of his own, based on his advisers' infallible formulas, for the development of Veraguas and its campesinos. Here's what Father Héctor Gallego thought of them, after some toning down by Monseñor Martín Legarra, who'd replaced Vásquez Pinto as bishop of Veraguas:

> I cannot do less, general, than express my fear that this attitude of ignoring them can only adversely influence the campesinos, animated as they now are with the desire to participate in the development program, [or to mention] the concern of community leaders over . . . the elaboration of programs for Santa Fe that don't take into account the campesinos' studies and analysis.

When Gallego sent that letter, he was a dead man. On the other hand, he'd nearly been one eight days earlier when his rancho was arsoned. "If it be not now, yet will it come." Gallego was ready.

If he was nervous, he gave no outward sign. He kept to his punishing schedule of center visits. On Monday and Tuesday, June 7 and 8, he was in Panama City for a course on the views of the Brazilian "liberation" theologian Hélder Câmara. On Wednesday, he worked on the land with campesinos. Less than three weeks had passed since he'd lost most of his possessions in an attempt on his life, yet he went about his occupation normally.

"The joyfulness of infinite play . . . lies in learning to start something we cannot finish."

On the night they were going to make him disappear, Wednesday, June 9, 1971, Padre Héctor went to bed early. He was staying with Jacinto Peña in a two-room adobe house with a thatch roof. Another campesino, a man named Leonor, was staying there also. Later on, the regime made much of that peasant's name to slur Padre Héctor, but campesino men can have names like that—Leonor, Isabel, Carmen—without being women in disguise or homosexuals. Half an hour or so before midnight, a vehicle stopped outside. A man began calling softly, "Jacinto, Jacinto." Peña woke, but Padre Héctor answered.

"Who is it?"

"Where can we find Héctor Gallego?"

"I'm Héctor Gallego."

"I have to talk with you."

Peña heard the door open. Then he heard voices. He got up and stood inside the curtain that separated his room from the front room where Padre Héctor and Leonor slept. Padre Héctor stood at the door in his undershorts facing two men in dark shirts. The men said they had a capture order for him. Padre Héctor asked what it was about.

"It's from a superior."

"If you have an order, tell your superior that I'm very sorry, but I can't go, because I'm very tired. Tomorrow morning at eight, I'll be at the diocese, and from there I'll go by the cuartel and turn myself in."

The men insisted: Padre Héctor had to go with them. Padre Héctor repeated that he couldn't. Their talk went on like that for several minutes, all three speaking in whispers. The order was from a superior; they had to take Héctor. He wasn't going to move, but he'd see them tomorrow. He was going to Santiago in the cooperative's station wagon. As if to prove this, he turned round to Leonor.

"You can go with me early, isn't that so?"

Leonor, still in bed, said yes, he would go with Héctor, but the men insisted that Héctor go with them. One of them switched on a flashlight and handed Padre Héctor a paper and shone the light on it, repeating that they had an order for his arrest. Padre Héctor examined the paper. He seemed convinced by it but repeated he couldn't go. Well, said one of the men, there would be consequences. Padre Héctor said he wasn't moving that night.

"I accept that I have to go, but I'll go in the morning, because it's inhuman that I leave for Santiago at this time of night. I'll go in the morning. I worked on the land all day, and now I'm resting. I want to rest, and I'll be up early to be at the diocese at eight o'clock. You can come and get me at the diocese, or I'll turn myself in at the cuartel."

At that, one of the men asked Padre Héctor if it was his house.

Padre Héctor told him no, the house wasn't his. He slept there because he had no house to sleep in. The man said something in a very low voice, and Padre Héctor answered that he didn't want anyone else involved in the matter. Well, the man said, if the house wasn't Padre Héctor's, they were doing wrong to talk there. They were keeping other people from sleeping. Why didn't Padre Héctor let them ask him a few questions outside? Padre Héctor said, "All right, let me get dressed." Peña didn't hear if anyone answered, but Padre Héctor came away from the door and began to put his trousers and shirt on. At that, Peña stepped through the curtain to Padre Héctor and asked him, very softly, what was the matter. Padre Héctor made a sign for him to keep still and go back to his room. Peña obeyed.

Padre Héctor got dressed and left the house. He moved very slowly. Peña went to the door and looked out through a crack. The two men were on either side of Padre Héctor. The three walked slowly up toward the road. The cooperative's Commander station wagon was parked off the road at an oblique angle to it. Another vehicle was parked on the far side. The three disappeared between the Commander and it, and a second or two later Peña heard two cries—or two squeals, as if someone were trying to cry out with his mouth muffled. Peña ran out at once, but when he reached the Commander, the vehicle parked beyond it, a jeep, started up, and its headlights came on, and it drove off. Peña cried out, "Eey!" but could do nothing.

Peña watched the jeep speed off toward town. His eyes followed it as it turned toward the road to Santiago, the only road there was out of Santa Fe.

That was the last anyone admits to having seen Héctor Gallego. When he was taken from Peña's house, he was lost utterly, as if the earth had swallowed him up, though it seems he still had a few days to suffer. Peña collected some friends and went after the jeep, hoping to catch up with it on the way to Santiago, but the Commander broke down and they lost half an hour fixing it. The next morning, Bishop Legarra went to the cuartel in Santiago, asking after Gallego. He was told that the Guardia Nacional knew nothing of him, or of any order for his arrest. News media owned by the state took the line, echoed later by General Torrijos, that Gallego's kidnapping was part of a plot by "reactionary forces," specifically the "oligarchy" and the CIA, to discredit the government and weaken the people's resolve in future Canal treaty negotiations. Materno Vásquez, then minister of government and justice, ascribed Gallego's disappearance to "enemies of the government and people" and described Gallego himself as a "collaborator and friend" of General Torrijos whose whereabouts the government were earnestly seeking, but when Legarra hired a Mexican investigator to look into things, the government denied him a visa to enter Panama.

Meanwhile, a tremendous furor arose, the most intense revulsion toward the dictatorship in all its years of existence, before or later. Few Panamanians had heard of Father Gallego, but Archbishop McGrath, who had ordained him and recruited him for service in Panama, pronounced a homily on him the Sunday after his disappearance, and other priests throughout the country gave sermons about him, and laymen spoke and wrote of his work and his friendliness, of his dedication and his self-denial. Bishop Legarra spoke of him from the pulpit, and while he could in the media as well. His outrage was sustained and eloquent. He tore to shreds the government's feeble excuses and feebler attempts to shunt the blame onto others. In Omar Torrijos's Panama, people didn't go round pretending to be *guardias,* or flashing fake arrest warrants. If the government had nothing to hide, why didn't it let the church investigate?

Then, all at once, the church ceased denouncing Gallego's abduction, stopped calling for clarification of it. On July 18, thousands gathered at the Church of El Carmen on Vía España in the capital, the largest multitude since 1968. Their cry was for justice, but as he was to do fourteen years later with regard to protests of Hugo Spadafora's murder (and particularly in the case of Winston Spadafora's hunger strike), McGrath turned the public's fury aside with vague, abstract murmurings, and stopped his subordinates from speaking out—in other words, helped the dictatorship weather the crisis.

What his motives were is hard to say. Perhaps he feared an open conflict between church and state. Perhaps he feared for his personal safety. The excuse he used to bar further protest from the pulpit was that the regime's opponents were exploiting the Gallego case politically—hardly a convincing reason for abandoning one's own. His subsequent eagerness to associate himself with Torrijos in the matter of the Canal treaties and his eulogies of Torrijos when the tyrant was killed suggest that he, like so many others before him, fell to the seductions of power, thought of all the lovely things power could do if one surrendered to it instead of resisting. In any case, the church stopped its campaign.

Stopping Bishop Legarra was another story. To begin with,

Legarra was a Basque, and as such tenacious. Worst of all, he'd been in the Philippines in 1941 and had survived the Japanese occupation: he knew all about tyranny and didn't like it, and didn't scare very easily either. He kept right on speaking of Padre Héctor in sermons, even after he was relieved of his diocese.

As far as the Roman Catholic church is concerned, Father Héctor Gallego, who died for its tenets, is still officially missing, as though he had been taken by extraterrestrials, instead of by men with a warrant for his arrest. In Santa Fe, the campesinos hung his picture on the cross at their flimsy church, along with a sign reading, "GIVE HIM BACK TO US ALIVE." That hasn't done any good either.

A little over a year later, a Spanish Capuchin, Father Pedro Hernández, who'd served temporarily in Panama while assigned to the diocese in Barranquilla, Colombia, told reporters in that city a story he said he'd heard from one of the two men, both of them *guardias,* who'd taken Héctor Gallego from Jacinto Peña's. To subdue him, the story went, when he resisted, his captors knocked him unconscious with their revolvers. He didn't come to, and they took him to a military hospital, where he was diagnosed as having a fractured skull. When doctors operated to relieve this condition, he suffered an embolism that left him partially paralyzed. At that point, General Torrijos was informed, and supposedly declared, "He must be made to disappear; a missing priest is better than one who's crippled." Gallego was, therefore, put on a Guardia helicopter and thrown, alive but paralyzed, into the sea.

This tale can only be falsehood, though very likely it contains some pieces of truth. The part it assigns to Torrijos is past all believing. Suppose he had nothing to do with Gallego's abduction but learned of it only when the priest had been injured, and this accidentally, because of his captors' zeal—or suppose he himself had ordered Gallego arrested, so long as he hadn't ordered him to be harmed—then all he had to do was produce the man living (partially paralyzed, totally so, or whatever) and see to it that those who had harmed him were punished. Torrijos and his regime would have gained by it. Hardly anything could have done them more good. To suggest that Torrijos ordered a crippled priest murdered, and thereby stained himself with unneeded guilt, just to protect a pair of inept G-2 goons, is to suggest that he was half-witted, especially since by dumping the goons he'd have gained credit. Imbecility was not one one of Torrijos's defects. Nor, for that matter, were the goons inept. How delicately they played on Gallego's sensibility! Others might suffer because of him. Others were having their sleep disturbed. No, the story is surely untrue, and may have been leaked by Noriega to Father Hernández to absolve the G-2.

"When two men ride the same horse in the same race," goes a Czech proverb, "only one can win, the man in the front." Torrijos pretended to help the campesinos, made giving them dignity his favorite pose. Gallego actually did what Torrijos pretended. Héctor Gallego was the man in front. Almost certainly without the least intention, the priest was making a fool of the general. He wouldn't stop, and so he had to be murdered.

That he was tossed from a helicopter is probably true, as it is that Omar Torrijos gave the order. As for who was in charge of the tossing, that looks like Noriega. Torrijos habitually referred to him as "my gangster." The job was in line with his talents and/or pathologies. We can even hear him proposing the method: "Let's see if he's saintly enough to fly." That Noriega arranged and supervised the tossing was voiced throughout Panama and gave rise to the following incident, amusing and incriminating too:

As chief of intelligence, Noriega had an office at Guardia headquarters. One wall was decorated with a huge blowup photo of Noriega himself—his shoulders anyway, and part of one profile—going out an airplane door during parachute training at Fort Gulick, in the Canal Zone. One day in the mid-1970s, Dr. Roberto Arias, Arnulfo's nephew and, incidentally, husband of Dame Margot Fonteyn, the ballerina, visited Noriega in his headquarters office, saw the photo, and said (having, like his host, a sense of gallows humor, along with plenty of chutzpah in his own right), "I assume that's the last picture of Padre Gallego." At which everyone ducked, as in an oldtime western when someone calls Black Bart a liar, but Noriega just sat there laughing, hands held iguanishly at his chest: "Heh, heh, heh. Heh, heh, heh."

In 1986, while sectors of the U.S. government were coming to consider Noriega more of a liability than an asset, Seymour M. Hersh, of the *New York Times*, discovered derogatory information about him. Some of it appeared in the *Times* that spring. More was published in 1988 and ran, in part, as follows:

> Father Gallegos [*sic*] . . . was seen being forced into a helicopter identified by witnesses as belonging to Panamanian intelligence forces.
>
> There were repeated and widespread reports in subsequent years—never publicly confirmed, until now—that the popular priest had been thrown

alive from the helicopter, and clung to life for a few days more. The United States Army, which operated a large communications intercept site in Panama, quickly learned much of the story. General Noriega was overheard joking and bragging about the incident to a colleague, saying that he learned an important lesson: Always kill a man before throwing him out of a helicopter. One American official, who reviewed all the intelligence about Panama before the 1978 debate on the Canal treaties, said that General Noriega's presence on the helicopter was confirmed by a member of the Panamanian military who participated in the murder and later told American agents about it.

Gallego's injuries thus came after he was thrown from the air not before, were the result and not the cause of his tossing. Torrijos, the caring leader, ordered the murder. Noriega, his gangster, thereby gained a hold on him.

Meanwhile, scattered about the hemisphere and Europe, Panamanian exiles watched in anguish as Torrijos consolidated his power, and fit himself into the international picture as protégé simultaneously of Washington and of Moscow, and wrapped himself in ersatz respectability. In San José, Guillermo Sánchez felt the Costa Rican government's growing coldness toward him—in repeated orders to present himself at police headquarters and repeated threats that he would be expelled—and concluded that, if he were going to be persecuted, he might as well be in Panama. That was at the beginning of June 1971.

Then, as he was making final preparations to leave, he noted in the San José daily *La Nación* declarations of a Monseñor Vásquez Pinto denouncing the disappearance of a Padre Gallego, neither of whom Sánchez had ever heard of. That the matter had to be serious struck him, however. Till then, *La Nación* had been wholly pro-Torrijos. So it happened that he returned home in the midst of the crisis. Very likely this was a good thing for him: the dictatorship had more pressing things on its collective mind than harassing another minor opponent.

In San José, and elsewhere during his exile, Sánchez had heard contradictory reports about the people's attitude toward Torrijos. Even in his own family, opinions differed. The day after his return, he began a week of going about the capital on foot and in buses—to the public market, to cafés in the old part of town—reading the expressions on people's faces, noting the timbre of their voices, when they heard or mentioned the names of men in power. At week's end, his diagnosis was clear: the people detested Torrijos and all the Guardia, and all their servile civilian functionaries. Nothing had changed in his two and a half years of exile. The regime's monopoly on the means of communication hadn't damaged the people's critical faculty, or made them stop wanting to choose their own leaders and participate in national decisions. The dictatorship was incompatible with the nation. The people rejected it with every part of their being and were outraged that one man, with neither culture nor statecraft, should arrogate the right to decide for all. This rejection of Torrijos and his regime was not due to Padre Héctor's abduction. That was merely the drop that made the glass spill over, a seed that served to crystallize people's feelings, to make precise what had been vague and obscure.

A great relief came over Sánchez. Years before, in Argentina, he'd known what it was to oppose a dictator, Perón, who had the support of the country's masses. It was something else when the people were on your side. For the first time in years, he felt part of a collective. Something had tormented him during his exile, but he hadn't known exactly what it was. Now it came to him. What had tortured him was his political solitude, the soiled conscience of a person margined from community, whose sole concern is for himself. There and then, that July, with his countrymen oppressed by a stupid crime, Sánchez regained at a stroke his inner peace and his will to struggle.

TRADING ON PATRIOTISM

On October 11, 1971, Omar Torrijos and his companions in tyranny celebrated the third anniversary of the Guardia's coup with a huge rally in the style of those held in Cuba. The murder of Héctor Gallego had cost the regime its credit with the people. Its revulsion had hurt supporters' morale. The aim was to restore both, regain the political initiative—and in passing impress outsiders with the revolution's momentum and popularity. No expense was spared of money or effort, and the thing became a model for rites to come—the seventh-anniversary bacchanal, for instance, which consumed the next year's medicines budget for Santo Tomás Hospital, and the 1978 reception for Jimmy Carter.

The site was Fifth of May Plaza in Panama City—funnel shaped, more than two hundred yards long, and about eighty yards wide at the wide end. A platform three stories high was set up against the façade of the Hotel Internacional, making a sort of superbalcony with room for ten or twenty people, and from there, resplendent in a white uniform and peaked cap, Torrijos harangued the multitude.

And multitude it was; the square bulged with people. Across its breadth, and back to where it funneled into Avenida Central, people were packed against each other. They lifted their brown faces toward the platform, holding signs, stretching sloganed banners—over 100,000 people in a country whose whole population was 1.4 million.

Most were public employees. Bureaucrats, functionaries, paper pushers. Secretaries, file clerks, receptionists, typists. Drivers, messengers, porters, janitors, charwomen. All the employees of all the government offices: the ministries and the autonomous institutes; the directorates, the tribunals, the departments; the provincial administration and the municipalities of Panama City and its outlying suburbs. And all the teachers of all the public schools, all the garbagemen, meter readers, and telephone linemen, the postal workers and the men who mucked stalls at the racetrack and the dancers of the National Ballet—all those who took the Maximum Leader's balboa in the capital or Colón or nearby towns. They were the rally's base, the big battalions. Each bunch had its spot assigned in the plaza. Every supervisor had a list. Roll was taken before the speeches started, and whoever wasn't there could sleep late the next morning. His days of public employment were over.

In close were the student groups and the labor unions Torrijos had given in usufruct to the communists, with operating funds from the national treasury, with government stipends for their officers. They were the shock troops, the assault units, jammed under the platform and to either side. They were expected and ready to yell their heads off, to chant the orthodox liturgy in chorus, at the proper rhythms, on cue.

Finally, there were the campesinos. They got five dollars each and a trip to the capital, were trucked in from their hamlets in the interior and then trucked back again that night. For authenticity's sake, or its simulacrum. Few would have come willingly without the money, but they were Omar the Compassionate's chosen, the chief beneficiaries of the revolution and its chief supporters, according to orthodox dogma. They supplied a necessary rural flavor, as well as more bodies and throats. A number would be left behind later, would get drunk or lost or both and miss their rides. Midnight would find their bodies collapsed in doorways, inert as the corpses of fishes washed up on the shore after an oil spill.

(Sometimes eggs got broken making these omelets. Sometimes attendance had to be encouraged with more emphasis than a mere five dollars or the threat of losing one's livelihood might supply. In June 1978, when Jimmy Carter shared the platform with Torrijos, a mishap of sorts occurred in La Chorrera, a town twelve miles west of the capital, across the Canal. A man named Román Vega, a native of Capira, a bit farther west, refused to board the bus and began urging others to get off it. The *guardias* on duty had no choice but to arrest him and instruct him as to the errors he'd been making. In the course of the lesson, Señor Vega stopped breathing. That is to say, someone's hand slipped. That was always what happened, according to orthodox dogma, whenever someone stopped breathing in Guardia custody. The rally was a success, though, and that was what counted. Carter, it seems, never learned of the incident. It took some of the zip out of his comments about Panama's progress in human rights, but the crowd was nearly as large as that drawn by Arnulfo. You can get a lot of people to a rally if you're beating people to death if they don't go.)

The buildings fronting the plaza on its west side were festooned with red-white-and-blue bunting. Opposite, against the columned front of the old Panama Railroad Terminal, now housing government offices and a museum, was a five-story portrait of the Maximum Leader. He was displayed from thigh up, hatless, in battle dress, standing in a relaxed pose with his left foot on something—a rock, perhaps, or a tree stump, or the severed head of an imperialist-oligarchic dragon. His left arm rested against his raised left knee, his right hand on the butt of his pistol. He gazed in half-smiling approval down on the throng, framed on each side by huge red-white-and-blue drapings.

The flesh-and-bone Torrijos approved also. He was thrilled, he believed the whole business. Actually, there was little authentic enthusiasm. The claque near the platform yelled and chanted on cue, but otherwise there was no fervor. Except for two moments. One came near the beginning of Torrijos's speech when he held up a copy of a new labor code. It was destined to hurt production and swell unemployment, but no one knew that yet except the entrepreneurs and managers in the private sector who hadn't been consulted in its preparation. The people in the plaza thought it would help them and responded with a spontaneous ovation.

The other ovation came when Torrijos referred to the Canal Zone, when he asked Fidelishly, "What people on earth puts up with the humiliation of a foreign flag nailed through its heart?"

Those at the bottom of the plaza could see the flag he meant if they felt like it. Its stars and stripes were flying behind their right shoulders, a hundred or so yards off in Shaler Triangle, just inside the Zone. Panama's flag flew beside it, but that was no solace. Two flags flying there were one flag too many. And worse, whether they felt like it or not, they could see Ancon Hill, along with people in most parts of Panama City. The massive, jungled butte loomed over the city, site of headquarters, U.S. Southern Command. No flag stood on its summit, only communications antennas, but that was no solace either. Panama's flag should have been up there, on the high ground. And everyone who'd come from the interior had come through the Zone—Panama's land, controlled by foreigners—on his way to his country's capital.

At that moment, and during succeeding references in that speech and thereafter, Torrijos had his listeners' approval. When he denounced U.S. control in the Canal Zone and the treaty that provided for it, he had the people of Panama behind him. He was doing nothing new. Every Panamanian leader since Panama's founding had made similar denunciations. Few if any were as self-serving as Torrijos. None was more adept at milking the issue for personal benefit. In exploiting the sovereignty issue, Torrijos simultaneously strengthened his tyranny and acquired an international reputation as a liberating leader. The reputation was no truer than anything else about him, but his time saw the eclipse of the Canal Zone and new treaties with the United States.

To understand these events and their effect, though, one has to know how the Zone came into being, the how and what of the original treaty. It is a fascinating story, a tale so bizarre no novelist could have got away with inventing it, but it can't be told well in a few paragraphs and takes one back to the turn of this century, so we have put it at the back, in an appendix, where the reader may peruse it at leisure. Here, meanwhile, are the essential items.

The key figure behind the original treaty was neither a Panamanian nor an American but a Frenchman named Philippe Bunau-Varilla, who stood to make a great deal of money if the United States were to choose Panama as a canal site.

The United States was willing, the Panamanians eager, but Panama was a province of Colombia, and the Colombian senate rejected the Canal treaty. (It should be made clear that the isthmians were Panamanians even while Panama was part of Colombia. Panama had known periods of full independence, as well as periods of loose federation, and a number of separatist gestures after strict union was imposed in 1886. Life there, besides, had its own special character, a blend of informality and sophistication born of its being a tropical place and a crossroads. It formed residents there into a separate nationality.)

Bunau-Varilla undertook to help Panama achieve independence by providing money and persuading the United States to help, requiring in return that Panama appoint him ambassador in Washington.

With the separatist movement successful and U.S. naval vessels guaranteeing Panamanian independence, Bunau-Varilla sat down in Washington and wrote a Canal treaty with much more in the way of concessions than the United States needed or had asked for in the treaty Colombia had rejected.

New envoys were on their way by train from New York to take over negotiations when Bunau-Varilla and Secretary of State John Hay of the United States signed the treaty, leaving Panama's government the choice of accepting it or having U.S. protection withdrawn and Panama reconquered by Colombia.

Panama accepted; Bunau-Varilla took the money and ran to Paris and lived to a ripe old age in conspicuous splendor.

So much for the how. Now for the what. Here is what the original treaty provided—though it is useful first to sketch what the United States had deemed enough in the treaty rejected by Colombia.

The treaty with Colombia, which passed the U.S. Senate 73 to 5, contemplated a zone ten kilometers wide (five on each side of the canal line) use and control of which would be granted to the United States for one hundred years, with the grant renewable on U.S. option. Colombian residual sovereignty was explicitly affirmed in article 4 and implicitly protected in what the treaty refused to give the United States: the right to make laws or to enforce them. Use meant building and running a canal. Control meant the United States would regulate the canal and the railroad across the isthmus. A joint U.S.–Colombian commission of two persons named by each country's president would "establish and enforce police and sanitary regulations," while three sets of tribunals would operate: Colombian, for civil disputes between Colombians, or between Colombians and non–U.S. foreigners; U.S., for civil disputes between Americans, or between Americans and non-Colombian foreigners; joint U.S.–Colombian, for civil disputes between Americans and Colombians, or between nationals of other countries, and for all criminal and admiralty cases. Defense and policing would be provided by Colombia, unless and until it asked the United States to help, though in "exceptional circumstances" the United States might defend or police unilaterally. The United States would pay $10 million in gold on ratification and $250,000 in gold every year, the money being the same in both treaties.

The Hay–Bunau-Varilla Convention (to give its proper diplomatic name) also proposed a zone, but one expanded to ten miles (not kilometers) in width. Everything else it gave the United States was swollen also. Besides use and control of the zone, the United States was granted occupation "in perpetuity." Then, to be on the safe side, the treaty, with a splendid gesture, included "any other lands and waters *outside* the zone . . . which may be necessary and *convenient* for the construction, maintenance, operation, sanitation, and protection of the . . . Canal" (authors' emphasis).

So much for the zone and its use. What does "control" mean? As the reader will by this time already have grasped, whatever else may be said about Bunau-Varilla's procedure, he cannot properly be accused of pussyfooting. So also with control. Article 3 deals with that matter, and one may scan it forever and find no joint commissions or separate tribunals or any other bitty-bit and halfway measures. Besides being simple, the article is clear, and besides being simple and clear, it is brief also, so it may be quoted in its entirety:

> The Republic of Panama grants to the United States *all the rights, power and authority* within the zone mentioned in Article 2 of this agreement and within the limits of all auxiliary lands and waters mentioned and described in said Article 2 *which the United States would possess and exercise if it were sovereign of the territory* within which said lands and waters are located *to the entire exclusion of the exercise by the Republic of Panama of any such sovereign rights, power or authority.* (authors' emphasis)

All the power the United States would have if it were sovereign! There is nothing like it elsewhere in the law of nations. There is nothing like it in the law of persons either, except the medieval *jus primae noctis* or droit du seigneur, which granted the feudal baron the right, power, and authority to bed a vassal's bride, the right and so forth he'd have if he were her husband—but observe, the grant was good for the wedding night only, a single night (albeit one of some importance in the married lives of most couples), whereas the rights and so forth Hay–Bunau-Varilla granted were Uncle Sam's to enjoy till the twelfth of never. Article 4 throws in rivers, streams, lakes, and other bodies of water. Article 5 makes the whole thing a monopoly, not just on canals but on "any means of communication . . . between the Caribbean and the Pacific"—in perpetuity, *naturellement.* And article 7 gives the United States the authority to maintain public order, not just in the zone but "in the cities of Panama and Colon and the territories and harbors adjacent thereto in case the Republic of Panama should not be, *in the judgement of the United States,* able to maintain such order" (authors' emphasis).

In article 1, the United States undertook to guarantee and maintain Panama's independence. Given what followed, however, one might at first glance wonder why. Why didn't Bunau-Varilla just hand the whole country over in a straightforward treaty of annexation? Annexation confers responsibility, that's why. Had the United States annexed Panama, or any part of it, it would thereupon have been obliged to extend the rights and privileges of American citizenship to the territory's inhabitants—just as, if the feudal baron married the girl, or installed her in the manor as his concubine, he'd then be obliged to feed and clothe her, and do likewise for any brats she bore, and that would have ended up costing him money. The trick of droit du seigneur, of *jus primae noctis,* was that you had the fun but escaped the annoyance. So likewise with Hay–Bunau-Varilla.

* * *

"Do not begin your marriage with a rape," warns Balzac. A healthy relationship might have been hard to achieve between partners so unequal in size and strength, but the treaty destroyed all hope of one's forming. Each nation was schizoid toward the other. "I took the isthmus!" crowed Teddy Roosevelt. To Americans, Panama was at once a host and a chattel. To Panamanians, meanwhile, the very agency that brought redemption—independence, economic benefit, and end to disease—simultaneously brought degradation. Profound admiration of the United States coexisted with the bitterest resentment, often in the same person. The Canal became a great source of national pride, the Canal Zone a bottomless well of humiliation.

Ah, the Canal Zone! Who could see it and ever forget? The power it didn't need and hadn't asked for harmed the United States more than Panama. For one thing, it fostered blind arrogance, as too much power always does. De facto sovereign power in perpetuity wasn't required for the canal project, but when all semblance of justification for it faded, when Gorgas and company had wiped out yellow fever, when Goethals and company had built the Canal, exercise of U.S. sovereignty intensified, till what one had was a trumped-up alien world, vaguely Americanesque not really American and as artificial as a space station, plunked down in the middle of the green tropics. It had the Stars and Stripes flying above it, and an American governor (though no elections), and U.S. courts and post offices and police, but no free enterprise, no private business. It had the U.S. armed forces and the Panama Canal Company, a botched clone of the British East India Company owned by the U.S. Department of War. Everyone in the Zone worked for the U.S. government, lived in a government house, bought in a government store, watched movies in a government movie theater—all subsidized, so they cost next to nothing—and carried a government ID card. Without showing a card, no one could go anywhere—except to Gamboa Penitentiary. It was open to all, without regard to race or nationality, though nonwhite Panamanians got preference.

English was spoken and displayed on all signs. One could be born and live a long life and die without ever learning a word of Spanish—a number of Zonians actually achieved this!—for one need never leave the Zone. There were hospitals and cemeteries, schools and churches, and every sort of civic association, from the American Legion to the YMCA. There were, besides, for much of the Zone's existence, two wage scales and two payrolls (one paid gold, one paid silver) and everywhere twin sets of toilet facilities for U.S. citizens and non–U.S. citizens. The whole place was as beautifully groomed as a theme park, and after 4:30 P.M. there were no lower classes (domestics excepted). No American could be lower class in the Canal Zone, be he never so poor in money, culture, and intellect. Lesser breeds lived in the republic, or in their own special communities tucked away out of sight. There were no proper upper classes either, though the governor and his top bureaucrats were fawned on, as were generals and admirals.

It wasn't an evil place, but it was offensive. It offended Panamanians deeply. It also offended the Declaration of Independence and the Constitution of the United States. Excessive rights, power, and authority lured the United States from its moral grounding, away from its openly proclaimed values of liberty and justice for all toward the dark side of its heritage, racism and bullyhood.

Too much power clogs thought processes also, the way too much cholesterol clogs circulation. Panama? No need to think about that. Panama was signed, sealed, and delivered: full power, just as if the United States were sovereign. For how long? "Till a' the seas gang dry, my dear, / And the rocks melt wi' the sun." Just as decades later, when all power was vested in the Guardia Nacional and General Manuel Noriega was *comandante en jefe,* when he was on the CIA payroll and let Shultz and Casey pick Panama's president. No need to think about Panama then, either. Excess power gives the illusion of safety, making it more dangerous than no power at all.

Besides, all power addicts, and sovereign power addicts sovereignly. Every Panamanian leader from Amador on protested the perpetuity clause and article 3 of the treaty, but the United States clutched them ever more tightly. Neither was required practically, but early on, the addiction set, and both became, in a sense, truly needed—the way a child needs its teddy bear.

The addiction was physical as well as psychological. Hay–Bunau-Varilla gave the United States the right and capacity to defend the Canal, but the military and naval bases authorized under the treaty for that purpose were also useful in defending the southern flank of the United States. As time passed, the bases' primary purpose dwindled. Insofar as it remained valid, it was merged with defense of the United States. But overseas bases to defend the United States, its interests, and its allies are touchy things to arrange politically, and also terribly expensive. The sovereign power conferred by the treaty was wonderfully comfortable to fall back on.

Meanwhile, besides costing Panama much more of its sovereignty than Panamanians had freely agreed to, Hay–Bunau-Varilla cost them money. Zone commissary stores, subsidized by the U.S. government, undersold Panamanian retailers. Zone clubhouses charged less for beer and Zone theaters for movies than did counterpart establishments in the republic. Worse, all manner of economic activity, from pierside hotdog stands to industrial parks, that the Canal might have generated, and Panamanian entrepreneurs founded, and Panama and its people benefited from—all that never happened, because under the sovereign power enjoyed and exercised by the United States, the Canal Zone was the sole spot on earth where pure communism was practiced, where private enterprise was banned. There it lay like a tumor in Panama's midsection. The Zone was injury as well as insult.

Nonetheless, the Zone had its charm. The meeting-mating of North and South, of West and East, which Kipling praised and Conrad shuddered at, may have begun as rape, but it ended more like the coupling of the praying mantis, with the superimposed element getting devoured. There was charm in the moment of superimposition triumphant because the moment was brief, the triumph illusory—temperate superimposed on tropic, technology superimposed on biology, prissy hypocritical superego superimposed on lush self-glorying id. One can glimpse it in the Canal though the Zone has vanished (disestablished by the treaties of 1978), the mechanical superimposed on the natural. Take the stretch from Pedro Miguel to Miraflores, as seen from Bruja Road on the west bank—or, rather, as not seen, since the point is that from there the Canal is invisible, and what one sees (blinks at, cannot get used to) are elephantine oceangoing vessels, superstructures and three or four meters of hull, gliding along the top of a foresty ridge as in a dream or hallucination. Here and there as well on U.S. bases, one can still get a zonish whiff of empire in manicured spruceness superimposed on fecundity. The officers' club by the golf course at Davis, for instance, a chintzy club, a boring course, but sip gin and tonic at dusk on the veranda, gaze across the fairway at the jungle, and you might be in Ceylon or Sumatra, somewhere east of Suez at the turn of the century.

The true charm of the Zone, though, is gone with the wind. R. M. Koster recalls it most vividly in connection with the Tivoli Hotel in Ancon, a five- or six-story white wooden structure on a bluff above Panama City, the largest and most notable example of Early High Gringo Imperialist architecture, completed in time to house Teddy Roosevelt when he visited the Canal works in November 1906, and torn down (alas!) during the 1970s. It had a front porch with rocking chairs on it, from which one could look down on Panama in both senses of the phrase, and on which Mr. John Gunther was said to have composed the Panama section of his best-seller *Inside Latin America* without ever setting foot in the republic. It had a spacious, somnolent, high-ceilinged lobby with softly whirring overhead fans, and ancient black bellboys with Barbadan accents and wide eaves and excellent ventilation that made air-conditioning unnecessary and a great mistake when it was put in in the 1960s. And in the cocktail lounge, one wall was floor-to-ceiling mesh screening, so that every afternoon from March through December the rain fell just beyond your table—fat gouts that hit the tree leaves with audible ploppings, six or eight perhaps and then a deluge that would have made Noah gasp.

The Tivoli was the chief magnet for angry mobs during the flag riots of January 1964 and also the post of U.S. Army marksmen putting counter–sniper fire into Panama City. What happened was that the United States of America, through blind arrogance, occlusion of the thought processes, and addiction to power, caused an arrangement that was bizarre at the time of its conception, that insulted and injured one party while offending the principles of the other, to be prolonged well past the point where it made any sense, where people could live with it in any comfort—the diplomatic equivalent of leaving oily rags stuffed in a warm cupboard till they ignite spontaneously. The immediate cause was a confusing U.S. directive as to whose flag might be flown where in the Canal Zone, which led to a tussle between two groups of schoolchildren in which a Panamanian flag was torn, which led to an angry mob's formation and its attempt to enter the Zone, and police action to prevent this, and the shooting death of a Panamanian student. But if the directive had never been issued, something else would sooner or later have set off disorders. Four days of rioting ensued along the border between the Zone and Panama. Twenty-one Panamanians died, fifteen from small-arms fire by U.S. forces. Four Americans also lost their lives. Nearly five hundred on both sides were wounded or injured. The casualties, in other words, were modest by the standards of our barbarous century, but they were sufficient. Panama briefly broke relations with the United States, for which the business was acutely embarassing, and in December of the same year Presidents Marcos Robles and Lyndon Johnson jointly declared the intention of the two countries to replace Hay–Bunau-Varilla with a new treaty arrangement between them.

That was the good news. The bad news was that conditions for doing this painlessly, simply, and well had disappeared abruptly at about 7:30 P.M. on Thursday, January 9, 1964, in the vicinity of Shaler Triangle, when a .38-caliber bullet from the revolver of a member of the Canal Zone police entered the right shoulder of twenty-year-old Ascanio Arosemena, the first casualty, traversing his right lung and severing his aorta. Then, later, the moment was missed for doing it decently. In the end, of course, it got done because it was necessary, but in the manner of a sloppy divorce case, with maximum damage and minimum benefit to both sides.

The declaration of December 1964 was the first gesture of willingness by a U.S. government to change the basic agreement in Panama. It did not come freely but rather in grudging acknowledgment of unpleasant realities that had, so to speak, made their tormented way through clogged thought processes into official consciousness. The United States had legitimate interests in Panama that required some sort of relationship with that country, but Panama, reality said, was uncomfortable with the status quo, to the point where maintaining it had become somewhat a matter of force and was liable to be more so in the future. At the same time, reality continued, the status quo conflicted with expressed U.S. principles, so that while use of force was, in letter, legal, no moral authority was behind it. Finally, in the weird, looking-glass world that Mr. Johnson and his advisers saw all around them, the smaller and more feeble a country was, the less freedom the United States had to use force against it in the absence of overwhelming moral right. Change, therefore, was in the U.S. national interest.

But that, alas, was the only argument for it. Changing the arrangement in Panama promised no political payoff for the Americans who took part in the effort, no increase in their power or electability. Much the reverse, it would be costly. The current arrangement was the most one-sided ever established between two nations not at war with each other. Any change, however slight—let alone the sort of change that would satisfy Panama and put the United States on firm moral ground—would oblige the United States to give up something, and that would be unpopular with people and devilishly hard to explain. Every map that showed Panama showed the Canal Zone bisecting it, with the initials "U.S." printed alongside. The people would think the United States was giving up territory. And the Canal! It wasn't what it used to be, couldn't be defended against bombs and missiles, so the U.S. Navy had to some extent written it off. None of the big carriers could pass its locks, nor could the supertankers and ore carriers. But every kid had heard about it in grade school. What it was was a national shrine, a holy place in the American religion of material progress through technology and grit. Fooling with who owned the Canal would be a big headache. No question of it, a new treaty with Panama would cost those who made it. Teddy Roosevelt had a big banquet in Panama, and now someone else would have to pick up the tab.

As it happened, however, the time was propitious. December 1964 saw the United States at the apogee of its power, prestige, and prosperity, on the threshold, so it seemed—though the semblance turned out to be only a mocking mirage—of eliminating poverty within its borders, and obstacles to its will beyond. Its government was rich in political capital. Mr. Johnson had just been reelected by a landslide. So the declaration was issued, and negotiators were named, and the basis of a new arrangement was worked out and embodied in three draft treaties. These were ready in the late spring of 1967. Under their provisions, the Canal Zone would cease to exist as a juridical entity, control of the Canal would pass to Panama at the end of the century, and the United States would keep its bases till then and be able to renegotiate their retention thereafter. There were, besides, economic provisions, an immediate share in Canal tolls for Panama, and so forth—quite a bit of money and substantial indirect benefits as well.

Each side, in short, got what it most required: Panama its sovereignty in the Canal strip, the United States its bases on the isthmus. As for the transfer of the Canal, and for the end of the U.S. presence except as a prolongation might be negotiated with a fully sovereign Panama, a nice round date was picked, December 31, 1999. This roundness was an important provision, a way to avoid the appearance of precipitous retreat by the United States.

As might have been clear at the time, and is certainly clear today, twenty-two years later, the arrangement devised in 1967 was about what was possible, what was in the cards, given the nature and identity of the two parties, along with their aims and needs and bargaining leverage. The treaties signed in 1977, though different in structure and denser in detail, present the same solution. Nonetheless, the 1967 treaties remained drafts. President Marcos Robles was unwilling to sign them.

His reason, and it was certainly valid, was that with an election campaign in progress the drafts could not receive the measured consideration they deserved. More to the point, perhaps, the drafts were so far from providing satisfaction that Robles's collaborators urged him to let them lapse lest they draw the people's wrath down on the Partido Liberal.

People's wrath? Far from providing satisfaction? The reader may justly wonder at such statements, for the 1967 draft treaties not only represented a vast improvement over Hay–Bunau-Varilla but were just about what Panama ended up with anyway. The treaties' terms in themselves were but part of the problem. There was, besides and crucially, the gap between what the treaties provided and what Panamanians aspired to.

To Panamanians, the December 1964 declaration was an admission of error by the United States—not a confession of guilt, an avowal of protracted wrongdoing! For signing a treaty with Panama drawn up by a Frenchman, for extorting its ratification, for imposing its degrading terms all those long years. Wrongdoing and guilt for the Canal Zone, for its dual wage scales and payrolls, for its signs in English, for its mountie-hatted cops. For a flag torn, for blood spilled, for indignities heaped up over six decades, so that Panamanians came to regard any new arrangement not merely as a means to future equity but as reparations for damages present and past. Anything, thus, that the United States might offer freely, no matter how wished for till then or intrinsically valuable, automatically became insufficient, next to worthless in fact, in the appreciation of some Panamanians, for reparation implies punishment, and punishment pain, and pain reluctance. Divorce lawyers, judges, and jurors will understand. What could the United States possibly give up that would compensate for such prolonged insult and abuse, for the resentment felt by ordinary people of the country, and felt suddenly, too, for till then they'd not allowed themselves to feel it? Had the United States offered Texas and California, New York and Iowa, the whole country, some Panamanians would have remained unsatisfied. Only the spectacle of a United States abjectly begging on bended knee for mercy would have satisfied some.

Then there was the problem of U.S. bases. No aspect of the de facto sovereignty conferred on the United States by Hay–Bunau-Varilla was so onerous as the right implicit in it for the United States to quarter soldiers in Panama. Both the 1967 drafts and the treaties ratified eleven years later address this question by ending the U.S. military presence at the century's close. However, both also contained and contain clauses granting the United States the right to reintroduce troops in the case of a threat to the Canal, with the United States free to decide what a threat is. Here was a substantive reason for dissatisfaction with the 1967 drafts and perhaps the main reason why Robles declined to sign them. Long years before, when Panama was first faced with the problem, President Manuel Amador Guerrero gave guidelines on it in a letter to Eusebio Morales, author of Panama's Independence Proclamation and, at the time of the letter, first secretary of Panama's embassy in Washington: "They [the United States] can do what they please because they have the force, but we must not authorize it by signing anything." Robles did not care to be the first Panamanian to authorize the presence of U.S. troops on the isthmus. He left that honor to Omar Torrijos.

In sum, for reasons of both substance and sentiment, no treaty that the United States would agree to could be signed and presented for ratification by a Panamanian government unless that government was one of two sorts. Either it must enjoy the confidence and support of the people as expressed in an overwhelming electoral mandate, or it must be willing and able to curb free expression and crush dissent.

Hay–Bunau-Varilla, therefore, continued in force, though both parties to it wanted it replaced, and each day that passed made doing so that much harder. Panamanian aspirations could only rise as each day prolonged a degrading arrangement, while making concessions to Panama grew more and more difficult as U.S. power, prestige, and prosperity declined. Meantime, politicians in both countries were under increasing pressure and temptation. In Panama, the pressure was to ask for more and more, and to demand immediate satisfaction. The temptation was to play on the people's passion for political gain. Politicians in the United States were pressed to be stingy, to cling to the letter of Hay–Bunau-Varilla though their country's national interest lay elsewhere. U.S. governments were tempted to procrastinate, to push the problem around on the plate, as it were, to get safely out of office without chewing on it, to let those who came next suffer the indigestion. Such, then, was the state of treaty relations between the United States and the Republic of Panama when the latter suffered military takeover and fell off the edge of things into tyranny.

* * *

In the summer of 1969, almost a year after the Guardia took power, Torrijos began dropping hints about resuming treaty negotiations. And was roundly snubbed by the Nixon administration. The United States would help him kill democratic opponents and otherwise oppress the people of Panama but could not (so went the leak to the *New York Times*) "engage in long-term commitments with . . . the 'military-type, provisional' government" he headed. These scruples faded with time, however, or with the regime's consolidation of power. On October 25, 1970, Mr. Nixon was at Camp David and suffered a number of Third World personages to be passed in and out of his presence like beasts through a dip. Puppet President Lakas got half an hour (between Yahya Khan of Pakistan and Ethiopia's Emperor Haile Selassie), long enough to learn that the United States would renew talks. Meanwhile, however, Panama had formally rejected the 1967 draft treaties as a basis for them.

The step enraged at least one Panamanian. This was Diógenes de la Rosa, perhaps the best-prepared person in Panama on treaty matters, who'd served on the team that negotiated the drafts and was destined to serve again under Torrijos. He was in San José when the foreign ministry's note was made public and vented his fury to Guillermo Sánchez, then still in exile. "The morons have no conception what it cost to drag those concessions from the gringos. Now they have to start over from zero and renegotiate everything we won!"

But anger was clouding de la Rosa's judgment. Rejecting the drafts had nothing to do with stupidity. Years later, on a flight between Panama City and the interior, Graham Greene asked Torrijos the basis of his political ethic, and Torrijos indulged himself by answering honestly. "The same as his," he said, pointing to the pilot.

"Not to fall." As with everything else during his time as a tyrant, his first (if not only) thought regarding the treaties was of staying in power. From that perspective, rejecting the drafts was smart. The United States had only so many concessions to make. Starting negotiations over from zero enabled Torrijos to take credit for winning them all.

The drafts, therefore, were no good. So said the ministry's note. So said all declarations on the subject. The fault, besides (so the note and all statements suggested), was not that the United States had ceded little but that the "oligarchy" and its lackeys hadn't cared or dared to demand more. The same lie, in short, put forth on every issue by Torrijos and his companions in tyranny. All Panama's history, to hear them tell it, was a pointless stumble by night through a putrid swamp gulled on by craven traitors, till at last Omar the Redeemer brought the dawn and led his people to the airy uplands. Viz, Omar, and only he, cared about campesinos. That was the lie Héctor Gallego died for. Now only Omar cared about sovereignty either. As if Amador and Arango hadn't lived! As if Ascanio Arosemena hadn't died! As if de la Rosa and Sánchez and two million others hadn't known that they were Panamanians until the advent of Omar Torrijos, who in his infinite loving kindness informed them!

But lying doesn't alter fundamentals. The same countries were addressing the same problems. The treaties Omar the Redeemer heroically won look a lot like the drafts he scornfully rejected. Both dismantle the Zone and the Canal Company. Both set up a binational commission to run the Canal until the end of this century. Both give the Canal to Panama at midnight, December 31, 1999. Both make Panama meanwhile a partner in toll revenue. Both provide for U.S. military bases. Both affirm a U.S. right to defend the Canal. The approach is a bit different in the two efforts. The Guardia gains in the second, at the expense of productive sectors. But where it comes to redressing Panama's grievances, in the matter of benefit to their country supposedly supreme to all Panamanians, the six-year process that culminated in the Torrijos-Carter (or Carter-Torrijos) treaties of 1977 resembles nothing so much as a long, sweaty, circular trek (and a noisy one also) around the mulberry bush to the point of departure.

With one notable difference. Article 7 of Hay–Bunau-Varilla gave the United States the right to maintain public order in Colón and Panama City as well as the Zone. In 1936, though, the U.S. Senate abrogated it as both unnecessary and demeaning, and nothing remotely like it was in the 1967 drafts. To win ratification of the Torrijos-Carter treaties, however, the Senate attached a reservation (named for Dennis DeConcini, Democrat of Arizona) which gave the United States the right to intervene anywhere in Panama. If anything, therefore, the treaties brought down from the mountain by Omar the Redeemer were less favorable to Panama than the 1967 drafts he spurned.

On the other hand, it's grossly unfair to Torrijos to measure his treaty dealings by what they brought Panama, unfair to him and to his associates. Panama wasn't their *patria.* Insofar as they had one at all, it was the Guardia, and mainly they were too immature morally to seek more than the short-term good of themselves and their families. What one wants to know in gauging their competence is how much a policy benefited them—firmed their grip on the country, increased their freedom to push other people around, multiplied their chances to loot and pillage, camouflaged their malignity in the eyes of the dupable, or otherwise improved their careers as predators. Viewed from this angle, Torrijos managed things masterfully, and nothing more masterfully than the sovereignty issue. The moment he touched it, he put it to work, and year after year it slaved dutifully for him.

Here he is, for instance, in Fifth of May Plaza, October 11, 1971, at the rally we described at the beginning of this chapter. First, some clamorous swagger in the third person about what will happen if the treaty talks fail: Torrijos, he blares, will go at the head of the people. Where isn't mentioned. Those who care to may suppose he means into the Zone. Then, abruptly, he seems to leave the issue.

"The only criticism legalists have . . . is that we're illegitimate children of the *patria.* Illegitimate, very well. But I remember the parable that often it's the illegitimate son who saves the family honor, the same honor legitimate children stained."

Only criticism? Not exactly. There were, besides, murder and other little flaws. Illegitimacy, though, is the defect Torrijos admits to, and see, at once, the sovereignty issue mends it. This Galahad among governments, illegitimate but pure of heart, will cleanse the stains made by its legitimate but recreant predecessors. And for years he had the sovereignty issue to trade on.

Part of the delay came from starting over at zero, and when the two sides were finally back where they'd been in 1967, great wrangling took place over minor details: what, exactly, would be transferred exactly when during the interim between ratification and the year 2000. That battle was fought, literally, house by house through residential sectors of the Zone like Curundu. There was, besides, hard bargaining over money, amounts and method of payment also. Torrijos and company wanted as much money as possible displayed in the treaty, while the United States preferred it to go under the table as aid. Each government, that is, tried hard to fool its constituents.

Delay was also occasioned by events. Panama, being a dictatorship, had no treaty ratification problems. The case was very different in the United States. It was senseless for the United States to conclude negotiations till the moment was propitious for ratification, and once the Watergate affair blossomed, no such moment was destined to occur during the rest of Nixon's administration or the interregnum of Gerald Ford. A good moment certainly existed before that, during the months that followed Nixon's reelection, but U.S. zeal to treat with Panama seems to have been dampened, and the moment thereby lost, because of an event originating in Panama. On July 8, 1971, only eight days after treaty talks were actually resumed, a twenty-four-year-old Panamanian named Rafael Richard, traveling on a diplomatic passport, was arrested at JFK Airport, in New York City, with eighty kilos of heroin in his luggage.

Many years later, before a U.S. Senate subcommittee, Floyd Carlton, a notable drug smuggler and personal pilot to both Torrijos and Noriega, told what had happened. We've made his statement the epigraph to our book. One of the first things Torrijos did on taking power was get in touch with the men who traded in drugs, so that by 1971 a bustling heroin connection went via Panama through the good offices of Moisés "Monchi" Torrijos, broad-buttered elder brother of Omar. Monchi's part, or part of his part, was outfitting couriers with official passports to spare them the embarrassment of customs searches. So said or sang Rafael Richard when embarrassed with two suitcases full of horse. So may have echoed Richard's uncle Guillermo González, an old friend and ex-bodyguard of Monchi's and part of the drug ring, when Richard lured him to New York on instructions from U.S. Customs agents. González was sentenced to seven years in prison. Richard was released after a short stretch, probably because of his cooperation. And Monchi was indicted in the Southern District of New York on charges of conspiracy to smuggle narcotics into the United States. The indictment was sealed so as not to alert those mentioned in it, but in March 1972 the information leaked and caused a stink. Panama charged that the United States had made the tale up to torpedo the treaty talks and declared three U.S. drug agents non grata, but Torrijos himself admitted that the charges were true. "Monchi's only moving five kilos a week," he told Jack Vaughn. "Why make a big thing of that?"

The treaty talks plodded on for years, from June 30, 1971, to August 11, 1977, affording Omar Torrijos an opportunity (of which he took adroit advantage) to dance on a world stage. He engineered a meeting of the UN Security Council in Panama in March 1973 and got a resolution from it, which the United States vetoed, urging prompt attention for Panama's just aspirations. In September of the same year, he won the support of the so-called nonaligned nations and, in November, of twenty-four Western Hemisphere countries. He went to Cuba to meet with Fidel Castro in January 1976. Two months later, the Yugoslav dictator Tito visited Panama, and in June Panama joined the nonaligned nations. One could almost hear the great head of Teddy Roosevelt prophesying doom from Mount Rushmore.

Teddy's neighbors on the cliffside might have contended that America wasn't constituted as an empire and oughtn't to have become one in the first place. Nonetheless, Torrijos made news. He also used the treaty talks to justify oppression, to tighten his and the Guardia's hold on Panama. With Panama locked in a mortal struggle with the richest, strongest nation on earth, any dissent (so the line went) was high treason. So for scrawling some anti-Torrijos graffiti a fourteen-year-old could get his genitals wired for pain by Colonel Noriega. The gravity of the crime demanded that the land's chief security officer bring his handy pathologies to bear on the case, and other dissenters were similarly discouraged, or beaten, or submitted to mock execution, and sometimes someone's hand slipped, and the execution wasn't mock at all.

Discouragement or no, dissent continued. By 1975, economic growth was down to zero, from 8 percent per year when the Guardia seized power, and some traitors suggested that the regime was incompetent, or corrupt, or both, when everyone knew that all Panama's problems were the fault of the imperialists and the oligarchs. So early in 1976 a number of these traitors were packed into exile, although the constitution, the same one enacted by Torrijos in 1972, expressly forbade exile as a sanction. A phony plot was concocted and a bunch of prominent dissenters included in it, from Miguel Antonio Bernal, the Trotskyite law professor, to Rubén Darío Carles of the Chase Manhattan Bank, and when people gathered to protest the measure, goons were sent to discourage them.

This was opposite Parque Urracá in Panama City, outside the offices of the Association of Business Executives (APEDE), which met on the evening of the exilings to pass a resolution in protest. An evening early in the dry season, with the breeze swung round off the bay, hence fresh and welcome, but the palms still lush, not yet patched as they would be by April. Kids played in the park. Cars went by along Avenida Balboa. Lovers strolled and joggers jogged on the far sidewalk beside the parapet above the bay, and beyond it shimmered the lights of high-rise apartments perched on the crest of Punta Paitilla. Two or three dozen people were gathered informally outside the APEDE building, not shouting or giving speeches, just discussing events. At eight or so, a bus pulled up at the corner, and two or three minutes later all the lights went off in the whole neighborhood. Goons armed with knives and iron bars piled from the bus and attacked the people.

R. M. Koster and his wife were twenty yards off on the sidewalk beside the park. They'd just left the corner and were walking home, and then lights went out, and they heard angry shouts and terrified screaming and turned and saw the melee outlined confusedly by the headlights of passing vehicles. Right beside them, eating an ice cream cone and watching also, was a uniformed *guardia.* "Why don't you do something?" Otilia Koster screamed at him. The *guardia* grinned at her and licked his ice cream, then turned back, still grinning, to watch the violence.

7

SNOWING THE SENATE

"SOVEREIGNTY, THE PANAMANIAN RELIGION"

The moon-faced smile of General Omar Torrijos beamed down from billboards, brown eyes bulging froggishly below the floppy brim of a green campaign hat.

"WHAT I WANT FOR MY PEOPLE IS WHAT I WANT FOR MY CHILDREN"

And indoors, posters of the general. The general kneeling to fondle a half-naked campesino tot. The general glowering from amid a group of officers. The general in fatigues and pistol inspecting an agricultural project. The general in dress suntans with palm branches of rank at the epaulets.

"IF I FALL, RAISE THE FLAG AND KISS IT AND CONTINUE FORWARD!"

Omar the Redeemer, Omar the Compassionate, Omar the Maximum Leader.

"WHO GIVES LOVE GETS LOVE"

On billboards and posters, in the capital and along the highways, and if you don't like it, keep your dissent to yourself, or you may get your tender parts wired by Colonel Noriega!

Sovereignty was a millennial religion. As Omar preached it, the people of Panama had reached paradise in 1903, had won the promised land of milk and honey, only to be driven from it at once by the gringos and the *rabiblancos* with the flaming sword of Hay–Bunau-Varilla. The new treaty brought by Omar the Redeemer would restore that paradise lost, would work their salvation—the spiritual purity of a *patria* clear of foreigners and material splendor as well. "A billion in reparations!" is what he promised in one of his speeches. It surprised no one who knew him—he drank all day long—but he liked the sound so well that he took to repeating it. Paradise regained, that's what he was preaching.

Torrijos was not alone in deception. As early as 1969, with Nelson Rockefeller's visit, the American government began deceiving itself about Panama, not only lying about the Guardia and its dictatorship—that the one was a force for social justice and the other no dictatorship at all—but exercising the will to believe its own falsehoods. As time passed, the American government, no matter who happened to be in charge of it, was less and less disposed to see or hear evil or speak evil of Torrijos and company. Jack Hood Vaughn, as competent a person on Latin America as carried a U.S. passport, left government service shortly after Nixon took office but kept in close touch with friends and former colleagues in the State Department, who as a rule were always happy to have information from him. But whenever he tried to report something derogatory about Panama—Monchi Torrijos and drugs, for example—he felt, he said, "as if I had manure on my shoes: whoever I was speaking to grew restless; I'd start telling, but they didn't want to know."

Then, too, there was deliberate disinformation. When Jimmy Carter took office, the American government set out to present Torrijos and company as good guys, deciding that no treaty would pass the Senate if the American people were told the truth. According to Senator Robert Dole, forty-four file drawers full of documents about the drug dealings of Monchi Torrijos and friends of the general's were wafted from the Justice Department to some point unknown on orders of Attorney General Griffin Bell and given a security classification so that neither the press nor U.S. senators could get to see them. But the ones who were disinformed mainly were Carter and company. It's likely the American people knew Torrijos for what he was. He'd come in, after all, by force and held no election. U.S. support for the treaty turned on the issue of fairness, not on the character of Panama's government or main leader. Carter's men ended up brainwashing themselves. Dr. Robert Pastor, for example, Carter's national security adviser for Latin America. R. M. Koster had the unspeakable misfortune to hear a lecture from Dr. Pastor—in Panama! in the lobby of the El Panamá Hilton!—on General Torrijos's commitment to social justice. Hamilton Jordan, for another.

"Ham Jordan thought Torrijos was the greatest guy in the world."

And Torrijos stole but didn't flash his thievings. He murdered but didn't leave mutilated corpses around to nauseate his gentle gringo patrons. This "moderation" was a great advantage to him, and a great discomfort to his opponents, who (given the violence elsewhere in the region) sometimes found themselves apologizing for Panama's *relative* lack of victims.

Not all apologized. Some, like R. M. Koster, lacked manners for that. In March or April 1981, a few months after Ronald Reagan took office and a few months before Omar Torrijos was killed, a fan of Koster's novels gave a little party for him in Washington and invited a few people who knew Panama. Panama was much conversed on, and at one point a lady whose husband had been a high U.S. official in Panama said that, after all, Torrijos wasn't "that bad."

"How many people," Koster asked her, "would Ronald Reagan have to have tossed out of helicopters before you decided he was a bad president? If he started with your husband, would one be enough, or would he have to toss your children out too?"

The lady's error was entirely human. She would never have *her* lovely child tossed from a helicopter. Besides, as the wife of a foreign official, a member of the diplomatic corps, she hadn't really lived in Panama. She might not have even really lived in this century. In the summer of 1987, when paramilitary goons with automatic-loading shotguns—among them convicted killers and certified maniacs—prowled the streets of Panama City, firing into people's living rooms, it came to Koster (who was too young for the war in Korea and too old for the war in Vietnam) that he might have missed the twentieth century, the true twentieth century in its unique charm and splendor, if he hadn't chanced to settle in Panama and end up living on one of those goon-prowled streets. The lady was wrong in her assessment of Torrijos, and would now think twice before repeating her error, but the error was human; anyone might make it.

Finally, Torrijos shared an attribute with Ronald Reagan that Koster wasn't thinking of when he linked them for the instruction of the diplomat's wife. Both had the gift of being judged gently. Some people, that is, get by, slide by, slip by with conduct that in others would cost dearly. Their fellow humans don't want to notice their faults (much less their crimes, if they commit any) and look the other way, sometimes even turn the other cheek! rather than be forced to condemn them. The gift shows clearly when set against its absence.

One imagines what would have happened to Jimmy Carter had someone in his White House sold Khomeini a peashooter. Some folks get no leeway—and shouldn't if they're in authority, but should rather be held to account for all their acts. Meanwhile, however, some get away with murder. By means of a particular charm, evidently, an appearance of bashfulness, an appearance of frankness, a certain boyishness, a certain bluffness, a look or smile that says, "I know I'm no genius, I don't claim to be clever, but my instincts are good, my heart's in the right place." Torrijos, like Reagan, had it. It was what enabled both to have authority without most people's seeing the damage they did their poor countries.

A boyish charm, an appearance of frankness. Time and again, it came through for Torrijos. Millions of dollars disappeared: well, that was the crowd around him. People disappeared: ah well, someone's hand slipped. And his charm worked with special potency on U.S. senators.

This was in the fall and winter of 1977–78 when he was doing what was Carter's job, properly speaking, rounding up votes for treaty ratification. Carter came to the White House determined to do a treaty with Panama. It and the Camp David accords were the sort of thing he'd sought the White House for, the noblest part of his political ambitions: the reconciliation of long-standing enmities, the resolution of old conflicts. So as soon as he took office, in January 1977, negotiations were put in high gear, and in August the two sides reached agreement. Torrijos, brainwashed by his own rhetoric, didn't much care for the product. There was no billion in reparations, for example. Next he learned, with considerable annoyance, that he'd have to sell that product to the U.S. Senate. What followed was, in a certain sense, his finest hour, his undisputed triumph as con man, and the first of three instances in which he saved Mr. Carter's hide.

Carter had got himself in a terrible mess through ignorance of a basic political axiom, that you mustn't promise what you can't deliver. It was the sort of thing he did all the time, the reason why he looked so inept so often, a main cause of his failure to be reelected. For example, while campaigning in 1976, he promised he'd make the U.S. government run efficiently, a thing Jehovah himself would think about twice before promising, something far tougher than parting the Red Sea. So in debate with President Ford that October, Carter promised he'd never give the Panama Canal away, though he must have known that any new treaty would do that, and though he planned to try for a new treaty. Then he let his negotiators reach agreement with Panama's, thereby in effect promising Panama a treaty, though he didn't have the votes for ratification. Then he decided to get the votes by blackmail. He staged an extravagant signing ceremony and invited every chief of state in the hemisphere, with the idea that now the Senate would have to vote yes or make the president of the United States look foolish. All this did was deepen the mess by widening the promise. Now all those chiefs of state needed Carter to deliver, or they too would look like a bunch of dopes, but what Carter didn't know was that the only way to blackmail a U.S. senator is by being able to hurt him with his constituents. If the president's stature had mattered, the Senate would never have made a fool of Woodrow Wilson by rejecting his League of Nations treaty. So now it was up to Omar Torrijos. His hide was on the line too; so he had to save Carter's.

The signing took place at the Pan American Union in Washington, on September 7, 1977, and was the largest convocation of heads of state that the city had ever witnessed. In those days, practically every country in Latin America was in the hands of a military despot, so that looking on from the dais were monsters worthy of Lugosi and Karloff—Videla of Argentina, for example. Graham Greene reports Torrijos as being unhappy with having these gentlemen present, as if he weren't cut from the same cloth! It was sad to see Panama represented at so historic a moment by a person who held power by force and not by election. He was at least a Panamanian, however. None was present at the first treaty's signing.

What Torrijos and Carter actually signed were two treaties, one dismantling the Canal Zone and transferring its contents (the Canal included) to Panama in stages culminating at century's end, the other providing for the Canal's neutrality and joint defense. The United States clearly gained much and lost very little in restructuring a relationship long out of fashion and in conflict with its traditions and heritage. Such restructuring was the best way for the United States to protect its national security interest on the Isthmus of Panama. The alternative would have been to shed blood in defense of Hay–Bunau-Varilla, a policy with which the American people would soon have been uncomfortable and that world opinion would have condemned at once. The Canal is too easily put out of commission to be a strategic defense asset nowadays, and as for the U.S. bases on the isthmus, the treaties assured their existence till the year 2000. They were also supposed to produce a Panama friendly enough to extend their existence thereafter, and for the rest of Torrijos's time, and on into the tyrannies of Rubén Paredes and Manuel Noriega, Panama was Tío Sam's great chum. The falling-out that occurred in the wake of Hugo Spadafora's murder had nothing to do with the treaties signed in 1977. Finally, if prestige counts for anything, the United States gained prestige by concluding new treaties, and would surely have lost prestige by clutching the old.

Panama, on the face of things, gained immensely. To begin with, Panama regained its heartland, the transit zone between the oceans, the region's prime tract since the sixteenth century. More, these five hundred square miles were for the most part highly developed, with the cities of Balboa and Cristobal and numerous towns, with roads and utilities and bridges and dams, with extensive port facilities and a railroad and hundreds of buildings, industrial and residential. Much of this would be Panama's in two years' time, assets valued by the world bank at 6.3 *billion* in 1983 dollars. *All* would be transferred within twenty-three years. Finally, there was the Canal itself, a source at once of wealth and of status. Few of history's conquests have been so grand; few conquests by force of arms, fewer still by diplomacy. Or so, on the face of things, it seemed. Yet from twelve years' perspective it is frightfully clear that the treaties have done Panama nothing but damage.

Panama was a country with cancer, a conquered land pillaged by vandals. Anything that might have benefited Panama had Panama been healthy, had it been free, merely fed the cancer, strengthened the barbarians. A cancer can do nothing useful with what one feeds it. All it does is grow till it kills the body it lives in, and thereby itself. Barbarians can do nothing useful with roads and ports and hydroelectric stations. Those belong to civilization, which barbarians are ignorant of and despise. It took the treaties, in fact, to show just how barbaric the Guardia is. Of all the lands and buildings turned over to Panama in 1979, pursuant to the new Canal treaties, hardly anything was put to productive use. The Guardia ended up with more installations. Some officers' girlfriends got duplexes. That was about it. And if one collects symbols, the Canal Zone Library ceased to exist, though its doors had been open to readers of all nationalities. Its facilities became the office of Colonel Luis Córdoba, who directed the torturing of Hugo Spadafora.

If the treaties benefited at least one of the parties to them, they were bad news for both the men who signed. They left Jimmy Carter with an exposed right flank that the Republicans attacked with effect and gusto until the man was voted out of office, and as for Omar Torrijos . . . For Torrijos, the treaties were a priceless asset so long as they were only an idea, on the order of a magical steed that could lift him out of any political predicament. But the moment they achieved actual existence, they turned into a white elephant. No sooner had he set his name to them, for instance, than they obliged him to start paying, in this case to wander from his principles and grossly liberalize his rule. The treaties had to be ratified, you see, for which purpose he'd scheduled a plebiscite. To be held on September 23, only sixteen days after the signing and barely a month after the texts were released. His contempt for democracy was as firm as ever. Those treaties were strewn with his broken promises. The last thing he wanted was an informed vote. But then Jimmy Carter told him, with no minced words, that the Senate would never pass the treaties unless the people of Panama endorsed them, and up there in the U.S.A., where the senators lived, no endorsement was valid unless it was preceded by free discussion.

Now, Omar Torrijos hadn't had Floyd Britton murdered so that Panamanians could have free discussion. That wasn't why he'd had Héctor Gallego killed either, or all the others killed or jailed or exiled. Free discussion was something he and the Guardia had got along very well without. But now the treaties obliged him to allow some, and the people of Panama took full advantage. The government put in its best people, Rómulo Escobar to start with. Torrijos, too, campaigned, though in Colón he was booed so badly that he fled the scene, with his bodyguards shoving a path for him through the multitude. The "No" side was represented by a group of lawyers organized for the occasion and numbering some of the country's best minds, from Mario Galindo and Alfredo Ramírez at center-right to Carlos Ivan Zúñiga and Fabián Echevers at center-left. They spoke on radio and TV and at public meetings, and it was a tonic after nine years of pedantry and propaganda and pap to hear the country's business discussed with wit and acuity by men till then constrained to silence. As honest men, they set out to criticize the treaties on their merits, and they made a number of points: that the new treaties contained no safeguards for the rights of Canal workers such as he been prominent in the 1967 drafts Torrijos had contemptuously rejected; that the neutrality and defense treaty authorized the existence on Panamanian soil of U.S. military bases, something Panama had never done till then; and so forth. Insensibly, however, criticism of the treaties graded to criticism of the regime that had subscribed them. Without realizing it, the lawyers were anticipating the future, as good minds sometimes can. Not in so many words but in substance, without the perspective of time but hence with great insight, they were making the argument we have made above on the basis of fact: nothing could be good for Panama so long as Panama was under Guardia tyranny; nothing brought by the tyrants could have any worth. No one could have imagined the stupidity and contempt for their country and countrymen that the Guardia was to display vis-à-vis the lands and so forth transferred to Panama under the treaties, but the lawyers had intimations.

On the other side was what the treaties brought in concrete terms—land, facilities, and so on—along with the promise (still unfulfilled) of boom times. Torrijos milked this last hope successfully. The people believed, wished to believe, that the treaties would bring a shower of money, if not the deluge Torrijos assured. The vote was about 65 percent to 35 percent "Yes" in Panama City.

In the countryside, however, particularly in Indian regions, things went harder for the government. "No" carried the province of Bocas del Toro, in the process nearly causing the death by apoplexy of Gerardo González Vernaza, a cousin of the Maximum Leader's and of the Santa Fe storeowner most outraged by the brief ministry of Héctor Gallego. González was charged with putting Bocas behind the treaties, and when the province embarrassed him, he lost all control of himself and dashed into the street and tried to throttle the first Indian he saw. His bodyguards pried his hands from the man's throat and dragged him back, at which point he screamed, "Why'd you vote 'No'?" The Indian looked at him with the exasperating impassivity that is his race's richest patrimony and that many mistake for indifference. "Because of the 5 percent sales tax," he said calmly. What the treaties might bring, sovereignty included, was vague and abstract to those who lived far from the Canal and the Canal Zone. The dictatorship, however, was all too palpable. Hadn't it just had its hands on the man's throat?

In Colón, too, the treaties took a thrashing. In the San Blas Islands, "No" was almost unanimous, to the point where the Indians celebrated the result by running a Stars and Stripes up the flagpole. The capital's vote, nonetheless was overriding. Guillermo Sánchez, who observed the proceedings closely and voted "No" himself, calculated that if the votes had been fairly counted, "Yes" would have won nationwide by perhaps 58 percent to 42 percent. But, of course, the votes were not counted fairly. The nature of the counters made such impossible. Besides, the treaties needed a two-thirds vote to pass the U.S. Senate, and Omar the Redeemer was not going to show up with less. The count as officially reported therefore gave "Yes" 68 percent, but whoever cooked the thing got a bit sloppy, so that, by the government's own figures, 117 percent of the electorate voted.

In any case, the plebiscite was over. Panama had ratified the treaties. The ball was in the U.S. Senate's court. But now the treaties exacted another payment. Torrijos had had to allow free discussion—and could scarcely stamp it out, not for the present, not with all the world peering at Panama. Now, for his next sacrifice, the next strip of his hide the treaties demanded, he had to get the Senate to vote right also—and up there the fools counted votes straight. He had to do Carter's work, save Carter's hide.

Jimmy Carter and Omar Torrijos deserved each other. Torrijos was a general whose whole store of martial experience was getting shot in the butt while fleeing a bunch of students. Carter was a president entirely without political talent and savvy. He was far, far above taking the American people into his confidence and explaining why the United States needed a new Canal treaty. There were good reasons. Doing the treaty was in the national interest. But Carter wouldn't explain that to the people. He had more important things to do. Which aides got to use the White House tennis courts when? Carter had to wrestle with questions like that. He didn't think of preparing public opinion for a little thing like disencumbering the United States of its greatest overseas achievement, preparing opinion first, then concluding agreement, when a good climate for ratification existed. That would have been too much like politics.

One almost feels sorry for Torrijos. On October 14, not a month after the big signing gala, Torrijos was back in Washington on Jimmy Carter's request. The tennis season must have been over, for Carter had time to read the papers and find out that his Canal treaties were in big trouble, so he called on Omar Torrijos to help him out, to "clarify" certain passages, to join him in declaring that the United States could intervene militarily in Panama to keep the Canal open, and could send its vessels to the head of the line, if and when the United States decided a threat or an emergency existed. Back home in Panama, Torrijos maintained that he'd signed nothing, had given nothing away, but he can't have enjoyed making that declaration, particularly when one of his own negotiators, Dr. Carlos López Guevara, he of the little mustache and the Harvard degree, began pointing out to anyone who'd listen, in a Panama filling up with reporters, that giving U.S. ships priority of transit took a big chunk of neutrality out of the neutrality treaty.

But there was scarcely time to fret about that. The treaties now claimed yet another slice of Torrijos. The colder the weather got in Washington, the more convinced U.S. senators became that they couldn't in conscience vote on the Canal treaty without investigating matters on the ground, and besides senators there were all kinds of so-called opinion makers—Ambassador Angier Biddle Duke with a delegation, the Reverend Jesse Jackson with another—craving to make the Panama scene also. And who was supposed to convert them, get their votes or get them to get somebody else's? Omar Torrijos, that's who. He had to do what Carter should have been doing. He had to romance a bunch of gringos, *icarajo!*

The senators, of course, got the most attention. The first bunch arrived just after Thanksgiving, led by Robert Byrd, the majority leader, and including Metzenbaum of Ohio and Sarbanes of Maryland. They met with businessmen in Panama City, then went over to the Zone to see U.S. civilians and officers attached to Southern Command—ordinary junketing so far, but then they entered the world of Omar Torrijos.

By Twin Otter aircraft. The Otter is made in Canada and is as safe as anything else in the sky, but is pint sized and buffetable by thermals, compared with something ponderous by Boeing. When you're up in one, you know you're flying, know you're in an alien element. So Torrijos was getting to them already. A good part of his impact on this and succeeding groups lay in his world's being alien and exotic, seemingly simpler, straighter, sterner, and thereby sexier than the citified senators' regular habitat. It was a world by Jean Jacques Rousseau with its back-to-nature theme and its noble savage (in floppy green campaign hat, in green fatigues with pendant .45 pistol), and by Douanier Rousseau, too, in its bold images and violent colors.

The flight was to El Porvenir, on the San Blas Coast. From there they crossed the lagoon in an outboard-motored *cayuco.* That crossing intimidated the senators: putt-putting slickly across the breeze-rippled lagoon in a long, low, gaudily painted dugout with the noble savage sprawled smiling in the bottom, not minding if the seat of his trousers got wet, and his guests crouched apprehensively on the thwarts in their suit jackets and leather-soled oxfords. Across a lagoon in a dugout toward a low horizon of breeze-swayed palm trees—not the senators' normal thing. And on the island there was a session with the Indians: chunky, mahogany-skinned Indians in gaudily colored sarongs, and bare-breasted Indian women with gold rings in their noses. To whom the general dispensed unintelligible wit and wisdom. Did the senators know how the San Blas had voted? Did they know that the San Blas had run up a Stars and Stripes? Not likely. They knew it was a show put on to impress them, but they were impressed nonetheless.

The next show was in Los Santos, two hundred miles west of Panama City on the Azuero Peninsula, where the movement for independence from Spain had begun, an effort consummated on November 28, 1821, 156 years to the day earlier. Torrijos led an impromptu parade down the main street, with the senators marching along beside and behind him. Later on that afternoon, however, things got a bit less pleasant for the noble savage. This was at Farallón, his seaside retreat eighty miles west of the capital, where he and the senators sat down around the dining room table for a discussion that lasted five or six hours, drawn out by the repeated need for translation. Senators got up from time to time, but Torrijos was onstage for the whole session. He showed them fancy footwork, sidestepping their questions about human rights, weaving away before they could back him in a corner, but the senators kept coming at him, and sometimes they got to him. Why military government? Why not press freedom? Why not political parties? One can almost hear Torrijos's teeth grinding.

"I don't like dictators," Howard Metzenbaum told him.

"I don't like them either," Torrijos shot back, crossing his fingers under the table maybe.

Late afternoon in late November. It will have rained before dusk, then cleared. Men sitting around a table in their shirt sleeves in an airy informal beach house in the tropics. A dining room that gave on a *sala,* a *sala* that gave on a terrace that gave on a lawn, a lawn that gave on the beach and the Pacific. Saying (not in so many words but nonetheless clearly), "Look, General, if we're going to do this deal . . ." And he's saying, "Hold it! Wait a minute! I've got a deal!" And they come back, "No, you've got an agreement with Jimmy Carter. Now you're going to have to give us something, so we can go home and make your agreement stand up."

Hear his teeth grinding. Everyone wanted a chunk of Omar Torrijos to take home and feed his constituents. "I met with General Torrijos, and I told him he has to change this, and he has to change that . . ." When *he* did a deal, he delivered, *¡carajo!* The plebiscite went over, didn't it? It was Carter's job to stroke Howard Metzenbaum, to kiss Bob Byrd behind the ear.

No matter, he kept his head, he gave a performance. Not as smooth as those he gave later on, once he'd figured it all out and come to terms with what he'd have to suffer, but all the more impressive for being his maiden effort. Byrd pushed him hard, but he didn't push back. He knew Byrd's role. He knew he had to get along with the majority leader, or he could kiss the treaties good-bye. He surprised and impressed his guests with his knowledge. The discussion would go along, and just when he seemed out of his depth, mystified by some clause in one of the treaties, Torrijos would come up with a pertinent comment. He was gifted at listening. Draw the speaker out, draw him out further, then nip him on the flank that he's exposed. That way you don't have to know much to look knowledgeable. Most important was the impression he left that "he understood the problems the senators were raising and that he was serious about doing something about them. The senators went away feeling that here was a man interested in their concerns and was willing to do something to move the ball forward."

That fall and winter, Omar Torrijos probably saw more U.S. senators than Jimmy Carter did. Unquestionably, he was more effective with them. Very soon he had his act pat, certainly by January when Minority Leader Howard Baker showed up with a contingent of Republicans—a key visit, since Republican votes were crucial in putting together the two-thirds margin required for treaty ratification. Torrijos took them to Contadora Island, where much of the negotiation had taken place, and the footage of him strolling on the beach with the Honorable Jacob Javits—Torrijos stabbing his finger, jawing away, Javits with his suit jacket under his arm and his bald pate glistening resplendently, while a leash of scribbling reporters plodded behind them—put one in mind of Lewis Carroll's Walrus and Carpenter. By then, even before then, Torrijos had perfected all his numbers: the scenic tour, the tropical informality, the boyish charm, the strong-man-cum-man-of-the-people manner. He took the Honorable George McGovern to Coclesito and led him on a blistering four-mile trek to a jungle swimming hole, then jumped in fully clothed and joshed his guest for not joining him. The two of them posed for stills sitting on a boulder above the river looking like overage urchins, Tom Sawyer and Huck Finn.

But listen to Jack Vaughn, who was present at some of the sessions and talked with others who caught Torrijos's show:

> You got a toast-of-the-country reception. A box of Cuban cigars, a decanter of liquor, a top-of-the-line *guayabera* to wear around and look like an

old Panama hand. And everyone got a sombrero in his right size. Then a helicopter ride to Farallón. That's where he preferred to take them, anywhere from a couple of hours to a couple of days. There were five or six beautiful hammocks strung in the entrance where you could have a rum and relax a little, go to sleep in the afternoon if you felt like it. He always had attractive women there too. And there was always an enormous spread, shrimp and lobster and interesting *interiorana* food, often venison. The "real Panama," away from the Zone and the capital. There was the deal where he had half a dozen girls in bikinis to go swimming with you at this lovely, isolated beach. He had an uncanny ability, looking at a VIP, to know if he was the raunchy type who wanted girls around or if he was prudish and straitlaced, or maybe he wanted a more intellectual presentation. And, where do you want to go, what can I show you? He'd taken them in a helicopter for short sightseeing trips, and they'd get off and go around and meet the natives. A very carefully orchestrated, devastatingly effective show. None of these guys had ever seen a caudillo, or if they'd met Trujillo or Somoza it was in a Washington setting. The effect on a gringo politician was, "This guy has real power, he can make things happen." He really did a job on the Senate.

Uncanny ability? Well, not that uncanny really. Torrijos, you see, had an intelligence officer—he was also a gangster and a bagman, a torturer and a familiar fiend—who got him all kinds of useful information. And where did it come from? From his good friends in the CIA, that's where. As late as late 1987, after the Senate passed a resolution condemning Noriega, the CIA was still feeding Noriega information on the private lives of U.S. senators and their aides. The CIA, through Noriega, was a partner in Torrijos's con game.

Lieutenant Colonel Noriega. There was a certain honesty to him in those days, or perhaps it was merely cynicism and chutzpah. In Panamanian slang, "stool pigeon" is *sapo,* "toad." Noriega's office was full of little ceramic toad figurines. It also had TV monitors displaying sensitive parts of Guardia headquarters, and paintings of little girls weeping that took on a sinister tinge when one considered who'd put them there. This decor was memorialized by Sally Quinn in a profile in the *Washington Post.* R. M. Koster escorted her to Noriega's office, and Noriega took one look at her and excused himself and came back reeking of eau de cologne—a natty little guy in a blue business suit, bouncy, full of energy, victim (it's true) of a bad acne problem, so that his cheeks looked like the landscape at Verdun, shell holes and pools of mustard gas, so that the people called him Cara de Piña (Pineapple Face), but his eyes could twinkle, went glassy reptilian only now and then.

In those days, too, he had a sense of humor. Koster was at the airport, along with every other journalist in the country, the day in July 1979 when Edén Pastora and the Rigoberto López Brigade came in with Cardinal Obando y Bravo and the political prisoners they liberated (Daniel Ortega included) after seizing the National Palace in Managua, the great feat of arms of the Nicaraguan civil war. The journalists had been waiting for hours to ask Pastora questions, when Colonel Noriega came strutting across the tarmac. "What's going on, Colonel?" asked Koster. Noriega shook a finger: "Yo no sé nada." "Then can I report that Panamanian military intelligence knows nothing?" Koster grinned and held out his pencil and notebook. Noriega grinned back at him pointing the finger: "Do that and I'll hurt you."

Noriega was on hand for the Byrd group's visit, unobtrusive in sport shirt and slacks, having quiet conversations with the visitors. What struck one American as the two talked was his cynicism. The whole business, to Noriega, was only an act with which to gull the public. The senators had to pretend human rights concerned them. Torrijos had to pretend their pretense was real. But men of the world, he and his listener, for instance, knew better. The difference between Noriega and Torrijos intrigued the American, as did Noriega's role in the ratification process.

The difference didn't intrigue those who suffered their tyranny. Noriega and Torrijos were diseases, one with clear symptoms, one without.

Still, one almost feels pity. The crow Torrijos ate to get his treaties! One humiliation after another. Humiliations came in an endless dribble, each one scarcely bearable and in accumulation so tormenting that had he known beforehand what he would suffer, he would never have begun. It wasn't just the entertaining of men he must have despised, smiling at men who believed (or anyway claimed to) that power should come only through election and shouldn't be used to have men who mock you murdered. No, he had to adopt their ninny creed! He had to promise *he* would have an election, a direct election for president in 1984 where the people, supposedly, would choose who would govern. He had to promise to permit free speech, and not some empty token, either, but newspapers his government didn't control. He had to promise to follow his own constitution in the matter of Panamanians he'd sent into exile. His constitution forbade exile, so he had to promise to let the exiles come home. What business was it of a bunch of gringos what his constitution said or whether he followed it? He had, in sum, to promise to respect people's rights—as if who had rights in Panama were their business!—and worst of all, he'd have to keep his promises, at least in part, at least for a while. Once the Senate voted ratification, the House of Representatives had to vote implementing legislation, and besides his government was a money junkie, as we mean to show in the next chapter. He didn't want the gringos to cut off the money. And as if all that weren't enough, all those degrading smiles and debasing promises, he had to swallow reservations imposed by the Senate and still sweat out the ratification vote.

Debate on the Carter-Torrijos Panama Canal treaties began in the U.S. Senate in January 1978 and continued intermittently for nearly three months. For fourteen years, every administration since Lyndon Johnson's had pursued the goal of modernizing U.S. treaty relations with Panama, but had pursued it at a stealthy creep, without telling anyone where they were headed or why. Now Carter had speeded things up and concluded new treaties yet still hadn't explained them to the public, preferring to let the senators do that for him. Moreover, in sending the treaties to them for ratification, he neglected to define the issue clearly, so that the debate ranged well beyond its proper concern, which was whether the treaties were in the national interest, to consider the character of Panama's government. A curious circumstance thereby ensued: each side was exactly half right and half wrong; each had one foot on solid ground and the other in the mush of make-believe.

Some senators and other political figures responded to the Canal's symbolic importance as incarnating the myths of American know-how and altruism, and especially as recalling a simpler era, the nation's young manhood, as it were, when America acted boldly on the world's stage without annoying second thoughts and guilt tremors. These were treaty opponents. To them—and, one assumes, to their constituents—clutching the Canal preserved not only the myths but a hope of return to the bygone era. Abandoning it and sovereignty in the Canal Zone somehow meant the end of national greatness. They viewed the treaties, then, as dangerous lunacy, if not as part of a vast, semisecret conspiracy to destroy the nation's pride and dismantle its defenses as a prelude to delivering it to the Bolsheviks. Irrationality of this sort generally characterized the treaties' opponents when they considered the treaties themselves. But let them turn their attention to Torrijos and company, and instantly they recovered use of their reason. Here's an example that illustrates the thought process perfectly, though the treaty opponent involved wasn't a senator but a former film actor named Ronald Reagan: "The United States, not content with giving away the Panama Canal and leaving the hemisphere defenseless, now does business with criminals who in this country would be in prison." Wrong about the hemisphere's defenses; right as rain about the criminals, though when he became president, Reagan lost his prudishness in regard to dealing with them.

On the other hand, a majority of the senators had no trouble distinguishing substance from symbol with regard to the nation's defense, prestige, and other interests. These supported the treaties. They saw that clinging to de facto sovereignty in the Canal Zone would provide neither strength nor honor, and would no more bring back the days of Teddy Roosevelt and the Big Stick than would wearing a bustle or a wing collar. On the other hand, the principles on which the United States was founded—national self-determination, for instance—once the visionary dreams of revolutionists, were now rights to which all peoples aspired, Panamanians included, and which they could legitimately seek by diplomacy or violence. The United States would do itself much more good by adhering to the spirit of its heritage rather than to the letter of Hay–Bunau-Varilla. So, in general, the treaties' proponents kept touch with reality when discussing the treaties and why they should pass. But when, instead, they considered Panama's government, they straight away went sailing off into cloudland, fantasizing apostles of social justice such as rarely existed anywhere on the planet and certainly not in the Panama of Omar Torrijos. It was hallucinating for those who knew Panama to hear men swerve from madness to sanity in the same sentence, then hear other men make the same swerve, but in reverse.

In March 1978, as the decision neared, and as the debate more and more outlined the division, careful counters realized that while the treaties had a clear majority behind them, they were a few votes short of the needed two-thirds. At which Jimmy Carter, who had campaigned on the slogan "A leader for a change," who was, besides, paid to lead—that is, chart a course and persuade the people it was a wise one—who had a "bully pulpit" but hadn't used it, preferring a stagy spectacle and blackmail, found not just relations with Panama (which would have been plenty) but his whole foreign policy, including hope for Mideast and SALT agreements, in hock to the Panama treaties and a few senators. So when Dennis DeConcini, Democrat of Arizona, who'd been a senator less than fourteen months, no longer in fact than Carter had been a president, came to the White House with a deal, Carter had little choice but to agree. What DeConcini wanted, the price of his vote and maybe one or two others, maybe enough votes to make the difference, was to tack a reservation on the neutrality treaty embodying the "clarification" Torrijos and Carter had made the previous October. What the DeConcini reservation in effect did was write into the Carter-Torrijos treaties something beyond Hay–Bunau-Varilla's article 7 (which, anyway, had been junked in 1936), whereby the United States got the right to intervene militarily anywhere in the Republic of Panama when it deemed such action required to keep the Canal open.

The debate on the Carter-Torrijos treaties entered its final phase on March 16. The vote on the neutrality treaty would come that afternoon. Depending on how it fared, passing the second treaty would be a formality or not worth attempting. In Panama, Radio Liberdad, the government's station, broadcast the proceedings in Spanish translation, while the Southern Command Network in the Canal Zone carried them live. In the house on Fiftieth Street, Torrijos and aides had two sets tuned. First Byrd introduced and the Senate accepted an amendment that took some of the sting from DeConcini's proposal without much changing its substance. Then DeConcini introduced his reservation, and it passed without debate, on a voice vote. At once, Radio Liberdad broke from its coverage of the Senate: Dr. Rómulo Escobar would make a statement. But much to the surprise of everyone listening, Escobar (speaking, of course, for Torrijos) declared that the reservation was "potable." It was a very lame pronouncement after so much demagoguery and so much bluster, and blasphemous too if sovereignty was in fact the Panamanian religion. There was nothing inside Torrijos, nothing firm. All his talk about sovereignty and dignity was merely that, talk.

At 5:30, when the vote was about an hour off, flatbed military trucks with salsa bands on top of them began pulling up in front of public buildings and into the main plazas of Panama City. Pickup trucks with rum, beer, and soda followed. State employees, held at their posts past quitting time, were trooped down to partake. Much the same thing happened elsewhere throughout the country. Radio Liberdad interspersed its coverage with assurances that Byrd's amendment had detoxified DeConcini's reservation. *Also sprach* Omar! Panamanians had his leave to rejoice when the treaty passed.

And pass it did, with a vote to spare. In Panama, fireworks went off, car horns tooted. For three hours, while the free booze and music held out, people salsa'd in the streets and rode around in Guardia trucks, each with a picture of Omar the Redeemer. A good party, though not as lively or spontaneous as the one four years earlier when Roberto Durán had won the lightweight boxing crown. By ten, the crowds had filtered off, leaving a litter of confetti and broken bottles.

At about seven, Torrijos spoke to the nation. His hair was mussed, his voice monotone and rambling. He shuffled his notes more than referred to them. Often he leaned forward on his left elbow and grasped the table mike with his left hand. Often he clasped his forehead with his right. He seemed not drunk or drugged but rather drained utterly, and what he said was odder than how he looked. Had the vote gone wrong "the next day there would have been no Canal." Guardia units would have destroyed it, and would destroy it if the United States ever intervened in Panama's affairs. The Guardia, he said, "should never lose its capability of destroying the Canal." His vanity had been bruised very badly. He complained about the insults heaped on him during the debate, though all he'd been called was drug peddler, thief, and dictator, all of which titles he'd earned. He spoke well of Carter, however, and gave the American people a backhanded compliment, saying the treaty opponents were unworthy of the people's decency and fairness. Then he appealed for national unity and, in his avatar of Omar the Compassionate, offered a great boon. The exiles could come home, even Arnulfo, and political parties would be allowed to exist. There, truly, was a generous leader! Under pressure from the United States, he gave back to the people a little of what he'd stolen from them!

In the now-doomed Canal Zone, the evening was tranquil. Everyone had expected the treaties to pass, and such firebrand antitreaty Zonians as had existed were by then long gone from the isthmus. Someone at Southern Command Network TV was a diehard, however, or maybe merely a wag. Canal Zonians who tuned in the late movie saw Ronald Reagan in a thing called *Desperate Passage.*

The second treaty was passed on April 18. Exiles began returning thereafter. Arnulfo's return, though, had the government skittish. At length, a poll was commissioned to gauge its impact. This decision, which involved paying good money to a Marxist sociologist, shows what different lands the government and people of Panama lived in. The government lived in the land of Omar the Compassionate. The people, on the other hand, while willing to respond honestly to, say, a market survey for a new product, would rather not bare their souls to strangers inquiring out their opinions of Arnulfo Arias. They lived in the land of Manuel Noriega, Torrijos's torturer and familiar fiend, for whom the inquisitive strangers might be working. The finding of the poll was that no more than twenty thousand Panamanians would turn out to greet Arnulfo on his return.

Did the government believe this figure? Partly. It had grown mentally obese from ten years of munching its own propaganda, during which time Arnulfo had been absent, and scarcely mentioned. He must, the government was convinced, have been driven from people's hearts by Omar the Redeemer, certainly from those of the generation come to political maturity since 1968. In due course, therefore, Arnulfo was advised that he might come home. On the other hand, collectively the regime retained a few lean neurons, all of which counseled prudence. Arnulfo, therefore, was told to return on Saturday, June 10. Jimmy Carter and a number of Latin-American presidents were expected in Panama six days later for the ceremonial exchange of treaty ratification instruments. They would take the spotlight from Arnulfo. And, just in case, he was forbidden to cross into Panama from Costa Rica and then drive to Panama City, as Torrijos had done in December 1969, or to use Tocumen International Airport. He might charter a small plane and land at Gelabert Airport, a small strip right on the bay near the capital's center, where what passed for a terminal building could hold no more than fifty or sixty people.

As June 10 neared, a mood of lethargy came over Panama, a great indifference, especially as concerned Arnulfo's arrival. On the seventh or eighth, Guillermo Sánchez ran into Eric Arturo Delvalle, son of Sánchez's old chieftain in the Partido Republicano, now one of Torrijos's firmest supporters among *rabiblancos,* and destined to be puppet president during the tyranny of Manuel Noriega. Not even twenty thousand, said Delvalle, and Sánchez had nothing with which to refute the prediction. The morning of the tenth came seasonably muggy, a palpable weight of moist air on one's chest and shoulders, and a torpor so profound as to confirm Sánchez's worst fears. The city was as if in coma. And at about one, the greasy sky opened and let down a deluge. There went the welcome! Arnulfo was due to touch down at three. If the rain acted seasonably, it would last until nightfall, and it was said, and not by accident either, that a Panamanian crowd would face bullets before facing rain. Those who've seen it rain in the tropics will understand. Still, Sánchez went to the airport, where he ran into a number of acquaintances, including R. M. Koster, who was reporting the event for *Newsweek.* That was at about two-thirty, and what passed for a terminal building wasn't yet full, but people kept arriving, and toward three the place began to get very crowded, so since the rain had slackened to a drizzle, some people (including Sánchez and Koster) went out on the runway apron and waited there. Then, just at three, an odd thing happened. Off beyond the south end of the runway, over the bay, the sky cleared abruptly, casting a stream of light under the heavy clouds that covered the city, and from that stream of light the plane appeared, looking very small and fragile, hence very brave. It hung in the river of light above the water and first seemed not to move, then came on bravely, and as it approached the shore, it brought the light with it, as if it were parting the clouds, peeling a rift back, so that by the time it touched down and began to trundle toward where the people were waiting, the rain had further slackened and then stopped altogether. In a novel or movie, it would have been corny. In real life, the effect was deeply stirring.

There were no *guardias* visible at the airport—in fact, neither Sánchez nor Koster nor anyone they discussed the event with saw a single *guardia* all the rest of the day—but some *arnulfistas* formed a kind of honor guard making a path through the crowd, which suddenly seemed to number four or five hundred, between the plane and what passed for the terminal. With that, the door of the plane opened, and Arnulfo appeared. There was a momentary hush, during which a working man near Sánchez said, in an ordinary voice but in the hush heightened, "He looks newer than Torrijos!" using *nuevo,* "new," rather than *ioven,* "young," as if to say "in better shape," "more serviceable." Then madness broke out and continued for hours.

What one realized, driving ahead of Arnulfo toward the center of town as Koster did, then walking when the streets were too packed with people for driving, was that the whole country had turned out. One realized it even more clearly if, like Sánchez, one walked along with Arnulfo. Twenty thousand? There were twenty times that between Fifth of May and Santa Ana plazas! And every balcony was full besides! There were campesinos who'd risen at two in the morning and walked miles to the highway to get a bus to the capital. There were people from every district in every province. They'd found their own way and paid their own way and were happy. Red-yellow-purple *panameñista* banners fluttered everywhere. Impromptu *pachanga* combos blared. The truck Arnulfo rode on like a carnival float was awash in ecstatic humanity. He smiled and waved and took cheers and now and then halted his progress and got down and bathed in the love that foamed around him. It took him four hours to go the three miles from the airport to Santa Ana, but the jubilation only grew. He spoke for over an hour, and at every pause the crowd chanted, "Presidencia, presidencia!" Had he cared to lead them the twelve or so blocks to the building, he could have tossed Lakas out and slept there that night, though what would have happened once the crowd dispersed can't be guessed at. The people were telling Arnulfo they hadn't forgotten, and that they ought to have backed him more firmly, in the first days after the coup, when the strike was called. But the word was for Omar Torrijos also. They were telling Torrijos they preferred being free men and women, that they'd rather chose their own leaders, thank you, that he might command their obedience by fear, because he was backed by cutthroats with weapons, but that he could never command their allegiance. That was their message to Omar the Redeemer, which they sent the only way they could, the same message they sent Manuel the Repugnant ten years later by coming out for Arnulfo's funeral. They didn't get a chance to express themselves often, but when they did they were eloquent.

It was a terrible blow to Torrijos's vanity, the worst he ever sustained, one he never got over. He was at Farallón that weekend, in seclusion, but he had Arnulfo's welcome filmed from a helicopter, and at ten that night he watched the film along with the Guardia general staff and a few close aides. "Now we know who the real leader of the Panamanian people is," he said when the film was over, "but he'll never return to power while I'm alive." He also heard excerpts from Arnulfo's speech, and it too was a blow. Arnulfo called him a psychopath for proposing to destroy the Canal, Panama's greatest asset, and denounced the regime's corruption and Monchi's drug trafficking—nothing people didn't know and mutter in private, but the first public dissension in ten years. Like the people's actions, it couldn't go unanswered, and four days later Torrijos replied. He sent a message to the people and to Arnulfo, and to Jimmy Carter, too, if he was interested, and Torrijos was eloquent also in his fashion.

There was a group of university students who opposed the regime and the treaties and who planned a demonstration for Thursday, June 15, to protest Jimmy Carter's visit. The leader was a young man named Jorge Camacho. Koster knew him. That is to say, he'd heard him speak and seen him in action. They were tear-gased together one morning that spring outside the U.S. embassy on Avenida Balboa, where Camacho and company had gone to throw red paint and Koster to pick up a little of *Newsweek*'s money. Camacho was about five feet eight inches tall. His arms and shoulders suggested body-building. He was very bright and apparently fearless, an odd combination. He had taken numerous lumps for his love of freedom but persisted in it at once fanatically and with a cheerfulness fanatics usually lack.

These students, Camacho and company, had their demonstration planned for Thursday morning and meanwhile were holed up in the Faculty of Law on the university campus so as not to be arrested before they had a chance to put on their protest. In Panama, as in most if not all of Latin America, police are forbidden by law to enter the university precincts, a law Torrijos had to pretend to respect or lose credit with the neighbors who were supporting him, some of whose presidents would be arriving on the sixteenth. On the other hand, Torrijos wished to prevent the demonstration, and send Arnulfo and the people a message, and generally reestablish his tyranny, which had lost much of its snap of late, and for that sort of problem there was no one better suited than his gangster and familiar fiend. After dark, then, on Wednesday the fourteenth, Noriega sent a bunch from the progovernment Federación de Estudiantes de Panama (FEP, Panamanian Students' Federation), whose leaders were paid from state funds. They were armed with pipes and crowbars, and their mission was to break into the Faculty of Law and flush the dissidents out and off the campus so they could be arrested and jailed without the government's seeming to violate university autonomy—and in fact they managed to break into the building and set fire to a couple of classrooms before Camacho and company forced them back out. Noriega then sent in G-2 agents. One of them, wearing black, crouched in the back of a gray pickup truck and sprayed the building with bullets from his Uzi as the truck sped by. Others then opened up with small arms. One antigovernment student evidently was killed by gunfire, and a number were wounded. Soon enough the dissidents surrendered, whereupon G-2 agents murdered Camacho and another of the group's leaders, named Demóstenes Rodríguez, and the FEP students gave the rest a terrible clubbing. The total was two dead and three hundred hospitalized. The Social Security Administration Hospital, where they were taken, was sealed. Parents of the dead were told they could collect their son's corpses when Carter's visit was over.

The government used the violence at the university as a pretext for ordering all radio stations into a single network under government control for the duration of the dignitaries' stay in Panama, but more important was the message it sent the people and Arnulfo. The government media blamed the incident on Arnulfo and the other recently returned exiles, accusing them of abusing the liberties granted them by Torrijos. This may sound insane or cynical, but there is no reason to suppose that Torrijos did not believe exactly that. He had been generous; they had taken advantage. His answer to the people and Arnulfo Arias was that he and the Guardia had the will and means to continue their tyranny, and that if and when they chose to injure his vanity, they would pay in blood. A man had his dignity, after all. They chose to upstage him on the eve of the American president's visit. How did they like being murdered? How did they like being beaten with pipes?

It was really a most economical operation. A message, a pretext, and Camacho dead too. Camacho had to die for exactly the same reason as Floyd Britton and Héctor Gallego: he mocked Omar Torrijos just by existing. Britton was the revolutionary Torrijos talked about being. Gallego was the caring leader Torrijos pretended now and then to be. Camacho was a patriot. He believed in sovereignty and national dignity, words and phrases that were just talk to Torrijos. Hence he mocked Torrijos, hence he had to be murdered. The mere existence of Jorge Camacho made those words and phrases rattle emptily inside Torrijos like pebbles in a gourd, and the anguish of it was unbearable.

Camacho's father was a petty functionary of some sort. For years afterward, he could be seen at protest marches wearing a jacket and tie and carrying a cardboard sign with his son's name on it. He was at every march, not out in front or otherwise ostentatious, but there—until the crackdown in 1987 ended the marches. In more fortunate countries, such as Panama once was, sons remember their dead fathers.

Carter's visit featured a rally in Fifth of May Plaza. The platform was there again, against the façade of the Hotel Internacional. The crowd was there, too, somewhat bigger than on October 11, 1971. A bigger effort had been made to collect it in the vain hope of outdoing the crowd drawn effortlessly by Arnulfo. The attempt would have been pathetic but for Señor Román Vega's being beaten to death in La Chorrera for exhorting people not to go. "When two people are riding the same horse in the same race, only one can win, the man in the front." Torrijos could not outdraw Arnulfo Arias, not even with Carter and other presidents alongside him.

The rally had some innovations. One was the cream of the American government, from Andy (Young) to Zbig (Brzezinski), on the platform. Another was a press platform opposite it from which R. M. Koster had a good view of the roll-taking operation that went on before. Every government department had its appointed place in the plaza, and there was much bustling about by supervisors with clipboards. Torrijos, too, had a new look, not drunk but not sober either. He seemed to have snorted something on the way from the exchange-of-instruments ceremony to the rally. His hair was disheveled and his grin lopsided, and as Carter spoke he hogged in beside him, staring at the American president from a distance of eight or ten inches and at each of Carter's pauses leering down at the crowd and pumping his right arm to cheerlead. Carter did well not to show disconcertion.

His speech had nothing memorable in it except for a sentence about human rights. Panama, he said, was making progress in this area. A man had been murdered that very morning for exercising his human right to free speech. Students had been murdered and beaten for that two nights before. But what makes Carter's sentence chilling in retrospect is that, bad as it was, the state of human rights in Panama was better that afternoon than ten years later.

Carter's visit, despite its including a rally in Fifth of May Plaza, was not, properly speaking, the denouement or resolution of the scene with which chapter 6 begins. That came on October 1, 1979, when the Canal treaty went into effect, when the Canal Zone ceased to exist as a juridical entity, when the Panamanian flag was raised on Ancon Hill. The flag raising took place at eight in the morning. The weather was good. It was a moving spectacle. Americans could feel both proud and sad for their country: proud that it had freely relinquished a role which had never really fitted it but which it had nonetheless played with more decency than most other nations; sad that it could not have done so at such a time and in such a way as to have advanced democratic values in Panama. Panamanians, likewise, were liable to have mixed feelings. In one sense, their country was at last whole. In another, it was sick unto death.

Later that morning, a ceremony took place in Curundu, about half a mile from Fifth of May Plaza, in what till that day had been the Canal Zone. Jimmy Lakas and Walter Mondale spoke, as well as the Mexican president, López Portillo. At least a hundred thousand Panamanians walked through parts of the former Zone to attend. There may have been twice that many, for many came from the interior and from Colón, but they were very quiet, very orderly, like children on their best behavior, as if the ghosts of the old Canal Zone police might at any moment spring up and chase them back into Panama City. And like children they looked about them wide-eyed. Everything they saw was now Panama's. Panama, on the other hand, belonged to the Guardia. There had been and would be much demagoguery about how the fruits of the treaties would be put to optimum social use for the people. It was all lies. The people, no doubt, suspected as much, which may have been another reason why they were so quiet that morning.

That morning, Omar Torrijos stayed home. It was the most decorous thing he did in twelve years as a tyrant.

8

TORRIJOS THE POLITICIAN

For all his ranting at the 1971 rally, Torrijos found political illegitimacy rankling. Either he guessed or had heard directly from Nixon that though talks might be held, the United States would never make a treaty with a Panama openly under de facto rule. There was, besides, the matter of personal preference. Your Noriega has the honesty of gutter birth and wears the label of tyrant proudly. Torrijos, petty bourgeois, craved respectability. He and his crew were therefore at pains to procure some before going all out regarding sovereignty.

Essentially, it was a camouflage problem, and not a very tough one as such things go: make the whore look from a distance like Old Mother Hubbard. Nothing of substance was to be altered. That is, changes made since the coup were to be preserved. All those with power would still be in uniform. All those with real power would still fit into a small room. Panama would still be run to please their whims and appetites as these were modulated by Torrijos, and the only true political institution, the conduit along which support and petitions flowed upward, commands and favors downward to rank and file, would still be the Guardia Nacional. The thing, though, would now look more or less like democracy to those who didn't look closely, as well as to those who wished to be fooled, because of a plywood or pasteboard façade of legality and a few mock-up institutions.

The key tool in building this Potemkin village was a subdivision called the *corregimiento.* The verb *corregir,* "to correct," gives the noun *corregidor,* "corrector" or "magistrate." A *corregimiento* is where this personage operates. The office and jurisdiction were established by Alfonso XI of Castile in the fourteenth century and later exported to Spanish America. In Panama, lines were redrawn in 1904, after independence from Colombia. *Corregimientos* were made roughly equal in physical area. They were unequal in population, which was why Torrijos found them handy. A few, in urban centers, were densely inhabited: more than 15,000 voters, for example, in Bella Vista, Panama City. One or two, meanwhile, had fewer than 100. Most had fewer than 1,000—in other words were easy to manipulate if you controlled public funds and the means of violence. What Torrijos did (though exactly who thought it up no one now seems sure of) was decree the election of representatives, one from each *corregimiento.*

In the old system, a majority of the deputies represented a majority of the country. Now tiny communities all but lost in the jungle sent representatives to the assembly, and that was wonderful, but you could form a majority in that assembly from the representatives of about 3 percent of the populace, and that was worthy of wonder also. The point of Torrijos's scheme was 180 degrees from democracy, to enable a detested minority that had imposed tyranny by force to go through the empty motions of democracy while tightening its grip on the country.

Besides employing grossly unequal constituencies, the election for representatives proceeded under the most antidemocratic conditions imaginable, with the means of communications controlled by the government and all political parties outlawed. All but the PDP, the communist party, but it hardly counted since, even as the sole party extant, it had only a handful of adherents. No parties meant no party nominations. There was what the government called "free nomination." Any resident could run in his or her *corregimiento* by getting a certain small minimum number of signatures, with a maximum of five candidates per slot, the five with the most signatures qualifying.

This system, it will be noticed, is child's play to rig if you are the one authenticating the signatures. Anyone you really don't want can be kept off the ballot. If you're hoggish, all the candidates can be yours, to the point where it doesn't matter who gets elected. That was what happened, partly through the regime's efforts and partly because its opponents, forbidden from participating collectively, refused to participate as individuals. To do so, they held, would legalize the swindle. In private, they reasoned that staying out cost them nothing. Few if any would be permitted to win, certainly not enough to control the assembly, while by not taking part they saved themselves money and denied Torrijos the chance to claim he had whipped them. In *corregimiento* after *corregimiento,* therefore, the voters' only choice was between regime flunkies.

The job of getting these qualified as candidates was done by an outfit called the Dirección General para el Desarrollo de la Comunidad (DIGEDECOM, General Directorate for Community Development). Torrijos established it in July 1969 and put one of his boyhood buddies in charge, Angueto Riera Pinilla. DIGEDECOM never fulfilled its assigned mission, which was to promote development in backward areas, but became instead a bureaucratic monstrosity, a font of *botellas* and booty for regime faithful. It spent enormous sums and produced nothing, except a certain number of newly rich, but it did enable Riera to range the countryside and get to know people in every far-flung cranny. When elections were convoked for representatives, he decided that his hour had come, since these would elect the next puppet president, but above all he wanted to proceed correctly. He went to Torrijos and asked if the general had picked his man yet. Torrijos said no, not yet. Would the general mind, Riera asked next, if he sought the office? No, said Torrijos again, no he wouldn't. Then, said Riera, he'd try, using DIGEDECOM. *Adelante,* said Torrijos, go right ahead. Riera, after all, was his boyhood buddy. Torrijos may also have thought that Riera and DIGEDECOM might infuse some excitement into the campaign, over which no one was very enthusiastic. With that, Riera went off and began organizing, and DIGEDECOM took on the look of an ersatz political party, anointing candidates and spending money and doing what it could to get people elected.

The elections were held in August 1972. Everyone was obliged to vote, with heavy penalties for abstainers. But since in most of the races only dictatorship hacks were running, many people cast blank ballots, or put insulting messages into their envelopes, or simply filled them with toilet paper. Still, 505 representatives were elected, and labeled "the people's power" and cited to meet in New Panama Gymnasium. Before they could do so, however, all dignity was driven from the proceedings, along with any remaining pretense of democracy.

At an informal meeting the night before their convening, the representatives, a majority anyway, endorsed Angueto Riera for puppet president. In the meantime, though, Torrijos had promised Lakas that he might stay on—had either forgotten his chat with Riera or had come under Lakas's sway, as in times past—blackmailed, bullied, bluffed, it didn't matter. Torrijos and the Guardia staff therefore threatened Riera with all kinds of horrible reprisals if he didn't withdraw, and the next day, at a solemn ceremony attended by the cabinet and the diplomatic corps and the gorilocrats in their dress uniforms, with Monseñor McGrath in attendance as a gate-crasher (for he sought the seats of power as the sparks fly upward), Lakas was elected unanimously.

R. M. Koster, meanwhile, was fearing for his sanity. In February that year, he'd published a novel called *The Prince,* set in a fictitious banana republic. About two years before, while composing the book's twenty-fourth chapter, it had pleased him to imagine a cynical potentate who finagled a bogus assembly into existence and installed it in the national gymnasium and manipulated its deliberations and actions. Now Torrijos was doing the very same, even to the group's venue! Coincidence? Koster couldn't conceive it, the odds were too great. More likely, God was plagiarizing him.

Riera, for his part, was acting predictably, adhering with scruple to all probability's laws. A day or two before, having canvassed the 505 and counted votes carefully, he'd concluded he would certainly be the next president. Hence, everyone he knew and many he didn't would soon be dropping by to congratulate him. All, most likely, would be thirsty. He had, therefore, laid in a stock of refreshments—rum, whisky, vodka, gin, and so forth. Seeing his hopes smashed, he refuged in his house, gathered his few authentic friends about him, and immersed himself in silent communion with Bacchus. Some hours later, he began to speak.

"Yo soy el Excelentísimo Señor Presidente de la Republica!" he began hoarsely, with all the strength of his lungs, and proceeded to issue decrees and make appointments, to dismiss commandants and ambassadors, to find replacements for them among the faithful who were drinking beside him. The world outside had already forgotten him, but Riera continued, in the tyrannical mode of drunks everywhere, to exercise his imaginary mandate, promulgating laws, making proclamations, delivering grandiloquent orations, till at length he was overcome—not by the general staff, not by Torrijos, but by alcohol. With that, he disappeared from public life as if the earth itself had swallowed him up, and no one has ever heard of him again.

Besides being unrepresentative, the representatives had no power. They met once a year for the month of October to hear a report from the puppet president and approve laws prepared by the executive—that is to say, by the Guardia general staff—laws they had no power to amend. In theory, they were free to disapprove them, but in practice the least hint of any indiscipline would at once ignite the gorillas' fury, and bring browbeating, threats of reprisals, and so forth, till the measure that had been in trouble regained strength miraculously and took its due place among the laws of the land. As when, in 1980, the representatives, meeting in the old legislative palace adjacent to Fifth of May Plaza, were at the point of rejecting an unpopular treaty with Colombia, the building was surrounded by soldiers with orders to let no one out till the thing passed. Thus instructed, the representatives reviewed the treaty and found it much less offensive than on first reading and passed it by a healthy majority.

During the rest of the year, the representatives served as councilmen in the districts where their *corregimientos* were located, while a small number, chosen for loyalty in the manner of prison trusties, got to serve on a so-called legislative council, which rubber-stamped bills that couldn't wait till October. The plumpness of their salaries, however, somewhat consoled the representatives for the vacuity of their offices, and as people palpably close to if not in power, it was hard to deny them credit and even harder to collect. In short, they lived well, and in Panama City during their annual session, they disported themselves with conspicuous merriment, giving much custom to the capital's restaurants and cantinas and (since most were male) ladies of the evening, entirely in the manner of representatives elsewhere, those with real functions and actual clout.

During the first meeting of the first assembly, in October 1972, the representatives were supposed to draft a constitution. The decree stipulated a maximum of one month for this endeavor, much too short a time to do the job. In fact, a draft was prepared well beforehand and passed to the members for rubber-stamping. They complied at once without offering a single change. This document commends itself to the attention of scholars as the only such to mention a specific individual. In the course of 276 articles, it pretended to define the structure of Panama's governance. Then in article 277, at last, it got down to business, recognizing Omar Torrijos as the "Maximum Leader of the Panamanian Revolution" and conferring upon him the power "to coordinate the entire work of public administration, to appoint and remove members of the Cabinet and of the Legislative Commission, to appoint the Comptroller and Deputy Comptroller of the Republic, the Directors General of autonomous and semiautonomous institutions, and the Magistrates of the Electoral Tribunal." Without pausing for breath, article 277 further empowered Torrijos to appoint the chief law and law enforcement officers and (with the approval of the cabinet he himself named) to celebrate contracts, negotiate loans, and direct foreign relations.

Thus the dictatorship begat the Assembly of Representatives of Corregimientos, and the assembly rebegat the dictatorship, the same proxy dictatorship as before but now baptized with hogwash as constitutional. The whore was now refurbished to look respectable—from a distance, of course, to those who wished to be fooled. The government of the United States, for instance, could now afford to be seen in public with it.

Practically speaking, Torrijos ran Panama out of his hat. Wherever he was, there was Panama's government. He spent his time mainly in three houses: a house on the beach at Farallón; a house on the model cooperative at Coclesito, where he kept his favorite pet campesinos; a house on Fiftieth Street in Panama City. Anyone he needed to see was brought to him, usually by helicopter if he was in the interior. His wife, whom he had married in 1954, lived a few blocks from the house on Fiftieth Street with their three children, but by the mid-1970s he rarely went there and never spent the night.

Torrijos got drunk every day. Every night, that is, he went to bed plastered. After 1972, on some fifty occasions, Jack Vaughn never saw him when he wasn't drinking. On the occasion when Torrijos referred to his brother Monchi's drug trafficking, he and Vaughn rode around Panama City in an air-conditioned van with one-way windows—the twentieth-century equivalent of Harun al-Rashid's tours of Baghdad. As they talked, Torrijos swigged from a bottle of Chivas, which when not swigging from he held clasped between his thighs.

Torrijos's main drinking partners were Rodrigo González and Ernesto Pérez Balladares, "Rory" and "Toro." They were also his chief economic advisers. The combination is not as odd as it sounds, for during most of Torrijos's time as a tyrant Panama's economy was on a binge, guzzling borrowed Eurodollars and petrodollars—in fact, almost any sort of borrowed currency. While not drinking with Torrijos, Rory managed the copper mine at Cerro Colorado, a wonderfully profitable enterprise for everyone but the people of Panama, though not an ounce of ore was ever extracted. Loan after loan came through for feasibility studies and development surveys. Everyone had a grand time till the morning after.

A key figure in the carousing was Nicolás Ardito Barletta, "Nicky." He'd studied economics at Chicago, and the phrase "economic planning" rang in his title; nonetheless, his function was in another line. Barletta was a minstrel, a singer of tales: tales that enabled Panama to borrow money, and tales that enabled Torrijos to hide where it went. Instead of a lute or lyre he had his own person, his earnest good looks, his excellent English, his first-rate Ph.D. These helped sustain the illusion wrought in his tales that Panama's economy was actually planned, and planned in accord with the science of economics as formed and taught by Milton Friedman and George Shultz, not a haphazard slush fund for the enrichment of brigands. Barletta gave Torrijos a valuable dimension of respectability, in the view of men who counted in the United States and in Europe, bankers, politicians, civil servants, directors of international organizations. His prostituting of his person and schooling was invaluable in the looting of Panama's credit.

Also in Torrijos's entourage was José de Jesús Martínez, "Chuchú." He was a professor who lost his post at the National University because of the coup, then later joined the Guardia as a private and became a member of Torrijos's escort. The sad part was he thought he was making progress. Somehow he found it manly to serve with a force that oppressed its own country, and meaningful to be a poltroon's court philosopher. Along with Rómulo Escobar and Gabriel García Márquez, Martínez helped make Torrijos respectable to the intellectual left in Latin America, a class which (like bankers in the United States and in Europe) has more influence than it merits.

Escobar and Gabriel Lewis were good examples of what Torrijos meant by his boast of hitting with left and right simultaneously. They were left and right in background as well as in politics, pure *pueblo* (common people) and *rabiblanco,* respectively, and potent instruments both. Lewis had as much savoir faire as Escobar had intellect. For years, as Panama's ambassador in Washington, he successfully presented himself as living proof that Torrijos and Panama's succeeding tyrants were pro–U.S., thereby doing them great service and his country great harm.

As for what the men around Torrijos were after, some like Jimmy Lakas were getting rich, and some like Escobar were getting even, and some like Juan Materno were getting ahead, but all were indulging a fascination with power, as were the general's literary groupies. Power is the right and capacity to survive others, is always based on death and people's fear of it, and confers a feeling of invulnerability that is highly enjoyable to those with a taste for it, as enjoyable (it seems) as sex, yet longer-lasting. Some who crave the feeling, however, are too poor in spirit to come by power directly, hence seek a beggar's high in its effluvium. R. M. Koster noticed a cognate phenomenon at a brothel in Pamplona, Spain, in July 1953. At least two dozen men slouched outside the place, too poor to go inside and partake but so fascinated that they hung around, as it were sniffing.

Torrijos liked to denigrate those around him, especially the intellectuals among them, as in the terrible insults he rained upon Escobar, before a houseful of important guests, when the latter got drunk at Torrijos's forty-eighth birthday party. No one with self-respect would have borne the treatment all received at one time or another, but then no one with self-respect would have been in Torrijos's entourage to start with. At times, too, however, he showed these hangers-on affection, for he couldn't bear to be alone. He and they were well matched.

Like many *interioranos,* Torrijos was superstitious, but with him it was more than a quirk, a method of thought. He didn't analyze things but rather played hunches. He wouldn't go step by step on a linear path but would let a thing mull in his head till an answer came to him, by feeling if you will, or intuition. People trained to reason things out find this method bizarre and often look down on it, calling it "feminine," but there's no evidence it isn't well suited to fields like politics, and certainly it worked well for Torrijos. By his own measure, he was successful: he stayed in power. Like all successful politicians, he kept his word to his peers, lying only to aides, adversaries, and the public. When he became commandant, infighting among top Guardia officers ceased. This can only have meant they could trust him to deal with them fairly.

He had two great assets. One was his flexibility, which is another way of saying he believed in nothing. He forged a heterogeneous coalition symbolized in the persons of his adviser-collaborators Rómulo Escobar and Gabriel Lewis, Chuchú Martínez, and Rory González. *Rabiblancos* and communistoid revanchists, leftist intellectuals, and greed-ridden bourgeois—all these sorts supported Omar Torrijos. Second was his ability to keep silent, never opposing anything anyone said, thus allowing all to believe he was with them. Everyone could have his own Torrijos.

Properly speaking, though, he was not devious. He pumped Jack Vaughn openly for information. "Tell me about Linowitz and Bunker," referring to Sol Linowitz and Ellsworth Bunker, the chief U.S.

treaty negotiators. Or, "What do you think of Kissinger?" Every conceivable question: his curiosity was never ending. And all the time, too, he openly curried favor. Every time Vaughn arrived in Panama, he found a gift from Torrijos, or a helicopter waiting for him at the airport, or a car and driver at his hotel. And Torrijos paid in kind for Vaughn's opinions, trading information freely in return. About *mi gangster,* for example, about Tony, his executioner and familiar fiend:

"I realize a lot of people think I've become wealthy, but I'm nothing compared to Noriega. Noriega's my bagman. A lot of people think it's Rory, but Noriega is my principal guy. He's the funnel for our big money operations, but he dwarfs me in terms of wealth. He is really one rich gangster."

Torrijos had millions, of course, business interests, real estate holdings in Spain and elsewhere, but by standards in vogue in Panama in the time of the tyrants his greed was moderate. Where power corrupted him mainly was in his vanity. He couldn't bear benefaction. He'd grovel for it when his need demanded, but then his benefactor had better watch out. Somoza and Boris Martínez learned that the hard way. He couldn't bear incorruptibility either. That's the lesson Floyd Britton and Héctor Gallego learned. Such people mocked him merely by existing—and threatened him also, for he tyrannized mainly by corrupting.

Despite his considerable political talents, things were never easy for Torrijos after the passage of the Canal treaties. To begin with, verbally abusing the United States was a form of spiritual masturbation to which he and his entourage were addicted, on which the great part of their self-esteem seemed to depend. There was no question of their giving it up, but adopting the treaties obliged them to curtail the practice in public, and meanwhile here and there to say something friendly about (for example) President Carter's statesmanship, or the American people's sense of fairness, thereby doing themselves psychic damage, for it's always damaging not to be yourself. More, since the new treaties supposedly resolved all differences between Panama and the United States, their adoption denied the Torrijos regime, at least temporarily, use of a traditional Panamanian policy employed in one way or another, justly or not, by every Panamanian government since Dr. Amador's and continuously by Torrijos himself: that of blaming problems on the gringos. It is true that within a few years, through the unremitting stupidity of U.S. governments, the dictatorship recovered use of the policy. But not fully. For best results, while blaming the gringos, one pointed (or shook one's fist) at the Canal Zone, but now the Zone was gone forever.

But none of this was the principal damage, nor that the pledges Torrijos made to gain U.S. Senate ratification for the treaties weakened his hold on the country and whetted the people's appetite for democracy. The main damage done by the treaties was that the instant they were adopted, all justification for the dictatorship vanished—the justification Torrijos claimed for it, since no valid justification had ever existed. As of nightfall on March 16, 1978, Torrijos could no longer claim that Panama was locked in a deadly struggle with a world power and that any dissent aided the adversary. This was twaddle, of course, but Torrijos claimed it. It gave him something to say, and may have been believed by his supporters, and helped them calm their consciences, those who had them. Once the treaties were adopted, no scrap of justification remained for Panama's military dictatorship. From then on, those who perpetuated it did so strictly from greed or power lust or sadism, or from all three.

These, unfortunately, proved sufficient. The dictatorship endured. But in a maimed fashion, altogether without the vigor that characterized it at times during the prelude to the Canal treaties. It is very hard for human beings, no matter how vicious, to proceed without any moral purpose.

Torrijos seems to have grasped this, if not very firmly. He seems to have had an intention to end the dictatorship—but only a weak and intermittent intention such as the road to hell is proverbially paved with ("I will be true to the wife, / I'll concentrate more on my work"), the intention of a lush with three drinks in him, and another waiting close at hand on the bar, to cut down on the booze someday in the near future. He spoke of his and the Guardia's withdrawal from politics. He even acted. On October 11, 1978, he let article 277 of the constitution expire, the article that named him head of the government and gave him all sorts of special powers. On that day, too, his government offered and his assembly passed constitutional amendments moving Panama "toward a democratization of the governmental system," with direct, popular election of the president in 1984, along with a legislature whose districts reflected demography.

But what laws say doesn't matter where laws aren't followed. On October 12, 1978, constitutional changes passed the day before not withstanding, Torrijos still ran Panama just as he pleased. The commandant of the Guardia could still toss the president from office, and did so on four occasions in the next ten years. And democracy doesn't come in fractions. No amount of fiddling with the governmental system made the slightest practical difference so long as the Guardia—and Torrijos was part of it—had the means and will to tyrannize. And the Guardia kept both, with the enthusiastic urging (as if such were needed) of its dependent flatterers and flunkies, and the material and moral support (both were very useful) of its patron the United States of America.

Power is sweet. It is also addictive. Sadism and greed are hard habits to break. Both are self-perpetuating in institutions like the Guardia Nacional, with each brutalized and corrupted rank dumping its filth on the rank below. And if anyone, gorged with power or sick of brutality or gagging at the stench of corruption around him, had the good intention to end the tyranny and make Panama clean again, he was instantly forced to pinch it from his mind by fear of his colleagues, or fear of having to pay for his crimes. So Panama's oppressors, like those they oppressed, were powerless to end the dictatorship. The dictatorship lurched on, bereft of even the ghost of a moral purpose, a source of damage to itself and the country, till those who were part of it were as wretched as those who were not, neither having a country fit to live in.

On that same October 11, Torrijos chose a new puppet president, a trim and agile puppet to replace the rhino-jowled, hippo-sterned Jimmy Lakas. This was Aristides Royo, a lawyer then not quite forty whose good looks and glib tongue commended him to Torrijos as cosmetic to Panama's image. In this respect, he was less a figurehead (whose nautical associations suggest seaworthiness and thus intrepidity) than a hood ornament, and his presentable shallowness was admirably captured by Senator Paul Tsongas of Massachusetts, who told R. M. Koster that Royo looked like a Jordache advertisement. Royo had been briefly minister of education and had a chance to display his servility to those in uniform on the occasion of a teachers' protest. When he refused to receive their representatives, the protesters sat down in the street outside the ministry, causing a major rush-hour snarl. The sergeant directing traffic, on learning the problem, went to Royo's office and told him to come down and speak to the teachers and get the street clear, and Royo at once complied in every particular.

Besides being minister of education, Royo had been one of the treaty negotiators and had had a leftist background while in school. Otherwise, he had no qualifications, but the position did not call for many. He handled the day-to-day details of administration, made speeches, and cut ribbons. All decisions were still made by Torrijos, in consultation with his disparate advisers and, of course, with the Guardia general staff.

Torrijos, for his part, had a new hobby: Nicaragua. He was helping topple his benefactor Somoza and put the Sandinistas in power.

This effort became more or less public in October 1977, when the Sandinistas' best field commander, Edén Pastora (nom de guerre: Comandante Cero), retreated into Costa Rica and was interned. The Costa Ricans allowed him to go to Panama, supposedly to stay there out of mischief, but within a week he had returned to Nicaragua via Cuba, with the advice and consent of Panamanian authorities. Panama's and Torrijos's involvement in the Nicaraguan civil war did not become all-out and open, however, until August 1978, after Pastora seized the National Palace in Managua and taking most of the legislature hostage. The hostages were traded for political prisoners through negotiations in which Panama's ambassador played a leading role, and these, Pastora, and his soldiers were extracted to Panama on Panamanian civilian and Venezuelan air force planes. The lot were then debriefed and tended to medically in the Guardia cuartel at Tinajita and then sent on to Havana. From then on, Panama was openly a rest area for Sandinista fighters, a transit point for Sandinista recruits on their way to Cuba for training, and, most significantly, the Sandinistas' chief source of weapons.

This provision of weapons, it should be stressed, was not a philanthropic endeavor. Fat profits were made in Panama from Nicaragua's agony, chiefly by Colonel Manuel Noriega. He set up a thing called the Club de Caza y Pesca (Hunt and Fish Club), which was legally empowered to import firearms, and thus to obtain export permits in the United States. The club's president was a former G-2 agent named Carlos Wittgreen. Its agent in Miami was a Guardia captain named López Grimaldo, who was also Panama's vice-consul. López ordered the weapons and got the export permits. Wittgreen took delivery in Panama and saw them safely on their way. The money rolled in.

Until March 1979, when Nicaraguan authorities found recoilless rifles, rocket launchers, and machine guns under a load of tires that had just crossed the border from Costa Rica. A check of the serial numbers with U.S. authorities established that the weapons had been manufactured in the United States and sold by Johnson Firearms of New Jersey to Universal Firearms, Miami, Florida. Universal then shipped them, on valid export permits, to Club de Caza y Pesca in

Panama City. When the story broke, Wittgreen got indicted in Miami (alas, in absentia) and López Grimaldo had a spot of trouble. His diplomatic status saved him. The only ones really hurt were the U.S. weapons manufacturers and wholesalers. From then on, Noriega bought mainly in Europe.

A buyer was Mike Harari, an Israeli, once and perhaps still a high Mossad officer. Harari's involvement suggests that Noriega sold to both sides, for Israel backed Somoza to the bitter end, his father having been one of the first to recognize that country's existence. Noriega is known to have helped both sides later, remaining buddies with the Sandinista commander and president of Nicaragua, Daniel Ortega, while facilitating U.S. aid to the contras. The weapons were stored at the Guardia base adjacent to Tocumen International Airport, outside Panama City, and then moved by air to Costa Rica, usually aboard aircraft the Guardia confiscated from drug traffickers, flown by soldier-of-fortune pilots (who earned $2,000 per trip), and convoyed by Panama air force fighters—this not to protect the transports from interdiction but to keep the mercenaries flying them honest, since anyone flying a load of arms around Central America could get himself a deal quickly enough. The arms then came under the watchful eye of Juan Echevarría, the Costa Rican minister of security, who was Noriega's partner, and while many then went northwest to Nicaragua, many more were still in storage when the war in Nicaragua ended and were later marketed in El Salvador and elsewhere, as well as to the Sandinistas' enemies the contras.

Then there was Dr. Hugo Spadafora and the Victoriano Lorenzo Brigade. Spadafora was bored with being vice-minister of health and sickened by the corruption around him and teetering on the brink of a crisis of conscience as Torrijos's fake revolution got harder and harder to believe in. He needed a spritz of action and danger, a cleansing immersion in a new cause. With Torrijos's approval, he raised a force for the war in Nicaragua.

Victoriano Lorenzo, for whom the outfit was named, was a populist *guerrillero* cognate to Mexico's Emiliano Zapata and Nicaragua's Augusto Sandino (though earlier than both), active on the liberal side in Coclé and Veraguas during the 1899–1902 civil war. The volunteers themselves ranged from overweight intellectuals to ex-*guardias* but were mostly idealistic university students. They trained for a few weeks on Coiba Island, then went on to a camp in Costa Rica, their number by then pared to about one hundred. There was no question of their fighting as a unit—they had no command structure, no veterans, no NCOs—though that seems to have been Spadafora's original intention, and though the Torrijos regime and others gave that impression in references to "Spadafora and his Panamanians." The volunteers were parceled out among existing formations and seem to have fought as well as anyone else, there being recruits from all over the world serving with the Sandinistas. Panama, meanwhile, had a public relations presence in the struggle against Somoza and put itself openly in the forefront of supporting the Sandinistas.

Helping the Sandinistas was a way for Torrijos to conciliate the domestic left as the phoniness of his revolution grew more and more patent and as he snuggled up to the United States, stroking senators and holding still for affronts like the DeConcini reservation. It was also a way to gain foreign allies, to cement his alliances with Presidents Carlos Andrés Pérez in Venezuela and Rodrigo Carazo Odio of Costa Rica, and to keep his hand in with Castro and the Cubans. Panamanians, meanwhile, like most Latin Americans, loathed Somoza. Opposing him gave Torrijos a new and popular theme for bluster after their orgy of unfulfilled bluster over the treaties. And Somoza, though no one knew it, had saved Torrijos's career as a tyrant. Torrijos's vanity, bruised by the memory of this temporary dependence, demanded Somoza pay for having helped him. Storing up credit with the Sandinistas also paid off in power and prestige.

The United States had invented the Somoza dynasty and had supported it unstintingly for decades. Now, as Noriega would do in 1988, the current Somoza had united every decent person in his country against him, while nauseating much of the international community, so that at last, belatedly, the thinking portion of the U.S. government realized that the dynasty was doomed. There was nothing to do but end it as quickly as possible, but on no account should Somoza himself be captured. He was so bespattered with crime that those who'd used him as an instrument were badly soiled also. His capture would mean a trial; a trial would bring the whole mess out in public. A deal, therefore, had to be cut: shortening the war and saving some lives in return for Somoza's safe conduct out of the country. Unfortunately, however, the U.S. government did not have the Sandinistas' confidence. Torrijos, on the other hand, was able and willing to serve as go-between. So, as the Sandinistas closed in on Somoza's bunker, Torrijos, at Carter's urging, met with the Sandinista leadership at Puerto Limón, Costa Rica, along with with Presidents Pérez of Venezuela and Odio of Costa Rica, and persuaded the Sandinistas to let Somoza fly out to Guatemala, thus sparing the U.S. government much embarrassment.

Manuel Noriega made this sort of usefulness a rich source of power. What Torrijos craved and got from it mainly was importance, a chance to play a role on the world stage. There's the key to Panama's increased involvement in Nicaragua as of summer 1978. In June of that year, Torrijos shared a platform with Carter, but then, with the treaties done, he was shoved to the wings. At which his vanity suffered painful withdrawal symptoms, so he sought and found ways to push back into the limelight. There, also, was the key to another of his international adventures, providing a haven for the Shah of Iran.

The Shah fled Iran early in 1979 with his queen, Farah Diba, and settled at length in Mexico. In October, he went to New York for medical treatment. While he was in New York Hospital, on November 4, 1979, Iranian revolutionaries broke into the U.S. embassy compound in Teheran, captured the sixty-six Americans who were inside it, and held them hostage against the Shah's delivery to them to answer for crimes committed while he was in power. Jimmy Carter responded oddly. He was chief executive of a country whose territory had been forcibly invaded without provocation or warning, and whose officials stationed there had been taken prisoner—roughly the situation (though in miniature) of Franklin Roosevelt in 1942, after the Japanese invaded the Philippine Islands and captured its garrison. Carter's response, however, was that of a summer camp director upon the kidnapping of some of his charges. Instead of defending the country's honor and sovereignty, instead of obliging Iran to respect the United States, Carter concentrated on the hostages, moving heaven and earth to secure their release.

His first move was to unload the Shah, supposing foolishly that he could placate Khomeini and the revolutionaries. Unloading the Shah, however, proved tricky. On November 30, the Mexicans went back on their promise to let the Shah return after his treatment. Nor did anyone else seem to want him. Henry Kissinger, who had his nose deep in the business, compared the Shah to the Flying Dutchman. Actually, he was more like the garbage barge that wandered the Caribbean endlessly (or so it seemed) during the summer of 1987. No one wanted either, nor could the rejectors reasonably be blamed. Then, lo and behold, Panama agreed to receive him.

Torrijos was in Las Vegas, Nevada, when the idea came to him, watching Panama's great boxer Roberto Durán defend his lightweight title. Soon feelers were out between Washington and Panama City, and on December 11 Hamilton Jordan arrived at the house on Calle Cincuenta to do the deal.

Jordan and Torrijos had met at the treaty-signing ceremonies two years before and had instantly become the fastest of buddies—younger and elder brothers, one might even say, with Jordan calling Torrijos "Papa General." They had in common a fondness for drink, along with contempt for culture, schooling, and intellect, for norms and forms and rules and traditions in general, and for them especially as they concerned public affairs, for statecraft as an art and a profession, and for careful preparation as opposed to just winging it. A pair of cowboys, in short. Adolescent charm and impulsiveness were, in fact, their only endearing characteristics—and this only to those few amused by such traits. Fellows of that sort are dangerous at the helm of anything, even a skateboard.

On the occasion of arranging the Shah's asylum in Panama, Jordan was amateurish in the extreme. He went alone to Panama and saw Torrijos with no other American present, communicating solely through Torrijos's interpreter, who seems to have been Chuchú Martínez, though the U.S. ambassador to Panama, Ambler Moss, a Spanish speaker, was in the house on Calle Cincuenta in another room. He presented a request from Carter, made in the cause of world peace and in the name of the American people, that Panama take the Shah of Iran temporarily, a request that Torrijos instantly granted. Without conditions, according to Martínez, but eight years later Torrijos's first cousin, Colonel Roberto Díaz Herrera, disclosed that Torrijos received $12 million, apparently to spread around among Guardia brass, and the disclosure has a great ring of truth to it. Jordan then placed a call to Jimmy Carter, who breathed "Thank God!" at the news and then thanked Torrijos in Spanish. Four days later, the Shah and entourage arrived in Panama.

Here is Jordan's subsequent comment on the business: "Months of debate in the councils of our government had preceded the decision to allow the Shah to come to the United States. Omar Torrijos, sitting alone in a private house in Panama, puffing on his cigar, had made his decision in seconds." Jordan had the honor to be chief of the White House staff, yet shows his contempt for American democracy, with its intricate machinery of checks and balances, and his envy of the petty despot for having no such restraint on his use of power.

Martínez says that Torrijos's motive in accepting the Shah was to help Carter get reelected, to prevent a Republican, Ronald Reagan especially, from winning the White House in 1980. That may have been so. The $12 million, one feels sure, didn't hurt either, along with sugarplum visions of extortion, the Shah being rich and sick and friendless. Even before Jordan left to tell the Shah he was going to Panama, Torrijos was thinking of selling him a house of Rory's, and not a day passed during the Shah's stay when he wasn't pestered with this or that scheme for investment—a trap he never fell into (he was from the Middle East after all) but an annoyance that must have shortened his life. Mainly, though, the move put Torrijos back in the majors. That was his payoff for taking Carter's garbage.

The Shah's sojourn in Panama was generous of ironies. He was, not, for example, at all eager to go there, complaining to Jordan that Torrijos was a dictator. Jordan parried the complaint by insisting that "Torrijos was an honest man who was attempting to democratize his country." Was Jordan the world's biggest liar or biggest booby?

If the Shah didn't like Panama, the Panamanians certainly didn't like him. They had plenty of their own bloodthirsty thieves and saw no need to import others. There were anti-Shah demonstrations and Guardia repression, including an instance of spectacular brutality perpetrated against Dr. Miguel A. Bernal.

Four days after the Shah's arrival, Wednesday, December 19, Dr. Bernal organized a protest march to begin at 4:00 P.M. at the Church of Don Bosco. This was in Perejil, a part of Panama City built in the boom times during World War I—a large church with a Florentine bell tower set back from Avenida Central and faced by three-story wooden buildings painted blue-green, with shops at street level and apartments above. The Guardia had blocked traffic six blocks above, where two-lane Central becomes four-lane Vía España. About fifty or sixty people had collected on the sidewalk in front of the church and in the street before it, watched by a few people on balconies and by about a dozen foreign journalists, including two U.S. network TV film crews, who'd come down for the Shah but hadn't seen him and who hung about in the languid poses such people assume when on an assignment where there isn't much of a story. Also on hand were Majors Roberto Armijo and Julián Melo of the Guardia Nacional, and their driver and escort, and three or four *sapos* slouched in the mouth of a side street opposite the church steps.

The season hadn't turned, though by then it should have. The sun was out, but there was no breeze. Heat and moist air pressed down. A priest came out of Don Bosco and pulled the doors shut. In one of the apartments, a radio, on at full volume, called the fifth race from José Remón Racetrack.

A little before 4:30, demonstrators stretched a pennant across the street. It said something about the Shah and had swastikas on it. Dr. Bernal went toward the church. Majors Armijo and Melo went after him and stopped him on the sidewalk below the church steps. The programmed march, they told him, couldn't happen, "on orders from above." The constitution, Bernal reminded them, granted the right to demonstrate peacefully, the constitution put through by the military regime. By way of an answer, the two majors laughed at him mockingly.

Bernal turned and went up on the steps of the church. He had taken off his suit jacket and his tie but nonetheless looked more formal in his long-sleeved white shirt than most of those gathered below him—a well-built man in his mid-thirties, half an inch or so under six feet. He began to speak through an electric megaphone, very earnestly, his voice and shoulders charged with anger, but before he had said more than a few sentences, about two dozen *guardias* on motorcycles roared up with sirens blaring from the direction of Plaza Cinco de Mayo, followed by a patrol truck and two sedans full of G-2 agents. An opponent of the regime who was monitoring the Guardia radio that afternoon remembers hearing the signal for the attack, which was called Operación Relámpago (Operation Lightning, or Blitz).

The cyclists formed a V and drove at the demonstrators. They fled back and into the side street and to the church steps, and when they did, the cyclists halted. Dr. Bernal went down to speak to their commander, Captain Tomás Herron, but before he could say a word, Herron howled, "Here's Bernal!" and began striking him with his *tolete.* The G-2 agents piled from the cars and rushed up the church steps, shoving people aside with their left hands and flailing at others with the yard-long heavy hoses they carried. Then they turned back to Dr. Bernal.

In front went Captain Fritz Gibson, very tall and thin, of Barbadan ancestry, the most feared person in the G-2 after Noriega, nicknamed bilingually "Sangre" and "Captain Blood." He clouted Dr. Bernal in the face and seized his shoulder and hurled him toward the others. Dr. Bernal was pushed and dragged along and across the sidewalk while hoses thwapped heavily against his neck and shoulders and popped down onto the back of his head, and when he reached the street, the G-2 men bunched around him hosing him fiercely, hosing his back and shoulders and his hands where he held them clasped at the back of his head. He stumbled forward, bent low under their blows, and behind him stood Captain Blood, pushing a G-2 comrade with his left hand so as to have room to swing his hose, down and down and down, onto the back of Dr. Bernal's neck.

While this was happening, Doña Elvia de Wirz, who had been pushed up the church steps against its locked doors, rushed down and grabbed a G-2 man's hose arm. She was an elderly lady, gently bred, from the *rabiblanco* Lefevre family, and had served as Panama's envoy to Switzerland, but she rushed down to aid Dr. Bernal. So did Professor Víctor Navas. He and Doña Elvia were hosed and arrested, but their courage gave Dr. Bernal a moment of respite. People on the balconies, however, who threw water down on the *guardias* and G-2 men, only made them more angry, so that some rushed into the buildings to club in their homes.

When Dr. Bernal fell, as of course he had to, someone caught his left ankle and dragged him along while G-2 and uniformed *guardias* hosed him and kicked him, a slowly moving cluster of avid men—like ants, perhaps, dragging something too large to carry. They clustered about Dr. Bernal's twitching body, dominated by Gibson, who raised his hose arm high in the air before each blow and howled obscenities. At length, they reached the patrol truck, parked across from the church and about thirty yards down from it. They stood up, more or less sated, and one kicked Dr. Bernal two firm kicks in the stomach, and then they stoked him in back with Doña Elvia and Professor Navas and other prisoners who had meanwhile been collected.

When Dr. Bernal was taken from the patrol truck at La Comandancia, he began convulsing. "Take him to the hospital," said the duty officer. "Let him die there. Mi Coronel Noriega wants him dead." But when he was put back in the truck, he began vomiting. "Clean the truck with your tongue!" the driver ordered. Navas and Dr. Carlos Morales (also under arrest) got some water and washed the truck down, first sitting Dr. Bernal down against a wall. When the patrol truck arrived at Santo Tomás Hospital, a *guardia* who had ridden on it tried to handcuff Dr. Bernal to a stretcher and have him taken to the military wing, "by order of Mi Coronel Noriega." Dr. Edison Broce stopped him. "Tell your colonel that *médicos* command here. This patient's not moving."

Dr. Miguel Antonio Bernal was admitted to Santo Tomás Hospital semiconscious, convulsing, and bleeding internally. While he was in the emergency room, his hemoglobin dropped from fourteen grams to six. His head and body began to swell grossly in a syndrome that Panama's doctors were familiar with as attendant on hosing. He underwent surgery to stop his hemorrhaging and drain fluid from his brain. He survived.

Dr. Bernal recovered, though he suffered brain damage and for a time was unable to speak. No one, in fact, was killed in the Guardia's repression of anti-Shah demonstrations. The price Panama paid was modest, no more than a pittance for enabling Omar Torrijos to collect a bribe and preen as a world figure and play at the same table with the big boys. Lucky Panama, fortunate Dr. Bernal, to be so serviceable so cheaply!

Dr. Bernal's ordeal was documented by two U.S. network TV crews. The footage was never aired, no doubt because in those days Panama's tyrant was a certified good guy. We will, however, be glad to arrange a showing should Jimmy Carter and Hamilton Jordan care to view the result of their policy.

The Shah probably had no idea of the turmoil his arrival caused in Panama. For security reasons, he had disdained Rory's house in Chiriquí and stayed instead in a house owned by Gabriel Lewis on Contadora Island. The house was comfortable but the island itself claustrophobically tiny, and the sense of being trapped (which the Shah must have felt very poignantly, having nowhere else on earth to go) was further accentuated by the constant presence of G-2 goons and a platoon of frogmen camped on the beach below. Queen Farah, too, had her discomforts. Torrijos (the expansive host) "found her very desirable." He kept sending Chuchú to her to tell her "he would provide her with anything she wanted," and tried to get her off alone with him somewhere. And for relief he took her and the Shah to lunch with Mike Harari, assassin and arms dealer. And Noriega arrested one of their aides and held him incommunicado. And the monthly bill for their guards' food was $21,000. Asylum in Panama wasn't much fun.

In March 1980, the Shah and Farah went on to Egypt. The sense of constriction and menace had gotten to them. They accepted the hospitality of Anwar Sadat. Omar Torrijos went back into the wings for good. On the day of the Shah's departure, however, he gave evidence that, though a coward, a thief, and a murderer, he was perhaps most despicable in his bad taste. "He sent word to Contadora that the Queen's room was not to be touched. 'I didn't sleep with her, but at least I'll sleep in her sheets,' he told one of his friends."

It fits him exactly.

* * *

Torrijos's last effort to give his regime some semblance of moral purpose had to do with educational reforms proposed by the communists, who'd been given the ministry of education to play with. Panama's teachers opposed them because they were stupid, and although they were neither malicious nor much imbued with Marxist-Leninist doctrine, the people were suspicious of them on instinct, as they were by then of whatever the government proposed, and also out of hatred for its authors, for in Panama anticommunist feeling intensifies as one descends the socioeconomic scale. Resistance to the reform, ably managed by Miguel Bernal and Manuel Solís Palma, acting for the teachers, focused what had hitherto been a diffuse and inchoate resistance to the dictatorship.

The teachers went out on strike on August 31, 1979. The government replied by withholding their paychecks, thinking to break the strike quickly, since most of Panama's teachers lived hand to mouth on less than $300 monthly, and supposing they would have little sympathy from people who had made sacrifices to buy books and supplies and school uniforms. The tactic boomeranged. A radio station took up a collection, and within hours a crowd of people, many of reduced means, was lined up outside in the street waiting to make contributions—a marvelous advertisement for the teachers' cause and evidence of a solidarity with it that went across class and professional boundaries. The strikers took over the Republic of Venezuela School, near Plaza Cinco de Mayo in Panama City, and despite a constant Guardia presence around it for weeks all day long and late into the evening, people went to stand outside the building and show their support. Then, on October 9, the teachers announced a march and got a permit from the Guardia to hold it.

They announced it for 3:00 P.M., but it started late, partly because everything starts late in the tropics and partly because at 3:00 P.M. it was raining, a light but persistent rain that continued till about four, by which time the march was at last under way. No more than a thousand or so were on hand when it started, and none of them expected what was coming, any more than had the Guardia when it issued the permit, or else the thing would never have been allowed. The route was east along Avenida Justo Arosemena from the school, then north four blocks to Avenida Central, then west past the Church of Don Bosco to and through Cinco de Mayo, and on along Central through the old part of town, past Plaza Santana to Plaza Catedral. The officers of the teachers' union marched in the front, and every twenty yards or so there'd be a group with some school's flag or stretching a banner denoting some organization, but at the start there weren't a lot of people. R. M. Koster, working for *Newsweek* but in his heart a marcher, felt exposed in a way no one does when a crowd's large. Camacho's father was there, of course, in tie and jacket, holding a small cardboard placard with his murdered son's name on it, but at the start the march was certainly thin, with the whole thing filling the street for only two blocks. The funny things was, however, that if, after six or eight blocks, you happened to look round, you saw the whole street behind you filled with people all the way back to the school where the march had started. The head of the march kept advancing, but the tail didn't move, not for more than an hour after the march started, for people kept arriving to fill the street up.

Who was there? Teachers, of course, and doctors and nurses, and dentists and others in health care. They were among the most militant in those days because of the deterioration of health services, what with medicine money going for rallies and so forth, and the way politics was infecting the hospital system. And other professionals, and private-sector employees—the middle class, in short, and those on the fringe of it who, like Camacho's father, had special grudges. That was who was there at the start. But toward five o'clock one began seeing people . . . Toward five, when the head of the march was near Don Bosco, those marching there could look left, downhill, at intersections, and see Justo Arosemena four blocks to the south packed sidewalk to sidewalk with marchers. The march advanced like a string pulled out of a box, and the other end never came out, there was no end to it! By five, you had more than half a mile of avenue filled with people, and Panama's middle class just wasn't that big! Guillermo Sánchez had started with the teachers, but he was more of a stroller than a marcher, and by five o'clock he was more or less in the middle, and those walking beside him certainly weren't teachers but people who'd probably never been inside a school. By then who was there was the people of Panama—except, of course, for government employees. They couldn't afford to march, wouldn't risk being caught at it, but all the balconies were filled with people. Many government employees participated that way.

A huge multitude, in short, two or three hundred thousand, counting those who looked on in approval from sidewalks and balconies, chanting anti-Guardia slogans along with the marchers. As Sánchez's part of the march entered Plaza Catedral—and marchers were still coming in two hours after those in the lead did—a friend turned to him and said, "We've made a great procession, and without the saint." By "saint" he meant Arnulfo Arias. The march was against the dictatorship, not for any leader. And entirely peaceful, too, even good-humored. Many marchers had their children with them, walking beside them or in their arms—the best proof of peaceable intentions. And though the Guardia, prudently, kept out of sight, there was no theft or vandalism. That was the rule for all Panama's protest marches. All lawbreaking, if it came, came from the government, the supposed custodians of law and order. If violence occurred, it was always the work of the Guardia, or of the government's goon squads or paramilitaries.

It was a fine way to spend an afternoon, marching in a multitude, chanting rhymed slogans. It was hot, of course, sticky hot in October, and if it rained you got a little wet. Your feet hurt that evening. Your thighs and calves were stiff the next day. It was good, though, to know you were right and weren't alone. An afternoon spent that way was better than a day at the beach. It vented your anger, even made you feel brave, gave you the impression you were resisting. But the marches had no political meaning, and may even have prolonged the dictatorship's life, since in venting anger, in providing the impression one was resisting, they reduced real opposition and resistance. No doubt, the marches hurt Torrijos's vanity, but they didn't hurt his ability to rule.

On July 31, 1981, Omar Torrijos was killed in a plane crash. He was on his way to Coclesito with his latest girlfriend, a dental school classmate of one of his illegitimate daughters. A thunderstorm was in progress. His plane hit a mountain and exploded, the same plane he'd been in with Graham Greene when he told the latter his political objective. Everyone on board was killed.

There have been many allegations that Torrijos was murdered. Those suggested as being to blame have been, variously, the Cubans, the CIA, and Manuel Noriega. Torrijos's brother Moisés has claimed to have learned from a CIA agent, a supposed friend of Omar's, that the agency did the assassination. Chuchú Martínez is certain that this was the case. Graham Greene has doubts but thinks it might have been. Roberto Díaz Herrera, on the other hand, says it was the

CIA with Noriega. A story has been told about a bomb put on board Torrijos's plane at the last minute by a CIA dupe who thought it was a transmitter. This story features an American officer described here as a colonel, there as captain, who supposedly showed up at the field in Penonomé just before Torrijos's plane took off. The dupe, supposedly, was one of Torrijos's bodyguards, a corporal name Machasek. The bribe was supposed to be a quarter million—a bit high, one thinks, just for planting a transmitter, high enough to alert the most dupable dupe. How and when it was paid, the story doesn't say. Machasek isn't talking: he died in the crash. No proof of any sort is provided.

We think Torrijos's death was accidental. Both motive and opportunity seem scanty for an assassination. In March 1981, Cuba and Panama collaborated in a rather foolish adventure, the former training and the latter arming a group of *guerrilleros* introduced into Colombia. The Colombians captured them at once (probably on a tip from the United States) and extracted from Torrijos a denunciation of Fidel Castro delivered via a regime-controlled newspaper. This is a flimsy motive for an assassination, however, especially since Panama had been, was still, and would go on providing an invaluable bypass for Castro, whereby Cuba received U.S. technology and exported its goods, principally seafood, to the U.S. market. As for the CIA, why on earth should they murder Omar Torrijos? Every favor Washington asked, he performed promptly. Noriega had something to gain but not much. Torrijos's death speeded his rise to the top, but assassination is a risky business. One can get caught in the act, one can get caught afterward. The gain has to be great or the idea's stupid. No one has accused Noriega of being dumb. Far from Torrijos's being a threat to him, there is reason to believe he had Torrijos thoroughly blackmailed. Finally, would Noriega have killed Torrijos without leave from his CIA paymasters? We doubt it. Then there's the problem of how the thing was done. It's not that easy to get a bomb onto the aircraft of a national leader wary of possible attempts on his life. The odds against being able to plant a bomb when there happens to be a thunderstorm on the plane's route are prohibitively high for credence. We think Torrijos's death was accidental.

There is one circumstance, however, we feel we must mention. By July 1981, Ronald Reagan was in the White House, accompanied and advised by activist ideologues of nearly unbelievable bumbleheadedness—the idiots who gave us Iran-contra. Torrijos was Washington's faithful hound, but he covered himself by putting out anti–

U.S. rhetoric and visiting people like Qaddafi and Castro—not people at all, in the view of Colonel North and others like him, but demons straight from hell's deepest pit. As ideology is a substitute for thought, it may be that people in Reagan's government noted Torrijos's rhetoric and the mentioned visits while paying no mind to his record of loyal service. It is just possible that Reagan's bumbleheads were stupid enough to murder Omar Torrijos in order to get the CIA's star "asset" Manuel Noriega. Not likely but possible. If there's one thing our story teaches, the story of Panama in the time of the tyrants, it's that one should never rule out stupidity as the motive force behind U.S. policy.

Torrijos was fortunate in some respects to die when he did. It was already a lot less fun holding power in Panama than it had been while there were so many borrowed billions to send flying and the treaty issue to ride around the world on. The predicted post-treaty boom never occurred, mainly because the regime lacked the wit and credibility to put the treaties' bounty to sensible use. The soiled linen of scandal was already showing. Panama's credit was drying up. Torrijos was already somewhat depressed. His luck was that of a man who throws a huge party and dies just when the fun is beginning to flag, before he gets the bill or the hangover.

Torrijos's death was widely rejoiced at in Panama, in some homes noisily, with dance music at full volume, in some cantinas with such glee that the Guardia had to close the places down. Between the man himself and his poses, between the reality all to clear in Panama and the myth so avidly gobbled elsewhere, there were sidereal distances.

Guillermo Sánchez spent an unpleasant evening. He had to write a column but couldn't use his customary jocular tone. Nor would he speak well of Torrijos just because he was dead. He ended up recounting a few anecdotes that did not reflect ill on the dead man but said that he couldn't be pardoned for his irresponsible and thievish rule. The paper's editorial, which he also wrote, cost him no effort: a word of condolence for the family, a harsh judgment of the man himself, and a call for a constituent assembly and a prompt return to democracy as the only way to face the perils ahead. The next evening, however, he got drunk, even though in rigorous logic he shouldn't have celebrated. His livelihood, after all, seemed in peril. As things turned out, there was no danger. The Guardia and the *proceso* were endlessly productive of targets for gallows humor.

R. M. Koster, for his part, worked hard almost all night, but with satisfaction of two sorts. The *New York Times* had called asking if he would write something on the event for its op-ed page. He was alloted only 750 words, thus had to work very hard to find the right ones. He discovered, however, that few things are so satisfying to compose as a tyrant's obituary. By 4:00 A.M., he was satisfied with the words he had chosen. And he remains so. One sentence in the last paragraph was even prescient: "The only certainties for Panama's future are turmoil and unease." The sentence may not seem hard to think up. The future of many countries has the same certainties. But Koster would have liked very much to believe that Torrijos's death would bring some improvement. Try as he might, he could not. He was satisfied to be writing Torrijos's obituary, but he did not celebrate Torrijos's death.

Turmoil and unease was surely what Panama got. Would Torrijos, had he lived, have brought anything better? Possibly. In many Latin countries, there is a more or less regular cycle whereby military dictatorship of greater or lesser harshness alternates with more or less democratic civilian rule. In Panama, which modern militarism spared until 1968, the victim had no resistance to the disease. Thus the seizure has been unusually long and painful. It is just possible that had Torrijos lived he might have been instrumental in allowing Panama to recover more quickly. We don't mean to romanticize him. He was a tyrant, a murderer, and a thief. But he had political insight and two defects that might have proved useful. A few weeks before he died, he accurately predicted the result of the election scheduled for 1984, telling the Peruvian novelist Mario Vargas Llosa that the opposition would win if it united, and that if it didn't unite it would still win. Since Torrijos was vain, it is possible that his vanity, his desire to figure honorably in Panama's history, might have led him to allow the opposition's electoral victory to prosper politically. Finally, besides being vain, Torrijos was a coward. Some twenty years after Panama came under military tyranny, and solely because the tyrant of the moment, Manuel Noriega, turned against the United States, the U.S. government at last decided that it was in the U.S. national interest for democracy to be restored in Panama. Noriega resisted this decision. Had Torrijos lived and found himself in the same situation, being a coward he would have backed down. Panama would have been better off had Torrijos never been born, but since that happiness was denied it, Panama might have been better off had he lived a bit longer.

The Guardia certainly lost by his passing. Its ranking officers no longer had a trusted arbiter of their ambitions and jealousies. Colonel

Florencio Flórez, the chief of staff, succeeded Torrijos as commandant, but he was only a temporary solution. Koster required no prescience to advise the readers of the *New York Times* to expect a power struggle between Paredes, Noriega, and Díaz Herrera. One could hear their grunts and groans, wrestling for advantage, even through their protestations of grief.

The funeral ceremonies were ghastly. There was the Guardia staff, grouped round the coffin, on which reposed symbols of the defunct's power, his dress uniform and his canteen, the one he carried always filled with Scotch whisky—or a replica, since the original probably didn't survive the crash. And Flórez took the canteen and raised it on high, like a priest with the chalice, or a witch doctor about to munch a totem animal.

"Now I drink the substance of my commander!" he intoned. And a transfiguring substance it was, for after gulping a swallow or two, he at once began orating with the arrogance of the dead man himself!

One touch, though, was fitting: naming the new airport Omar Torrijos. Fifty million, after all, had been swindled building it.

9

LA PRENSA, THE SACK OF PANAMA, AND RUBÉN PAREDES

Roberto Eisenmann's grandfather immigrated to Panama early this century and prospered in business. His father stayed and prospered further. Eisenmann continued the tradition. But unlike many well-to-do Panamanians, he never fooled himself about the Guardia's takeover or collaborated with Panama's tyrants. In January 1976, while serving on the board of the Asociación Panameña de Ejecutivos de Empresa (Panamanian Association of Business Executives), he spoke some truth at a public meeting about the dictatorship's economic policies, for which, a day or so later, as he was driving his children to school, his car was stopped and boarded by goons with machine guns, and without being charged with a crime, much less convicted, in the clothes he had on, with what chanced to be in his pockets, he was put on a Guardia plane and shipped out of his country, one of a dozen business and professional leaders so treated in that swoop. Two years and two months later, after being shunted about in South America, he was in Miami on his way to prospering there when the U.S. Senate passed the Neutrality Treaty, and Omar Torrijos, as per his pledge to Robert Byrd and others, announced that exiles might return. Eisenmann called the others sent in January 1976, and on a day they all converged on Panama. That was in April 1978.

Eisenmann was then a few years shy of fifty, tall with slightly stopped shoulders and thinning blond hair and blue eyes that belied him absolutely. They were watery. He, however, was either firm or pigheaded, depending on whether or not one agreed with his views. He was glad to be going home, but he was not grateful. He was not even willing to live and let live. He spent the flight meditating on what he and others could do to promote democracy in Panama, and hit on the idea of establishing an independent, responsible newspaper. It was a fiendish idea of deliberate cruelty, like turning the kitchen light on when the roaches are feeding.

It took two years to get the paper started. That it started at all was a surprise to some. Neither Eisenmann nor those who joined him on the board of directors had any knowledge of the newspaper business. Fabián Echevers, the paper's first editor, was a lawyer, as was Ricardo A. Arias. Ricardo Bermúdez was an architect, Ricardo Arias Calderón a philosophy teacher. What they had were democratic convictions, and the courage of them, and the good sense to make some wise decisions. To put out a full-scale daily, for example, despite the costly plant that such implied. To raise the required million from many investors, none putting up more than five thousand dollars—this to spread the financial risk thinly (for who knew how long the regime would tolerate truth) and to preserve the paper's independence, to keep it from becoming the tool of one person or party. To call it *La Prensa:* the word means simply "the press," but the name is hallowed, charged with memories of other struggles against tyranny in Latin America, *La Prensa* of Managua's struggles against the Somozas, *La Prensa* of Buenos Aires and the struggles against Perón and other Argentinian despots. And finally to run it on a businesslike basis, since the press can be free only if it is self-sufficient economically.

Economics was the reason why the regime allowed the paper to publish. When Torrijos and the Guardia general staff discussed the matter, the arguments on both sides were nicely balanced. Everyone knew it was simpler to govern the country, and much simpler to loot it, if one controlled all the means of communication. On the other hand, Torrijos had made pledges to Jimmy Carter and to numerous senators with regard to liberalizing his rule. It would be inconvenient to break them so quickly. What tipped the balance was the regime's own experience in publishing. It had stolen four dailies from the Arias family but had never managed to make them pay their own way, though all four were run by experienced professionals and had the Guardia's resources behind them in the matter of bullying merchants to advertise in their pages. Let the paper open, Torrijos decided. In six months it would have to close.

At first, he seemed to have judged correctly. By the time *La Prensa* began to publish, in August 1980, the public had developed expectations of it that no mere newspaper could fulfil, that the oracle of Delphi could not have satisfied. Meanwhile, its directors, though clever and cultured, were new at the game, and it is not true (though Otto von Bismarck said it) that "journalism is the only profession that requires no training." More, every Panamanian is an expert on everything. People who rarely even glanced at newspapers, much less had thought about them with care, acquired instant yet very firm beliefs as to what and how *La Prensa* ought to be and generously passed them to Eisenmann and the others, who had no idea what weight, if any, to give them. The format, for instance. It was too serious, some contended. Others found it not serious enough. All it was, in fact, was innovative. For example, it had no "jumps," no "turn to page this or that" to finish a news story. Nonetheless, the format and everything else were complained of, and although for a short time the paper sold wildly, thereafter circulation dropped abruptly.

One day Guillermo Sánchez, who was contributing weekly essays on cultural subjects, came by the paper to drop off his piece and ran into Eisenmann. The two hadn't met till then, but Eisenmann invited Sánchez to give his opinion of the paper and of the criticisms people were making. Sánchez advised him to pay them no mind, and certainly not to change the paper's format. The whole paper could be a little more lively within the format already chosen, but mainly there had to be a clear distinction between news stories and opinion pieces. The news had to be presented with rigorous objectivity, even when it favored the dictatorship, *especially* when it favored the dictatorship. *La Prensa* was new; the public had to get used to it, and would never do so if the format kept changing. But its success or failure depended entirely on its credibility. These thoughts echoed Eisenmann's own inclinations, and from then on he and the others in charge were not distracted by peeves from without.

Shortly after that meeting, Sánchez went to work at *La Prensa,* correcting proofs at first but with widening responsibilities as time went on. In the street, he still heard griping about the paper. The most vitriolic came from opposition politicians, all of whom disliked *La Prensa* out of spite while craving to make it the instrument of their personal ambitions. One day, Sánchez heard the leader of an opposition party declare in full seriousness, "The most important job now is to wipe out *La Prensa!*" Another had made some banal comments over the radio and was miffed when the paper didn't pick up on them—out of charity, thought Sánchez to himself. "It should have been the lead story," the politician maintained in righteous indignation, "with a six-column head, with my picture!" Meanwhile, when Sánchez ran into government figures, in cafés or in the homes of mutual friends, they made fun of *La Prensa*'s amateurish reporting and tentative editorial line. "Why don't you hit us harder?" they would say grinning. "We see your arms swinging, but we can't feel the punches." In time, they came to wish they'd kept their mouths shut.

On August 19, 1980, scarcely two weeks after bringing out its first issue, *La Prensa* began its first exposé—this of a most aromatic swindle-in-progress cooked up by government insiders in cahoots with counterpart crooks in Venezuela. It involved an unneeded bridge over the Canal five miles from an adequate one already in service, to be built for a mere $150 million by a Venezuelan outfit, Van Dam, S.A., and a Panamanian firm, Sosa y Barbero. Van Dam had so far tried bridge building twice, failing both times. Sosa y Barbero had never come close to so vast a project. Still, contracts to both had been let without any bids, and the project itself approved without plans or studies, at the highest possible speed and in hermetic secrecy, till *La Prensa* got wind through an anonymous phone call. Swindle and exposé then proceeded in tandem, the one in no way deterred by the other. On the twenty-second, the government borrowed $100 million for the project. Three days later, *La Prensa* came out with details on the bidless contracts. And so on for two years till the scheme petered out. By then, tens of millions had been sent flying, without a brick laid or a girder erected, including $4 million to the ex–puppet president Lakas for inspecting work never begun, much less completed. So, score it Swindlers 1, Exposers 0? No, not quite.

On October 10, 1980, scarcely two months after bringing out its first issue, *La Prensa* began to rescue Panama's history from the falsifiers who'd been kidnapping it piecemeal. It was the eve of the twelfth anniversary of the coup, so *La Prensa* ran a two-page interview with Colonel (forcibly retired) Boris Martínez, coup maker and onetime Guardia commandant. Martínez spoke some truth about his benefactee Omar Torrijos, and *La Prensa* published it. At the time, it didn't seem to make much difference, but Torrijos appreciated its importance. It was the hardest blow ever struck him, he told a friend. A great deal of hot air had been spent inflating Torrijos. Now there was the supposed colossus—*Mi General,* the Maximum Leader—

reduced in a few plain words to his natural size: coward, drunk, and traitor.

La Prensa was already fulfilling its mission. The effect was not yet apparent, but that was because the mission was educational, and a teacher's work rarely shows effects at once. Panamanians were not so much taken in by the government's pap and propaganda as they were bored to somnolence by it. In the absence of truth, those not directly harmed by the dictatorship turned their attention from the country's affairs and dozed off in a moral siesta. In telling plainly what Panama's tyrants had done, what they were about, and what they were planning, *La Prensa* was waking people to the tyranny around them and teaching them to be angry at its crimes and lies. The people didn't wake fully or get truly angry until June 1987, but *La Prensa*'s work started almost with its first issue. That's what promoting democracy is: waking people up and making them angry.

This was civic duty, but not entirely. It was right and proper to wake people to the sad fact that thieves were stealing their country; it was a clear benefit to those who were wakened. But there was an egotistical element to it also. People who couldn't sleep, who were already angry—Eisenmann, Echevers, and others like them—woke up those who were sleeping, as insomniacs will. They couldn't sleep, so nobody else would. The insomniacs took their lumps, but they had fun also, waking people up and making them angry and especially landing swift kicks on the scrota of Panama's masters. Fighting tyranny is surely serious business, but it is not necessarily solemn.

Everyone connected with *La Prensa* took part in this work of rousing people from sleep and to anger, but the sharpest stings came from a column of short notes, "En Pocas Palabras" (EPP, "In a Few Words"), at the bottom of the last page of the first section. The column was contemplated in the original plan of the paper but did not begin appearing until October 1980. Its first incumbent was Miguel A. Bernal, the law professor, one of those exiled in January 1976 and *La Prensa*'s first foreign-news editor, whom we saw being hosed for patriotism in the last chapter. He established the column's location but soon found he couldn't do it and foreign news too. EPP then passed round the newsroom like flu or measles until Guillermo Sánchez ended up with it. The arrangement was that he would cook it from unused scraps of other people's news stories. As was bound to happen sooner or later but actually occurred almost at once, one night there were too few scraps to fill the column. Sánchez asked advice from Fabián Echevers. Now, Echevers is usually the most genial of men and, more than genial, sympathetic, but he earned his law degree at the Sorbonne and on Wednesday evenings, when the moon is full (or perhaps it is on new-moon Thursdays), imagines he is back in Paris and in self-defense adopts the French national character, delighting in the distress of fellow humans and seeking as best he can to exacerbate it. When Sánchez asked piteously, "What should I do?" Echevers replied without lifting his eyes from the copy he was reviewing, "Use your imagination."

Sánchez stalked back to his work station, his chest stuffed with rage, his system awash in adrenaline, and imagined a distinguished excretologist of Heidelberg and that scholar's professional evaluation of certain policies of Panama's government. Then, since Bernal had established the practice of illustrating the column with a photo of whoever figured in it most prominently, Sánchez cribbed a likely likeness of his imaginary coprographer from the cover of a children's book. Then, feeling much relieved, if not in fact exalted by his efforts, he went home and slept peacefully. On waking, though, he felt much trepidation, calmed only by the hope that Echevers had dumped the column before putting the issue to bed. But no, when the paper arrived, there was Herr Doktor Schmockfurstensteiner, gat toothed and melon headed, and there were his outrageous remarks. Trepidation swelled and persisted all day, yet when Sánchez arrived that evening at *La Prensa,* he was neither sacked nor scolded, nor scorned telephonically by a single reader. At that, a great clearness came over him and he decided he could get away with anything, and if not, in for a dime, in for a dollar. From then on, he disdained the leftovers of others and instead filled up the column with his own comments, and at times even produced his own scooplets. From then on, he gave free rein to his born-again Marxism, and "En Pocas Palabras" proceeded at a Grouchovian slouch, though mainly without imaginary Germans.

Like Groucho himself, the column was entertaining. Now and then, a joke misfired. Here and there, a whole column trudged a bit wearily, for Sánchez turned one out six days a week. And some people, of course, insisted on taking him literally, a fatal error, as when he illustrated some comments on a Panama-Cuba trade agreement with a close-up photo of a Sumerian tablet and was complained to by a pair of old duffers, co-breakfasters at his café, for not translating the text into good Christian Spanish. Most of the time, however, most people found EPP amusing. The least likely places, in fact, harbored EPP fans. In 1982, in the time of the tyrant General Rubén

Paredes, after *La Prensa* had been closed down on his orders, his puppet president, Ricardo De la Espriella, summoned the directors to the palace to discuss the conditions on which it might reopen. Eisenmann and the others were waiting in an anteroom when De la Espriella's secretary tiptoed up. "Don't let him make you drop 'En Pocas Palabras,' " she whispered.

EPP amused astringently. Not all its stings were inflicted on Panama's tyrants and the sycophants around them. These received plenty of torment via ridicule—and ridicule's stings are especially painful to Latins, and even more so to Latins in uniform. But the people of Panama also were stung by the column. The more clearly Sánchez displayed the people's oppressors as ignorant, oafish, corrupt, and/or insane, the more keenly the people felt the effects of oppression. There was an odd element of schadenfreude to Sánchez's columns: the pain (or disgrace or discomfort) one laughed at was often one's own. The stings, besides, stayed in one's flesh when laughter subsided. Thus "En Pocas Palabras" woke people and taught them anger.

One Sunday, finding nothing he felt like commenting on in the news, Sánchez amused himself by alluding to a vast espionage apparatus supposedly at the column's service. His agents were everywhere, Sánchez gloated, even in Mi General's private office, even in his latest conquest's boudoir! Sánchez forgot the whole thing when he filed his copy, but the fantasy took on a life of its own, sprouting from the idly tossed seed like Jack's beanstalk. Anonymous hands began Xeroxing sensitive documents and sending them to EPP at *La Prensa.* Disembodied voices poured terrible confidences into Sánchez's telephone. Strangers hissed at him from shadowy doorways to pass him hair-raising secrets of state. Unsought informants proliferated and approached him, till it seemed that one of Stalin's old nightmares had traveled to the tropics and taken on flesh, that everyone in Panama was a spy and conspirator. One evening, a council of state was called at great urgency to discuss an appalling catastrophe: because of fraud and bungling, the hydroelectric plant at La Fortuna was $250 million above budget. The regime was desperate to keep the news secret until some offsetting good news might be dredged up. Only those expressly concerned were told of the meeting, only the top people, Guardia and civilian, and some of them had trouble getting in. "All these precautions," grumbled Edwin Fábrega, head of the state energy authority, "but that SOB Sánchez will have the whole story in his column tomorrow." Said and done! The very person Fábrega grumbled to told Sánchez everything! The real network came to surpass Sánchez's invention, so that without doing anything that resembled investigation he became the best-informed person in Panama, and those who were not amused in the least by his column, the U.S. ambassador, for example, had to read it just to know what was going on.

And in the time of the tyrant General Manuel Noriega, when darkness spread over Panama—a chill darkness not relieved by the heat and sunlight that drenched the country daily—tormented men whispered horrors to Sánchez, and he vented their anguish in his column. The column became the country's confessional or psychiatrist's couch. *La Prensa* became the country's conscience.

La Prensa had its press and offices out past the business and banking district of Panama City in its own building on, ironically, Eleventh of October Street, the only connection between the paper and the coup that put the Guardia in power. The whole place was state-of-the-art, and the paper's content was worthy of its excellent physical plant. Its domestic news coverage was accurate and impartial, its foreign news as extensive as that of any daily between Miami and Rio. Besides "En Pocas Palabras," there were columns of opinion representing all points of the intellectual compass, both locally produced and syndicated, and the Sunday magazine had first-rate, in-depth feature articles. By the end of 1980, circulation was rising steadily and merchants were taking more and more ads, so that before *La Prensa* was a year old, its stockholders (most of whom had put their cash up as a matter of conscience, without expecting ever to see it again) were allowing themselves to feel like successful investors.

The paper's success, however, was not proved until October 22, 1981. Well before that, Guillermo Sánchez's acquaintances in the government had ceased mocking *La Prensa,* but not until October 22, 1981, could Eisenmann and his associates feel certain that it had "arrived" and that they were proceeding correctly. On that day, at about five in the afternoon, a dozen or so hoodlums sent by the puppet president of the republic and armed with crowbars and machetes attacked the newspaper, smashing windows, typewriters, the head of a pressman, and that of the director of the Central American Institute of Business Administration, who had come by with a press release about scholarships his institution was offering and whose suit and tie made the hoods think he was a director.

The attack confirmed that *La Prensa* was doing its job, and ended up helping the paper do it. Damage was spectacular but superficial. The hoodlums, no smarter than usual, didn't know that the reporters nowadays work at computer terminals that feed the "brain" that composes a newspaper's layout. The smashed typewriters were in the accounting department. Meanwhile, the mess made the evening news on both TV networks and was documented in detail by *La Prensa* itself, for the next day's issue came out on schedule. The result was a jump in circulation. The attack made reading *La Prensa* an act of protest, and as such a source of pleasure and satisfaction, beyond the stimulation, amusement, and feeling of being informed one normally derives from reading a good newspaper. The resources of the dictatorship itself were now, as it were, mobilized promoting *La Prensa!*

To do so, of course, was to promote opposition. Effective opposition to the dictatorship came only when *La Prensa* found its voice. Thereupon, its most effective harping came on the subject of money.

Now, there was money in Panama, plenty of it. Along Avenida Balboa in the capital, and clustered thickly on Punta Paitilla, new office and apartment buildings towered twenty and thirty stories above the bay. On weekday mornings and evenings, the six lanes of Calle Cincuenta were clogged with new cars. New restaurants had opened in Obarrio and Cangrejo to feed the executives of newly arrived foreign banks and newly established foreign corporate offices. The banks came because Panama was a dollar area where U.S. banking rules didn't apply. The corporations came because of the banks, and because of the new restaurants and buildings. There was plenty of money and more was on the way, the big drug money of the 1980s, but it was concentrated among a tiny few, many of whom weren't Panamanians. Panama's prosperity in the time of Torrijos—or, rather, the illusion of it—was based on the government's spending borrowed money, and in the late 1970s the illusion began fading. The public sector dominated the economy. An entire class worked for the state directly, a class of semi-educated paper pushers mainly specialized in attending rallies. The state was, besides, the private sector's main customer, and the only purchaser of some goods and services. This swollen state, this ballooned public sector, had been run for ten years like a chain letter. Now, with inflation rampant, it was running down, for Panama was running out of credit.

In 1983, the National University of Panama brought out a little pamphlet about the state's finances, which *La Prensa* was happy to reprint. All figures came from the state's own publications. Here is what Panama borrowed between 1968 and 1982:

15,197,070,053	U.S. dollars
230,882,875	Swedish crowns
115,240,000	Japanese yen
74,356,043	Venezuelan bolivars
40,000,000	European credit units
17,000,000	Kuwaiti dinars

This figured out to well over $10,000 for every human in the republic, the highest per capita national debt in the world. About 60 percent of the budget went for debt service, the world's worst ratio of debt to revenue. Criminally stupid (or stupidly criminal) bankers had met and fallen in love with Panama's stupid and criminal tyrants. Now, very late in the day, the bankers grew nervous, and Panama's credit began drying up. So the state ran more and more sluggishly and slowed the private economy with it. So wages lagged behind prices. So (since the state remained a money junkie) taxes were jacked up and new taxes invented and water and light bills padded to squeeze out more cash. So unemployment climbed, so people suffered, so people already suffering suffered more. So Panama began displaying new sights, scenes never before witnessed, though people got used to them: women with babies at the breast asking for handouts; men tramping from door to door looking for work; children from five years old up begging at intersections, stretching hands out to cars that whizzed by; prostitutes of both sexes working the street corners. These new sights blended in with the new high-rises and restaurants.

Economic woes begat opposition even when it had nothing to coalesce around. The exilings of January 1976 came in response to criticism of the regime's economic policies. In November of that year, students demonstrated against economic inequities and were brutally punished for their impertinence. R. M. Koster's witness of seven *guardias* hosing one twelve-year-old dated from then. Widespread opposition blossomed, however, when *La Prensa* began inquiring into the whereabouts of all those borrowed billions.

Some must have gone to good use, that much seems certain, though we hold this on faith more than on actual evidence, faith in the science of statistics, not in the wisdom or honesty of *Gorilla gorilla panamensis.* It seems statistically impossible for so much money to have been entirely wasted and thieved by so few. The signs on Avenida Perú, for example, when it was made a one-way thoroughfare. The money spent on them went to good use. Much, though, was bungled away and more was swindled.

The State Sugar Bungle was a side effect of Torrijos's pact with the left. Private farmers grew sugar in Panama, but not extensively: enough for local consumption and the U.S. quota. Cuba, of course, grew sugar on a grand scale, but not because doing so was advantageous. The sugar market was chronically unstable. Sugar's labor demands were seasonally uneven. Most of Cuba's soil was unfit for anything else, though. That was the reason why Cuba grew so much sugar. Panama's communists, however, suffered from acute Cubanitis, to the point where they all spoke with Cuban accents and called Torrijos *comandante* à la Fidel. Cuba raised lots of sugar; ergo, Panama should do likewise. That is what they urged Omar Torrijos. No doubt they dreamed of mammoth harvests and volunteers from all over bringing it in. Perhaps Torrijos recalled the famous photo of Castro posed heroically in a cane field brandishing a machete on high. Whatever the case, the state went into sugar, and boldly too, early in the 1970s.

God, fate, or happenstance was malicious. A year or so after Panama planted, the European crop of beet sugar failed. The Panamanian state made a great killing. But instead of quitting while they were ahead, or at least realizing that they had been lucky, the fools in the Ministry of Agriculture assumed that the world price of sugar would stay on the moon forever and not only planted all the sugar they could but bought and assembled a number of sugar mills also, flogged onward by the Japanese manufacturers. Others in other lands were just as foolish—the Philippines (where Marcos tyrannized), for example—so that production zoomed and demand hit rock bottom and lay there comatose for years and years. But now the Panamanian state was stuck fast in sugar. It had to keep planting its fields to keep its mills running to keep its employees busy—all at a loss. Some of the borrowed billions were got rid of that way.

Other bungles included the campesino cooperatives and the community juntas. By 1980, some 250 million 1970s dollars had been spent on them to no good use. Campesinos didn't benefit, nor did those in the barrios. Insiders made money, so maybe they should be called swindles. Or misappropriations, since the main idea behind them was to buy a political base for Omar Torrijos. The idea flopped in one sense but worked in another. Torrijos's popular support never materialized, either in the countryside or in the cities, which is why he never held a straight election. On the other hand, he fooled Hamilton Jordan, and a number of other geniuses in the United States.

Torrijos's base was in the United States, after the fashion of many Latin dictators. And the insiders who got rich certainly loved him, so the funds expended did buy some support. But call them what you will, bungles or swindles, whatever, the cooperatives and the juntas got rid of money. They sent a borrowed quarter billion flying.

The Spanish Bus Bungle-cum-Swindle starred Monchi Torrijos. While Panama's ambassador to Spain, Monchi served as middleman in a deal whereby Panama bought almost three hundred huge buses, fifty-passenger jobs, from Pegaso—without bids, of course. The thing was to get the deal done, 30 million early 1970s dollars, because Monchi was getting $10,000 per bus. That was the swindle part. The bungle part, which was really expensive, was that these were buses designed for long hauls on the highway, whereas Panama bought them for use in the capital. Stop and go in traffic wrecked their transmissions. Go and stop burned out their brakes. Half were out of action by the end of one year. Cannibalizing kept others running awhile. The deal, however, was pretty much a dead loss, another way to get rid of borrowed money.

There were, besides, the National Slaughterhouse Bungle and the National Cement Plant Bungle and the National Banana Corporation Bungle, all not merely failures but textbook examples of how to waste public monies while damaging private interests as well. The cement plant, for instance, was supposed to produce for export, but its production cost per bag was more than double the world price. It drove one private firm from business and forced another to lay off workers and cost $30 million more to build than was budgeted. The Bayano and Fortuna dam projects were over budget, $60 million and $250 million, respectively. At Bayano, too, we pass from bungle to swindle, for when the dam was complete, with the water rising, someone realized that the land that would soon be flooded contained a great deal of marketable timber. At once, at forced marches, using state employees and equipment hurriedly transferred from other projects, the timber was harvested and sold to Cuba and the proceeds pocketed by the Guardia general staff.

The New Airport Swindle, while not the grossest pulled off in the time of the tyrants, was a model of its kind from start to finish. Exhaustive studies established what was required: lengthen the existing airport's runway and put up a second terminal building. A whole new airport, however, would cost much more money, so more could be skimmed from the top and scammed in construction. Personnel and equipment of the Ministry of Public Works were used extensively, as well as trucks from the Guardia's civic action program, but firms run by insiders charged and collected bundles all the same, and the work dragged on for years, and the costs were incredible. The original lenders, made nervous by constant overruns, finally balked at lending any more. By appealing to Latin-American solidarity, the government managed to get money from Venezuela, the 70-odd million bolivars mentioned in the study referred to above. The total sum was obtained in successive wheedlings, and at one point the Venezuelan president, Carlos Andrés Pérez, asked if Panama was in fact building an airport or a launching site for space vehicles. At length, however, the new airport got built, whereupon the Guardia took over the old one and made it a base for drug and weapons smuggling.

The National Finance Corporation Swindle was an *atelier* of swindles, a swindle workshop, a house of swindle in the high-fashion sense, with handsome new collections each spring and fall. The corporation itself (Corporación Financiera Nacional, COFINA) was set up wholly owned by the government in 1975, supposedly as a bank for developing industry. Its first general manager was Pedro Rognoni, part of Omar Torrijos's right-hand punch in the sense of his being a businessman adviser. COFINA had the backing of international agencies like the World Bank and also got lines of credit from merchant bankers for ventures that received its approval. To get an enterprise okayed for financing from or through COFINA, those behind it had to present a favorable study drawn up by reputable financial analysts. That, anyway, was what the law said, the decree under which COFINA was created. In practice, what you did was consult the firm run by Pedro's brother Mario, a stumpy chap, later noteworthy as one of Manuel Noriega's most useful and durable tools. For a fee, Mario would approve any wild scheme, and anything Mario liked was okay with Pedro. Later on, Pedro was followed by other managers, who had their own methods of pilfering. The principle, however, remained the same. COFINA was a swindle and the mother of swindles.

There were a thousand and one COFINA swindles: simple grabs where loans were pocketed and never paid back without anyone's ever going into business, and schemes that afforded multiple swipings—as in the Promarsa Fishing Swindle, where swindlers were set up in business to catch tuna (with a loan, of course, that was never paid back) and caught endangered shrimp instead. Torrijos himself partook of COFINA's largesse through a company called Karnes Chiricanas. But it couldn't last forever. By mid-1982, with 95 percent of its portfolio "nonperforming," the end came for COFINA. The World Bank marshaled what euphemisms it could in composing the obituary. "Poor project evaluation," said the World Bank, did COFINA in, along with "inadequate project supervision, and extension of credit based on political considerations."

There were many more scams than we've named, many, many. A whole book could be written solely on the subject of peculation in the Panama we are describing, a long book, too, and one that professional swindlers elsewhere could learn from. We suppose that no land can be totally free of corruption, that a small amount may lubricate government operations, that a certain level in any case is inevitable, though the level varies as one moves about in space-time. Different styles of corruption exist as well, varying from culture to culture. In the United States, for instance, while Reagan was president (to pick an example near in time of a country that is supposed to be well governed), the nation's credit was plundered somewhat as Panama's was for the benefit of a greedy few, but there the swindlers were more moderate, at least in relation to the size of the nation's wealth, and sometimes even took the precaution of changing the laws to make their swindles of preference technically legal. In short, they showed some respect for the borders of decency. In Panama that was not so. A lot has been said, often in very shrill tones, about corruption in the Philippines of Ferdinand Marcos, and surely the man was a thief, and his wife was a thiefess, and they had many thieves around them. But considering the sums made off with, and that Panama has one-fiftieth the Philippines's population, corruption in Panama was worse. Its corroding effect was especially damaging. Values collapsed. The concept of value itself all but lost meaning. Society's fabric was mercilessly shredded. People felt like fools for being honest, like weaklings for not partaking themselves.

Tyranny in Panama was structurally similar to that in the Philippines and other countries. A small bunch ruled by controlling the military. The Guardia, though, fostered no martial virtues, no duty, no honor. Its traditions were those of police in loosely run cities: bribe taking and summons fixing; a cut for protecting this illegal thing or that; beating up and shaking down small-time hoodlums; beating up and shaking down poor pimpless whores. Along came the United States of America, in the boundless stupidity of its brief moment atop the world's greasy pole, and encouraged these uniformed apes to feel brave and act masterful. They took power and ran amok indulging their appetites, which were about seven parts greed and three parts sadism. There was nothing inside or outside them to hold them back. Perhaps one should feel grateful that their appetites didn't run to setting up a workers' paradise or purifying the world racially, but they certainly were corrupt and they corrupted. Americans may grasp the effect by performing the following thought experiment. Take the police of, say, Hoboken, New Jersey. Expand them to where there is one for each one hundred residents in the United States. Now put them in complete charge of the government, the sole armed force sea to sea and border to border, running things in response to the proddings of appetite, as advised in concerns of the spirit by Jim Bakker, and in financial affairs by Ivan Boesky.

When the Social Security Swindle came to light (and we mean to take it up in a moment), Guillermo Sánchez asked a member of the board of directors of the Caja de Seguro Social (Social Security Administration, hereinafter called the Seguro, for handiness) how it was possible that he and others, themselves honest and intelligent men, had let the monstrous theft happen. The answer he got was that the military wanted it—there was nothing to do. Were he and other board members threatened? No, but *los militares* wanted it, so it was going to happen. In short, the board members and other civilian functionaries felt a reverential awe toward Guardia officers of a sort more properly shown to divinities. Their will be done! And the feeling persisted even when the foul mess was discovered and the board members found themselves spattered with it. Colonel This and Colonel That had said to do it, or someone else had said that's what they'd said.

Before the coup, of course, there'd been corruption, malfeasance, and misappropriation of public founds, but the cases were confined to an individual or a department. The Guardia inaugurated a new modality. Corruption infected the entire administrative apparatus. In the past, those guilty of administrative infractions were punished if and when they were discovered. Under the dictatorship, no functionary could be punished, no matter how insignificant his post, for chains of complicity stretched from him to the highest levels. If a single thread were pulled, the whole system would unravel. And that is what *La Prensa* did. It tugged at the exposed threads of corruption, at times no more maliciously, so it seemed, than a kitten, until the entire regime of tyranny nearly came apart.

Many of the dictatorship's big swindles had already taken place when the paper opened. The Social Security Housing Project Swindle probably produced the largest thefts of all, however. It was in mid-career when the paper got wind of it, at first (as it were) sniff by sniff, beginning with Augusto Vives.

Vives was one of the founders of the Seguro. For years, he was its chief actuary, but by the time *La Prensa* opened he was in retirement, partly because of his age, partly because he had suffered a heart attack, and partly because there was no place in the new order of things for a man of his probity. Like many clear thinkers, he had an excellent prose style, and he became a contributor to *La Prensa*'s "Contrapunto" column, mainly with nostalgic evocations of the Panama of his youth. He retained a paternal interest in the Seguro, however, and did a piece or two on certain disquieting developments he had noticed—that the Seguro had become irregular in issuing finacial statements, and that the few figures one could obtain didn't look right. The articles excited little interest, except perhaps among professional economists. One of these, Pepín Navas, published a few careful studies that also suggested things might be amiss, though the trouble looked more like lax management than anything criminal.

One day, Giovanni Carlucci, at the time president of Panama's real estate brokers' association, sought out Guillermo Sánchez to tell him something fishy was happening in connection with a Seguro housing project. Carlucci had nothing firm on which to base charges, not even names, but someone seemed to be up to something. Sánchez made a few cryptic references in his column, supposing the swindlers would figure he knew more than he did and call the thing off. Later on, in fact, he learned that they'd been alarmed, but such was the arrogance of Panama's kleptocrats, having gotten away for so long with so much, that those involved went right ahead as if nothing had happened.

People were now thinking about the Seguro, however, and Sánchez began to get anonymous tips. He learned that Monchi Torrijos was one of the housing project's building contractors, Monchi who didn't know a brick from a birdcage! He learned that Norberto Navarro had a contract also, and while Navarro was in fact a builder, he was also a crook, a crook from way, way back before the coup, a fellow who'd rather cheat you out of ten dollars than make a million honestly. Monchi involved, and Navarro! That was as good as a smoking gun for Sánchez. On his suggestion, two Partido Liberal deputies went to call on the Seguro's director, Abraham Saied, who happened to be Monchi Torrijos's son-in-law, to warn him that a scandal was brewing. Saied left them waiting in his outer office and sneaked out the back way. Obviously no warning was required, and the swindle was bigger than anyone had thought. That's where things stood on July 31, 1981, when General Omar Torrijos was killed in a plane crash.

Had the crash not occurred, Torrijos would likely have closed *La Prensa* that fall. He and others had seen their mistake in letting it open. Tyranny and a free press cannot coexist. To survive, one must destroy the other. In Panama, tyranny triumphed. *La Prensa* was closed down for lengthening periods, then permanently. Had Torrijos lived, the thing would have been over much more quickly. However he might prate of restoring democracy, however he might now and then believe his own prating, he would never have done so (even imagining his colleagues would have let him), lest Monchi and other members of the royal family find themselves on trial and then in prison. *La Prensa* stayed in business as long as it did only because Omar Torrijos died and for a time no new tyrant had his degree of power.

The problem with closing *La Prensa* was Washington. The Reagan administration was pretending to favor democracy in Latin America, hence was urging its protégés in Panama to pretend that they were speeding toward that goal. Summarily closing *La Prensa* did not fit that pretense. A goon attack was tried, as we've seen, but proved counterproductive. For a time, closing the paper down briefly was all Panama's masters could get away with. For a time, they could do no more than yearn for the golden days when they lied without fear of rebuke, when they stole without having their names bandied all over, when there were no independent voices in Panama. They still lied and stole, of course, but for a time they had to bear being nagged for it. Meanwhile, the immediate concern was arranging for who would be the new tyrant.

The ranking officer, Colonel Florencio Flórez, was not a contender, having no vocation as a dictator, though he ran the Guardia and perpetuated its rule until the power struggle was sorted out. Four men figured in it: Colonel Rubén Paredes and Lieutenant Colonels Armando Contreras, Manuel Noriega, and Roberto Díaz. By early in 1982, they had agreed—or at least had convinced each other they had agreed—to take turns as Guardia commandant. The deal was probably cut in January but was formalized, actually put on paper, on March 8, after Flórez had been shoved into retirement: seized, that is, and threatened with the death of his twenty-year-old son, until he agreed to bow out.

Contreras never collected his share of power. The others were probably conning him from the start. In 1987, after Robert Díaz had been welched on, Díaz made his copy of the pact public, intending (it seems) to discredit Noriega for betraying him. By then, of course, he and Noriega had betrayed Parades, after he, Noriega, and Parades had betrayed Contreras. The pact itself was a tissue of treason. In drawing it up, all four were betraying their country and would have been betraying the Guardia had it not been merely a gang of thieves and cutthroats with no more institutional standing than one of the drug cartels. In any case, Díaz's copy circulated widely in Xerox. Thus the terms of the compact are known, and also the airs put on by its signatories, for the thing is called "Historic Pledge of the Guardia Nacional for Patriotic, Ethical, Orderly, Natural, and Peaceful Institutional Organization."

The pact, which contains nine "Doctrinal Pledges," arranges the succession in the Guardia as follows:

Paredes	- February 1982 till March 1983
Contreras	- March 1983 till March 1984
Noriega	- March 1984 till July 31, 1987
Díaz Herrera	- July 31, 1987 till July 31, 1988

Pledge number 4 establishes that after Parades retires, the general staff will help him run for president, with things getting really scary when their help is spelled out as coming "in a normal, altruistic way, without the institution's involving itself in coercions to immoral or reprehensible acts." Pledge 7 has Díaz Herrera, when he is commandant, integrating his staff with that of President Parades, with a clear view to making the presidency of the republic a kind of board chairmanship to which Guardia commandants will be elevated on their retirement as surely as saved Christians are into heaven. In pledge 8, Paredes undertakes, as commandant and later as president, to safeguard the rights, aspirations, advantages, and privileges of members of the Guardia general staff when they leave active service, "in an ample gesture of comradeship and brotherhood." Pledge 9 names the pact after Torrijos "in memory of our great chief and teacher," certainly an appropriate appellation for a document at once arrogant and disgusting.

The tyranny of General Rubén Paredes was confirmed with the pact's signing and continued until August 1983. Through the summer and fall of 1981, meanwhile, and on into the new year, the Seguro swindle continued in progress, with the swindlers leaving loose ends of it draped here and there, and *La Prensa* coming along behind to tug at them. By March and April 1982—by the time, that is to say, when the compact was signed and the succession crisis over—each day's paper brought ever-more-redolent whiffs of more and more rats decomposing under the floorboards, and readers breathed them with mingled glee and horror, glee that someone was onto the thieves at last, horror that they were stealing Panama cross-eyed. Horror predominated. The Seguro was a beloved institution, one that the nation was proud of and had assumed, more or less without thinking, would not be defiled even by the dictatorship's greed-crazed cynics. Since 1940, it had provided a whole system of social welfare without taking a cent from the treasury. Nothing in Panama, not even the Canal, had been designed better. Now it was being plundered, possibly wrecked.

Panamanians, too, take pride in being worldly. They acutely dislike appearing naive. Ask one if he thinks public officials are stealing, and he will likely say, "Yes, that's human nature." But the very same Panamanian will be annoyed on reading that the public officials Pérez, Gómez, and López stole so-and-so many millions in such-and-such year. That would, of course, mean that Pérez et al. have been playing our Panamanian for a sucker, are exhibiting him in public as a fool. Besides being horrified, Panamanians felt insulted and angry.

Nor could the citizen hope, or the government charge, that *La Prensa* was mistaken or merely malicious. Each revelation came with ocular proof. Such was the arrogance of Panama's kleptocrats, having got away with so much for so long, that the swindlers had left their marks everywhere. Norberto Navarro paid bribes by personal check! And besides being clear and present, the swindle was vast. The stench rose to the dictatorship's highest levels. The dead hero's brother Monchi reeked of it. So did Major (retired) Antonio Suárez, late of the Guardia general staff and bosom friend of the new tyrant General Paredes. Other big shots would soon be implicated. And all was recounted in the sober tones of accountants, illustrated by photocopies of canceled checks.

But we had better describe the swindle first. More than one hundred million was made off with, over the course of about a year and a half, in two separate frauds wrapped around a housing project: a large but otherwise pedestrian loan fraud in which most of the money disappeared, and a wonderfully inventive insurance fraud that gobbled up the last six or so million.

It began with a Noriega tool named Guillermo Vega, a sometime journalist who put out a scandal sheet in the late 1950s so as to extort money from prominent people for not printing articles about them. That's when he and Noriega met, when Noriega was working as a lab technician, before he lied about his age and got a scholarship to Peru's military academy. Then, in 1969, nearly ten years later, when Noriega was commanding in Chiriquí Province and the anti-Guardia *guerrilla* was about over, Torrijos wanted Walter Sardiñas murdered and told Mi Gangster Noriega to arrange it. Sardiñas, his health broken, was holed up in a rooming house in San José, Costa Rica, and Noriega issued an open death contract on him with $25,000 put up by Torrijos. Vega transported the money, which makes him (we suppose) a bagman's bagman. Thereafter, as Noriega floated upward, so did he. In 1980, he was Panama's ambassador to France. His principal duties, however, had to do with Noriega's real estate holdings in France and secret bank accounts in Switzerland—generally, that is, with Noriega's financial welfare. In 1980, Vega came from France to approach Saied with an idea about the Seguro's financing a resort hotel and complex in Bocas del Toro that would cater especially to tourists from Europe. The Seguro was then extremely solvent, and the point was to get a lot of money flowing so that Noriega might get some of it for himself and other ranking Guardia officers, with lesser personages of course getting shares also. Saied thought the point was valid and liked real estate as the way to achieve it but believed low-cost housing would play better politically than a resort: the regime, after all, called itself revolutionary. Vega, thereupon, disappeared from the scene, but he'd done his part in getting the project started.

It wasn't supposed to be totally crooked. People who didn't deserve to were going to get money, but the country was going to get some housing too. That, anyway, seems to have been the idea, though no one killed himself setting up safeguards. No study was done to see what sort of housing was needed, where and when and how much and by whom. No bids were requested, no competitions held. Verbal contracts to build twenty-five hundred houses were awarded to four gentlemen named by Noriega, for he and the Guardia were to receive the main slice. Norberto Navarro got a contract for one thousand houses. Humberto Moran got one for five hundred. No one asked if they had land to build the homes on. No one felt like seeing any blueprints. No one wanted to hear about costs or materials or seemed to care when the houses would be done. The contracts were let, the promoters were advanced money. So they could get started building, that was what was claimed later on, though once a check was issued, the payee could send the funds to his aunt Eulalia for all anyone at the Seguro minded, and these loans were not secured by so much as a paperweight. And meeting the Guardia's needs was just the beginning. Officials at the Seguro went around asking people they knew if they wouldn't like to get into building houses, and awarded them contracts, and advanced them cash, though since these folks weren't fronting for officers, they had to kick back part of the advances.

Besides Saied, a bunch of Seguro big shots had their fingers in the housing scam. The tone of the thing is conveyed in the following incident involving Dr. Ricardo Fábrega, the Seguro's chief actuary. One evening after the scandal had begun perking, Giovanni Carlucci ran into Fábrega, whom he'd known for years, in Sarti's restaurant across the street from the Hotel Continental in Panama City—in the restaurant's men's room, to be exact. "I know what you guys are up to," said Carlucci. Fábrega didn't blink, much less break his stream. "You know I've been meaning to call you," Fábrega said. "How'd you like to have a hundred units?" Carlucci wasn't interested but couldn't help wondering how many contracts had been let in similar settings.

Saied and the others couldn't lay out ninety million all by themselves. They were the ones who bypassed Seguro procedures, such as having collateral for loans, but first the project had to be passed by the cabinet and the National Finance Commission. Then it had to go through the Seguro's board. Some directors pretended not to notice its weirdities. *Los militares* wanted it, after all. At least two were bribed by Norberto Navarro. And then there was the comptroller's office. Their okay, too, was needed, but not to worry. In Panama during the time of the tyrants, the comptroller did exactly the opposite of what he was supposed to. The comptroller made sure there was no effective control on how the people's money was disbursed.

All told, there were thirty-eight promoters. Hardly a one did so much as think about building, though when the scandal broke a few went scrambling around buying land and maybe had a hole or two dug on it. Virtually no houses were built, however, and the cash disappeared into private accounts.

That was the building fraud, crude but effective. Through it ninety million plus was sent flying. Now for the insurance fraud, Navarro's masterpiece, the matchless pearl of Panamanian swindledom.

When Norberto Navarro found out that contracts to build ten thousand houses were going to be awarded in the Seguro's program, a great clearness came about him (as they say in the old chivalric romances), he had a moment of illumination. The houses didn't exist and never would, but Navarro could see them in his imagination, and so clearly that he even saw what they lacked. Not one of those ten thousand houses had insurance. It came to Navarro, then, to insure the imaginary houses against imaginary risks, but using real insurance policies, with real premiums and real brokerage fees. From that majestic leap of imagination it was just a hop to using equally real policies, with equally real premiums and fees, to insure the imaginary owners of those imaginary houses, lest imaginary death snuff out their fake lives and cause an untimely lapse in the phantom payments they were making on their ghostly mortgages. We don't know if Navarro had read Gogol. In Gogol's novel *Dead Souls* a swindler named Chichikov buys up dead serfs whose names are still on the census rolls to use as collateral in business deals. If Navarro had read it, he may have owed Gogol a debt, but you still score it Panama 1, Russia 0. Navarro worked *his* con in very real life, and made off with perfectly real money.

Not all by himself. He spread the fruits of his genius around, as he was well advised to do for health reasons, considering the sharks who were swimming alongside him. Colonel Manuel Noriega, for example. He, too, went into the insurance business, with a spanking-new firm called Superseguros, S.A., run by Carlos Wittgreen the hunter and fisherman. Colonel (retired) Rodrigo García was in the insurance business. General Rubén Paredes was involved too. He stipulated that half the brokerage fees, a matter of $1.1 million, should go to the PRD, the government's party—this at a meeting in April 1982, in the Restaurante Galaxia, with Toro Balladares and Alberto Pons, the PRD's treasurer, information that came out only after Paredes had fallen from power. And $200,000 went to help finance the presidential campaign of Luis Alberto Monge in Costa Rica, an investment that showed a return when the headless corpse of Hugo Spadafora was found on Costa Rica's side of the border. And there had to be help from inside the Seguro. A single crook of genius thought it up, but it took a whole herd to make the miracle happen. And puppet President Royo was consulted, and puppet Vice-President Ricardo De la Espriella. The latter's cut was $115,000, for he headed the National Finance Commission, and its approval was required, what with the face value of the policies coming to $385 million, and the premiums and fees to nearly $7 million. A whole herd were made happy in the Seguro Swindle.

By April 1982, enough of its effluvium had seeped out for all to know there was rot in the institution. People were horrified, people were angry. *La Prensa* was loose, as it were, in the regime's boudoir glimpsing things not for the eyes of outsiders. The government had to do something to make it all stop, and on April 25, therefore, Dr. Abraham Saied resigned as Seguro director and was replaced by Dr. José R. Esquivel.

Esquivel will be remembered as Torrijos's minister of health in the early days of the fake revolution, and as one of those most to blame for the dismantling of Panama's public health system. The results of this bungle were not yet apparent, however, and Esquivel had a well-deserved reputation for honesty. His appointment calmed the public's fury. And since he was infinitely servile to those in uniform, Paredes and others thought they were out of the jam. Esquivel, though, had no inkling how bad the mess was, or that his heroes were up to their eyebrows in it. Early in July, while bustling about trying to locate the trouble and vindicate the regime by setting things right, he discovered and quoted a hitherto secret report the comptroller's office had sent to Dr. Saied about the fraud-filled housing program. Paredes, almost insane with rage, called him on the carpet at Fiftieth Street and told him to shred the report and stop talking to journalists. It was too late. Like the dunce in the children's story, Esquivel had knocked the lid off the caldron in which the infernal brew was bubbling.

First out was the insurance swindle. The perfume of unbuilt houses insured for millions was wafted about the land by *La Prensa* and a number of radio commentators. Then came a smell of neglected procedures in the granting of loans to building promoters. Then, with the public's nostrils thus assailed, Dr. Saied tried to leave the country and might have made it if he hadn't been piggish and decided to take his girlfriend along. He might cheat his country but not a princess of the blood royal. His wife, Monchi's daughter, Omar Torrijos's niece, tailed him to the airport and surprised the pair and had their exit permits lifted, and the country roared with laughter and howled in rage. The teachers and doctors, still bristling over the government's breaking the agreement by which the 1979 strike was settled, took advantage of the Seguro scandal to organize nationwide protests on July 13. Hundreds of thousands of citizens marched and demonstrated, chanting insults about the Guardia and the PRD. Even Paredes admitted the turnout was massive in the capital and the major provincial cities. On the twenty-eighth, another protest drew even more people. The regime seemed to teeter. Actually, the Guardia and its civilian apparatus had not the slightest thought of relinquishing power, nor had the opposition the means or will to oust them. What came was a readjustment, the first of four during the next six years in which pressure was relieved by dumping the puppet president.

In effect, the regime made a coup against itself—or, rather, went through some motions pretending to make one. One remembers it as a succession of TV programs, and these would have been very funny had they been fictitious, or set in a country where one didn't live or have friends. On Thursday, July 29, in the middle of the evening newscast, screens suddenly bulged with the jowls of Jimmy Lakas, and tremulous jowls they were on that occasion. "Fellow citizens," he began gravely, so that one's first supposition was that the network was running an old address of his made while he was still puppet president of the republic. But no, he was discussing the current crisis, which demanded (he said) that everyone pull together, putting aside personal rancor and strife. One might have thought that Panama had suffered an earthquake, or some other form of natural disaster, that the crisis didn't concern corruption of the very sort Lakas himself had so gorged on.

Lakas was followed by Felipe González, prime minister of Spain. He had come to power in the wake of General Francisco Franco's long dictatorship, during which the Spanish people suffered all manner of torment and privation, and he (González, that is) pretended to a belief in democracy, yet he thought military dictatorship just the thing for the people of Panama and missed no opportunity to nuzzle up to Omar Torrijos and his successors in tyranny. He gave a lecture on Panamanian history stuffed with evidence of his ignorance and contempt. "The Guardia Nacional," he said at one point, "is the spinal column of delivery of social services in Panama." Oh, that he were sitting on that column!

The first anniversary of Torrijos's death fell on Saturday. Had it been marked then, however, no one would have attended the solemnities. They were held, therefore, late on Friday morning, July 30, with the forced attendance of public employees, and were of course carried on television. The main orator was puppet Vice-President Ricardo De la Espriella. His address was a stern critique of the administration and a strident call for thoroughgoing change. It was as if De la Espriella were not in office, as if he'd never been in the government, and meanwhile looking on in approval were Paredes and a great skulk of Guardia officers, along with civilian officials and Royo himself, as if they, too, had been for years out of power, out of the country, out of the galaxy even, and had had nothing to do, nothing whatever, with the inept and useless government that De la Espriella was attacking.

At lunchtime, news came that Royo was resigning because of a throat ailment impeding his speech, and that De la Espriella would be installed that afternoon. At four, that spectacle was broadcast, live and direct from the presidential palace, with a host of big shots in full plumage. The feature performer was Aristides Royo, who held forth for half an hour with a vocal vibrance street vendors might envy. So was he caused to demean himself and emphasize that he was being tossed out. From time to time, the camera panned to his successor, pasty-faced and slight, looking adolescent not youthful, hunched with legs crossed in an armchair acres too big for him, his pinched expression filled with obscene joy. And at length the sash of office was pinned on him, puppet president by grace of the tyrant Rubén Paredes.

Then, lest anyone doubt who exactly was master, or suppose De la Espriella president in his own right, the transmission switched to Guardia headquarters and screens filled with the sweat-glazed face of the tyrant himself, eyes rolling like Idi Amin's, drunk with power. He declared all the newspapers closed—"As of now!"—and sat with head hung glaring balefully into the camera. Had he spat at it, had he bitten the head off a live chicken, no one who was viewing would have blinked.

That was Parades's finest hour. At that moment, tyranny in Panama achieved Ugandan primitiveness and malevolence, fitting prelude for Noriega's later abominations. Not Idi Amin himself outdid Parades that day in repugnance or bestiality. He was lifted out of himself, as it were, into regions of disgust normally beyond him.

Later on, when he'd been two or so years out of power, Sánchez and Koster ran into him in a restaurant. That was in November 1985, in the wake of the Spadafora murder, the day Sánchez came out of hiding. Paredes sent drinks over to their table, and they got up and went over and chatted with him a moment. Sánchez had gibed at him cruelly when he was tyrant, and certainly he deserved the gibes, but now he was no longer mighty, no longer important, somewhat a victim even and soon to be more so, with a drug-runner son murdered at Noriega's order. Neither Sánchez nor Koster had seen him before in person. Both remarked later how much smaller he was than he seemed on TV. He was, besides, soft-spoken and diffident, bearing out Malaparte's observation that dictators are, in psychology, violent yet timid. His timidity was on display there, just as his violence had been three years before.

The point of closing the papers was closing *La Prensa.* Only then could an effort be made to contain the scandal before anyone who counted was befouled—that is, any active service Guardia officers. The reason Paredes gave was that the newspapers were much given to insult, and shortly thereafter Archbishop McGrath committed the delinquency of echoing him, then of suggesting that norms of decorum be imposed on government and independent media alike—as if *La Prensa*'s clear obligation to call thieves thieves could in any way be justly or logically likened to the practice current in the government papers of calling its critics perverts and syphilitics.

Containing the scandal had two aspects. Both were facilitated by the fake coup. Having ordered the newspapers closed, Paredes ordered the arrest of "persons implicated" in the Seguro case. Even as he spoke, Ricardo Fábrega and two other Seguro chiefs were being picked up. The three were certainly guilty. The plan, though, was for them to take all the blame, and the inference Paredes hoped the public would draw was that Royo had been impeding the march of justice, but that now Rubén Paredes was firmly in charge, and had put in his own man, De la Espriella, justice had triumphed. The second aspect, therefore, was to have an investigation, *ma non troppo.* Changing puppet presidents allowed for other changes. Top on the list was booting Dr. Esquivel from the Seguro. He was replaced by Luis Alberto Arias, who was up to his ears in the swindle, a member of the National Finance Commission that approved both ends of the fraud, the $90 million in unsecured loans and the insurance of the phantom houses. Also out were the comptroller and *procurador.* Both had lied long and loyally for their military masters, but neither retained a drop of credibility. In as *procurador* was Rafael Rodríguez, on the recommendation of a Paredes adviser, Hernán Delgado, who was destined to figure in a curious incident. He ran afoul of Noriega without being aware of it till news of his death appeared in a government newspaper. He got the hint at once and left the country. Rodríguez was a young lawyer with a reputation for both honesty and efficiency, and his appointment seemed perfect from the government's point of view: a young fellow, inexperienced, and very flattered to have been picked for high office, who would follow the guidance of those above him in rank and age. Only a seer could have warned against the choice.

And the public humiliation of young Señor Royo. That was the most useful of all the steps taken in relieving the pressure on the regime, most useful for being most primitive. Many middle- and upper-class Panamanians were really quite content with the dictatorship so long as they could delude themselves as to its nature—believe it moderate, under control. The Seguro swindle made the delusion untenable, but now, with the ritual degrading of Royo, people could lie to themselves again. *There, the regime had been punished for going too far.* Witness of damage inflicted allowed people to feel that they, after all, controlled the government, while actually they were being facilely manipulated. Modern man is nowhere as clever as he thinks. All the great discoveries were made long, long ago. Driving a goat out into the wilderness really does work. Predators rend it to morsels, are for a time sated, and the rest of us can get on with our nice little lives.

The newspapers were ordered closed for a week. The idea was for *La Prensa* not to reopen. While the building was sealed, under Guardia control, the rotary press was booby-trapped so as to wrench itself to pieces when it was turned on. Fortunately, the operator was suspicious and took the machine apart piece by piece beforehand. Since the closure of the paper had not been gentle, with *guardias* clomping in flailing their hoses, Eisenmann and others of the staff took the precaution of having some witnesses with them when at length they were permitted to reenter the building—the Venezuelan ambassador, and Mr. Alan Riding of the *New York Times,* and the agent for the paper's insurance company. Everything had been smashed or broken into. Documents, files, and personal belongings had been carried off. Acid had been poured into the processing unit of the main computer. Even though the rotary press was saved, nearly $100,000 worth of damage had been done. For which Paredes accepted full responsibility. He said so on television. Almost at once, however, he changed his story and alleged "autosabotage." And so it stood and still stands officially, though in June 1987, after Colonel Roberto Díaz's declarations stripped the dictatorship's camouflage, Paredes recanted and admitted that the destruction had been done at his order with a view to silencing *La Prensa* once and for all.

Two themes were stated in this incident on which variations would be played with increasing frequency as the decade continued. There was, first, the theme of state vandalism, destruction of property irresponsibly ordained and gleefully accomplished by the supposed custodians of public order. Then there was the theme of U.S. pressure on the regime to allow the appearance of democracy. The substance of democracy was not wanted. No one of importance in the White House or Pentagon or State Department wanted Panamanians to be free, any more than such was wanted in Guardia headquarters. The appearance, though, was very much desired, which is why *La Prensa* was suffered to reopen after sabotaging it proved ineffective.

And ineffective it was, psychologically as well as physically. The paper got out a four-page issue on August 6, exactly a week after being invaded and sacked. All four pages were devoted to that calamity, but on the seventh the Seguro swindle was back on *La Prensa*'s front page. Lest anyone entertain sugarplum visions of the paper's being intimidated, there on page one, suitably enlarged, was a check drawn on the Seguro for one million dollars to a firm called Constructoras Agroindustriales, S.A., of Aguadulce, Coclé Province, with the explanation underneath that the firm's president was Monchi Torrijos.

The Ministry of Justice pressed the Seguro case, *ma non troppo.* Fábrega and the other two officials who were arrested were held not in La Modelo but in the Guardia cuartel at Tinajita, where each had a sort of air-conditioned suite, where all had all the liquor and visitors they wanted, where food was brought to them from the best restaurants in the capital and served by *guardias* in uniform. On September 1, Saied himself was arrested, but Tinajita wasn't swank enough for him. He stayed with the Fuerza Aérea, the Guardia air force, at Tocumen Airport. All were found to possess personal holding companies with shares in construction and/or insurance firms that had taken part in the swindle. One had time deposits that totaled over a million dollars. Five thousand pages of evidence had been accumulated, and the law denied bail to those accused of peculation in amounts over one thousands dollars, yet on September 6 Circuit Judge Manuel Batista set bail for all four, citing the absence of a prima facie case! Soon afterward, Batista was elevated to the Superior Tribunal as a magistrate in the pleasant town of Las Tablas, where Carnival is celebrated with more gaiety than anywhere else in Panama and where, as far as we know, he lived happily ever after.

In January 1983, the prosecutor assigned to the case turned over some twelve thousand pages of evidence to the judicial branch, asking that proceedings be instituted against Saied, Fábrega, Norberto Navarro, and others, including members of the Seguro's board whom Navarro had bribed. In May, the bribees were declared indictable, but the briber, Navarro, was provisionally absolved. The May 1983 finding was not final. Thereafter, Panama witnessed two fraudulent elections and four changes of puppet presidents, yet as of the dictator's fall in December 1989, the Seguro case was no further along.

The affair, however, had one final moment of drama. On July 28, 1983, almost exactly a year after he was appointed, Rafael Rodríguez, the *procurador* (who either in wisdom or innocence had not yet pressed his inquiries beyond safe limits), informed Paredes and the Guardia staff that puppet President De la Espriella had had guilty knowledge of the Seguro swindle and had in fact, along with Drs. Royo and Saied, been behind the payments made by the insurance swindlers into the coffers of the government's party, the Partido Revolucionario Democrático. What Rodríguez seems not to have known is that Paredes himself was thoroughly slimed with that offal, back to front, head to toe. Paredes himself had ordered the payments made at the April 1982 Restaurante Galaxia meeting, fully expecting to benefit from every cent of them as the PRD's nominee for president in the elections scheduled for May 1984. Rodríguez was walking into a buzz saw. He was summoned to Guardia headquarters at eight the next morning. There, in the presence of De la Espriella and members of the general staff, Paredes spoke to him in a manner he was later on ashamed to relate in detail and ordered him to resign his office. Panama, said Paredes, could not take "another throat ailment." What he meant, of course, without letting on to Rodríguez was that if Rodríguez pulled the chain on De la Espriella, De la Espriella might pull the chain on him. Rodriguez was allowed to leave the building, but when a few hours had passed without his resigning, he was sent for again, held more or less prisoner, and threatened with death by the Guardia's noisiest blusterer, Colonel Roberto Díaz. "If you want to be a martyr, martyr you'll be!" Díaz assured him, adding with his inimitable *délicatesse* that blood would flow and that he and his colleagues were as much dictators as any in Central America. With that, Rodríguez resigned (and who can blame him?), went to the bar association, accompanied by a large number of attorneys, gave a short press conference relating the events, took refuge in the Venezuelan embassy, and having obtained safe conduct left the country, from *procurador* to exile in one day.

Rodríguez's replacement, Efraín Villarreal, had taken his law degree in the Soviet Union and knew perfectly well how to pretend jurisprudence in a country where justice did not exist. All swindle investigations ceased in an instant. The Seguro case remains officially a mystery. The guilty are still unpunished, the victims still unavenged.

The eclipse of Paredes came with dizzying swiftness and recalled the childhood occurrence in which the panther silhouetted against one's bedroom window is transformed by the flick of a light switch into something commonplace and innocuous, a chair, a fold of curtain, a lampshade, a pillow. On July 29, 1983, one beheld him in full menace, every inch a despot, bully, and beast, roaring Rafael Rodríguez out of office and into exile. Then, and through the next two weeks, he was, besides, the certain choice for president in 1984, in his own estimation and in that of almost every Panamanian and outside observer. And he would be a president who governed, not just a chauffeur whom the Guardia commandant would tell to turn right or left, then exhibit as the fall guy if there was an accident. Yet by that month's end Paredes was finished, a poor fellow with no seat at the table or likelihood of getting one again.

Sánchez and Koster weren't surprised, though the collapse was abrupt, the deflation total. The wonder was, as they saw things, that Paredes had been so sure and full of himself, so certain of his invulnerability. The arrogance of the mighty is always amazing—astounding, fantastic, a marvel of God. Belshazzar must drink from the temple vases. Nixon has to tape himself. You'd think people at the top would be a bit smarter, but in practice they aren't. The clearest thinker, when surrounded for any length of time by flunkies chirping how great he is, how grand, how majestic, finds his brain poached like an egg, and Paredes wasn't very bright to start with. There he was, putting faith in the pact he'd drawn up with his fellow piranhas, though everyone in the Guardia had the same holy reverence for pacts and oaths and vows as Adolf Hitler. Why, the ink was scarcely dry when he broke it himself! In December 1982, he and his lovely chums Noriega and Díaz forced Armando Contreras into retirement, eight months early and without his promised term as commandant. It was absurd, besides, to think that he, Rubén Paredes, or anyone else could be a real president of the republic without first getting the Guardia back in the bottle.

And how Paredes wasted his moment of power! How the man abused opportunity! He was concerned about Noriega—as anyone not a total dunce had to be. He knew Noriega was dangerous, knew it better than most. So what did he do? He eased his anxiety by demeaning Noriega. He gave Noriega no scope as chief of staff, a post Noriega came into when Contreras retired. He countermanded Noriega's orders and blocked Noriega's favorites from promotion, made Noriega's life miserable, in short.

That is precisely how not to handle Noriega, the Noriega who feeds on ill treatment and insult so as to feel justified when he strikes. If you must deal with a Manuel Noriega, steer 180 degrees from the course of Paredes. Be as courteous to him as you are able. Show him every mark of respect. Do your very best to make him happy. Then, the first chance you get—you'll never get more than one—kill him. Without hesitation, above all without remorse. Shoot him with a silver bullet, then drive a stake through his heart.

Did Paredes suppose he had Noriega browbeaten? Was he unaware of the provocations he made? Each is hard to believe, yet both are possible. Arrogance, after all, is blind. Noriega bore the abuse with patience, and somehow Paredes managed to believe that Noriega would honor the pact and his promises.

The pact, of course, was secret, wasn't published until June 1987. On the other hand, Paredes was set to retire on August 12, 1983, and Noriega was set to take command of the Guardia, so if Paredes hoped to be president (and he did), the two had to have some sort of understanding. Guillermo Sánchez, however, told friends that Paredes would never make it—this despite the support Paredes was rounding up with the leaders of traditional political parties, as well as with the PRD, and despite the okay Paredes had received from Washington. General Wallace Nutting, chief of U.S. Southern Command, called Paredes "a beacon of the Americas," and Sánchez took that so seriously that from then on he referred to Paredes in his column as Faro Parlante (Beacon Who Speaks).

As for Koster, he showed a similar lack of awe for Paredes's future while lunching with Senator Alan Cranston early in August. Cranston was considering a campaign for the Democratic presidential nomination in 1984 and was making the trips that sort of thing requires. As they were sitting down, he told Koster, not without satisfaction (not to say pride) that he had breakfasted with General Paredes.

"I hope you ate well," Koster replied. "Otherwise your time was completely wasted." Koster was amazed, and had been so often, that an otherwise decent and clever man like Cranston, who held office by the vote of his free fellow citizens and knew exactly how Paredes came by his, could feel anything but nausea on meeting the tyrannical oaf.

"Isn't he going to be president?" Cranston asked.

"Five minutes after he takes off his Guardia uniform, he'll have no more power in this country than I do."

Koster's calculation was about right, though Paredes's illusions lasted a bit longer. He was as full of himself as ever at the change-of-command ceremony, taking leave of the troops and his country's armed service with martial pomp. An uninformed onlooker might have supposed him a soldier and imagined that he'd led these troops in battle instead of against unarmed compatriots, that he'd defended Panama instead of help sack it. Then he was saluted by Manuel Noriega, another ornament of the profession of arms, who referred in envoi to the parachute training they'd taken: "Good jump, Rubén!" The irony was wonderfully Noriegan, apparent within a few days and also long lasting. One couldn't think of Paredes without recalling it and, admiring Noriega's patience in revenge, marveling at Paredes's blindness in downfall.

Paredes turned to consolidating his candidacy, the timetable of which now contemplated the naming of key supporters to the cabinet. Time passed and nothing happened, so Paredes went to Guardia headquarters and collected Noriega and Díaz, and the three went to call on De la Espriella. The uninformed onlooker at this meeting might have thought Paredes was still Guardia commandant, for he roared at the puppet president with customary contempt and loutishness. De la Espriella assured him that the cabinet would be changed soon and handed him the list of appointments. "These aren't the men I picked!" roared Rubén Paredes. De la Espriella replied that his picks were more competent. "What has competence got to do with it?" roared Paredes. "Appoint the men I picked!" he roared and stomped out, Noriega and Díaz following.

The three stood for a moment on the steps of the palace. Then Paredes stomped to his car. Before driving off, he glanced in the side mirror. Noriega and Díaz Herrera were still on the steps. Then, as Paredes watched, they turned and went back into the building.

At that moment, Rubén Paredes grasped what had happened. He wasn't really bright, but he wasn't dumb either. Power had made him arrogant, arrogance blind, but now he saw clearly. A few days later, early in September, he addressed an open letter to the general secretary of the Partido Revolucionario Democrático, announcing his withdrawal from the presidential campaign. He had so recently been Guardia commandant, his letter said, that if he lost a bid for the presidency, the defeat would damage the institution. His time as tyrant of Panama had ended on August 12, 1983, but two or so weeks had to pass before he knew it.

10

OF THE CRIMINALS, BY THE CRIMINALS, FOR THE CRIMINALS

The man who took command of the Guardia on August 12, 1983, was at the peak of two demanding professions, had made simultaneous, mutually reinforcing, highly successful careers in politics and crime. On that day to a large extent already, and certainly within a year or so from it, Manuel Noriega was as close to being all-powerful in his country as anyone has ever been anywhere, and though Panama was hardly a force among nations, he possessed considerable influence in the world beyond. Meanwhile, his criminal enterprises and activities were making him one of the world's richest people. Either attainment would compel attention. Together they constituted something new. Under Manuel Noriega, the Republic of Panama became the first nation to have government of, by, and for its criminal element, and government for sale or rent to scum worldwide.

At the bottom of both careers was another in what is called "intelligence" and sometimes "espionage," though both terms mislead by being too narrow. Discovering hidden truth is part of the business, but so is making up and spreading falsehood, provoking error, undermining trust, sowing discord, manipulating, deceiving, injuring outright (as through "deaths put on by cunning and forc'd cause"), disseminating terror, promoting despair, and otherwise confounding for supposed advantage, with the link that it goes on clandestinely down in the slimed and roachy drains of statecraft. Supposed advantage, only supposed advantage, for if the purpose of the state is to advance the freedom and dignity of those within it (and no other purpose is legitimate), the state never gains by those aspects of intelligence work that go beyond collecting intelligence. If states prosper, it is despite not because of such efforts.

Spookery (to coin a term suggesting childishness and lack of substance, from "spook," an intelligence professional) is a form of combat, an especially savage form for having no rules. As a way to wage war while pretending to be peaceable, to be cruel while professing kindness, it congrues precisely with Noriega's nature. He was made for spookhood and it for him: "I am not what I am."

Except for his face. Oddly enough, his face is truthful, albeit involuntarily. The part most useful to most when they are deceitful openly proclaims Noriega evil.

Noriega may have been a *sapo* while still a schoolboy, a low-level informant for U.S. Army counterintelligence in the Canal Zone, reporting on leftist youth activities, a slightly higher-level snitch while at Los Chorrillos, but such duties scarcely qualify one as a professional. It was in 1966 that he put on spookhood, becoming the intelligence officer of the Guardia's Fifth Military District (Chiriquí) and a penetration agent for the CIA. He was, of course, disloyal in both capacities. Betrayal is the rock he built his church on. So we seek him first in the Niflheim of spookdom, misty putrid land of death and the dead.

Who were his case officers, his CIA handlers? There's no way for us to know, but one may have been Néstor Sánchez (no kin), a CIA veteran since the early 1950s, head of its Central American division, later a deputy assistant secretary of defense. He spent much time in Panama and had good things to say about Noriega when most Americans, frankly, didn't love him any more—in the fall of 1987, after the chancre burst in Panama, when Colonel Roberto Díaz's declarations made the evil of Panama's regime and tyrant patent. And in late February 1988, after Noriega had been indicted in Florida, when the visible part of the U.S. government was trying to lever him from power, Sánchez made a rush trip to Panama. A few days after this rush visit, a coup was attempted against Noriega, unquestionably with U.S. knowledge and approval, probably at U.S. instigation, and Noriega survived the attempt with ease, was laughing about it two minutes after it happened, just as if he'd known all along that it was coming, as if someone in the spooky part of the U.S. government had tipped him off.

Other CIA contacts of Noriega's were Duane "Dewey" Clarridge, head of the Central American task force that ran the secret war in Nicaragua early in the 1980s, and Joe Fernández and Félix Rodríguez and Tomás Castillo, associates of Clarridge's in that endeavor. Noriega was most accommodating to them in their work of getting weapons to the Contras, especially after Congress forbade them to do so. He happened to be in the arms-smuggling business, while helping Clarridge et al. facilitated his trafficking in drugs, but that's the way the world is: nobody's perfect.

Besides these, there were other CIA spooks whose names or cover names may never surface, those based in Panama over the years, doing spookery there or elsewhere in the hemisphere, moving money around and flying in and out of ugly, violent, nasty little places such as Panama was becoming. Noriega pampered them, made him glad to have him for a friend. Not just special treatment at the airport either, though that counts: a blind eye to this or that bit of tomfoolery—smuggling, say, or currency finagling—a spook might do to supplement his salary. And Noriega knew how to help a fellow relax, and how to film him while he was relaxing, so he'd never forget how much fun Panama was, or what a grand guy its chief spook, Manuel Noriega. He had a seaside retreat on the Azuero Peninsula, in western Panama, where U.S. officials got to star in porno movies, but anyone who knows Noriega and spookery would have guessed that much. Heinrich Himmler had Maison Kitty, where men worth blackmailing were recorded at frolic. Could Manuel Noriega have less, especially since technology now allowed one to watch as well as listen? Just like God, Noriega was watching. Noriega's kindnesses to colleagues in spookdom go a long way toward explaining the CIA's loyalty to him, and how it happened that, while the visible parts of the U.S. government were trying to oust him, he was in receipt of secret U.S. documents on the subject.

If the annals of human stupidity ever come to be written, the CIA's involvement with Manuel Noriega will surely figure prominently in them. It would be very interesting to learn how supposedly intelligent, sane men, one of whom currently resides in the White House, came to imagine that the purposes of the United States of America might be advanced by an entirely untrustworthy, totally amoral, sadomasochistic sociopath. And don't let George Bush whine and say he didn't know. It was Bush's job as director of central intelligence in 1976 to know what his important finks were up to. Bush's successor, Admiral Stansfield Turner, knew. Turner dropped Noriega from the CIA payroll. When Reagan came into office with

Bush as vice-president and William Casey directing the CIA, Noriega was reinstated at a salary of $200,000 per year, the sum that Bush is earning these days as president.

Casey was an amateur who seems to have enjoyed playing spookmaster more or less the way his boss enjoyed playing president. He could not hope to handle Manuel Noriega. He will have met men as greedy during his career on Wall Street, men as nasty, even men as ruthless, but no one so bloodthirsty, evil, and demented. In the United States and other more or less civilized countries, the Manuel Noriegas don't make it to the stock exchange. Those who are not violently dead by thirty or so are in maximum-security institutions for the criminally insane. That's one of the definitions of civilization. Noriegas don't run around loose, much less run their countries.

We'll tell you who knew how to handle Noriega: Phillip Smith and William Durkin of the Drug Enforcement Administration. If the report to the U.S. attorney general is accurate, the one submitted on June 18, 1975, by Michael A. DeFeo and others, Smith and Durkin proposed that Noriega be killed. The report calls him "Noryago," which is probably neither a misprint nor a misspelling but a missive from the ghost of William Shakespeare, who also knew how to handle Noriegas: "The time, the place, the torture. O, enforce it!"

Did Casey know, before he died, the extent to which Noriega had betrayed him and the United States? Many would say immediately that he had to have. He ran the CIA, he must have known. But the others who'd been made fools of might have kept it from him. We're speaking of men like Sánchez and Clarridge. And they may have kept it from themselves. Sánchez's testimony before the Senate seems ingenuous. He'd heard, he admits, that Noriega was dealing in drugs, but there was no proof. As if proof were required in spookdom. The entire point of spookery is that there are no rules. Then one thinks again and realizes that Sánchez and Clarridge didn't want to believe Noriega was betraying them. And if Noriega was betraying them, using their beautiful Operation Black Eagle as a cover for moving tons of cocaine to the States, then, who knows, maybe he'd been betraying them all along. Maybe he had them on film, you know, relaxing. It's easy to imagine how they might have kept the bad news from themselves.

By the time he took over as commandant of the Guardia, Noriega had them all blackmailed anyway, even if he didn't have any on film. In December 1982, the U.S. Congress passed the first of the Boland amendments prohibiting the CIA and the Defense Department from providing "military equipment, military training or advice . . . for the purpose of overthrowing the government of Nicaragua." But no law could stop Casey, Sánchez, and Clarridge. They went ahead and busted right through that law, with Manuel Antonio Noriega as their accomplice. Casey, Sánchez, and Clarridge had to break the law, even if it meant tons of cocaine shipped to the States and their being blackmailed by Manuel Noriega, because if the Sandinistas weren't overthrown . . .

It's hard to see what they were afraid of. Did they envision Nicaraguan armored columns sweeping across Texas, fanning out toward Kansas and California? Did they actually believe the twaddle about the Sandinistas exporting revolution, or the near twaddle about their arming the insurgents in El Salvador? Manuel Noriega armed a lot more insurgents than the Sandinistas ever dreamed of doing, out of healthy, wholesome capitalistic greed. We think Casey, Sánchez, and Clarridge wanted to play spook, that they liked spooking about in secret, playing nasty tricks on people who couldn't trick back. That's what we think the contra war was about. That's only an opinion, but one thing is certain: they weren't patriots. If they'd cared about their country, they would have obeyed the law. All the communists on earth don't pose as great a threat to the United States as fools in high places putting themselves above the law and defying the sovereign people who employ them.

It's hard for ordinarily respectful people to accept that a country the size and importance of the United States is being run by fools, even when that's the only construction that fits the circumstances. We were living in Central America and knew much more than we cared to about its troubles. We argued, along with many others, against Washington's obsession with Nicaragua. Nicaragua was a mess, but it wasn't important—not for the United States, that is to say—and if one was concerned for the Nicaraguans, what they needed was an end to war, not more of it. Panama, on the other hand, was important. The United States could walk away from Nicaragua, but not from Panama. The Panama Canal couldn't be moved. The problems the United States was going to have in Panama would make Washington nostalgic about Nicaragua.

Of course, the only things Noriega gave us were nightmares. We managed our own relaxing as best we could without the slightest help from him. And we weren't ideologues, so we could think. It was no solace to us that Noriega wasn't a communist, or that Panama's tyranny was, in the hairsplitting of Jeane Kirkpatrick, authoritarian not totalitarian. We're not sure even Kirkpatrick could draw the distinction while watching seven soldiers hose a small boy.

Who gained by the secret war in Nicaragua? One CIA asset did: Manuel Noriega. And Barry Seal, the pilot (who some say was also on the CIA payroll), is reported to have got $19 million in a year and a half out of his involvement in Operation Black Eagle. William Casey and company got a chance to play spook. Jeane Kirkpatrick got practice in hairsplitting. Nicaragua got more misery. Panama got closer to the abyss. But the United States got nothing, unless you want to count more cocaine addicts and more reason for the American people to lose faith in its leaders.

Was a grand design drawn at Langley back in the 1970s to make Noriega master of Panama, thereby to facilitate agency games? We see it more as part of a general policy of helping assets rise so as to enhance their usefulness—one thing then another thing, from helping him be useful to Torrijos (in the matter of background information on visiting senators, for instance) to getting him an invitation to speak at Harvard in February 1985. If anyone was designing things, it was Noriega. If there was a long-term master plan, it was his. We know the outcome: United States, instead of controlling him, was hoodwinked. We know that when the United States decided Noriega must go, the State and Defense Departments and the CIA suddenly and sickeningly discovered that none of them had a single agent in the Guardia or civilian part of the dictatorship. All faith had been placed in Manuel Noriega. We know that at a certain point when Noriega was chief of Panamanian intelligence, his G-2 and the CIA were pooling information and had access to each other's take. We see this as the result of a long seduction, with Noriega maneuvering tirelessly, step by step, making it easier, easier, easier, for the gringos to confide in and depend on him, all the while despising them more and more, despising them particularly for their condescension and sense of superiority to him that were the means by which he bound them in his web. And it was done gradually. One station chief let him go this far. Another let him go a little farther. No need to go on. Everyone knows how seduction works. One day, there was Noriega smirking impishly.

Army intelligence, we note, was never seduced. Individual army spooks were subverted, but INSCOM (the army's Intelligence and Security Command) did not roll over as an institution for Noriega, the way the CIA did. It even mounted an operation against him. This was called Landbroker, went off in 1982, and involved bugging

Noriega's house in the Altos del Golf section of Panama City—went off faultlessly, but the take contained nothing earthshaking, very likely because it didn't run long enough, Noriega's indiscretions being infrequent. Top brass killed it because INSCOM had omitted a mandatory procedure, the filing of a document called a Clandestine Intelligence Operation Proposal, which gets passed on to the CIA for approval. Had one been filed, of course, the CIA would have had the whole thing aborted before letting soldiers spy on its prize "asset." INSCOM was in a catch-22 situation.

Landbroker came in response to a series of affronts inflicted by Noriega while he was running the G-2. The most celebrated was the Case of the Singing Sergeants, involving communications intelligence and two or three army enlisted spooklings attached to the National Security Agency in the United States. The United States is first-rate in technical spookery, and NSA is tops in the country. It has a grid in Panama that can eavesdrop on anyone from the Rio Grande to Tierra del Fuego and even caught Noriega in a rare slipup, blabbing about how Father Gallego was dumped from a chopper. Noriega corrupted the sergeants with money and got hold of embarrassing intercepts of Omar Torrijos that solidified Noriega's power in the Guardia. He also got "sensitive technical materials, including manuals that described how various NSA systems worked." They ended up with Fidel Castro in Cuba. There was, besides, a breach of security at the 470th Military Intelligence Group, Efraín Angueira's old unit, whereby Noriega obtained secret information on U.S. military projects in Central America, and a female spook who was instructed to get close to him and wound up closer than anyone wanted, and an INSCOM officer stationed in Panama who bedded with and blabbed to a Guatemalan woman (perhaps at Noriega's relaxation retreat), who relayed the confidential information to Noriega. The last straw was when the INSCOM commander, Major General Albert Stubblebine, visited Panama and became convinced Noriega had bugged his hotel room. Landbroker was conceived on Stubblebine's return to Washington, along with operations against Cubans and Russians in Panama, but none brought any real benefit. In June 1986, a "former senior C.I.A. official who served in Panama"—which sounds like Néstor Sánchez, who by then was in the Defense Department—told Seymour Hersh that he thought "the United States . . . came out ahead" in its intelligence dealings with Noriega. It seems to us the United States was outspooked very badly.

A great and good friend of Noriega's was the Israeli spook Mike

Harari, onetime director of the death squads set up in the aftermath of the Munich Olympics outrage to provide a final solution for Black September. Here is a view of Harari as he was in those days:

> The director of Mossad's special operations was regarded by the inner circles in Israel as nothing short of a genius in intelligence work. He belonged to the tightly knit group that ran the country. . . . He had fought in the War of Independence as a member of the Haganah's Intelligence service and, by 1972, had accumulated a quarter of a century of experience in espionage.

Genius and experience both seemed to desert him, however, in July 1973, in the Norwegian resort town of Lillehammer, when he personally fingered the wrong man, not the terrorist Ali Hassan Salameh, supposed architect of the Munich massacre, but a café waiter named Ahmed Bouchiki, who wasn't even Palestinian but Moroccan.

We know, we know. Who can tell Arabs apart? What's one less anyway? The Norwegians, though, were entirely unsympathetic. Lillehammer hadn't had a murder in forty years. Norway itself had been more or less free of violence since the Nazi occupation ended, and the Norwegians liked it that way. They took great offense when, because of Harari's perfectly human error, his spooks put fourteen bullets into a peaceable resident as he and his pregnant wife strolled home from the movies. Worse, although Mike got away, because of his blunders six of his team wound up breaking the Eleventh Commandment, one Moses didn't bring but Mossad reveres, and were tried and convicted. The incident became a festering scandal, and Golda Meir had to cancel a program that till then had been murdering flawlessly.

Mrs. Meir was not so contrite as to honor Oslo's request that Harari be sent to Norway to stand trial. Nor was Mossad as stern as one might have expected. Harari remained in service, reportedly reaching the rank of general. He went, reportedly, to Mexico as chief of station. Reportedly he retired in 1978. He may actually have gone off Mossad's payroll. What he clearly seems to have been was a cutout, an ostensibly private person handling part of his government's nastier business. He still belonged to the group that ran his country. In 1982, Israel's ambassador in Panama assured Roberto Eisenmann, publisher of *La Prensa,* that Harari had no connection whatsoever with the Israeli government, then complained in the next breath that he, the ambassador, had just been fired from his post on

Harari's say-so. In any case, in 1978 he appeared in Panama, as if Panama hadn't sufficient killers without him.

Harari was then in his fifties but didn't look it. He showed no bulge of flab about his waistline. His hair, clipped short, soldier style, was still thick and dark. When walking, he held arms and shoulders forward aggressively. When out, he wore aviator-style Ray-Bans and kept shy of photographers. He was, he said, in the import-export business.

He got close to Omar Torrijos, whom he'd met earlier and who admired Israel and its security services. Torrijos took him to Washington for the treaty-signing ceremony. Torrijos took him to lunch with the Shah of Iran. He got close to Manuel Noriega, Torrijos's bagman, torturer, and intelligence chief. Harari and Noriega became business associates, Harari buying weapons in Europe for Noriega to smuggle to rebels in El Salvador, Noriega providing phony end-user certificates for Israel's secret arms sales to Iran. Observe Harari's Noriegan cynicism: lunch with the Shah, arms for the Ayatollah.

A photo of Harari, one of the few extant, shows him hooded by dark glasses, standing behind Noriega to Noriega's right. That, metaphorically, was his position once Noriega was tyrant of Panama. Harari was behind the Guardia's being renamed Defense Forces (PDF), which is what Israel's armed forces are called. This was soon after Noriega took over, on September 29, 1983, with the passage of Law 20, which gave the PDF very broad powers—administrative autonomy, for instance, and control of passports and immigration (we'll see why in a little) and the legal right to extract information from anyone "for motives of national defense and public security." It empowered the commandant to appoint and promote as he pleased and bestowed on every member, no matter how poor in rank or wit or culture, the authority to arrest any civilian, no matter how illustrious, on his or her own say-so, without writ or warrant. Whether Harari was behind the law itself, or Noriega's immediate invocation of it to promote himself general of forces with four stars, we don't know, but at the promotion ceremony Noriega called Harari "my mentor," and accorded him Panama's highest decoration.

Harari was behind the formation within the PDF of the so-called Special Anti-Terrorist Unit (Unidad Especial Anti-Terrorista, UESAT). We say "so-called" because between its institution on December 16, 1983, and the U.S. invasion of Panama in December 1989 it saw action but once, at dawn on July 28, 1987, when it assaulted a private residence occupied entirely by unarmed civilians, some of whom were small children—, and though no one was killed, we have it from people on the receiving end that UESAT performed with exemplary harshness. Harari was behind providing Noriega's G-2 with highly sophisticated Israeli electronic eavesdropping and surveillance equipment, and behind the sale to the PDF for $20 million of Israeli-made radar and control tower equipment that must have helped keep the gun and cocaine planes flying, and behind Noriega's having a bodyguard of Israeli veterans.

Harari was behind a good deal of the Israeli commercial activity in Panama, such as the establishment in Panama City of an office of ISREX, a subsidiary of the Clal financial syndicate dealing in civilian as well as military wares. He allegedly took a bite out of every Israeli firm that did business in Panama, so that Israelis themselves called him a gangster. He seems to have split the proceeds with Noriega, for he was given Panamanian citizenship and became Panama's consul in Tel Aviv.

Harari had a home in Tel Aviv with (as of the early 1980s) a professor wife and an intellectual son, whom he looked down on, and a daughter, his pride and joy, who had joined the military intelligence service. He was welcome everywhere in Israel, showed up on guest lists with the likes of Shimon Peres and Abba Eban. In Panama, he socialized little, but Panamanians who dealt with him found him affable. His Spanish was fluent but strongly laced with Italian, a language he learned in Venice after World War II, when he served with Palmah, smuggling weapons and illegal immigrants into British-occupied Palestine. He had a house in Noriega's walled compound in Altos del Golf, linked to Noriega's (so U.S. Army investigators found in December 1989) by an underground passage.

When Noriega fell from grace with Washington, the United States repeatedly asked Israel to get Harari out of Panama. Israel repeated the same disclaimer: Harari was a private citizen over whom the Israeli government exercised no control. In October 1989, a White House spokesman said the Israelis ought to be ashamed. We agree. If Israel hadn't liked what Harari was doing in Panama, Mossad would have found a way to make him stop.

Also shameful, at least in our view, was the aid and comfort Israeli personnel furnished Noriega's partners the Colombian drug lords in the matter of training their paramilitary units, and the Israeli government's refusal to honor a Colombian request for the extradition of Lieutenant Colonel Vair Klein and others. Israeli contacts with the drug cartels served Noriega's interest on at least one occasion, providing him timely warning of a contract let on his life. It seems possible, too, that Noriega received advice from Israel with regard to suppressing street demonstrations during the summer and fall of 1987. One is struck by the similarity between the tactics employed by the two defense forces, Panamanian and Israeli. The emphasis on beating people, for instance, even where it meant breaking into the homes of people not the least involved in protest and beating them in their living rooms and bedrooms, something never heard of in Panama until the PDF began it but characteristic of the Israeli Defense Forces in their dealings with Arab separatists. As for the practice current in La Modelo Prison in June 1987 whereby some political detainees had the gold inlays prised from their teeth with a screwdriver, it was first inflicted by Nazis on Jews (at the urging of a dentist friend of Himmler's named Hermann Pook) and may have come to Panama via Israel. Those in contact with survivors of the Holocaust are more likely to have heard of this barbarity than equally barbarous Panamanians.

In December 1989, while American and PDF units were still in combat, U.S. Army investigators entered Noriega's house in Altos del Golf and found, besides other odd things, a memorial to Adolf Hitler, complete with effigies and portraits. This might, in retrospect, make somewhat ironic Noriega's 1984 state visit to Israel, during which he was received with full military honors and given a tour of Israeli bases by the chief of staff, General Moshe Levy—except that anyone who cared to use his wits would have known that Noriega was Hitler's disciple. Hitler has disciples the world over. That he should have disciples in Israel may be the Holocaust's greatest tragedy.

Only God knows how many spooks were friends of Noriega's—professionals, we mean, officers of this and that country's spook services. What's certain is he knew the top Latin Americans. He cultivated their friendship and did them favors, such as framing the exiled Ecuadorean politician Abdul Buccaram with a planted half kilo of cocaine, or turning over the leader of the Alfaro Vive movement so that he could be murdered. All this paid off wonderfully in 1989, after the regime's flagrant election fraud and violence led the Organization of American States to send a commission to Panama to arrange for power to be transferred from the tyrant to the people's choices. Diego Cordovez, the Ecuadoran foreign minister, got himself named to the commission and effectively bushwhacked its mission, thereby buying Noriega a bit more time. And Noriega used his spook colleague contacts to further other of his interests, particularly his interests in the arms and drug trades.

Everyone on earth has private interests, dreams, desires, drives. People in or after power will say they wish to serve the collective, helping it toward ideal and practical goals, and sometimes such claims are honest and authentic. Private interests, however, always exist, contributing much if not most of the push. The rub is where private and public interests conflict, such as Manuel Noriega's greed and the welfare of others, beginning with that of the people of Panama—where the person holding power puts himself above the collective, where he doesn't care a fig for it to begin with, or where he confuses it with himself: "L'état c'est moi."

Hitler was an extreme case of the latter. His personal megalomania was so wedded to racial and nationalistic elitism that he could probably say with sincerity that everything he did from 1923 on was so that the German people might take its rightful place as master, thereby fulfilling the plan of evolution. Sincere or no, Hitler's projections of idealism inspired the Germans to exertion and sacrifice that even in a vile cause were sometimes majestic. Noriega could inspire no collective effort grander than getting a gang of perverts to ram things up some poor devil's behind, for he thought of nothing beyond his own gratification, cared for no one but himself, didn't mind if other people noticed, and would probably have held that everyone else was just like him, though some were hypocrites and wouldn't admit it, while others were too stupid to realize what was going on in their own hearts.

A variation on "L'état c'est moi" substitutes an organization for the individual and confuses its interests with those of the larger collective. This perversion of thought, when applied to the military, is at the bottom of traditional militarism in Latin America. In Panama, however, there were no soldiers, and no shred or scrap of soldier's ethic—duty, honor, country, courage, glory—to restrain men from abuses or temper their lusts. What happened in Panama, beginning with Omar Torrijos, and reaching its most complete expression with Noriega, was that structural militarism, a form of elitism, was infused with an ethos (if it may be called that) of radical individualism common to corrupt police and other criminals. The result was the narco-military state, a new phenomenon, where a national entity is controlled by its military establishment, and this in turn is controlled by a criminal clique, gangsters in uniform dedicated to enriching themselves via crime, characteristically via the traffic in cocaine.

Watch the thing spread from Panama to Honduras. In 1980, Noriega's counterpart spook there, chief of Honduran military intelligence, was a Colonel Leonidas Torres-Arias. Noriega drew him into the business of supplying weapons to the Farabundo Martí National Liberation Front rebels in El Salvador, FMLN. Noriega sat down with the FMLN leadership and worked out two routes for shipping them weapons and had Torres-Arias protect the one that used airstrips in northern Honduras. Then Torres-Arias did such a good job that Noriega drew him into the business of supplying cocaine to the snorters of Gringoland. The network of clandestine airstrips in Honduras and other parts of Central America was made to order for the traffic in cocaine as soon as the cartels came into being and light aircraft became the principal means of shipping the drug. And there you are: the Republic of Honduras was on its way to being a narco-military state, a goal it seems now to have reached safely.

Torres-Arias personally experienced a reverse of fortunes not uncommon among friends of Noriega's. Torres-Aries brought an associate into the arms traffic, a Colonel Boden, who commanded an armored division, and in 1983 Noriega decided to put them in direct contact with the FMLN leadership, perhaps so that they could run the business without as much oversight from him, for surely he had many irons in the fire. In any case, Noriega flew Torres-Arias and Boden secretly from Panama to Havana so that Fidel Castro could make the introductions. Word leaked out, however, about the two Hondurans' making the trip, so to save himself embarrassment and make a few tardy points with the dopes at Langley, Noriega passed details to the fellow who thought he was running him. The result was scandal in Tegucigalpa (Honduras). Torres-Arias and Boden were cashiered from the Honduran army.

Cuba's top spooks were friends of Noriega's of course, including Manuel Piñeiro (called Barba Roja, Redbeard), who coordinated Cuban assistance to guerrilla groups all over Latin America. Noriega worked with him in March 1981, arming and arranging the transport for a contingent of volunteers, among them some Panamanians, who had trained in Cuba in preparation for joining the M-19 *guerrilleros* in Colombia. When they came ashore, though, the Colombian army was waiting, having been put on guard by U.S. Southern Command after the volunteers' ship was spotted by a U-2 spy plane. It may have been through Piñeiro that Noriega got to know M-19's leaders, particularly Jaime Bateman, who traveled often to Panama to deposit the proceeds of M-19's kidnappings, though perhaps it was García

Márquez who made the introductions to Torrijos, for it was Torrijos who arranged Panama's involvement in the March 1981 expedition.

M-19 was one of the go-betweens that put Noriega in contact with the Medellín drug lords. He was already in contact with them by proxy, already somewhat in business with them through a Miami accountant named Ramón Millán. As early as 1976, Millán was flying regularly to Panama to launder the picayune five- and six-figure sums made back in the horseless-carriage days of coke smuggling. He would count and pack the money and take it to Panama, where tote bags full of cash raised no banker's eyebrows. A dummy firm would be set up for each deposit, a thing you could do for $250, $500 (bribes included) for while-you-wait service. Then the funds would be withdrawn, accounted for with a teller's receipt that specified no destination for them, and deposited in another account at the same bank in the name of another dummy corporation. Then they'd move to another account in a different bank. The money would mill around from bank to bank, churn from one dummy company to another, until it felt clean enough to head for the islands, Caicos or Curaçao, Nassau or Grand Cayman, to repose in an outwardly honest investment company controlled in one way or another by Millán's client. Then, at length, it came home to the United States in exchange for stocks or bonds or treasury instruments or other things that people buy with clean money. And while Millán was in Panama doing this business, he had the help of members of Panama's military, who were always glad to assist businessmen for a fee. Quite possibly Noriega was among them.

In 1979, however, things changed. By then, cocaine smuggling had found its Henry Ford, Carlos Lehder Rivas, and its General Motors, the Medellín cartel, and Millán was working full-time washing the latter's money. That year, the kings of cocaine contracted formally to use Panama's laundromat. The cartel sent Millán to Panama, and Torrijos appointed his gangster, Manuel Noriega, and Millán and Noriega sat down and worked out an agreement whereby Torrijos and mob would furnish security and other services (discouraging musclers-in by terror, for instance) for the cartel's money-laundering operations, with a fee of between 0.5 and 10 percent, depending on the services actually rendered. That agreement was evidently still in force when Noriega's direct contact with the cartel started.

What happened around 1979 was that Lehder, a cocaine smuggler from Quindío, Colombia, realized that soaring demand could never be met, or the booming U.S. market exploited efficiently, without a better transport system than the one in use late in the 1970s. In fact, there was scarcely a system at all. Cocaine went by boat and was nabbed by the U.S. Coast Guard, was secreted on jetliners, but U.S. Customs knew that. Couriers rode the Bogotá–Miami flights with cocaine in false-bottom bags and sewn up in teddy bears, with cocaine stuffed in hollowed-out Indian art objects, with condoms full of cocaine in their gizzards. Cocaine was shipped by every means but dogsled, but in so vulnerable and haphazard a fashion that one's customers could never be sure of supply, and if there's a class of consumer that needs peace of mind, that wants to know the product's on the shelf, drug addicts are it. Lehder's solution was airlift, regular relays of drug planes, each plane carrying hundreds of kilos per flight. Only that way could cocaine be an up-to-date industry.

Enter Jorge Ochoa and Pablo Escobar, smugglers from Medellín in Antioquia, importers and refiners also, big men in the cocaine trade and destined to be bigger. Lehder sold them on the airlift concept, and they undertook to provide regular supply, putting together ton-at-a-time shipments by combining their own cocaine with piggyback loads from small dealers, one to one hundred kilos packaged separately and coded for ownership. The broker in Miami, New York, or Los Angeles had a list of the codes and handled the accounting, and your shipment was protected against theft and insured against confiscation by U.S. authorities. You paid a fee, turned over a percentage to the big boys, but look at all they gave you for your money, and if you insisted on being independent, on spurning the cartel's generous offer, you could end up with your balls for breakfast, because Colombia is a very serious country.

Was business good? Business was so good by 1980 that Ochoa bought a navigation and communications system to track his planes with, and hired an engineer in the States to install it, and had four or five groups of pilots operating at any one time. In April 1981, the cartel had a summit meeting at one of the Ochoa family's ranches near Barranquilla, on the Caribbean coast—all the young cocaine barons, for the cartel was feudally loose in structure. The theme of the conclave was expansion, and in Miami during the months that followed, one of Ochoa's distributors alone coordinated cocaine flights totaling nineteen tons of uncut powder! More, the gaudiest days were still ahead, when the cartel went into business with Manuel Noriega.

Enter now the Movimiento Diecinueve de Abril (Nineteenth of April Movement, M-19). As of 1981, when the cartel got into high gear, M-19 had about twenty-five hundred active members and specialized in bold and showy urban guerrilla capers. It had begun on the right wing but had soon swung leftward, perhaps because it funded itself by kidnapping and therefore found the rich a convenient enemy. Certainly it had them properly cowed. No wealthy person in Colombia was without his private militia of bodyguards, mostly because of M-19, which had pulled off many daring and lucrative snatches, but on November 12, 1981, the group got too big for its britches. That day, it learned (in Blake's phrase) that "you never know what is enough unless you know what is more than enough," for that day it kidnapped Jorge Ochoa's little sister Marta from the University of Antioquia, where she was studying.

M-19 asked $15 million in ransom. Instead of paying, Ochoa called the dope dealers together and, from among the 223 who attended, raised a treasury of over $7 million, recruited an army of over two thousand torpedoes, and formed an organization called MAS (Muerte a los Secuestradores, Death to Kidnappers) that began hunting down M-19 members and anyone else connected with kidnapping. Two knowledgeable reporters put it as follows:

> MAS's verifiable acts were impressive. In January MAS captured the Antioquia province chief of M-19, stripped him, tied him up, dumped him in a vacant lot in northern Bogotá, and called the police. In February MAS smuggled a loaded pistol into a jail outside Medellín, where a convict used it to murder two street punks imprisoned as kidnappers.

By then, the guerrillas were suing for peace and talks were in progress. In Panama, for M-19's leaders had asked their friend Manuel Noriega to act as mediator, and MAS had accepted his good offices. Negotiations lasted several weeks, at the end of which peace was concluded. M-19 accepted a token payment of $535,000 and released Marta Ochoa unharmed on February 19, 1982. The whole episode had profound consequences. The cartel, at first a loose organization, became consolidated as a result of successful military action in a process not unlike the consolidation of the state in medieval times. It acquired an image of omnipotence, having captured M-19's chief in Antioquia, something the Colombian army had been trying to do for years. M-19 and the cartel moved from antagonism to cooperation. The chief consequence, however, in our view, was that Noriega and the kings of cocaine met, for that led directly to Panama's becoming the first narco-military state.

Noriega's direct dealings with the cartel began in June 1982. The point was this: the flight to southern Florida from northern Colombia went some twelve hundred miles over the Caribbean, counting the dogleg required to miss Cuban airspace. Routing the drug planes west over Panama, Costa Rica, Nicaragua, and Honduras, using the network of strips Noriega controlled by virtue of his being in the arms-smuggling business, made the flights considerably longer *but cut close to four hundred miles off the part that went over water,* the longest leg between points of refueling. The shorter that leg, the less fuel had to be carried, the more cocaine could be shipped on every flight, and with a kilo of unstepped-on cocaine going for from $60,000 to $80,000, those four hundred miles made a big difference. Meanwhile, using Noriega's strips, the cartel could fly its product to Louisiana and Texas, avoiding Miami, which was carefully watched, and utilizing a technique developed by the Lindbergh of coke pilots, Barry Seal, whereby the plane went in at low altitude and airspeed so that it looked on radar screens like one of the dozens of helicopters plying between the coast and offshore oil rigs. Noriega asked $100,-000 for the first flight, then kept upping his price until it finally stabilized at $500,000 and 1 percent of the load. And since Colombia was cracking down on the dopers, Noriega let the cartel set up a processing plant in Daríen Province. What with the fees for that and laundromat charges, by 1983 the cartel's man Millán was handing Manuel Noriega $10 million per month!

In the matter of the shipments, Noriega dealt with Pablo Escobar. A pilot named Floyd Carlton was liaison between them. Like many of the coke pilots, he'd done an apprenticeship flying weapons. It was Carlton who got word when the shipments were coming and who, at the start of the business, kept bringing the bad news that the price had gone up. Each time the bump was $50,000, and Escobar said that was typical of Noriega. He'd dealt with Noriega before, Escobar said, perhaps referring to the talks with M-19. And when Escobar sent a flight without telling Carlton—a misunderstanding, perhaps, since Carlton was in Europe at the time, but in Noriega's view an attempt to sneak a flight through without paying—some of Escobar's people were taken prisoner and (as Carlton later told a Senate subcommittee) "they were severely tortured, and they had limbs fractured." Noriega told Carlton about it, and asked him what the cartel thought about him. Did they think Panama was run by a bunch of Indians, that they could come in and do whatever they pleased?

Carlton and his close friend César Rodríguez started a small charter airline in 1978, when both were twenty-four, flying weapons for Colonel Noriega. To the Sandinistas, then to the FMLN rebels in El Salvador; assault rifles and hand grenades, and ammunition, and powerful mines they called *bombas vietnamitas.* They flew from a place called El Tamarindo, in Costa Rica, to strips in El Salvador, till on Father's Day in 1980 Rodríguez crashed an Aero Commander on one of them. Carlton, who'd just taken off, went back in and pulled his friend from the wreckage and got him to Panama, where he recovered, but the Salvadoran army found the plane and traced it to Panama and raised a big stink, in which the United States also participated. Noriega came through it, however, with no real trouble. He pretended to get out of the weapons business, but all he actually did was work out new routes, one of which (as we've seen) went through Honduras with Colonel Torres-Arias's protection, and the gun business went on as smoothly as ever.

Noriega liked Rodríguez, who was a free spender and had an adventurous spirit. They were close friends and had businesses together, including a private club on the top floor of the Bank of Boston Building that was later converted into the restaurant Windows. Noriega asked the manager of the Panama National Bank to approve a loan to Rodríguez. That was typical of how Noriega invested. He went into business but rarely put up any money, and we'll bet the bank didn't check César's credit either. The manager could either approve the loan outright or make sure he had a seat on the next plane out. Rodríguez was in the limousine rental business and had a company named Sud Export and Import. He opened a discotheque, called Open House, and every night it was packed. His restaurant was popular too, at least in part because people knew who owned it, a gun and drug smuggler and friend of Noriega's. By the time he was thirty, Rodríguez had made and spent millions, but then he and Noriega drifted apart. Rodríguez got into drug deals without Noriega. And the way he flung money around was no longer appealing, now that Noriega was what news magazines call a "strongman" and was beginning to worry about his image. And in October 1985, after Hugo Spadafora's unfortunate passing, when Noriega's image was gathering grime at high speed, Rodríguez bought a big house a block from Noriega's principal residence in Altos del Golf. Noriega sent for his close adviser, José I. Blandón, and Major Luis del Cid, his longtime henchman, and in their presence called César Rodríguez and told him to sell his house, and Rodríguez did so. Noriega remarked at the time that if Rodríguez kept flashing his money he'd end up like Hugo, and amazingly enough the prediction came true, or almost true, since Rodríguez wasn't beheaded. Five months later, he was murdered in Colombia, along with General Paredes's son Rubén, Junior. Neither one was beheaded. They were merely stripped naked and trussed up with wire and relieved of their eyes and tongues before being shot.

Another pilot who flew for Noriega was Enrique Pretelt. They went back at least to 1970, when Pretelt was working for a domestic airline and Noriega was commanding in Chiriquí. On January 9, 1970, Pretelt was piloting a DC-3 between Panama and Changuinola when one of the passengers, an eighteen-year-old mental retard named Jorge Medrano, took out a gun and said he wanted to go to Cuba. The copilot convinced him that they'd have to go to David first for refueling, and Pretelt advised the tower of the situation. Within minutes, the field was crawling with *guardias,* with Major Noriega in personal command, and as soon as the plane landed, it was surrounded. Medrano surrendered, but as that would not have helped Noriega's career much, Noriega had him shot dead and put out the story that there'd been no other recourse and that wholesale slaughter had been averted only through his prompt and decisive action.

Pretelt was short and slight with delicate features, and very light-skinned, a mark of his German ancestry. He and Noriega may have known each other before the hijacking incident. After it, anyway, they had many business interests in common. Whether Pretelt flew weapons and drugs isn't clear, but (according to Blandón's Senate testimony) after Ramón Millán disappeared from the scene, Pretelt was in charge of laundering the cartel's cocaine profits. He was captured in January 1990 and taken to Miami to answer charges.

A number of FDP officers were accomplices in Noriega's drug trafficking, men in whom he could place absolute confidence for being as pitiless and degenerate as he was, among them Luis Córdoba, whom we've seen at play with Dr. Hugo Spadafora, and Cleto Hernández, who General Paredes says murdered his son and who ran La Modelo at the time of its most disgusting abuses, and Luis del Cid, who had the honor of being indicted along with Noriega by a Florida grand jury, and Hilario Trujillo, whom Noriega considered worse than he was. On August 12, 1988, the fifth anniversary of his taking command, Noriega harangued a military review and, drunk on power if not on liquor or cocaine, warned his enemies, those who clamored for him to leave power, warned them in hoarse and terrifying tones, "Put up with Noriega, those who come after are worse!" and as an example he named Trujillo and Córdoba.

Nivaldo Madriñán was part of the cocaine ring, Madriñán the torture virtuoso who accompanied Noriega in a notable duet performed on the teenage son of a prominent jeweler. Madriñán was chief of the Departamento Nacional de Investigaciones, Panama's counterpart to the FBI and (one hopes) the only such agency run by a criminal. He detailed his half-brother, a man named Luis Quiel whom he'd put on as one of his agents, to make sure that the cartel's people weren't bothered and generally to administer the drug shipments, and Quiel did his job so well that he was given the courtesy rank of PDF captain, though he wasn't a formal member of that glorious band. And in a perfect epiphany of cynicism, Noriega made Quiel chief of Panama's Drug Control Unit, and thus liaison with the U.S. Drug Enforcement Administration (DEA), which had agents in Panama attached to the embassy. So when Quiel wasn't busy keeping the cocaine flowing across U.S. borders, he pretended to help the United States in its war against drugs.

Which the United States was only pretending to fight in the first place. What other construction can be put on events? That the United States was in fact fighting, but on the wrong side? That, too, can be argued. Noriega was making ten million a month in the drug game, and John Lawn, the DEA chief, kept praising his cooperation. On May 27, 1987, Lawn wrote him, "DEA has long welcomed our close association and we stand ready to proceed jointly against international traffickers whenever the occasion rises." As late as March 1989, fifteen months *after* Noriega was indicted in Miami for using his position "to facilitate the manufacture and transportation of large quantities of cocaine destined for the United States and to launder narcotics profits," the occasion was still arising. The DEA relied on the PDF to capture twenty-nine persons who'd been indicted for laundering $443 million of the cartel's cocaine profits, but the main man, one Eduardo Martínez, "escaped" from PDF custody and made his way out of Panama home to Colombia. So much for proceeding jointly.

The DEA's "close association" with Noriega worked wonderfully well for the agency's image, however. One of Captain Quiel's jobs was to discourage competition, so dopers who infringed Panama's borders without paying off Panama's tyrant were often turned over to the DEA's agents, thereby goosing the latters' productivity stats. And the DEA was allowed to cowboy a little, to play a bit fast and loose with Panama's sovereignty where and when Noriega pleased, as when its agents plucked a big-fish doper named Reed from his refuge near Portobelo, in Colón Province, and in "Operation Pisces" in 1987, which pretended to strike a blow against money laundering. And once every blue moon there was a plump bonus. There was, for instance, Alberto Audemar, a Colombian hit man whom Luis Córdoba laid hands on and who was shipped to the States without benefit of extradition, though Córdoba got $60,000. And in May 1983 Ramón Millán, the money washer, was arrested in Fort Lauderdale, Florida, while attempting to leave for Panama in his Learjet with $5.4 million in cash. Noriega tipped off the DEA, DEA tipped off Customs. Everyone looked good, everyone looked like a hero, but the Panama laundromat kept churning smoothly. The only change was that Quique Pretelt did Millán's job and collected his fees. That was Noriega's way of rewarding Pretelt. And Millán? Millán got tried and convicted on RICO (racketeering) statutes and sentenced to forty-three years in federal prison, one of those unlucky reversals of fortune that come so often to Noriega's friends.

Then there was the gentleman smuggler, the idiot gringo, usually in his twenties, who went down to Colombia or Peru or Bolivia and got hold of a kilo or two, with a view toward making a few bucks back in New Jersey or just having something to snort and lure the girls with. If fate routed him north via Panama (and Panama was where most of the airlines stopped), Captain Luis Quiel and cohorts were liable to nab him, and then, and then—then things became unpleasant. His arrest would be blared in the government newspapers as proof that Panama, too, was warring on drugs. His cocaine would be impounded and promptly sold. And he would be beaten several shades of purple and dumped in the basement of La Modelo Prison—no trial, no sentence, therefore no release date—till family or friends ransomed him home. The going rate was $20,000, and if the fool had loved ones, they paid. You, too, would pay if a loved one were in La Modelo, living on roachburgers, not wanting for companionship during the night. In March 1985, Guillermo Sánchez went through the dailies for 1984 and found that over a hundred Americans had been arrested for drug smuggling, though records at the Ministry of Justice showed that not one had been tried or was still in custody. Ring up another $2 million for Manuel Noriega.

Noriega wrote no letters praising John Lawn. None, in any case, have so far surfaced. But he too had cause to appreciate his "close association" with the DEA. Besides the DEA's convenience as a waste bin for dumping competitors, DEA agents in Panama shared information with Captain Luis Quiel's intrepid drug controllers, and Quiel of course shared it with Noriega, and Noriega too was generous, he too shared, passed tasty tidbits on to Pablo Escobar—that is to say, to the Medellín drug cartel—and to other traffickers with whom he was friendly. And so the little planes winged bravely northward, bearing their cargoes of solace to the crackheads and *bazuco* freaks of Gringoland. The little planes passed through the blockade—along with some that weren't so little, Barry Seal's C-123, for instance, that had a interesting postcocaine history, ending up being shot down in Nicaragua with Mr. Eugene Hasenfus on board. The DEA caught precious few of them, at least partly because of that "close association" that its chief John Lawn thought was so grand.

The very concept of a war on drugs became meaningless with Black Eagle and Supermarket, the CIA operations whereby weapons were secretly supplied to the contras in contravention of congressional strictures. In Black Eagle, Israeli stocks of captured PLO weapons were moved from Texas to Central America by means of Noriega's network of hidden airstrips. By 1982, when Black Eagle was running at full throttle, the typical pilot's career had described an ascending spiral from flying guns for the Sandinistas to kill Nicaraguans with to flying drugs for the contras to kill Nicaraguans with, but now with the U.S.A.'s blessing. Observe the delicate touch Noriega added: "Instantly grasping that drug pilots would be sitting in the cockpits of empty planes for the return flights, Noriega alertly filled the void by arranging for them to carry narcotics." The CIA, of course, was buying the gas, as well as protecting the whole operation against the impious meddling of law enforcement organizations, which put the U.S. government in the cocaine trade—that is, in the war against drugs but on the wrong side.

With Supermarket it got a little worse. There the weapons airlift was funded with cocaine money. For example, Felix Rodríguez of the CIA approached Ramón Millán of the Medellín cartel. Would his organization help a worthy cause? Could they spare a few bucks for the freedom fighters? And Millán gave $10 million. To begin with, he couldn't say, "I gave at the office." More to the point, the philanthropists he worked for simply could not afford to pass up the chance to win a few friends in Washington. Rodríguez was now assisting Donald Gregg. Gregg, a former CIA officer, was chief of staff to George Bush. Bush, meanwhile, besides being vice-president of the United States, was titular head and spiritual leader of a thing called the South Florida Drug Task Force, set up in February 1982 to help the suffering nation dig out of the coke blizzard—the point unit, that is to say, in the so-called, supposed war on drugs. The task force was commanded in the field by Admiral (retired) Daniel P. Murphy, former CIA deputy director, former chief of staff to Vice-President Bush, the very same Daniel P. Murphy who in the fall of 1987, when the visible part of the U.S. government was trying to winkle Manuel Noriega from power, flew down to Panama with Tongsung Park, of all people, the peerless briber, in a jet borrowed from a Miami arms dealer under indictment for smuggling, and "convinced Noriega that he was not facing a solid wall of opposition in the United States, but an array of divergent views that could be manipulated."

War on drugs? Baloney! By summer 1989, the price of a kilo of coke, FOB Miami, had dropped to around $14,000, and even the Medellín cartel obeys the law of supply and demand. The United States had two governments, and the one that counted was making love not war. Casey was in bed with the dopers. As was lovable Oliver North, as his notebooks show. As was George Herbert Walker Bush, now of 1500 Pennsylvania Avenue, NW, Washington, D.C. He can plead terminal ignorance if he feels like it, and maybe he can get people to believe him, but what passed for a war on drugs was actually something much different, a permanent, floating, Mongolian cluster-fuck involving the decision-making members of the U.S. government and the daddies of the cocaine trade, and it's not much of a mystery who was on top.

Millán routed the $10 million through a company called Frigoríficos de Puntarenas, a Costa Rican seafood freezing company that Noriega set up during the 1970s to market Cuban shrimp in the United States, one of a number of ways (as we'll see in a little) in which Panama's tyrants helped Fidel Castro. Noriega, who reportedly raised $20 million for the contras himself, passed the funds to Mike Harari, who used them to buy Czech and Polish weapons that were sent to warehouses in Honduras. And guess what? When the U.S. Congress voted humanitarian aid for the contras, Frigoríficos de Puntarenas, that famous font of mercy, received $231,587 in late 1985 and early 1986, Uncle Sam's way of telling Noriega that there were no hard feelings over the unfortunate passing of Hugo Spadafora. Floyd Carlton's airline also got money from the State Department's Nicaragua Humanitarian Aid Office. Other cocaine traffickers were similarly favored. What war on drugs?

In May 1984, Noriega furnished the drug lords extraordinary services, and charged (of course) extraordinary prices. Ochoa, Escobar, and company had found out what enough was by going a little too far, had arranged the assassination of Colombia's justice minister, Rodrigo Lara, and suddenly found the country too hot for them. Noriega was in the process of stealing an election but managed to provide sanctuary in Panama for the cartel's chiefs and platoons of their gunmen, as well as facilities for their celebrated meetings with former Colombian President Alfonso López and Procurador Carlos Jiménez, in which, in return for amnesty, they offered to repatriate their numerous billions, retire from the drug trade, and live cleanly as gentlemen should on the fruits of their labors. But now Noriega's twin careers came into conflict, as they were perhaps bound to do once he'd reached the summit of both. As the man running Panama, he came under pressure from Colombia to betray himself as the cartel's business associate. What to do? There was the cartel's lab in Darién. PDF Colonel Julian Melo was in charge of it on the Panamanian side, undertaking (for instance) to keep it supplied with ether, a necessary ingredient in processing cocaine powder from paste. Melo had collected a bribe of $5 million, $2 million of which he kept, with $2 million for Noriega and another million split up among a number of officers. As something visible in the way of anti-cartel action to mollify Panama's neighbors to the southeast, Noriega had the lab raided and Melo cashiered—this on May 29, 1984, while the chiefs of the cartel were still refuged in Panama but with Noriega in Europe, since, like his forerunner Alphonse Capone, he liked to be out of town when dirty work was done.

The chiefs of the cartel were not amused. They decided to kill Noriega, an idea that seems to have occurred to just about everyone who's ever dealt with him but that no one, alas, has followed through on. Mossad got wind of the hit and alerted Noriega. Noriega asked Fidel Castro to serve as peacemaker, and Castro mediated a face-saving deal whereby the cartel canceled its murder contract while Noriega returned the lab equipment, released the twenty-three Colombian technicians who'd been arrested, and made restitution of the $5 million. The last must have pained him cruelly, for like many wealthy men who grew up in poverty Noriega is notoriously stingy. There was, besides, the apprehension he must have suffered on knowing that the cartel wanted him dead. On the other hand, he got the Colombian government out of his hair and (for closing the lab down) collected another letter from Mr. John Lawn.

Castro had good reason to keep Noriega healthy. There was the deal whereby Cuba's shrimp and lobster catch was packaged as Panamanian produce and marketed in the United States, a valuable source of foreign exchange for Castro. There was the port of Vacamonte, on the Pacific, just west of the entrance to the Canal, where Cuba's fishing fleet docked and received maintenance through a firm called Servinaves, S.A. Another firm, Reciclaje, S.A., operated in the Colón Free Zone buying embargoed U.S. high-tech products for sale to the Cuban state, which then resold most of them to the Soviet Union. Noriega made money on all these activities and also had, as Castro's gift, sole rights to distribute Cuban cigars in Panama, a business Carlos Wittgreen ran for him, but Noriega was worth all this and more. Noriega passed on to DGI, Cuban intelligence, the details of Black Eagle and Supermarket, along with all manner of espionage against the United States—NSA data and manuals, as we've seen, and the information that enabled the Sandinistas to shoot down Barry Seal's old C-123 carrying guns and ammo to the contras, along with a chap called Gene Hasenfus, and thus precipitate the Iran-contra scandal.

Meanwhile, he spied on Fidel Castro for Bush and Casey. Noriega worked both sides of every street, as much (one feels) just to betray those he dealt with as for the money and power that double-dealing brought him.

Did he have other rackets? He did. He was in contraband of all sorts, to the detriment of Panama and other countries. The PDF general staff moved liquor and appliances and TV sets, recorders, sound equipment, cameras, and so forth from the Free Zone in Colón onto the internal market, defrauding the treasury of taxes and competing unfairly with local merchants. This scam was as old as the dictatorship, and now Noriega, as top man, took the fattest cut. There was, besides, contraband in rice and other commodities to take illegal advantage of Panama's price support system, and Noriega condoned it in return for a cut. Colombian coffee was imported and repackaged as Panamanian coffee and marketed in the United States as part of Panama's coffee quota, and yes, Noriega got a cut of this also. His man in the Colón Free Zone was Carlos Duque, and in 1988 Duque was rewarded for faithful service in contraband by being the government's candidate for president—a sordid boon, as things turned out, for not even Noriega could steal that vote for his puppet.

Noriega was in fencing, the purchase and resale of stolen goods. He had an interest in a company called Goldsil, S.A., which bought ornaments from burglars and melted them down and sold the metal ingots. Major Rafael Cedeño fenced stolen jewels for Noriega, and the Department of Investigations, Madriñán's outfit, fenced electronic items—stereos, VCRs, personal computers—and resold them in South America. We imagine Noriega got a cut of this also. What we can't imagine is anyone cutting him out. And the PDF perpetrated house-breaking, directing and protecting burglars who victimized opponents of the regime. In 1988, after Noriega's indictment, the chief of police in Balboa, Captain Moisés Cortizo, a West Point graduate, directed a systematic program of burglary against residents of the community, virtually all of whom worked for the Canal Commission.

There was a racket making identity cards for all the sailors of Panamanian-flag vessels, the crews (that is) of fifteen thousand ships, since Panama ranks second only to Liberia in flag-of-convenience merchant navy. One hundred bucks each for a card good for one year only, of which about $99 was pure profit. And a racket involving seamanship exams for every ship's officers that brought in about $3 million per year.

There were rackets involving the sale of passports and visas, grosser variations on the theme of selling his country that were facilitated when Law 20 gave control of passports and visas to the PDF. Noriega sold both wholesale and retail. A thousand or so passports went to Fidel Castro at about $5,000 each for use by Cuban secret agents, and probably (through resale, trade, whatever) to those of other Soviet-bloc nations. Individuals, meanwhile, could purchase them retail. The celebrated Spanish manipulator Ruiz Mateos owned one, for instance, and gentlemen residents of Macao and Singapore paid as high as $100,000 for a complete Panamanian identity kit—passport, identity card, and birth certificate. The sale of Panamanian visas to people from Hong Kong, Taiwan, and other areas with large Chinese populations was a big business, though somewhat seasonal in that Chinese tend to be imported in greatest quantity prior to elections, always somehow finding their names on voting lists.

More loathsome was the sale of transit visas to dissident Cubans, a traffic in human misery run in cahoots with Fidel Castro. It continued from 1980 till 1987 and netted about $80 million, most of which came from the dissidents' relatives in Dade County, Florida. Once in Panama, the refugees had to live in housing owned by Noriega's henchmen, paying what these felt like charging, and were continually vulnerable to extortions and shakedowns enforced by the threat that they would be sent back to Cuba. Meanwhile, they were forbidden to work, and since the wait for U.S. visas might drag on for years, they were often tempted to try illegal entry, putting themselves in the hands of people smugglers of at best intermittent honesty. Noriega got a cut of this commerce also. What most of the refugees did was try to earn a few dollars as street vendors. One could see them at every big intersection in Panama City, middle-aged men trudging from car to car in the oleaginous stifle of a Panama forenoon, with their cardboard trays of cookies or bags of lemons, forlornly waiting out years in an alien land.

How much was Manuel Noriega taking in? Millán testified that in the period 1979–83 he paid him between $320 million and $350 million, that Noriega would have him pay fees and deposit the money, that several accounts in several countries were used, that the Algemene Bank Nederland was Noriega's favorite, that he never missed a month sending money to France, two or three million dollars in every deposit—and drugs were only part of Noriega's income, and Millán's disbursements only part of that part, the largest part of the cocaine part to be sure, but Noriega had other cocaine income and was in the marijuana business as well. Meanwhile, the other rackets were cranking out money. Meanwhile, the general staff's companies were paying too—legitimate businesses the PDF general staff had muscled in on (Licores de Tocumen, for example) or set up, such as Explosivos Nacionales, which had a dynamite-importing monopoly. Meanwhile, like every other serious gangster, he'd used his crime proceeds to found or invest in many legitimate businesses. How much he was taking in only God knows, but here's a shot at what he was worth in the late 1980s:

He had a house in Altos del Golf, which he bought for $275,000 and made $780,000 in improvements on, and a house nearby in the San Francisco sector of Panama City, which was worth about $750,000, and a fortified mansion on forty-five acres of beachfront at Playa Blanca, on the Pacific, near the PDF Río Hato base, and it was worth at least $3 million. He had a house in Veraguas Province worth $185,000 and a ranch in Potrerillos, Chiriquí Province, with a house and a bunker and an airfield. It was worth about $1 million. He had a chateau in France and a Paris apartment and a villa in Spain and two villas in Israel, and a ranch in the Dominican Republic, and a penthouse in Caracas, and a house in Japan. These together were worth a bit more than $10 million. In Japan, he also had a small Buddhist temple worth $350,000, which he'd donated or meant to donate to charity.

He owned half the shares in TV Channel 2 in Panama, and a chunk of Editora Renovación, the company that published the regime's newspapers, and part of Visat, the cable TV company, and shares in Transit, S.A., and in Explosivos Nacionales, and in Licores de Tocumen and Equipajes Acompañados. These were all companies owned by the PDF, and Noriega's shares were worth, say, $6.5 million. In 1988, the PDF opened a bank called Banco Patria. Noriega's shares were worth $28 million.

He owned four retail businesses in Panama City, Más x Menos, which had two stores, and stores called PX and El Depósito and El Millón. These interests were worth almost $4 million. He had a large interest in the Riande hotel chain, which has three hotels in Panama and many elsewhere. We don't know how much that interest came to, but his piece of the Riande hotel in Tampa, Florida, was worth $1.5 million. He owned two apartment buildings on Punta Paitilla in Panama City worth $1.3 million together. He owned two buildings in New Orleans—whether office or apartment, we don't know—and a building in Santo Domingo, Dominican Republic. The three together were worth nearly $4 million. His known bank deposits were as follows: As of January 1, 1988, four numbered accounts in Switzerland of $125, $232, $126, and $150 million, respectively. As of May 21, 1988, five deposits in England totaling $23 million, and one at the Bank of Credit and Commerce International in Luxembourg of $27 million, and three at the Banque Nationale de Paris, Paris, totaling $28 million.

Added up, this comes to $772 million. His entire Riande holdings aren't included, nor is the seaside hideaway on the Azuero Peninsula, in western Panama, where his guests got to star in porno movies, and he no doubt has silent partnerships no one knows of, not to mention other coded bank accounts. A billionaire, in short, give or take a few million. Torrijos was right when he called him one rich gangster.

But not rich enough. The Hebrews, in their genius for discomfort—they invented sin and guilt, after all—conceived the simplest and most terrifying hell: Sheol, the Bottomless Pit. And that is what Noriega's greed is. Not just unsatisfied, not just never filled up. Not one of those hundreds of millions has yet touched bottom. His passion for money and his passion for power: neither has any bottom to it, for he himself has never been on firm ground.

He craved power and became a tyrant. He craved wealth and became a criminal. And the careers came in conflict. One Noriega attacked and injured the other. The strongman betrayed the drug trafficker, raided the cartel's cocaine lab, and nearly got the communal head blown off. Meanwhile, the trafficker (weapons and drugs) was betraying the strongman, vexing the strongman's gentle gringo patrons. The beast, in short, was so hungry that it gnawed its own flesh.

11

NORIEGA TYRANNUS

In October 1983, Noriega went to Washington. He came back with renewed support from the U.S. government and its pick for puppet president of Panama. This was Nicolás Ardito Barletta, Torrijos's court minstrel. He had since become a vice-president of the World Bank and was ideally fitted to helping U.S. leaders delude themselves and the public about Panama. He was handsome, youthful, and tall and spoke excellent English, was doctored in economics, had trained with George Shultz. The latter and his colleagues in Reagan's Washington wanted badly to pretend and even believe that Panama was on the road to democracy. They craved that illusion much as they craved the illusion of a war on cocaine, the thing itself being in both cases sadly incompatible with their cherished obsession of overthrowing the government of Nicaragua. But they weren't cynics like Manuel Noriega. They needed to fool themselves along with their constituents, so they pressed Noriega to keep Torrijos's promise of a direct election for president in May 1984. As for a candidate, had Disney come back to life and invented a Panama, a theme-park Panama that Americans would flock to, he would have have made its president in Barletta's image.

Noriega, being as much a realist as Shultz and Company were romantics, found he could live with Barletta. A man who had shamed himself and betrayed his country was always worth considering, and Barletta, besides, was an intellectual who had shamed and betrayed his intellectual heritage—not just Milton Friedman's conservative school of economics but the science itself, the very concept of a rational approach to the material side of existence. And not from necessity either; just to be within sniffing range of power. Noriega may have suspected that, once in the palace, Barletta might begin to give himself airs. He may even have glimpsed the grain of integrity that still lurked in Barletta's character. Yet Barletta would do. The gringos wanted him, he could be used, and if he ceased to be useful, he could be garbaged. In due course, Noriega had him nominated by the party Torrijos had founded and built with state funds, the Partido Revolucionario Democrático (PRD), and by a number of a parties otherwise bought or confected, but so as to make it clear to all who were interested that no substance would exist behind the façade of democracy he was putting up to please people in Washington, he first had the general staff "suggest" Barletta's nomination at a meeting held at the cuartel at Tinajita on January 6, 1984. Then he set about stealing the election for him.

He also had to steal it for some few hundred others, people who would support any infamy, no matter how foul, that he wished to perform or foist through the legislature, along with a whole bestiary of lesser political fauna (such as mayors and representatives of *corregimientos*) on whom the administration of his tyranny depended. Nothing, therefore, could be left to chance. Nothing was. The 1984 elections in Panama were a perfect mockery of democratic processes, with at least fourteen distinct forms of electoral piracy accomplished before, during, and after the actual voting through massive misuse of the state's authority.

The first step was to get the right people to the right levers of the state machinery. Puppet President Ricardo De la Espriella was given a list of replacements for his cabinet. He balked at naming them, and this is what happened. On February 13, when he was with his family in Chiriquí Province, Noriega sent a plane to bring him to an urgent council of state in the capital at which only he and Díaz Herrera were present. Díaz Herrera talked while Noriega looked on. Why hadn't De la Espriella made the appointments? They weren't good for the country, De la Espriella replied, and that was surely true, surely they weren't, but sixteen years had passed since the good of the country had mattered a fig in the decisions of Panamanian leaders, and that hadn't bothered De la Espriella before. He wanted to end his term with a few scraps of dignity, but that wasn't to be, and he should have known it. "You should think of your family," said Colonel Díaz Herrera—and all the while General Noriega looked on. "Do you know where they are? Are you sure of their safety?" De la Espriella's family were supposedly on their way back to the capital by car, but they were in Panama in the time of the tyrants, and though De la Espriella was president of the republic, his sole means of assuring their whereabouts and safety was to do whatever the tyrants required of him. Which was for him to resign, and he did so immediately. That doesn't surprise us. What we find strange is that there was no lack of men willing to replace him. His successor, in fact, had already been chosen. This was Jorge Illueca, sometime follower of Arnulfo Arias. He accepted the puppet presidency, filling out De la Espriella's term. He made the appointments Noriega wanted, and the theft of the election went forward.

Arnulfo Arias ran in opposition. He might have served Panama better by standing aside and putting his influence behind a less controversial candidate, for his presence in the race gave the dictatorship something to harp on, revived ancient enmities (thus preventing some men and women of goodwill from casting clear votes for civilian rule), and tended to confirm the U.S. government's urge to recognize Barletta no matter who got the most votes. His vanity, however, demanded he run and win back the office that had been stripped from his sixteen years earlier, and he was probably the opposition's strongest candidate. Once he was running, other opposition politicos had the choice of joining him with good prospects for victory or heading off on their own with little to show for it except (on the one side) confirmation of their integrity and (on the other) the onus of splitting Panama's democratic majority. Most joined. What one had, then, essentially, were two coalitions, a democratic alliance behind Arnulfo and a grouping of parties, some bona fide, some bogus, backing Barletta and de facto military rule.

Opponents of the dictatorship worried that sixteen years of propaganda might have deluded the people. They worried that Arnulfo's past record and age (he was eighty-three) might disqualify him, especially in the eyes of the whole generation of Panamanians who would be voting for the first time. They worried that Barletta's youth might be appealing. Hindsight reveals that their worries were groundless. A clear majority for change existed on economic issues alone. Compared to what it would be in a few years, Panama was still prosperous, but its prosperity was narrowly concentrated. The promised post-treaty boom had still not materialized. Unemployment was high and rising, as was the percentage of Panamanians living in misery, and aside from the most affluent classes, the only ones who enjoyed economic security (and might thus be expected to vote their pocketbooks for Barletta and dictatorship) were the state employees. As for political issues, compared to what it would be in a few years, Panama was still a paradise, yet except for government insiders and the members of the PDF themselves, Panamanians were angered by the omnipresent corruption and heartily sick of uniformed oafs lording it over everyone in the country. Arnulfo, meanwhile, had his fits of lunacy, but the worst of them had done Panama less damage than the least damaging of the tyrant's acts, and though he was eighty-three, he still had his magnetism. Noriega had so far restrained his sadistic impulses and those of the perverts around him, but he was scarcely a figure of reassurance, and Barletta was not exactly charismatic. Guillermo Sánchez, writing in *La Prensa,* said he had all the appeal of a smoked herring, and from one end of the country to the other, people laughed in agreement, even those who were committed to voting for him. Theft was the only way to keep him from losing.

The appeal of Barletta and the regime's other candidates grew in strength, however, as one neared Washington. There he was the overwhelming favorite, the unanimous choice of Washington insiders. Henry Kissinger was for Barletta. So were Lane Kirkland and the AFL-CIO, who actually gave money to elect Barletta and (without knowing, but without wanting to know, either) to perpetuate the crippling of Panama's labor movement. Here, as in other instances, Washington insiders, wonderfully knowledgeable about the intricacies of Washington's pecking order, mistakenly assumed themselves knowledgeable about everything else. Much odder and more complex was the attitude of insiders in Panama. Brainwashed by their own lies and unwilling to face the truth of their own uselessness, they were able to persuade themselves that they had a legitimate hope of winning, even as they broke every rule to win by fraud.

Highways were closed and bus owners intimidated in order to impede opposition rallies. State employees were excused from work for Barletta's rallies and bused to them at state expense. Those who registered in opposition parties or who were spotted cheering for Arnulfo instantly joined the unemployed. Barletta posters and banners and T-shirts were produced in government buildings by government employees on government time from materials bought with government money, and Barletta campaign aides traveled in government cars run on government gasoline and lubricants. Government-owned newspapers had nothing but good to speak of Nicky Barletta and nothing but bad about Arnulfo Arias. Government checks,

150,000 every two weeks, carried Barletta advertisements, along with phrases to the effect that, if he lost, no more checks would be forthcoming. And government funds, at least $25 million, were poured into the Barletta effort.

Registration fraud was pervasive and systematic. A number of parties were certified on the basis of imaginary registrants, thus giving the dictatorship an overwhelming majority on the tallying board, which seated one representative of each certified party. This circumstance, in the end, proved decisive, enabling the dictatorship to falsify the vote count.

A goon attack on Guillermo Sánchez must be counted as one of the steps in the theft effort. At 7:30 in the evening on April 28, as he was standing on a corner near his home waiting to hail a cab to go to *La Prensa,* two large young men approached him. One asked what time the kiddie rides closed down in Parque Urracá across the street, and when Sánchez turned toward him to answer, the other hit him a shot that sent him flying. But as they moved in to finish the job by kicking, a car came by and stopped and two men got down, and three sturdy young fellows jogging that night in the park happened to be within sight and ran up shouting—a double miracle, since at that hour the corner was usually deserted—and Sánchez's assailants took prudent flight, leaving him no worse for wear excepting the lump on his jaw and a few scrapes and bruises, along with the intense annoyance of not having thrown a punch, being (like every good Panamanian) a fan of boxing. The attackers' mission, he thought then and thinks now, was to put him in the hospital till after the election, since if it had been to put him into the next world, the attackers would have used knives. Instead, it furnished him the best part of that night's column.

A final preelection measure was more effective. On April 30, a week before the voting, five days after Mr. Sherman Hinson of the Panama desk of the State Department in Washington announced that the United States would send no observers to Panama, since the electoral process there would be honest and pure, uniformed members of the Panama Defense Forces took over the computing center of the electoral tribunal and placed all its functionaries under arrest. Then, behind doors with armed guards holding them, a crew of programmers contracted by the PDF and directed by a German code wizard redid the electoral rolls for the whole country, dropping twenty-five voters registered in opposition parties from the list at each of the four thousand voting tables. Thus, one in every eight

Panamanian voters was cybernetically disenfranchised and one hundred thousand votes summarily lopped from the opposition's possible total!

This might have seemed sufficient to most tyrants. Noriega, though, was leaving nothing to chance. For the actual voting, therefore, thousands of spurious credentials were issued and all members of the PDF were declared eligible to vote at any table, whether or not their names appeared on its roll, for they were charged with defending their country and preserving its public order, duties that required their total freedom of movement. And move they did, indeed very freely. Most spent election day in ceaseless pilgrimage from table to table voting for Nicky Barletta and the rest of the dictatorship's ticket.

Skies were fair most of that day over most of the country, and the people of Panama came out in great numbers to seize their first opportunity in sixteen years to say whom they wanted and didn't want as leaders. At every table, a number found their names inexplicably missing from the roll, and always members of opposition parties. At every table, as well, people in uniform showed up and voted, as was their new right, although their names weren't listed. Nonetheless, and by a clear margin, Panamanians rejected militarism and its works, rejected Manuel Noriega and his flunkies. We don't mean the dictatorship lacked adherents. Panamanians were not yet at the point reached in May 1989, when the vote was unstealable, when a majority of the PDF themselves voted against Noriega's candidates. In upper- and middle-class quarters, Arnulfo and Barletta ran evenly. In the barrios and the countryside, however, where support for the regime would have been strongest had its prattle about revolution not been all lies, Arnulfo and other opposition candidates triumphed overwhelmingly.

This outcome was not immediately apparent on election night, as the ballots were counted at the tables and the results sent in to district and then circuit tallying boards, but the PDF knew first by virtue of its occupation of the electoral tribunal's computing center, and by midnight the word had gone to the government coalition's representative at the circuit level: impugn the results of tables where Barletta lost so that they would not be included on the circuit tally sheets. And dutifully the petitions were filed. The stated reasons were often puerile, even absurd. In the San Miguelito suburb of Panama City, the PRD representative impugned sixty tables before the tally sheets from them reached the circuit board. God alone knows what arguments he concocted for petitioning the annulment of results he hadn't seen, but the electoral tribunal functionaries knew what was good for them and accepted all sixty petitions. And so it went at circuit after circuit. As the sun came up on the morning of May 7, hundreds of table results were successfully impugned, so that their final outcome would have to be determined at the national level.

Now, this was supposed to be done in public, in the main hall of the legislative palace in Panama City, beginning on the evening of Monday, May 7, and by 4:30 that afternoon, with unofficial reports from throughout the republic indicating that Arnulfo was pulling ahead, a large number of opposition sympathizers had gathered around the building, partly in celebration, mainly to prevent the count's being cooked, which was of course what the dictatorship intended. The PRD, too, sent a group of adherents over. They marched about shouting old Torrijos slogans, and exchanging insults with the others in a mood of increasing animosity, but no clash occurred, because the PRD group found itself badly outnumbered and withdrew. At that, the opposition crowd grew euphoric, and danced about and sang and shouted vivas, and then ran a purple, red, and yellow *arnulfista* banner up the flagpole outside the palace, from which the national flag had been lowered at sunset.

That was the high point of freedom in Panama since 1968. A few minutes later, at 7:00 P.M., tyranny reasserted itself in the form of a goon brigade identifiable by caps bearing the insignia Comando Especial del PRD (PRD Special Commando). This actually comprised two separate groups. One was a group of party toughs armed with baseball bats and led by one Humberto López Tirone, a politician who had suffered exile at the hands of Panama's military and then had, inexplicably, joined them. The other was a PDF paramilitary force, Fuerza Siete (Force Seven). It was composed entirely of out-and-out criminals armed with hand- and submachine guns, led by a notorious bank robber and hood named Silverio Brown, and backed up by snipers who had got up into buildings around the palace. These combined bands began beating and shooting the opposition partisans in the full view of armed members of the Defense Forces, who of course defended nothing but their own persons and prudently withdrew inside the palace and barred the doors. This after Brown had briefly burst inside waving a pair of revolvers, until a uniformed PDF officer went up to him and put an arm over his shoulder and persuaded him to leave, for TV cameras were transmitting from inside the building. And from outside as well. Viewers of U.S. television may remember Peter Arnett broadcasting for CNN from in front of the palace and doing a kind of tap dance as ricochets skipped by his ankles. Footage of Brown himself blazing away with both guns into the crowd was carried round the world by satellite, and his picture was in *La Prensa* the next morning, but no order for his arrest was ever issued. Why should one have been? He was merely doing what he'd been told to do. When he ceased to be useful, however, he was garbaged. Exactly three months later, Fuerza Siete was disbanded and a number of its members murdered. Brown himself was shot to death by Lieutenant Colonel Nivaldo Madriñán in person. "Shot while trying to escape" was the official determination, though when his body was delivered for autopsy, his hands were still cuffed behind his back.

Firing continued until 10:00 P.M. Till then Fuerza Siete ruled the center of Panama's capital. The body count was three dead and eighty-odd wounded by bullets. Many more were beaten. One, a pregnant woman, miscarried as a result. Another, Father Fernando Guardia, S.J., gave the following explanation for his injuries: "I stayed to watch what was occurring so as to be a witness to something I could not otherwise believe, that such official brutality could take place in Panama."

Within three years, though, such scenes became commonplace.

The operation was entirely successful. Opponents of tyranny in Panama were driven from the streets and sufficiently intimidated not to protest by demonstrations (the only weapon they possessed) the theft of the election. Later that evening, the National Tallying Board, on which the dictatorship enjoyed a majority by virtue of its having registered bogus parties, voted to forsake its duty to decide the multitude of impugnations and to turn the task over instead to the electoral tribunal itself. That effort then proceeded behind closed doors and included the following decisive monkey business:

(a) False circuit and table sheets were confected for the Guaymi Indian District in Chiriquí (Circuit 4.4), perhaps the most blatant act of fraud in the whole process.

(b) The votes from the San Miguelito Circuit were juggled, and the juggling was then used as an excuse for not including in the final count the impugned result from the sixty voting tables from the neighborhoods where Arnulfo had his greatest strength.

This final piracy was sufficient. It was drawn out over three weeks because a great many races had to be stolen. Besides giving the dictatorship a majority in the legislature, it successfully pared the tens of thousands of votes Arnulfo had won by, despite all the previous fraud and theft. Barletta was ruled the winner by 1,713 votes.

The president of the electoral tribunal, Dr. César Quintero, abstained from voting for and signing the resolution certifying the faked results. That he lacked the courage to tell the world (from the horse's mouth, as it were) the full and precise details of the faking is something we need not blame him for. The world knew perfectly well that the tyrant Manuel Noriega used fraud and force to frustrate the wishes of the people of Panama. The United States of America, democracy's supposed champion, knew with particular clarity and thus shamed and betrayed itself egregiously. On the morning of May 7, the U.S. ambassador to Panama, Everett Briggs, called on the papal nuncio, Monsignor Laboa, scandalized by the monstrosities committed by the PDF and its civilian accomplices. Even though the United States favored Barletta, said Briggs, he was recommending that it recognize Arnulfo, whom he calculated as having won by at least 60,000 votes. Nor was Briggs lying. In 1987, after the chancre burst in Panama, the *Miami Herald* cited a State Department source to the effect that dispatches from Briggs recommending that course of action were in the department's archives. But in the blindness of arrogance the United States refused. The next day, Wednesday, May 9, after warning Laboa of what his government was obliging him to do—*While the fakery was in progress, with those murdered on Monday evening still not buried!*—Briggs went to the electoral tribunal and congratulated Quintero (whose resignation was still three weeks off) on the purity of Panama's democratic election.

The day was not without its moment of fun, however. On May 7, Rigoberto Paredes (the former tyrant's nephew, of whom more in a moment) had gone on one of the morning radio talk shows to vilify the voters of his circuit, calling them reactionaries and ingrates, for not electing him to the legislature. On Wednesday, May 9, a little before Briggs called on Quintero, Rigoberto returned to the show to apologize. The voters had, in fact, chosen with wisdom. "My votes appearing!" Rigoberto crowed. And so they were, out of thin air, along with Nicky's, till both were falsely certified winners.

On May 7, 1984, the ring of evil closed around Panama, and on the ninth it drew tight, for on those days the Defense Forces went to war against the people. Something similar had happened in Argentina during the 1970s. Now, alas, it was Panama's turn, with the difference that, in Panama's case, the United States joined the aggressors.

In 1968, after the coup, the people of Panama adjusted to military tyranny more or less as the people of France and the people of Holland adjusted to occupation by the Wehrmacht after their countries were conquered in 1940. A few resisted and were killed or exiled. Some collaborated. Most turned away into their private lives. This unwilling but passive majority was exploited. Much of their labor went to enrich parasites. They were denied a say in their country's business and thus degraded to the status of children. They were lied to incessantly, but they were not assaulted. They were under tyranny, not attack. The tyrants put out twaddle about revolution that no more justified their rule than twaddle about a "new order" justified Hitler's, but when ratification of the Canal treaties removed even this fig leaf and left the dictatorship naked in its predatory purpose, the people of Panama continued to put up with it, on the one hand fearful and on the other somewhat mollified by the scraps of borrowed millions that fell their way. But when the regime reformed the constitution and scheduled a direct election for president, and for a fairly apportioned legislature, the people assumed that their opinion was being sought and came to believe that their will might count for something. Those in power would try their best to stay there. They would very likely pull all manner of tricks. But if the people spoke against them with sufficient clarity, giving opposition candidates obvious margins, those candidates would be suffered to take office. So the people of Panama came to believe. Therefore they voted in good faith, and therefore they went out to celebrate and defend their triumph. Why else, if it didn't mean to honor their will, had the regime gone through all those motions?

The motions, of course, were not entirely voluntary. The regime was under pressure to *look* democratic from its squeamish patrons in the United States. But that wasn't the problem. The problem was that Panama's masters were cruelly self-brainwashed. Incessant lying had taken a terrible toll. Even as they were preparing to steal the election, they entertained the delusion that they would win legitimately. Even a murderous thief like Rigoberto Paredes was (as we've seen) outraged at his constituents for not electing him. He and others, including Manuel Noriega, arch-cynic and realist, thought that the people loved them, or at least respected their firmness and appreciated what they'd done for the country.

We're not kidding. We know them. We've spoken with them. Both of us talked, over the years, with dozens of top figures of the dictatorship. They actually believed they helped the country! Even when their whole time in power had been unmasked as a drunken, bloody shamble to disaster with Panama dumped in a cesspool and held under, apologists existed for Omar Torrijos, and for *El Proceso* and *¡La Revolución!* Even in 1989, with Panama in the final stage of dismantlement, the thieves still believed that people loved them and went out and held an election, confident they could get within stealing range.

The parents of lies love their offspring just the way other people love theirs. Tyrannical power's chief prey are the minds of its wielders. If Martínez, Torrijos, Paredes, Noriega, and company had had the honesty to judge their performance truly and truly gauge people's opinions of them, they'd have been far too honest to practice tyranny, whose beginning, middle, and end are nothing but lies.

Noriega and company, couldn't imagine the people's loathing of them. There was never a question of their leaving power unless and until they were forced to do so, but they gave a contrary impression by holding an election, and they held it only because they were certain they'd win. They'd win because the people loved them, or at least respected their firmness. How often the cruel mistake their vice for this! They'd win because Barletta was a World Bank economist and because Arnulfo was an old man, because of all the money they spent on advertising and on flashy consultants hired down from the States. They'd win by browbeating and intimidation. Then, just to be safe, just to be sure of a landslide, they took out 200,000 votes of insurance. Purging the voting rolls and multiple voting brought them almost that much. And when they lost anyway, they were devastated.

What a blow that must have been! Just because tyrants and bullies can't respond to other people's pain, don't imagine they don't feel their own. Noriega and company had to be hurt to the quick. The thing to do, of course, wasn't to hurt them but to scrape them from the country like shit from one's boot, but the people of Panama hadn't the means to do that. All they could to was gather in the streets to celebrate their triumph and try to defend it, and that was an intolerable provocation. Thus provoked, Noriega and company went to war against the people, partly to stay in power and mostly to punish the people for hurting their feelings and to make the people love them after all. We know the last sounds crazy, but recall whom we're dealing with. Force is the rapist's approach to love.

So the ring of evil closed around Panama. Its military, previously content with occupying and exploiting the country, now went to war against the people. On May 7, 1984, the first shots were fired by

Silverio Brown, and on the thirtieth the opposition alliance's offices were laid waste and people beaten and property destroyed, including (just to be on the safe side) humans and property in neighboring offices, and so the skirmishes went until June 1987, when Roberto Díaz's declarations brought the nature of the regime out into the open and hostilities became general. Meanwhile, Dr. Hugo Spadafora was kidnapped, played with, and beheaded, which was where we began. That was on Friday, September 13, 1985, and by then Panama's tyrants, having worked hard and skillfully at it since Friday, October 11, 1968, and with help from abroad, had reversed the processes of civilization and made Panama a place of darkness.

* * *

Now for some supporting players, beastlings formed in Noriega's image whom he kept around him. Captain Heráclides Sucre, for example, was cashiered by Rubén Paredes for committing mass murder—nine Colombians and one American, low-level drug traffickers. The Colombians had mutinied and deserved a lesson. The American saw them being taken away. Sucre had them all machine-gunned. On the day after Manuel Noriega took command, Sucre was back in the Panama Defense Forces with full rank and privileges. Noriega had learned from Torrijos, who'd reinstated the murderer Orejita Ruiz, and now, again, there were no restraints at all on people in uniform.

Captain Fritz Gibson, "Captain Blood," was the officer who'd led the savage public beating given Dr. Miguel Antonio Bernal. He murdered the union protester Yiyi Barrientes, and only God Himself knows how many others. In an ecstasy of cynicism, Noriega, then still chief of the G-2, made Captain Blood liaison with the pope's security unit when John Paul II visited Panama, and though Gibson retired soon afterward, having reached the mandatory age, Noriega, once he was commandant, recalled him to duty with the rank of major.

Captain Felipe Camargo was a specialist in torture—not an artist like Nivaldo Madriñán, whose Satan-given talents set him apart, but an earnest scientist trained in the latest methods of torment in Somoza's Nicaragua and Castro's Cuba. Noriega gave him scope to practice his science. He was the sort of officer Noriega favored.

And criminals from abroad, he collected these also. Steven Kalish was a marijuana smuggler who caught Manuel Noriega's fancy. He paid Noriega a bribe of $300,000 in September 1983, a down payment on use of the Panama laundromat, and within a few months the two were in business, along with César Rodríguez and Quique Pretelt. Kalish acted for Noriega in purchasing aircraft. Noriega gave him three Panamanian passports, and the cream of Luis Quiel's take of DEA information. And when Noriega went to Washington in November 1983, in part to discuss the supposed war on drugs, he made the trip in Kalish's jet.

Far weirder was Colonel Mohammed Ali Seineldin, veteran of the "dirty war" waged by the Argentine military against the country's civilian populace during the 1970s, in which perhaps ten thousand were murdered while in detention, mostly by torture. Seineldin was liaison between the army and the Alianza Argentina Anticomunista, a right-wing paramilitary outfit in which professional soldiers got to moonlight as terrorists. He was one of the continent's great criminals, but despite his spending the Falkland Islands War in absolute safety, he confected a hero's reputation for himself and thus escaped prosecution when Argentina recovered civilian rule. He was too dangerous, though, to have in the country and was sent as military attaché to Panama. No doubt, few other places would have taken him, but in Noriega's Panama he was at home.

Despite his name, Seineldin is a Christian, and a fanatical one at that, though badly tinged (it would seem) with the Manichaean heresy. He believes in an active force of evil subversion—we're not making this up; Seineldin has discussed it with journalists—which so far has launched five terrible offensives, the first culminating in the Crucifixion, the last in progress right now, today. And in this fearful offensive, according to Colonel Seineldin, *the entirety of civilian society in every country has been won over by the kingdom of evil.* Everyone not in uniform, therefore, is a legitimate target.

Did he get along with Manuel Noriega? Noriega decorated him personally. Noriega gave him PDF units to train. And in December 1988, Noriega gave him transport and money so that Seineldin might return to Argentina and lead a military uprising.

Luckily for the Argentines, the uprising didn't work, but that wasn't the fault of Manuel Noriega. And, in return, as one sadistic sociopath to another, Seineldin, a devotee of the Virgin of the Rosary, prayed for Noriega, and initiated him into certain mystic rites in response to which, in the spring of 1988, units of the PDF carried effigies of the Virgin from one part of Panama to another.

Seineldin's occult beliefs and twisted mysticism were especially congenial to Noriega, who is intensely superstitious and quick to put faith in outlandish cults and rites. Colonel Eduardo Herrera, who broke with him in 1988, once accompanied him on an official journey and shared a hotel suite with him and thus had occasion to watch him dress. A black ribbon went twined at his waist inside his underpants, and narrower ones at his ankles inside his socks, and in his shoes went little slips of paper with names written on them—all this, as Noriega explained, to protect him against spells cast by his enemies. On New Year's Eve in 1987, he summoned the whole general staff (of which Herrera was at the time a member) to celebrate with him at Playa Blanca, to the great annoyance of all the officers, who would rather have been almost anywhere else. Shortly before midnight, General Noriega, a huge amulet hung about his neck, led them down to the beach, where his personal sorcerer, a Brazilian named Ivan Trilha, had built a bonfire. Noriega had the officers sit round it and bow their heads while Trilha muttered spells, and then sprinkled a fine powder on the embers before sharing it with the congregation. Then they had to rise and go down to the water's edge, and turn round and toss the powder back over their left shoulders toward the sea. There followed much similar mumbo jumbo. The ceremonies, in fact, continued for hours.

Papito Almanza was Noriega's sorcery consultant, a costume designer and friend of Pretelt's who gyred in a number of eccentric orbits, *santería,* witchcraft, and the like. He made several trips to South America on Noriega's behalf, conferring with specialist witch doctors, procuring amulets, a *camándula,* and similar knickknacks. Through Almanza, Noriega contracted Trilha, in whom he at one time placed absolute trust—among other goofinesses having a huge illuminated cross erected to Trilha's exact specifications on a small island opposite his beach mansion—to keep off hostile spirits, though all it could be proved to keep away were nesting seabirds, frightened by the racket of its diesel generator. By 1989, Trilha had somewhat fallen from favor, and Almanza's lot was even worse. He somehow ran afoul of Noriega's wife, Doña Felicidad, who sent two goons round to his house to give him a beating. He cleared out the next day for Miami.

Omar Torrijos's coterie of advisers, leftist intellectuals on the one hand, nonideological men of affairs on the other, did not cease with his death to crave nearness to power or chances to fatten at the public trough, and since their talents were proven—that is, they were able liars, inventive thieves, and practiced grovelers with very strong stomachs—most of them passed to Torrijos's successors in tyranny, like the widows of patriarchs to their dead husbands' brothers. Thus one saw in Noriega's train Rómulo Escobar and Renato Pereira, and Mario Rognoni. Two others of his close collaborators, however, were peculiarly characteristic of his rule.

Rodolfo Chiari was minister of justice in Panama when fellow citizens of his were being shot and beaten in their own homes as part of the military's war on the civilian populace, when those who peacefully protested the lack of justice in Panama might have their gold inlays prised out with screwdrivers, when Señores Endara and Ford, the president- and vice-president-elect of the republic, were assaulted on the street—the world saw it on television!—while armed soldiers looked on in approval. To hold any post in a ministry of justice in a country so ruled is, first of all, to live a lie. Even to be such a ministry's porter or charwoman is to collect a salary under false pretenses and thus inconsistent with personal honesty. To be minister, to sign one's name above that title on letters, to respond to it in public, to sit at the minister's desk or ride around in the minister's limousine, is to shame oneself beyond imagining, yet Chiari was pleased to be minister. The person who made him a minister was one of the world's fouler criminals. He and other expressed their pathologies at will anywhere in the country. No one within Panama's borders was safe from their depredations, and if one of them—Noriega or Córdoba or del Cid—chose to torture one of Chiari's children, there was nothing Chiari could have done to prevent the crime or to gain redress once it was committed. Yet Chiari was pleased to be minister of justice. Clearly, even the wretches in La Modelo's basement had a more valid claim to self-respect. Clearly, anyone who put a bullet through Chiari's head would have been doing him an inestimable service, granting him release from indignity, curtailing the dishonor he heaped on his own head.

The reader will no doubt suppose Chiari an upstart, a fellow like Noriega up from the depths in whom the will to self-improvement has become twisted, for in such a Chiari the cynicism implicit in being minister of justice in a country where no justice existed would be comprehensible, if not pardonable—"I had no justice, so neither will anyone else!" Nothing, though, could be further from the truth. Chiari's family has been rich for over a century. His name, till he disgraced it, was perhaps the most honored in Panama. His ancestors were conspicuous proponents of civil liberties before Panama's separation from Colombia. His grandfather and namesake was one of Panama's founding fathers and president of the republic. His uncle Roberto Chiari was president also, and a man of demonstrable courage and patriotism, for it was he who broke diplomatic relations with the United States over the flag incident in January 1964. Noriega's justice minister enjoyed every advantage of wealth and social position. He wasn't born to squalor, he chose it freely. And in choosing him as his instrument, Noriega wonderfully advanced his designs. Having Rodolfo Chiari close down *La Prensa* and other independent media, thus stifling freedom of speech in his country, having Rodolfo Chiari sit as minister of justice while the human and civil rights of Panamanians were being systematically violated, was a telling blow not just at Chiari's class but at the very idea of a free society in which honor and wealth are gained by serving the collective.

Another characteristic instrument of Noriega's was Rigoberto Paredes, by pretense a political organizer, in practice a goon squad leader for whom a seat in the puppet legislature was stolen in 1984. Viewers of U.S. television may remember him on "Nightline" in the summer of 1988, gamely trying to defend Noriega and assuring Mr. Sam Donaldson that his questions were "very eeenteresting." On election day in 1968, in the space of one hour, Paredes kicked a pregnant voter in the stomach, stole a ballot box in the Bella Vista quarter of Panama City, and in the gasoline station across the street from the Boulevar café, in full view of two dozen café patrons, shot one young man to death and gravely wounded another. The Guardia coup that fall saved him from prison. His nephew Rubén (later both general and tyrant) saw to it that charges against him were dropped and that he prospered. Yet when Noriega shunted Rubén aside, even when Noriega had Rubén's son murdered, Rigoberto stuck with Noriega. As blood is thicker than water, so is slime thicker than blood.

Noriega's chief political operative was José I. Blandón, his emissary to Fidel Castro, for example, on the occasion of the cocaine cartel's intent to have him murdered. Blandón had been part of Torrijos's "left-hand punch" and served Noriega with great competence till angering him with his honesty. This in 1986 when Noriega developed presidential ambitions, an affliction suffered sooner or later by all male Panamanians, with the sole exception of Guillermo Sánchez. Noriega's criminal career was by then an open secret. Blandón suggested that he forget the whole thing. Noriega exploded and sent Blandón into gilded exile as consul in New York. It was Blandón, however, whom Noriega called on in the fall of 1987 to engineer his return to the United States's good graces. The plan Blandón worked out, however, was undercut by Admiral Murphy's visit and repudiated by Noriega—at which Blandón, whose children were pressing him to break with Noriega, and from authentic if belated patriotism, not merely broke but, as it were, defected, testifying against Noriega before the U.S. Senate and two federal grand juries in Florida. He first took the precaution of enrolling himself in the witness protection program and getting his family out of Panama. One child, however, remained, a mentally disabled teenager whose special therapy included residing on a farm and tending his animals, all pets really, though they were farm animals. And here is what Manuel Noriega did: He sent soldiers to the farm, in combat rig, and they made the sick child watch while they slaughtered his calf and killed or carried off the rest of his animals.

Noriega kept two mistresses. First in order of acquisition was Gabriela Deleuze, Miss Panama 1965. She has title to the Paris apartment and has lately served her country as cultural attachée to its embassies in France and Spain. In 1984, to divert from her some of Doña Felicidad's jealousy, Noriega married her to a PDF officer, a captain in the so-called antiterrorist unit. He did not attend the wedding but sent a large floral arrangement whose ribbon bore the following reference, conscious or no, to Teddy Roosevelt: "Now you're going to know what a big stick is." How Noriega came by this information on the captain's equipment we don't know.

By 1987, Vicky Amado had become Noriega's reigning paramour. She is now about thirty-five years old, is blondish and tall for a Latin woman, about five seven, an inch taller than Noriega. She has, of late, become a little plump. She possesses proven appeal to successful gentlemen. The boxing champion Robert Durán, a prominent politician, and the president of a large bank, preceded Manuel Noriega in her affections. She had a husband who was killed in a car crash in the late 1970s. Noriega came into her life in the early 1980s when the Banco Ultramar, owned by Venezuelans, failed with all her money in it. She appealed to Noriega. One of the Venezuelans was in Panama. Noriega had him arrested till he restored Miss Amado's funds. Other depositors weren't so lucky.

Miss Amado was, supposedly, much influenced by the musical drama *Evita,* which played in Panama in Spanish a few years back. It is she, supposedly, who stiffened Noriega's resolve when he was wavering toward flight in January 1988. Her opinion of him, supposedly, was behind a statement he made a little later: "A man proves his virility by staying in power."

On October 3, 1989, Noriega was briefly taken captive in an abortive coup attempt against him and extricated himself, so go the rumors, by calling Miss Amado, who then relayed his call for help to officers loyal to him. By then, so go the rumors, Noriega trusted only her and her mother to prepare his food. The latter, Doña Norma Amado, directed a public relations firm, which after Miss Amado's connection with Noriega become the sole purveyor of public relations services to the Panamanian state—the government, the military, the autonomous institutions, the national lottery, the Seguro Social, everything. The lucky father, meanwhile, Don David Amado, was given a racket that developed in March 1988, with the imposition of economic sanctions by the United States. Banks and stores stopped cashing government checks, so Don David was set up in the check-cashing business (no doubt with cocaine profits in need of washing) and allowed to take a 2 percent commission.

In October 1989, Vicky Amado's eleven-year-old daughter, who was attending El Colegio Internacional de Maria Imaculada (a private high school for girls run by the Catholic church, and the most socially prestigious school for girls in the country), was informed by her homeroom teacher that because of poor grades and frequent absences, she would not be promoted when the school year ended in December. Vicky went to see the headmistress, Sister Elsa Maria Schaus, and demanded that her daughter's teacher be fired. Sister Elsa Maria refused. Two days later, Sister Elsa Maria, a Franciscan nun of Peruvian nationality but a resident of Panama for twenty-six years, was given twenty-four hours to get out of Panama, for her own safety and the security of the state.

Luisa Sánchez, like the mothers of movie gangsters, lived in her old neighborhood until recently, in fact, in the tenement near the market where she raised Manuel Antonio—this despite Noriega's urgings that she let him install her in some place "more fitting." They got on well, however. He supported her and visited her frequently.

Swoop of limousines along narrow streets. Bodyguards leaping out before the mean building. Noriega struts between them as passersby gape.

* * *

> You'll see that everything's falsehood,
> You'll see that nothing is love,
> That the world cares nothing about you,
> It turns, it turns.
>
> —ENRIQUE SANTOS DISCÉPOLO,
> "Yira, Yira"

This sort of pessimism, this self-pity, implicitly justifies trickery, intimidation, and violence. Everything is falsehood, nothing is love. A host of losers agree, but there too, in six words, is Manuel Noriega, and every other tyrant, past, present, and future.

Add an intense self-loathing, a trait already noticed in Noriega and which, paradoxically, always accompanies self-love and self-pity. The latter account for his egotism, self-loathing for his compulsion to degrade who- and whatever he comes in contact with, a compulsion shared with despots in general. Compare, for instance, Malaparte on Hitler: "Like all dictators, Hitler loves only what he can despise."

Here, then, are some paradoxes Noriega displays.

War is peace: After the murder of Hugo Spadafora, with the declaration of war by his forces against the populace they pretended to protect, Noriega adopted peace as his watchword. The dove of peace, olive branch in beak, soared toward the stars of General Noriega's insignia on billboards all over the country. Nineteen eighty-seven the year when hostilities became open, with wave attacks by troops with shotguns against unarmed demonstrators, with people snatched from operating tables and taken to prison, he proclaimed the year of peace and had this slogan inscribed everywhere, even on the vehicles that carried the troops and that transported the wounded prisoners: "*1987, Año de la Paz: Seguridad sin Guerra*" (1987, Year of Peace: Security without War). And finally, when the country was almost in ruins, when thousands of Panamanians had fled their homes and other thousands were scrambling as best they could to do so, there appeared banners with the equation "M.A.N. = PAZ" (Manuel Antonio Noriega equals Peace). Cynical, of course, but inwardly honest.

Humiliation is dignity: Just as "virility is proved by staying in power," dignity is manifested by humiliating others. Invaluable here, however, is the tyrant's fund of remembered humiliation, which becomes a fund of dignity as he remembers having borne humiliation—for best results, stoically but, in any case, borne—and on which he draws for instruction as to humiliating others and justifying so doing. In this regard, observe the effect of the humiliation inflicted on Noriega by Paredes. Paredes blocked Noriega's designs, countermanded his orders, held back his favorites from promotion. Noriega bore it all with stoical dignity and later got even. Paredes's firstborn died in a ditch with his tongue and eyes plucked out.

Pain is ease: The experience of pain slakes guilt occasioned by prior atrocities, real or imagined. Hence the sadomasochist spends his time dreaming of pain, given and received, when he isn't actually inflicting or undergoing it. Simultaneously, through pain experienced—and in fantasy or actuality, pain remains pain—one stores up a treasury of authority or justification for atrocities to be performed in the future. Interestingly, with regard to the last, the pain that X receives or received from Y can authorize X to torment Z, and (more interesting still) the pain that B received from A can justify X to torment the whole rest of the alphabet. Hence the reported incident involving a PDF officer—a lieutenant whose name we don't know but clearly a disciple of Manuel Noriega—who prior to assaulting a person under detention asked him in mingled glee and rage why he, the prisoner, had shown disrespect for the lieutenant's mother, a woman whom the prisoner had never laid eyes on. The thought of his mother shamed gave the lieutenant the right to feed his perversion for inflicting pain and damage.

Finally, *victimhood is mastery:* The experience, real or imagined, of being a victim is, in these contexts, worth more than gold. If you can see yourself victim enough, you gain the right and drive to master all others, certainly to the glorious extent of putting things up their behinds, even to cutting their heads off.

Fair is foul and foul is fair:
Hover through the fog and the filthy air.

* * *

When the demonic finally spoke clearly in one case, an expression appeared on the patient's face that could be described only as Satanic. It was an incredibly contemptuous grin of utter hostile malevolence. . . . Yet when the demonic finally revealed itself in the exorcism of [the] other patient, it

> was with a still more ghastly expression. . . . The eyes were hooded with a lazy reptilian torpor. . . .
>
> —M. SCOTT PECK,
> *People of the Lie*

On August 11, 1983, a day before he took command of the Defense Forces, Noriega granted an interview to Migdalia Fuentes of *La Prensa.* Asked by her about the real Manuel Noriega, he replied in Latin, having taken it at the Instituto Nacional, "Ego sum qui sum," a self-description ("I AM THAT I AM") whose only previously recorded use was by Yahweh, on being interviewed by Moses.

Father of lies!

12

THE CHANCRE BURSTS

On June 1, 1987, when the Panama Defense Forces (PDF) announced the retirement of its chief of staff, Colonel Roberto Díaz Herrera, no one in Panama supposed the act voluntary, or doubted who had arranged it, or dreamed it would have dramatic consequences. Díaz aspired to top command of the PDF and was the only officer with a claim to it, hence Manuel Noriega's only rival. For years, despite public protestations of brotherhood in arms, it had been clear that one would get rid of the other. Now Díaz had lost. That was the end of him.

The PDF, after all, was the source of all power. Once removed from its ranks, yesterday's bully was strengthless. A succession of losers had proved that. The latest was Rubén Paredes, like Díaz a fearsome blusterer in his day. Díaz would take the sop tossed to him—a million dollars, so went the rumors, and the embassy in Tokyo for prestige, and for petty cash the consulate in Yokohama, which the incumbent milked for two thousand daily. He would go quietly. Noriega's grip on the country would be that much firmer.

His position with the United States seemed to be firming. In June 1986, Seymour Hersh came out with dirt on him in the *New York Times.* In retaliatory pique, Noriega, who probably thought the press was controlled in the United States as it was in Panama, sabotaged one of Ollie North's neatest ideas. This was the *Pia Vesta* scam, whereby a shipload of Soviet-bloc weapons bought by Mike Harari was to be passed off as Sandinista aid to the insurgent rebels in El

Salvador, then "discovered" by the Salvadoran generals, then turned over to the contras in Honduras—a way to disguise military aid to the latter while making the Sandinistas look more evil than they were, a double disinformation of the American people. Noriega, the middleman, confiscated both the ship and its cargo, while North and company watched in impotent fury. Later he added the insult of renaming the ship *Iran-Contra* and having it sailed back and forth through the Canal. Since then, however, things had been patched up. They were destined, as so often happens, never to be the same again, but for the moment both sides were trying. Noriega was behaving himself, and the United States was saying nice things about him, most recently through the lips of the Southern Command chief, General John Galvin, the week before Díaz Herrera's retirement.

Engineering that ouster was not a big chore for Noriega. Patience, in fact, was all it took, beginning with the self-restraint not to move against Díaz precipitously in the wake of his coup attempt in 1985. As a PDF officer, Díaz couldn't be murdered. That would make the other officers nervous. As Oman Torrijos's cousin, he was heir apparent to the fake revolution, the tapestry of lies that passed for a moral purpose among the PDF and its henchmen in mufti. Avarice was their only true creed, but none cared to admit it, so Díaz could not be brusquely garbaged either. Noriega seems to have been concerned enough also with his problems with the United States to have put off dealing with Díaz till that flank was secure, until he offered General Galvin a medal (on the occasion of Galvin's leaving Panama to take command of NATO) and Galvin accepted it. So he allowed Díaz his perks and his thieving but dealt directly with staff members and troop commanders, bypassing Díaz. Since the others knew who controlled the money faucet, as well as whom they wanted least for an enemy, Díaz Herrera was soon isolated. Meanwhile, till he was ready simply to announce that Díaz had retired and let Díaz deny it if he dared, Noriega (who, unlike Torrijos, was not vain, who liked nothing better than to be underestimated) intensified the whisper campaign that characterized Díaz as the real danger, the true threat to Panama's peace and prosperity, being (so the tales went) a confirmed leftist and far, far smarter than Noriega.

The last was a masterpiece of disinformation, for Colonel Díaz was a dunce. R. M. Koster, who had the misfortune to hear him talk for several hours, had never encountered anyone so mush minded, though he'd attended six Democratic conventions. Díaz had known Noriega for thirty years, had been to Peru's military academy with him, had watched his progress as Torrijos's gangster and as a ruthless criminal in his own right, yet he seems to have believed that Noriega had forgiven his attempt against him and would break the precedent of a lifetime and deal honorably with him in the matter of his promised succession to PDF commandant. Díaz was dunce enough, in any case, to have helped Noriega dump Rubén Paredes and yet feel hurt and outraged when Noriega dumped him—so much so, in fact, that he did what no one expected, least of all Noriega. He did not take the sop, he did not go quietly. He broke the code of silence every other PDF officer had adhered to, and as if just then realizing that Panama was an unhappy country, with a tyrant who treated people unjustly and a military that was corrupt, he went public with denunciations of both.

Not at once, though. He seems to have been dazed for a time. Then he tried to get Noriega to kiss and make up. On June 4, he asked his wife to set up a meeting with Noriega, first through Noriega's wife, then through the wife of Colonel Marcos Justine, now chief of staff. When neither woman would take his wife's call, he wrote Noriega a note recalling their long acquaintanceship and asking Noriega to call. The note was received but not answered. The next day, a local TV station aired an interview with him. That night, unhappy that certain slight criticisms of Noriega had been cut, he sent a complete tape to *La Prensa,* asking that the text be published in its entirety. The editor of the paper, Winston Robles, watched the thing through, found nothing earthshaking, and decided it could wait till Sunday. The next day, Díaz called him up and accused him of being scared to publish.

The remark annoyed Robles. He'd been fighting military dictatorship in Panama since the day it began and had suffered exile, calumny, and death threats. As for the paper, its presses had been sabotaged, its offices raided, its staff beaten by goons, its writers harassed with bogus actions for libel, and its publisher and top columnist forced to leave the country.

"Until a week ago," he answered, "you seemed to think we weren't scared enough. If you've got anything important to say, we'll put it on page one tomorrow morning."

"Then send a reporter," said Díaz. "I'm going to make sensational disclosures."

The first was that the house where he received *La Prensa*'s and six other reporters—a half-million-dollar mansion in the swank Altos del Golf section of Panama City, with spacious grounds and a bulletproof master bedroom—had been bought with his share of one PDF racket, the sale of visas to dissident Cubans. The PDF, he declared, had numerous rackets. It wasn't healthy for an officer to be honest. Torrijos himself had told him as much:

"Don't be a jerk, Roberto," Torrijos had told him. "If you get to acting too straight, you could 'catch cold.' "

Honesty hadn't been Torrijos's problem. He'd taken a twelve-million-dollar bribe for granting the Shah asylum in 1979.

And, yes, the 1984 election was crooked. The last touches of fraud were put on in Díaz's home.

And, oh yes, Noriega had arranged Spadafora's murder.

Sensational disclosures, no doubt about it, though they didn't scratch the surface of what had gone on or contain a word that was news to Panamanians. Everyone knew the PDF had rackets. Look at the colonels' houses, look how they lived! Everyone knew the election was phony. As for Spadafora's death, maybe Manuel Noriega didn't run Panama! Maybe Spadafora cut himself shaving!

The sensation was that one of the thieves was talking. One of the gangsters was breaking *omertà.* Other big shots had been sacked; all had kept silent. Not a word from Flórez or Contreras. Not a peep from Paredes even when they murdered his son. Never a leak, never the slightest admission, only a smooth carapace of lies. Now, though, it was suddenly broken. The chancre had burst, exposing Panama's sickness, a process at once painful and welcome as the necessary first step to recovered health.

A number of things happened immediately. To begin with, the majority of Panamanians, who had been against the dictatorship without actually battling it, all at once became powerfully agitated—that is, thoroughly angry and fed up. Meanwhile, most of the rest of the country could no longer be fooled or go on pretending.

There were a few on both sides who'd never done either. Your humble servants, for instance, knew very well what sort were taking over in October 1968: thieves and killers, thank you, though even we didn't know how voracious and ruthless until we began doing research for this book. Others, of course, knew also, those who went up on the ridges to fight them and those who were jailed the week they came to power, who were packed off into exile in the first wave, or who, isolated and cowed, could only stand looking. And a few on the other side weren't fooled either, clear-eyed opportunists, human pilot fish like Rigoberto Paredes, who joined in for a share of the loot and the power. But most who joined the regime were fooled or pretending, along with those who supported it passively. Panama didn't need an army, much less one that ran the country. It was as though Panama had somehow got stuck with a huge snow-removal department that wolfed most of the budget, whose top brass were involved in all sorts of rackets, and somehow this department was running the country. You had to be fooled or fooling yourself to support them, but now that Díaz was talking, those options were pretty much taken away, so that most of the regime's passive supporters went over to the opposition.

Similarly, people in Panama decided that those outside the country, particularly those in power in the United States, would also stop being fooled or stop pretending. No matter what Noriega had told his Harvard audience about the role of the military in Latin America, his idea of it was to traffic in drugs and cut people's heads off. If the United States cared to go on supporting him and the PDF, it would have to stand publicly for murder and cocaine, and that wouldn't be easy.

We held this view—we, and Sánchez. We were wrong. By the time crucial sectors of the American establishment finally stopped supporting Noriega and the PDF, the Panamanian people had been beaten to its knees and its resistance broken. We greatly and gravely underestimated that establishment's capacity for self-deception and pretense. Those who'd lied to themselves and the American people about the nature of Panama's tyrants were most unwilling to admit they'd been wrong. So the former U.S. ambassador Ambler Moss lobbied all summer and fall for continued U.S. support for Noriega, holding foolishly that there was no alternative to him. Idi Amin was available. So were Marcos, Bokassa, and Baby Doc. Any one would have been an improvement on Noriega, and did Moss really think that of two million Panamanians not one could have usefully replaced a degenerate psychopath? Meanwhile, those who lied to the American people about what they were doing in Central America, pretending they were making war against drugs and not making war against Nicaragua, had made Manuel Noriega their accomplice. So George Bush pretended he didn't know, said no one knew, Noriega was involved in the drug traffic. We were wrong, but we weren't alone. Many believed that the United States would abandon Noriega long before it even pretended to do so.

A final effect of Díaz's declarations was to suggest that the PDF was breaking up from within. This wasn't so, but many people thought so. No one knew in June 1987 just how foul the PDF's crimes were or how much money officers got by committing them, hence no one knew how strong the bonds were that bound them together. Defections came, but not quickly enough to make a difference.

In any case, by the admission of Roberto Díaz, till June 1 the second-ranking officer in the PDF and its dictatorship, the Defense Forces were corrupt, the puppet president and his government illegitimate, and the so-called strongman a perverted assassin. Few in Panama could support them any longer. It seemed, besides, that the United States would also withdraw its support in a very short time, and that the PDF itself was crumbling. The news, then, was that it and Noriega were finished. The news was that Panama was going to be free.

That, at least, was the conclusion Panamanians reached—not very wisely, as things turned out—by the time Díaz had been talking for three days. He talked nonstop, partly from sour grapes and partly from vanity, and partly from spite and partly to hurt Noriega and partly from fear of what Noriega would do in return, and partly too to ease his conscience. That he suddenly displayed a conscience was weird, as if he'd bought one or had one put in by transplant.

Being dumped had affected Barletta oddly also. A few days after he was driven from his puppetcy, in September 1985, he called the president of the Panamanian Human Rights Committee to complain that Díaz and Noriega had infringed his rights—through the threats, browbeating, and intimidation they'd used to make him resign his office. The person Barletta spoke with, Doña Otilia de Tejeira, was a very great lady. She earned an international reputation as an educator, the first woman in Latin America to be dean of a university, then came out of retirement in her late seventies to help protect human rights in her suffering country. She took note of Barletta's grievance with a straight face and refrained from inquiring, as we would have, why he had not come forward when the rights of hundreds of thousands of his fellow citizens were violated in the matter of his fraud-ridden election, or when his fellow citizens were being murdered and beaten to steal him the office he was now grieved to lose. We might even have asked why he didn't just shoot himself instead of bothering busy people with tripe.

Did Barletta act from stupidity or chutzpah? Well, he was only a puppet, before that a court minstrel. He stole no money, and as for power, craved and got only a sniff. It strains the imagination, yet one can accept that he may have been stupid enough to deceive himself as to the nature of the system he served, that he never realized it violated people's rights until his own precious rights were violated. We've already seen Dr. Carlos López Guevara, who couldn't grasp the nature of the system from the injuries it caused other people's children, but had to wait until it injured his own son. On the other hand, Barletta was dumped for suggesting (albeit while in New York City) that Spadafora's murder should be investigated by an agency independent of the PDF. He may have had the gall to believe that made up for all his previous work on behalf of the tyrants. And if so, he may have been right. In a little, we'll see him publicly applauded. Or perhaps Barletta craved to display some victimhood as a badge of having left the dictatorship and thereby rejoined the human species, as an application (so to speak) for readmission.

Díaz's case, however, was even odder. He had stolen millions, and still enjoyed them, was enjoying them even as he spoke, and would go on doing so, is doing so now. From the first, he'd shared in the PDF's power, and had shared as well in the pleasures of wielding it. He especially enjoyed emitting death threats, threats thoroughly stripped of all idleness by plenty of very real murders perpetrated by the dictatorship over the years. Here he was denouncing the system he'd served and served with, but only after it had expelled him, only when he could no longer hope to direct it in tyrannizing his country!

Oh, Díaz was going through a spiritual crisis. We forgot to mention that. Forgive us. He was in the process of accepting Satya Sai Baba, the first full incarnation of God in five thousand years, though he also placed faith in the Virgin of the Perpetual Help and a masseuse from Brickell Avenue in Miami. The masseuse practiced by candlelight and burned incense and muttered words in Sanskrit like the mystic who'd turned him on to Sai Baba's cult. And then there was the psychic Shama Calhoum. She told him he'd once been Alexander Pushkin, whom he'd never even heard of till that minute, and that (listen to this!) *Noriega was his enemy.* Some revelation! Díaz was as mush minded in his turning to God, as morally and intellectually dishonest, as he'd been while working for Satan.

He was the champion God sent, though, and he was talking. The confessional aspect was the most obvious, the one emphasized by Díaz's serenity and dramatized by the way he admitted his fear, for he was convinced Noriega meant to kill him, whether he talked or not, and that he could survive only if Noriega lost power. On the first night of his disclosures, he held out his hand to reporters so that they could feel how it trembled, and he often spoke of his home's being assaulted. In the end it was, and he fell into Noriega's clutches, and though Noriega did him no injury, his fear was certainly justified. Fear gave him a dignity, a seriousness, that he'd never possessed before and that he lost when the episode was over. It dramatized his status as a penitent.

Most Panamanians accepted him as such, and as a champion, moral rigor not being a very strong national trait, and his home took on somewhat the aspect of a shrine, as well as the aspect of a political headquarters. It was a garish place in execrable taste, powder blue with purposeless Greek columns and a pair of frumpish sphinxes painted gold, but for a while it was Panama's moral center of gravity. The high white walls around it were decked with banners. "JUSTICIA," they said, and "LIBERDAD." Cars filled with pilgrim well-wishers rolled by all day long, and young people camped in the street all day and all night. Within, in the front patio, were minor supporters. Even long past midnight, that space was crowded, and inside the house, by day in rooms where air conditioners whirred and pistol clips lay strewn about on coffee tables, or after dark outside in the rear patio, where the lawn sloped gently away toward the swimming pool and bugs fizzed to death in electric traps, the colonel sat talking, a slight figure in a sport shirt and loose slacks, sockless in canvas leisure shoes, bare right ankle slung up on his left knee, his hands moving nervously while everything else about him was serene, his face drawn by lack of sleep, by worry.

With him were his teenage sons, and his Venezuelan second wife, and a number of young men with Uzi machine pistols, who turned out to be no match for Noriega's commandos. Winston Spadafora was there, the murdered man's brother, and Father Néstor Jaén, the left-wing priest. Other members of the clergy were there also, as talismans against violence or at least witnesses to it. Some of them were there when the end came. The archbishop of Panama, Marcos McGrath, was a frequent visitor, but no one could tell exactly where he stood or what result he hoped would come of the crisis.

Dr. Miguel Antonio Bernal was there, the law professor. Where he stood was no mystery. He'd been exiled by the dictatorship back in the 1970s. We've seen him beaten almost to death protesting the welcome accorded the Shah of Iran. TV crews from two U.S. networks filmed that assault, but the footage was never aired, perhaps because Omar Torrijos was taking out Jimmy Carter's garbage, so that he and his goons were not supposed to be bad guys. That didn't slow Bernal down. When he recovered, he put his opposition to tyranny on the radio and caused the regime such trouble that the minister of justice, Rodolfo Chiari, banned him for life from speaking over the air. So he took his program into the street and broadcast by bullhorn every day at noon on a corner of Avenida Justo Arosemena. Bernal knew where he stood, and so did everyone else. He was at Díaz's house far into the night.

So was Aurelio Barría, the president of Panama's chamber of commerce. Like Bernal, he was in his late thirties, but there, apparently, the resemblance ended. Barría was a businessman, Bernal an intellectual, a former Trotskyite. Barría was new to opposing dictatorship. Bernal had been putting that first for his whole adult life. But Noriega was about to make Barría just as implacable an enemy as Bernal was. Earlier in the year, Barría had been out to the Philippines as an observer of that country's first free election since its dictator's fall. He saw a parallel between Marcos and Noriega. He was at Díaz's house the moment the colonel started talking.

Sam Dillon of the *Miami Herald* was there, the most knowledgeable foreign reporter to cover Panama since Alan Riding of the *New York Times* left the beat. And Tom Brown of Reuters, who was the first journalist Noriega threw out of the country. And José de Córdoba of the *Wall Street Journal,* and Alina Guerrero of AP. *Time* was there, and *Newsweek,* and a girl named Mary Speck, who said she was stringing for a Fort Lauderdale paper but who five weeks later had a byline with *U.S. News & World Report,* because nowadays, at last, the goons were bad guys, and Panama was on the front burner. Agence France–Presse was there, and Prensa Latina from Cuba, and TV from all over, all four U.S. networks and crews from Europe and South America. All these listened to the colonel.

As Díaz's confessions appeared, on Sunday, June 7, then in expanded form on Monday and Tuesday, Panamanians began reacting to them. Noriega and the state-owned media said Díaz was crazy. Opposition leaders, as surprised as anyone else, first said his charges ought to be looked into, then focused on his tale of electoral fraud and began calling for a recount. Among those who joined in was Nicky Barletta, the fraud's chief beneficiary for eleven months. Another unfamiliar voice deploring the fraud was Omaira Correa, who'd been elected to the legislature in 1984 and who'd formed part of the regime's majority. She was an instant convert to Díaz's views and not only called for a recount but invited the people of Panama to gather at her radio station on the afternoon of June 9 to demonstrate against the dictatorship.

A large number of citizens answered this call, including chiefs of opposition parties. Such as Dr. (of philosophy) Ricardo Arias Calderón, president of the Christian Democratic party, and Dr. (of laws) Carlos Ivan Zúñiga, president of the moderate socialist Popular Action party. Dr. (of medicine) Arnulfo Arias tried to show up but was prevented.

Also attending were a large enough number of riot troops. These had visored helmets and looked like Darth Vader's henchmen in *Star Wars.* Their elite company (if so martial a term may be applied to hoodlums whose only opponents are unarmed civilians) was officially designated Doberman, for its savagery, and had doberman-head insignia embossed on its trucks, but nonmartial Panamanians called all riot troops "dobermans," and we see no reason to alter that practice here. Some of them carried tear gas and shotguns. All had plastic shields and rubber hoses. Anyone who thinks the last don't mean serious business is hereby invited to think again. They are four feet long, willowy, yet quite substantial. An easy flick with one to thigh or buttocks will raise a welt the owner may cherish for days, while a healthy swat on the crown can cause brain damage, as Dr. Bernal, aforementioned, can, alas, testify. Citizens of the United States will be comforted to know that this equipment was paid for, at least in part, by their tax dollars.

Instead of waiting for the demonstrators to approach their lines, as was the usual practice in such confrontations, the dobermans attacked while the crowd was still gathering. Dr. Arias Calderón was hosed to the sidewalk. His wife, a diminutive and gentle matron, was not only hosed but dragged across the pavement, so that her legs were considerably scraped. Others were similarly ill treated. All, it must be noted, were making nonviolent use of their constitutional right to assemble publicly.

The crowd dispersed speedily, but instead of staying dispersed, as was the usual practice, rallied and flung taunts at the doberman. There ensued a tremendous street battle such as Panama was to see many of in weeks succeeding, in which the citizens took all the punishment yet seemed lighthearted, while the dobermans grew frustrated and more vicious, in which the citizens retreated precipitously as though headlong in flight, then flowed back whenever the dobermans stopped firing. They fired tear-gas grenades and bird shot, the former most conspicuously through the stained-glass front window of the National Sanctuary Church, where a number of citizens took refuge (for the battle spread out in all directions from its epicenter on Vía España), the latter most tellingly into people's faces. Those who were shot, of course, bled. Those who were gassed wept and strangled. Those who were hosed yelped loudly and fled if they could. Yet, paradoxically, the citizens' taunts seemed to hurt the dobermans more than the dobermans' weapons hurt the citizens. The dobermans, who mainly advanced, appeared fearful. The citizens, who mainly retreated, did not. And, overall, the dobermans, sweating terribly in their heavy fatigue suits, panting through their gas masks in the tropic heat, seemed more to be pitied. This odd business continued apace until nightfall.

Meanwhile, of course, people were being arrested. Ricardo L., a twenty-five-year-old proofreader and university student, was arrested at about 11:00 A.M., while the crowd was still gathering, well before the demonstration began or the dobermans attacked it. He was in an outdoor phone box on Vía España near the Hotel Continental and hadn't finished dialing when a doberman beat on the glass wall of the box with his hose.

"You!" the doberman shouted when Ricardo turned round. "You're under arrest for calling the person you're calling!"

Ricardo held out the receiver to show him there was no one on the line. The doberman repeated that he was under arrest and tried to pull him from the phone box. Other dobermans came up and began to swat Ricardo. With Ricardo cursing and kicking, three Dobermans hosed while two others pulled him from the phone box and dragged him to a patrol truck parked in front of the Joyería Rivera on the Vía España corner of the Hotel Continental.

As soon as Ricardo was in there, sprawled on one of the narrow benches that ran along each side of the truck, the doberman who'd assaulted him first said, "This one gets special treatment." At that, a large doberman jumped up into the truck and put his palm on Ricardo's forehead and began ramming the back of Ricardo's head against the steel wall of the truck. Someone told him to stop, and he did, but then a sergeant climbed in and put an electric stun gun against Ricardo's throat and shocked him repeatedly. The shocks brought spasms that stiffened Ricardo's limbs and threw him against the wall of the patrol truck.

Finally the sergeant stopped and got down. Three young men were being put into the patrol truck. They worked in a nearby store, Almacen Clubman, and had crossed Vía España to buy lunch in Cafetería Jimmy's. That's all they'd done, they told Ricardo, but they'd been arrested. Then a street vendor was put inside, along with several pairs of the cheap shoes he'd been selling—a tiny little fellow, whom the dobermans began beating because, so they shouted, he'd challenged them to a fight. Then a new doberman arrived. He asked if they needed help, and Ricardo was pointed at. "This one's the pet." The new Doberman jumped in and began punching Ricardo in the groin. Then he pounded Ricardo's face with his forearm and the side of his fist.

Ricardo had the sensation this couldn't continue. He was surprised but not frightened, for the whole business seemed unreal. Outside in the street in front of Radio Continente, where the demonstration was scheduled to take place, a crowd was collecting, people were milling about, as yet unmolested, and to Ricardo what was happening to him seemed a delusion. Ricardo cursed at the dobermans, which only made them more enraged. He neither cried in pain nor protested nor asked for mercy. His senses weren't tuned to his injuries, nor did he think of them. Later, he discovered it was useful to groan and complain. That calmed the soldiers a little, no doubt gratifying their sadism.

Other soldiers got into the truck and beat Ricardo. One, a very short man, grabbed Ricardo's beard. "Look, this one's got a beard, let's fix it for him!" He took a pair of pliers from his belt and gripped Ricardo's beard with it and began yanking, tearing hairs out. Then he did the same with Ricardo's mustache. He gripped only a few hairs, but the feeling was terrible. Then he took a razor blade from somewhere and passed it roughly over Ricardo's face, cutting his chin. Ricardo began to bleed and to sweat profusely. The sergeant with the stun gun returned and shocked Ricardo on the throat again, and he went into spasms. He couldn't guess for how long, he was disoriented, and all notion of time had passed from him. The boy with the bag full of shoes was shocked also, but only once. Ricardo was shocked again and again.

An officer got into the truck and pointed at Ricardo's face and asked him if he didn't know how to shave. Ricardo said he hadn't done it. Who had? The officer asked, and when Ricardo said a soldier, the officer beat him. Ricardo kept on saying a soldier had cut him, and the officer kept on beating him, mainly beating his head against the side of the truck, till Ricardo said he'd done it himself, and the beating stopped. Then the officer began giving him shocks on the neck, how many Ricardo lost track of, and he couldn't get his breath, and he couldn't see. He stood up violently and hit his head on the steel roof of the patrol truck, and he began to shout that he'd been blinded. He wanted to grab someone and tear him with his fingernails, but someone pushed him and he fell back on the bench. He wondered if he was blind or only imagining it. All at once he felt drained of all energy, his limbs were limp.

Later that day, Ricardo and others in his view were beaned and kicked, restrained with self-tightening handcuffs till their hands turned purple, denied use of lavatory facilities till some soiled themselves, hosed in the face for talking, interrogated and hosed in the kidneys for answering truthfully, for not admitting that they had broken laws. They had questions shouted at them, jumbled questions shouted in slurred voices, and when they couldn't answer, they were hosed, and when they asked what had been asked, they were hosed for asking. All were strip-searched and made to spread their buttocks and prodded there with billy clubs, and all were threatened repeadly with rape, especially a boy of about thirteen to whom Ricardo was handcuffed for a time. The boy cried constantly, sobbing and sniveling. He seemed very fragile, and anyone who saw him would know at once he wouldn't be mixed up in a demonstration. He was threatened with rape time and again, and was made to suck a chicken bone a soldier had been eating—this in the S-2 intelligence substation where Ricardo and others were interrogated. As Ricardo was questioned, lying face down on the floor of the substation, his questioner, Major Octavio Samudio, rested his foot on Ricardo's face, a small foot in an expensive, highly polished black shoe.

Later, in the G-2 courtyard, Ricardo and the others he was with were made to lie face down on the ground and were threatened with rape and had condoms held in front of them and were told they'd be put in La Modelo and raped by prisoners, most of whom had AIDS. At that Ricardo tried to get up, and someone put a foot on the nape of his neck and held him down, and a voice said, laughing, "Let's not fuck this one, let's burn him, go get gasoline," and Ricardo thought it a bluff, but then he smelled gasoline, and gasoline was poured over his legs. There he was, lying face down, shirtless and shoeless, his hands cuffed behind him, waiting to be set on fire, and down the line of recumbent prisoners someone cried out, and Ricardo thought the man had been set on fire, and at that all his body began twitching.

"Don't be such a coward!" someone said behind him, with a mocking laugh, and then, "All right. Take them inside and charge them."

This was how prisoners were taken and treated on June 9, 1987, the first day of open, general hostilities in the war waged by the Panama Defense Forces against the people they were sworn and paid to protect. As the war continued, treatment became harsher.

That same evening, the opposition's chief political instrument was fashioned. Its origins, like those of the crisis itself, went back to September 1985 and the murder of Dr. Spadafora. In its perverted cruelty, the crime departed entirely from Panama's norms, signaling a level of barbarism unknown till then in the country's history. Particularly affected was a class of young business executives who had grown up under dictatorship and had not as yet been active in public affairs. For them the murder, coming on top of years of blatant corruption and the 1984 electoral fraud, was a sort of threshold. They could not be bystanders any longer. What they did was begin a campaign for decency, for the "restoration of moral and civic values," through the clubs they belonged to, Rotary, Lions, Kiwanis, and the like.

This campaign was not directed openly against the government. Its main focus was the problem of drug abuse. But Noriega took it personally, as well he might. Any movement toward decency was a threat to him, and he bore the main responsibility for Panama's drug problem. The state-owned media attacked the clubs and their leaders with great savagery. Ricardo Acevedo, president of the 20-30 Club, was jailed on trumped-up charges and held until the multinational corporation he worked for threatened to pull out of Panama. Serafín Mitroti, president of Rotary, was found in a cheap hotel eighty miles west of the capital, a suicide according to the official verdict, but both of his wrists were cut to the bone, something one simply can't do unassisted, and his gold ring with an *M* in diamonds, a gift from his children, wound up on the finger of Nivaldo Madriñán.

Now, on the evening of June 9, in response to the government's charges that the crisis had been provoked, and was being manipulated, by partisan political figures to serve their ambitions, veterans of the decency campaign, meeting at the chamber of commerce and with Aurelio Barría and Gilberto Mallol as their chief organizers, formed the National Civilian Crusade. Twenty-six organizations were represented, including the Catholic church. Another thirty-nine joined in the next few days. The communiqué that was issued promised a campaign of civil disobedience, repudiated the "cowardly and brutal repression" performed by the dobermans that afternoon, and called for the immediate removal from office of all those implicated by Colonel Díaz until an investigation of his charges had been made. As the crisis continued, the crusade became more and more important, while the opposition parties and their leaders moved into the background.

Dr. Zúñiga, however, made at least one more prominent contribution. On the radio the next morning, he called on citizens to show their disapproval of the dictatorship by beating post and honking car horns at noon and 6:00 P.M. each day. A final touch came about by spontaneous generation. At six that afternoon not only were post beaten and horns honked; white handkerchiefs were waved all over the city. Little groups of smiling citizens stood on street corners throughout the capital, waving white handkerchiefs, while cars went by with horns honking and people stood in house windows beating pots. Thus the three Ps of anti-Noriega militants: *paila* (pot), *pito* (horn), and *pañuelo* (handkerchief). All announced sedition, and the last made your doberman rabid.

This became clear on Thursday, June 11, but by then two important things had happened. On Wednesday night, after a day of street violence in which seventy-odd citizens were wounded by bird shot and one lost an eye, the crusade called for a general strike. In response, at twenty minutes past midnight on Thursday morning, the government declared a state of emergency and suspended the rights to freedom of movement, expression, and assembly, to security of domicile, privacy of correspondence, and private property, and the state's obligations to abide by legal formalities, to advise arrested persons of the charges against them, to allow them benefit of counsel, and to process writs of habeas corpus. Dawn found the capital occupied by soldiers and the citizenry apparently cowed, but at noon people began beating pots, honking car horns, and waving white handkerchiefs.

Along Fiftieth Street in the banking district, the strike had not had much effect. Government pressure kept most businesses open, and the state of emergency had many people thinking twice about showing opposition. Later on, after rights were restored and the regime took to simply disregarding them, the people stopped thinking twice. The more disgusting the repression became, the more willing people were to take punishment in order to show disagreement. In any case, most businesses were open. At noon, people came out onto the sidewalks and began waving handkerchiefs. The dobermans hosed, gassed, shotgunned, and arrested them, and perpetrated much violence against property, but nowhere with such frenzy as at the Banco del Istmo. Why there is a mystery. Puppet President Delvalle was a stockholder. But these were the genuine article, the doberman's Dobermans, parked across the street in blue-gray patrol trucks with pooch's profile embossed. Waved at with handkerchiefs, they charged the seditionists, and when the latter fled into the bank and locked the glass door, the troops smashed it in and followed.

Katia P., twenty-five, a junior executive of the bank, was at her desk on the second floor when a colleague rushed in, hotly pursued by three dobermans armed with hoses. One of these seized Katia by the hair and dragged her downstairs, where soldiers were smashing everything in sight, typewriters, computer terminals, everything—then out of the building. There, three other female bank employees were being hustled into the back of a patrol truck. Katia pleaded with her captor to be allowed to go with these others. By way of an answer, he hosed her on the ear, then lifted and shoved her into another patrol truck and climbed in behind her.

The truck was packed: five or six civilian prisoners, a dozen or more dobermans. Katia was the only woman. She was pushed on top of a prisoner with a bloody head wound who was half lying on the narrow bench that ran along the side of the truck compartment. Right away the truck began moving.

The soldier who'd captured Katia stood over her. He wet his hand in the wounded man's blood and smeared it over Katia's face and neck. He reached his hands into her blouse. He grabbed her hand and pressed it to his crotch, then against the crotches of soldiers nearby. All the while he kept shouting. They were going to the jail, he shouted. She would be put in with criminals, She'd "do the favor" for all of them. They hadn't had a woman for a long time. Was she a virgin? he shouted. Did she have a boyfriend she "did the favor" for? Was she good? He and his friends would have her, too, before the criminals. Didn't she know that rights had been suspended? That they could do whatever they felt like with her?

When the truck entered the grounds of Santo Tomás Hospital, a soldier sitting next to Katia whispered that he would help her. He was taking a risk, he said, but he wasn't like the others. They would stop to take the wounded man off. She should try to get out then.

As soon as the truck stopped, Katia stood up. Pushed by the soldier beside her, who pretended to hold her, and despite the threats of the soldier who'd captured her, she got to the back of the truck, where hospital personnel could see her. An orderly helped her down.

Katia P. was taken into the prison wing of the hospital and treated for trauma to her ear. Then a resident to whom she'd told her story insisted that she needed special treatment and moved her into another wing. She rested there for a while and then went home.

Fourteen-year-old Eidinai Piñeda was in a playground in the working-class barrio of Pueblo Nuevo, for schools had been ordered closed the day before. Someone must have been waving a handkerchief nearby, for a patrol truck pulled up and dobermans armed with shotguns entered the playground. Eidinai and the other children there began running. She tripped on a board and fell, twisting her ankle. As she lay on the ground, she saw a soldier aim his gun at a younger girl. "Señor, no!" Eidinai cried. "We haven't done anything!" The soldier fired and the girl fell down bleeding. Eidinia went to pick her up. The soldier aimed his gun at her. "Señor, no!" said Eidinai. "We haven't done anything!" The soldier kept his gun aimed at her. "If you shoot, I'll accuse you." With that, the soldier fired at Eidinai.

Eidinai Piñeda and Kathia Villareal received multiple bird-shot wounds. Both were hospitalized at the San Fernando Clinic. Kathia, who was nine years old, underwent successful surgery to remove her spleen, which had been damaged by pellets, and to remove pellets from her left lung.

Aurelio Barría, the chamber of commerce president, was arrested just after noon, picked off the street in front of the chamber of commerce by G-2 agents in an unmarked car. He spent the next five hours in the Balboa Police Station, naked, with a hood over his head, being shouted at by a number of angry voices, berated, taunted, vilified, threatened. Besides being threatened with death, he was threatened with rape. The death threats were vague, the threats of rape specific.

Here, as in the ordeals of Ricardo L. and Katia P., we have a peculiarity of the Panama Defense Forces since the ascension of General Manuel Noriega, a trait, no doubt, imparted by their commander, like the Swedes' intrepidity under Gustavus Adolphus, or the discipline of the French when led by Turenne. We mean the PDF's obsession with rape, homosexual if possible, heterosexual faute de mieux. Rape—in person, by proxy, or just via threat—may even have replaced bribe taking as the chief incentive in a PDF career. People of both sexes arrested during the summer of 1987 suffered rape while in PDF custody, and as far as one can gather, not a single person detained for political reasons was spared the threat of rape, often with the garnish that it would be performed by AIDS carriers. In fact, opponents of Noriega rightly took as an attempt at intimidation the ostensibly innocent disclosure, made in July by the minister of health, that there were AIDS carriers in La Modelo Prison.

Barría was not intimidated by his experience. Much the reverse, he emerged from it more firmly opposed to tyranny than ever. So too with the populace. Noriega was training Panamanians to be stubborn, and his attempts at intimidation became ridiculous at noon on Friday, when a special mass was celebrated at the Church of El Carmen on the request of the crusade, and he had the church surrounded by troops in battle dress and camouflage face paint, bristling with hand grenades and automatic weapons. This was Batallón 2000, supposedly an elite unit named for the year when Panama was scheduled to take over the Canal, but for all their firepower they seemed ill at ease, mainly eighteen-year-olds from the countryside out of place among peaceful citizens on Vía España, and the palm-lined Avenida Federico Boyd.

The churchgoers were certainly not daunted. They included an unexpected yet welcome attendee, Ms. Susan Davis, daughter of the U.S. ambassador to Panama, Arthur Davis. This gentleman, a former Denver businessman, a former chairman of the Colorado Republican party, had by his actions during the crisis given proponents of democracy cause for hope. His embassy had reacted to Díaz's charges with a communiqué supporting "efforts to have the facts clarified in a manner just to all," and simply by standing for truth and justice Mr. Davis had set himself well apart from preceding U.S. envoys. He was, in fact, the first U.S. ambassador to Panama since Jack Hood Vaughn in the mid-1960s to be recognizable as an American in his official behavior—that is, to favor democracy over dictatorship, civilian over military rule, respect for the lives and well-being of U.S. citizens over short-term compliance with the short-term policy of the U.S. government of the moment and decency over barbarism. On Thursday morning, June 10, when PDF troops surrounded the home of Dr. Arias Calderón, putting him, in effect, under house arrest, Ambassador Davis paid Dr. Arias Calderón a visit (having first called puppet President Delvalle and said he was going to), thereby causing the troops to be withdrawn. Now he was giving the resistance to tyranny further comfort, for no one could believe that his daughter—the first lady, as it were, of the embassy, since Mr. Davis is a widower—would appear at the mass unless the ambassador (and, by extension, the government he represented) approved.

That night the rumor throughout the capital was that Noriega was leaving, and that a provisional government would be established to oversee elections. The next morning, an effort was made to bring this to pass. Opposition party leaders appealed to high officers of the PDF to dump their commander. The go-between was Gabriel Lewis Galindo, the former ambassador to the United States, who had spent years helping Americans, influential ones mainly, fool themselves about Torrijos, Paredes, and Noriega. The colonels, however, weren't buying, and their answer was so vehement (as it had to be, lest Noriega doubt their sincerity) that Lewis Galindo took the first plane out.

Still, though the dobermans persisted with tear gas, hoses, and bird shot, though the PDF in general persisted with cruelty of increasing harshness, citizens persisted with horn, pot, and handkerchief. The tyrant had no ease or respite. It was a season of liberty. Ferdinand Marcos of the Philippines and Baby Doc Duvalier of Haiti had both been thrust into uncomfortable exile, and now Manuel Noriega found the people of his country seeking the same for him. Being a monster, it turned out, wasn't all fun.

During most of June, Noriega seemed to teeter, scrambled around like a roach in a paper bag, trying to find the right response to his problems, while citizens continued to display sedition and dobermans to make them suffer for it. Then, at month's end, his frustration exploded in a response that damaged him and gave his enemies hope.

Since and because of the murder of Hugo Spadafora, a certain receptiveness had existed in U.S. congressional circles for the proposition that the dictatorship in Panama ought not to enjoy U.S. support. The attitude centered among certain congressional aides, particularly Deborah de Moss, who worked for Senator Jesse Helms, F. Marian Chambers of the House Committee on Foreign Relations, and Gregory Craig, chief adviser to Senator Edward Kennedy. Later these were joined by Dick McCall, Alfred Cumming, and Randy Scheunemann, aides (respectively) to Senators John Kerry, Bob Graham, and David Durenberger. We mention these staffers because staffers rarely get mentioned yet are responsible for much of the useful work the U.S. Congress does, and because they do credit to their employers. In any case, on June 26, 1987, through the good work of these aides and their principals, Kennedy and Helms in particular, the Senate passed a resolution calling for Noriega's departure from Panama. The vote, 86 to 2, reflected how hard it had suddenly become to fool oneself (or pretend to) about Noriega. But neither the vote nor its text gave the measure significance. The purpose of such things for most who take part in them is to get themselves off the hook of previous action and enable them later to say, I told you so, and while such resolutions purport to influence policy, in general only those voting pay them any attention.

So it seemed with this one. After all, the State Department had been put out with Noriega since he fired Barletta, and that made no difference. The Pentagon loved the PDF and the tyrant, "professional" soldiers and a valued ally. The CIA clung to him. The DEA was his faithful hound. As a counterpoise to the Pentagon, Langley, and the executive branch, the Senate vote seemed to count little.

Noriega, however, decided it was important and thus made it so. For over a year, he'd been saying that criticism of him in the U.S. press and Congress, as well as acts of his opponents in Panama, were all part of a vast and sinister plot by U.S. reactionaries to prevent Panama's getting the Canal in the year 2000. As an attempt to revive the sovereignty issue, to engender support on nationalistic grounds, this lie did Noriega no good but little harm either, and he clearly wished to believe it. Only in violence could he find any ease. Now he had the puppet legislature restore the right of public assembly, and on the last day of June gave the Senate his answer: a mob of hooligans egged on with a public harangue by Rómulo Escobar and led by government figures proceeded to the U.S. embassy, consulate, and Information Service library for an hour of rock throwing, while armed PDF units looked on in approval. And, that night, paramilitary goons tore down and carted away a memorial statue of Roosevelt—the good Roosevelt, Franklin not Teddy—that had stood more or less unremarked for forty years.

This spree must have pleased the participants and calmed the general—how thin-skinned these bullies are, how they hate being criticized!—but did not increase his internal support and hurt him terribly in sectors of the U.S. government that paid no attention to Senate resolutions. It brought an immediate protest, and a suspension of aid. Nothing Noriega could have done would have been so effective in making the Reagan administration consider withdrawing support for him. Then, as if to make Reagan jealous, as if in spite for being jilted, he brought Daniel Ortega down from Managua for a vow of Sandinista solidarity.

Internally too, Noriega lurched leftward—as much, we suppose, from necessity as by design, for his main civilian support now came from Cuban-line communists. Only the rich were against him, he said. But this message was cruelly undercut by the arrangements he had made for celebrating his daughter's wedding, scheduled for July 11. The Marriott, the newest and most splendid hotel in the country, was booked in its entirety, all twenty stories, to house guests from abroad, and a jet chartered to bring the bridegroom and his family from Santo Domingo. Moët & Chandon (by appointment, wine merchants to the tyrant of Panama) had made up special labels for the champagne, and each of four thousand guests received a bottle with his invitation, along with a Baccarat crystal champagne glass with the happy couple's initials engraved upon it.

So much for Noriega the man of the people, but he seemed to have swallowed his own populist poppycock, for he briefly adopted the strategy of trying to outdemonstrate the crusade. A "sovereignty" rally was called for the ninth, and all stops pulled out to generate ardor for it, but when the crusade called a march for the tenth—five marches, in fact, each starting from different parts of the city, all converging at the Church of El Carmen—it was soon clear the numbers were not with Noriega. So puppet President Eric Delvalle, who (as fraudulently elected vice-president) had succeeded Nicky Barletta when the latter was deposed in 1985, went on TV proposing a truce. Pots were beaten all over Panama even as he was speaking. No truce, replied the crusade, till Noriega got out. So Delvalle issued a decree banning both marches, an unconstitutional decree since all rights were in place. Pots were beaten again. The crusade said it was marching.

Noriega decided to smash the march, and put the crusade out of business, by cruelty and terror. He seems consciously to have imitated Israeli procedures in territories occupied by Arabs, methods which, in turn, seem patterned on those of persecutors of Jews. Lieutenant Colonel Eduardo Herrera, who had seen these methods in action as Panamanian military attaché in Israel, was recalled and put in charge of the operation, though another reason for his appointment may have been his reputation for honesty, which made him the leading candidate in U.S. military circles to succeed Noriega as PDF commandant. And two items were added that gave the episode, no matter how great its debt to Israel, a distinctively Noriegan touch: a paramilitary force was put in readiness, and certain preparations were made at La Modelo.

To begin with, Major Cleto Hernández, the murderer of César Rodríguez and Rubén Paredes, Jr., a G-2 product and longtime Noriega familiar, was assigned temporarily to the prison with more authority than the nominal commandant and assistant commandant, Lieutenant Colonel Eric Aguilar and Major Ricardo Garibaldo.

Then, between 7:00 and 8:00 P.M. on Thursday, the ninth, the most aggressive offenders in the prison were removed from the galleries and collected in a large ground-floor holding pen called La Preventiva, and told they were being shipped to Coiba Island to make room for the expected influx of political prisoners. Despite the move's suddenness, it produced lightning riots of theft in the galleries, as the Coiba bound tried to get clothing, blankets, containers such as paper cups, and especially money, all of which might make the difference between life and death in the penal colony, where inmates are systematically starved and treated with almost unimaginable harshness. Between 10:00 and 11:00 P.M. two consignments of prisoners were removed from La Preventiva and put on buses for Puerto Mutis, where the launch for Coiba docked, leaving the twenty-odd strongest and fiercest who had fought their way to the cell's rear. These were then advised that they would not be sent to Coiba until later, that on the next day political prisoners would be put in with them, and that they might do as they pleased with these "rock throwers" without fear of punishment.

This was how the dictatorship prepared for July 10, 1987. Then the hour of the wolf came to Panama.

You may have seen part of it on television, the people in white, carrying white flags, walking toward the lines of visored soldiers, walking forward and being shotgunned, walking forward again. Compact masses of men and women in white, filling the street and stretching blocks and blocks backward, being shotgunned and pressing forward, being shotgunned again. On Vía España beside the Republic Bank Building, and on Vía Argentina near the university, and on Samuel Lewis at the Sanctuario Nacional, a large Catholic church, and on Calle 50. On Federico Boyd the route went steeply uphill, and the dobermans were on the crest, so the marchers broke and dissolved at the first volley, but elsewhere they pushed forward again and again. Under a brilliant white sky, on an afternoon refreshed by pleasant sea breezes. Panamanians attempting to exercise their newly restored rights to public assembly and freedom of transit, offering no violence, merely receiving it.

How many marched? At least one hundred thousand. And all along the five routes, people watched from their windows and waved white handkerchiefs, and draped white towels and bedsheets from the sills. And got shotgunned for it, if they weren't lucky, for when the marchers broke (as they had to, of course, after two or three volleys), the dobermans went crazy.

They rushed forward shooting, hosing, arresting people. They fired at the windows that showed white. They fired gas grenades into buildings and shot people as they fled out. A large number of marchers took refuge in the National Sanctuary Church, which might have done them some good in the Middle Ages, but not in Panama in the time of Manuel Noriega. The dobermans fired tear gas in through the windows and shotgunned people point-blank as they tried to get out. Drove them back in and gassed them. Shotgunned them point-blank as they tried to get out. Just people, you understand. Not insurgents or foreign invaders. Then charged into the church, shotgunning and hosing left and right—*inside the church,* you understand—and grabbed people and dragged them out, hosing them as they dragged them, and flung them into patrol trucks and took them to prison, beating them on the way.

And complained to them also. It was still Panama, after all. So sometimes the dobermans, instead of beating their captives, or when their arms were weary, complained to them. The dobermans, it turned out, had been confined to barracks since the crisis started. Not allowed home for six weeks, though some lived only a block or two from headquarters. Not allowed to see their families, and the food was terrible, and it was all the opposition's fault.

More PDF brutality, this time expressed toward its own troops? Or simple stupidity, not rotating units so as to give the men leave? Neither. The PDF was *afraid* to let them go home, afraid their wives and mothers and sisters would scold them for being bullies, afraid the neighbors would let them know how hated they were by all those who didn't wear uniforms.

Then the paramilitaries came out, though they were on no one's TV footage. For which viewers can count themselves lucky. Ugly goons, the sight of them makes one's flesh crawl. Not odd, Noriega got them out of prison and from worse places. In April 1988, Dr. Jaime Arroyo, formerly chief of mental health programs in Panama, was horrified to recognize a murderer he'd ordered committed as insane hefting an assault rifle in a paramilitary formation. That afternoon, they traveled six to a mini-van and appeared in all parts of the city as if by diabolic conjuration—sleek-skinned assassins in jeans, in fatigue trousers, in bulletproof vests, many with little numbers tattooed on the insides of hairless forearms. Armed with riot guns: cut-down, auto-loading, twelve-gauges with pistol grips. They came down the street R. M. Koster lived on, prowling slowly, turning as they walked, pointing their weapons, and he went out on the street for a close look at them, for that response somehow eased his terror.

He eyed them, they eyed him, and they prowled by, but on other streets they fired into windows and smashed doors in to shoot people in their own living rooms and dragged men out and flung them into the vans. Prisoners were taken that weekend all over the capital: marchers, people whose houses showed white, men with white shirts on.

William Bright, thirty-three, a businessman from La Chorrera, twelve miles from the capital, a dual citizen of Panama and the United States, was gassed from the Sanctuario and arrested as he ran out.

Dr. Andrés Berroa, a thirty-seven-year-old radiologist, had finished his tour at the Oncological Hospital and was too tired to think about marching. He was on his way to visit his brother Alvaro, was in his brother's apartment building, at his brother's door, when paramilitaries rushed up the stairs and grabbed him. He resisted for a moment on impulse and got bashed on the upper arm with a shotgun barrel, a bruise he kept for two weeks. What's wrong, he asked, what's it about? "This is war!" his captor replied. At that, Berroa's brother, who had heard the commotion, opened the door and was captured too.

A Lloyd Aereo pilot, a Bolivian, stepped out of the Hotel Continental to see what the fuss was and got grabbed five meters away and taken to prison.

A young Belgian, in Panama to see his fiancée, was plucked off the street and beaten severely and taken to the G-2 and interrogated as a spy.

Everyone with white on was at risk. Their cars too: cars were abused and arrested. As in the unhappy case of the two U.S. citizens stopped on the night of the tenth at a roadblock in front of the El Dorado shopping center, two gringos new to the country who worked for a building contractor on one of the bases. They'd been to the beach that day and had the unspeakably bad judgment to leave a white towel on the backseat of their Wagoneer. So the poor Wagoneer had all its windows shotgunned, and then was impounded, and the two gringos were hauled off to La Modelo Prison.

Ah, La Modelo! Who could see you and ever forget! The first stop for those taken on the tenth was La Preventiva, and the Coiba reprievees were waiting for them. As each political detainee was shoved in, he was assaulted and robbed. Got his eye blacked and/or his lip busted. Robbed of valuables, naturally, but also perhaps of his shoes and/or of his shirt, of whatever took a robber's fancy. William

Bright was one of the first to enter. He thought he was going to be sexually assaulted—he'd been threatened with rape, of course, on the way over—and he resisted. In an instant, he was against a wall with a knife at his throat, the wielder a man of forty-odd wearing jeans whom Bright had seen at the Balboa Police Station in the uniform of a PDF sergeant. The sergeant, who was in and out of La Preventiva all night long supervising the criminals, calmed Bright down in a hurry and relieved Bright of his watch and his wedding ring and the few dollars cash he had on him. After that, Bright stood by the door telling new entrants to take it easy, to turn over their valuables and they wouldn't get hurt. Some were robbed down to their underwear, a few of gold fillings.

The gold, the money, the pawnable loot was passed through a slot in the wall to a guard outside, for the actual robbers got but a small share of the proceeds. And above the slot was a window that gave on the guardroom, from which the guards browsed these scenes of brutality, grinning and laughing.

La Preventiva is thirty feet square, with a tap in one wall and two scoop-out toilets—bowls, that is, without plumbing. The floor was slimy with water and excrement. By nightfall, three hundred men were packed inside. The heat was intense. The stench was incredible. A lone bulb burned palely high up at the ceiling, and all night long the guards came to the little window and shouted for the men to stand up, for the men to kneel down, for the men to raise their hands, and so forth.

Sometime after midnight, the sergeant in jeans came in with marijuana cigarettes for the criminals who'd been working as harassers. The smokes calmed them down, but then a young woman was thrust inside, what looked like a young woman to the politicals, in high heels and pedal pushers and a pink blouse. Actually it was a male transvestite. And frequent visitor at La Modelo evidently, for the criminals greeted him by name, by nom de guerre, Carolina. With great enthusiasm, the reason for which was immediately evident, for (following what seemed an established pecking order) they at once began to make sexual use of him. With his consent at first, or at least resignation, and then despite his pleas and protests, his whimpering and tears—twenty or more acts of oral and anal intercourse, with wisecrack accompaniment from those who'd already coupled or were waiting their turn and cuffs, ear twistings, and curses to encourage Carolina. To the horror and shame, of course, of the politicals, for whose benefit no doubt the performance was staged. Every man in there had to fear he might be used similarly. Each had to be shaken to witness that living nightmare.

When it had been going on for about fifteen minutes, Dr. Berroa was called to by a man whose face he recognized but whose name he didn't know, a person, he guessed, who knew he was a physician. Then he was pulled through the press of squatting, standing men to where a man of fifty or thereabouts lay in evident anguish, sweating profusely and hyperventilating. Suspecting that the man was having a heart attack, Berroa cleared a little space around him to give him air, went to the door, and told the guard outside. So what? was the reply.

"If it's his heart," Berroa said, "he may be dying."

"Let the son of a whore die. I don't care."

For the next hour, till long after the criminals were done with Carolina, Dr. Berroa went back and forth between his patient, whom he couldn't help, and the guard, whom he couldn't move. Finally, the latter gave in. He and a colleague came in and dragged the sick man out, dragged him along the floor and up the step out of the cell. When he was released three days later, Berroa learned that a man had died of heart failure in Santo Tomás Hospital that morning, but no mention was made of the dead man's having been a prisoner, and since Berroa never knew his patient's name, he never learned for sure what happened to him.

In the morning, the political detainees were told they would get six months' incommutable confinement. All would get the same. No trials would be necessary. None had been allowed to see a lawyer. None had been advised of the charges against him. These rights are guaranteed by the Panamanian constitution, and had been fully restored, but suspending rights wasn't Noriega's style anyway, so it's hard to understand why he did it. Noriega's style is to keep the rights in place and then violate them. Violation causes maximum humiliation, along with maximum pain, and besides, in Spanish "violate" and "rape" are conveyed by the same verb. Nearly two hundred writs of habeas corpus were filed on behalf of political prisoners taken on July 10, and not a single one was processed.

The political prisoners' next stop was the galleries. They were put in one at a time. Again they were robbed, though now the guards got no part of the proceeds. On the other hand, very few had anything left worth stealing, which sometimes made the regular residents angry. At least two men arrested on July 10 were raped. And the filth, the stench, the misery, the despair. Ah, La Modelo!

Ah, the savagery, the mass arrests, the planned abominations for those arrested! And the practice, in force in emergency rooms of public hospitals (and noted by Physicians for Human Rights following a visit to Panama by a team from that organization), whereby PDF sergeants did the admitting, whereby people with shotgun wounds got no treatment, or got it at a PDF infirmary after being arrested—not to mention incidents where soldiers invaded wards and treatment rooms, and pulled patients from their beds, or from the hands of doctors ministering to them! All to intimidate opponents, to cow them into suffering tyranny kindly. Armies of occupation are often savage in reducing uprisings by civilian populaces, for they have no claim except force and are greatly outnumbered, and this army was, besides, a criminal enterprise of, by, and for degenerate sadists. Later on, this approach proved effective. When Noriega had his back to the wall and no longer cared what anyone thought of him or his government, he cowed opposition easily with terror tactics. He would have cowed it in July 1987, if the detainees could have been held hostage in those hideous conditions, but the events on the street, and reactions to them, were reported by the independent media. An immense stink arose at once, at a time when Noriega and company still had pretensions to appearing civilized. "Beyond all the limits of necessity," said Archbishop McGrath, and others in and outside Panama joined in. All those taken on the tenth were released on the fourteenth, no doubt because of pressure from within the PDF and the civilian apparatus of government, for the regime was still responsive to public opinion and hopeful that the crisis might blow over. The effect of it all was to make the opposition tougher, and to convince Noriega that free speech had to go.

There was another reason for the pain inflicted that weekend. The crusade's persistence in marching on July 10 personally discomfited Panama's tyrant. He had to cancel the festivities planned for the eleventh. His daughter's wedding was celebrated on the eighth, in the chapel on the PDF base at Fort Amador, with only a handful of guests in attendance. A clear and palpable humiliation, and what was he going to do with all that champagne? Good reason, in short, to make his enemies suffer. Drunk and tearful, he complained that Díaz had ruined his life. He'd take care of that son of a whore for sure. He knew he might have to leave power, but a lot of Panama would go with him.

Noriega seemed to teeter. The National Civilian Crusade announced a general strike for July 27 and 28, and worse news came from the United States. The Pentagon had apparently decided it could live without him, for abruptly, as a bartender does with a drunk, U.S. Southern Command cut the PDF off—stopped maintenance on PDF equipment; stopped gas for PDF vehicles; stopped all chumminess by U.S. officers toward their valiant Panamanian allies. And Washington announced it would sell Panama no more tear gas, and that economic aid would not be renewed, despite an apology from the puppet foreign minister, and payment for damage done to the embassy on the last day of June.

On Friday, July 24, *La Prensa* and the tabloids *Extra* and *El Siglo* published a public letter to Noriega by General (retired) Rubén Paredes, in which the former PDF commandant asked his successor to resign for the good of the PDF and the country. And that morning Paredes went on radio answering listeners' questions and suggesting that, if Noriega refused to resign, the officers of the PDF ought to remove him. He was the only obstacle to a settlement of the crisis and a menace to the health of the institution.

Were these acts by Paredes spontaneous? Probably not. At the time, they certainly looked like part of an orchestrated effort, a U.S. attempt at toppling Noriega by making it plain that he'd lost American backing while assuring the PDF that it wasn't the target, thereby nerving Noriega's colleagues to move against him. Paredes had been betrayed by Noriega and had done nothing. Paredes's son had been murdered, and again he'd done nothing. That he acted when he did suggested a plan.

Whatever the case, that weekend the jubiliation that had come to Panama nearly two months before, at the start of the crisis, redoubled. All summer the mood had been one of exhilaration—leavened, of course, at times with naked terror, as when the paramilitaries prowled, but essentially a mood of hope and confidence, a sense in the hearts of decent people, the vast majority, that is, of those on the isthmus, that they were stronger than the barbarians and hence would win. Odd country, Panama; odder still that summer. That summer, one could see—as R. M. Koster saw one afternoon at five, on his way to the Canal area to teach a class—a pitched street battle with demonstrators being clubbed and shotgunned (this in front of La Contraloría on Avenida Balboa), and two blocks off, in Parque Uraccá, a softball game in progress with fifty or a hundred spectators looking on absorbed. Koster felt exhilaration in the streets, for on every corner, so it seemed that summer, there were little bands of people waving white handkerchiefs. He felt the confidence in his own person, felt it especially one afternoon, riding back from La Modelo with a young man whose release his wife had negotiated, when he came on a caravan of government supporters waving Partido Revolucionario flags from their car windows, and sat laughing scornfully at them as they passed, even when the notorious López Tirone pointed an Uzi at him, cursing. That last weekend in July, then, jubilation reached an apogee. The gringos were dumping Noriega! The Defense Forces were dumping Noriega! Noriega was finished! Panama was going to be free!

As if in response to such longings, and (so it seemed) in confirmation of them, the dobermans disappeared from the capital. In the two weeks since the tenth, their presence had become more or less permanent, but now, with white handkerchiefs waving on every corner, they disappeared. People who had trips planned canceled them. People already abroad cut their trips short. No one wanted to be outside Panama when Noriega fell.

What no one knew, however, was that if Paredes acted with U.S. encouragement, it came from nowhere near the top. The real U.S. government was foursquare behind Noriega and was to remain so at least until winter, for when Admiral Murphy called on him in November, the word from the real U.S. government was to hang on. The CIA continued to back him even after he was indicted by two federal grand juries. John Lawn of the DEA was still seeking his cooperation as late as May 1988, and it is still unclear how many high officials in the United States, beginning with President Bush, may be bound to him, or be in his power, by blackmail.

What crossed no one's mind either was that Noriega's colleagues, though thieves, had already stolen a great deal of money and were more concerned about living to enjoy it than about stealing more. They knew perfectly well that Noriega was an obstacle, and a menace, and whatever else one wished to call him. They knew Manuel Noriega better than most, and the knowledge very likely gave them nightmares. He is not the sort one risks annoying idly. And suppose they risked and were successful. Where would they find a leader as ruthless as he to keep the PDF in power and thus save them from paying for their crimes?

The PDF's health was worse than Paredes suspected. The PDF, and Panama with it, had lost the ability to excrete.

By Sunday the euphoric mood was fading. There was no sign of anything's happening inside the Defense Forces in response to Paredes's actions, and that morning a twenty-three-year-old law student named Eduardo Carrera became the first fatality of the crisis—

first confirmed fatality, for there were people missing to go along with the more than one thousand wounded, two of them blinded for life. Carrera had been arrested on July 10 and badly beaten. His mother, a widow, sent him to the town of El Valle, ninety road miles from Panama City, in part so he could recuperate, mainly from concern for his safety. At about 3:30 A.M., he and some other youths were outside a cantina in the center of the town when two PDF corporals arrived, armed, in uniform, and drunk. "Down with Pineapple Face!" someone shouted. Corporal Eliécer Almengor drew his pistol. "Take it easy," Carrera told him. Almengor grabbed Carrera's shirt and shot him in the stomach. Under crowd pressure, the two corporals took Carrera to the town's health center but, finding the place empty, left him on the floor and fled. Carrera was dead on arrival at the hospital in La Chorrera.

That afternoon, wild rumors gripped the capital. Three buses full of convicts from the penal colony on Coiba Island had been seen headed east on the Pan-American Highway; they would be brought in after dark and let loose in the city. And so on. What Noriega was actually up to, however, was worse.

At twenty minutes to midnight, troops occupied the offices of *La Prensa, Extra,* and *El Siglo,* as well as Radio Mundial and Radio KW Continente, belonging to Dr. Zúñiga and Ms. Correa. Employees were hustled out and the places padlocked. These media, the regime said the next morning, were accused of having issued calls to sedition. They would stay closed until the investigation was concluded.

At 4:00 A.M., troops of the Batallón 2000 began blocking off the streets around Roberto Díaz's home in Altos del Golf. At 4:40, they opened up with machine guns at barricades Díaz's guards had set up at the corners of his block. The guards fired back for a few minutes, then withdrew to the house. There were fifty-three people inside, including five minors, four of them Díaz's children, one his nephew. Díaz moved them all into his bedroom. He and a few other men went into the master bathroom, whose window gave on the street. He had his guards put their weapons in a closet. According to those with him at the time, he couldn't believe that the PDF, troops he had led, would assault his house with his wife and children inside. He thought the attackers paramilitary goons of Noriega's and didn't want them provoked.

At first light, around five-thirty, troops who had moved in around the house, began firing tear-gas grenades through the windows while riflemen directed fire at the house itself. Shortly thereafter, two helicopters appeared overhead and began taking turns strafing the house with M-60 machine guns. Some spent bullets penetrated the bedroom, but the ceiling armor held. The main problem was tear gas. People breathed through handkerchiefs kept damp with water from the bathtub.

Sometime before six-thirty, the firing stopped. A man called out over a bullhorn identifying himself as a state prosecutor and calling on Señor Díaz to surrender "for the sake of your family." Díaz called out for the troops to be withdrawn. "You wanted it this way," the voice called back. Tear gas and rifle fire resumed, followed shortly by machine-gun and explosive fire (probably rifle grenades, perhaps bazookas) against the house walls. Just after seven, there were two loud explosions. Commandos of the antiterrorism unit had blown in the front and rear doors. At that, the fire became intense. The next thing those inside knew, commandos were in the bedroom.

Díaz and the others with him were brought outside into the front garden, the men hustled along with blows from gun butts. His wife, her mother, and the children were taken to the Venezuelan embassy. The others, forty-six in all, were put under arrest. The PDF announced later that morning that the "operation" had resulted in neither dead nor wounded. The claim seems correct. The closing of the free media and the capture of Díaz crippled the crusade and effectively discouraged PDF defection. Pushed into a corner, Noriega had reacted with vigor and aim, entirely reversing the situation with two easy swipes.

Tyranny, in short, wasn't finished in Panama. Not quite yet. Noriega retained the support of the Defense Forces and could put the fear of death into those who betrayed him. He therefore retained control of the government machinery and the apparatus of civilians who manned it. His regime had lost all authority but retained the means and will to rule Panama by force.

CODA

August 1987–January 1990

Three weeks after the assault on Colonel Díaz's home, R. M. Koster, hiking in Maine with his son, suddenly realized he could write about Panama. He'd treated themes from Panama's story in fiction. He'd sent private memos to politicians he knew. But he'd published nothing factual; he was afraid to. A phony name, he knew, would give no protection were he to write the kind of piece he craved to, one that whacked the bullies where it hurt most and that might affect attitudes in the United States and elsewhere. Now suddenly, however—just below timberline on Mt. Katahdin—he saw a way. There was a real person of at least equal skill and knowledge, believable as the author of a piece about Panama, yet out of Manuel Noriega's reach. That night he called Guillermo Sánchez in Miami.

Sánchez agreed to sign what his friend proposed writing, an indictment of military rule in Panama pegged to Díaz's declarations and the repression. Both men judged that the dictatorship would fall if only the United States would stop supporting it. The judgment turned out to be overly sanguine. Its underlying premise, though, was correct. The key to freedom in Panama was in Washington, and one of the keys to Washington was public opinion.

The article, fragments of which are preserved in the previous chapter, appeared in the December 1987 issue of *Harper's* with an apt title, "Panama Fallen among Thieves," supplied by the magazine's editor, Lewis Lapham. It attracted considerable interest and helped set the tone of Panama coverage. Sánchez and Koster at once began another, on the death of Dr. Hugo Spadafora. In the process, they worked out a mode of collaboration: Koster composed from Sánchez's Spanish drafts. Also published in *Harper's,* the second article helped fuel the disgust which the American people came to feel for Noriega and his regime. It forms the first half of chapter 1 of this book. The two were at work on the book; Sánchez in Miami and Koster in Panama, by the time the second article was published. Here their motives were historical not political, that Panama's story be fully told.

Meanwhile, the story continued. During the fall of 1987 and into 1988, the two governments of the United States struggled for control of its policy toward Panama. The visible government wanted Noriega ousted. It no longer cared to be seen with him in public, and had, besides, serious qualms as to his trustworthiness. Thirty years of policy, from building the Guardia into an army to supporting its rule to enacting the Canal treaties, had one underlying purpose: keeping the Isthmus of Panama in friendly hands. Did Noriega's regime fit that description? The visible government didn't think so. Its invisible counterpart may well have agreed, but its members had made Noriega their accomplice, had trusted him too deeply to risk making him angry.

It was inevitable that the visible government would win in the end, that a "nation conceived in liberty" would cease to ally itself with a criminal despot. Freedom of speech and the separation of powers ensured it. Apparently, however, the great aim was to keep Noriega happy until after the 1988 presidential election in the United States. This was achieved. Even thereafter the struggle was lengthy, and Noriega's friends apparently well positioned. Meanwhile, conflicting signals went out from Washington. No policy worth the name could be fashioned. Dealings with Panama were thoroughly botched.

Noriega, for his part, was maneuvering also. His problems hadn't ceased with silencing Roberto Díaz and the free media. The former accepted exile in Venezuela. The latter, though, were allowed to re-open as a concession to opinion in the United States, and even in the interim while they remained closed the National Civilian Crusade came back to life and resumed demonstrations. Street battles occurred almost daily all fall and winter. Paramilitaries made depredations. A marcher was murdered by them on September 1. Others were killed later. The dobermans sprayed violence almost at random, reaching a high point of sorts when they fired tear-gas grenades into medical wards at Santo Tomás Hospital. Panama's economy, meantime, was failing, and in Florida grand juries were hearing evidence as to Noriega's involvement in the drug trade. So either because he was weary of clinging to power or simply as a way to buy some time, he summoned José Blandón from New York and asked him, "Find me a way out with the gringos."

The plan Blandón drafted included elections in 1989 as already scheduled, reopening the media (which Noriega did in January 1988), a general amnesty, and restoration of civil rights. It also called for Noriega to step down as commandant no later than April 1988. Blandón sold the plan to leaders in Latin America, as well as to representatives of the Panamanian opposition, and cleared it with members of the (visible) U.S. government, including William Walker, deputy assistant secretary of state for inter-American affairs. Then the invisible government ambushed and smashed it. In December 1987, Admiral (retired) Daniel Murphy, former chief of staff to Vice-President Bush and commander of Bush's project, the South Florida Drug Task Force, flew to Panama and, Blandón says, advised Noriega he could stay on until after Panama's elections in 1989. Noriega, of course, might not have gone anyway, but now he ruled Blandón's plan no longer acceptable. With that Blandón defected from Noriega's service and went to talk to Congress and the grand juries.

Blandón's testimony made the indictments a certainty. Before Blandón, all the witnesses had been convicted drug dealers and, as such, not very credible. With Blandón, U.S. Attorney Leon Kellner had all he needed. The effect, though, took both U.S. governments by surprise. Until the indictments were handed down late in January (they were actually unsealed on February 5, 1988), senior representatives of the intelligence services, of the National Security Council, and of the Departments of State and Defense, had been assured (by John Lawn, among others) that there was no case against Noriega. Now any move toward quashing the indictments would put Kellner on everybody's TV screen with word that men at the top were protecting Noriega. With much wheedling, the State Department got him to hold off indicting the Defense Forces en masse as "a criminal enterprise." For the rest, a political virtue was made of necessity. U.S. officials convinced themselves that the indictments would brand Noriega an outlaw and flush him from Panama.

Their actual effect was exactly the opposite. They strengthened Noriega's resolve, gave him more reason than ever to hang on to power, as having otherwise to fear extradition. More important, they freed his hand. Fear of them may have restrained him before they were issued. Surely he did many things and held back from others in hope of regaining Washington's good grace, or to avoid falling from it entirely, but once the indictments were actually issued and the United States came out and called him a criminal, he could do as his instincts and pathologies urged him. Acting through his minister of justice, Rodolfo Chiari, he closed down every independent news organ and banned foreign papers and TV newscasts also, as likely to carry unflattering views of him. Then, having removed its rallying point, he beat the opposition to its knees.

On March 16, a putsch was bungled, bungled or betrayed. Colonel Leonidas Macías, commander of the Panama City police, attempted to overthrow Noriega. Not to restore democracy; to rehabilitate the PDF in the eyes of Washington so that it might continue in power. Noriega squelched the attempt with little effort, but it kept police from the streets for a few hours. This gave rise to rumors that Noriega had fallen, which in turn brought acts of premature jubilation, such as bonfires and impromptu celebrations. Here's what happened to one young man whom authorities alleged to have taken part, Nelson B., a twenty-eight-year-old mulatto-mestizo street vendor, married and the father of two children.

Early on the seventeenth, as he was taking a shower, men burst into Nelson's one-room home in San Miguelito, a working-class suburb of Panama City, and without presenting a warrant or explaining the cause, dragged him out with nothing on but a towel, though after some pleas they let him go back inside and put some clothes on. He was taken before the *corregidor* of the district and without any process at all, no reading of charges, much less a chance to refute them, though with considerable ill treatment—the *corregidor* personally hit him in the face—he was sentenced to a year in prison.

The next day, Nelson's sentence, and many others similarly imposed, were declared commutable on payment of a fine of $1 per day, but Nelson could not raise $365. He was remanded to Coiba Island. His mother contacted a private human rights organization, and it intervened, had the fine lowered, then paid it. On April 13, an order was issued for Nelson's release. The *corregidor,* though, took an interest in Nelson's case and used his influence to delay proceedings. Nelson was not released until May 27.

What impressed Nelson most about Coiba were the poor diet given the prisoners and their harsh treatment. There was plenty of food. The Defense Forces ran a large farm worked by the prisoners. These, however, were on starvation rations, and for stealing so much as a lemon or piece of yucca, prisoners were suspended in handcuffs from basketball rims and left hanging there for up to a week, during which time they received only water. Nelson saw one man who had been hanging for five days. His hands were monstrously swollen. His wrists were torn through to the bone and clustered with flies. There was also a punishment cell, very small and without ventilation, where offenders were sometimes suspended in shackles, or simply left to bake in their own excrement. During his first days on Coiba, Nelson felt great anxiety at the moans of men who were hanging or in the cell. He asked a fellow prisoner how he could bear it, and the man replied that one got used to it in time. And so it was with Nelson, he got used to the groaning.

Prisoners did forced labor. Guards carried bamboo scourges with the tips split into thin strips. They whipped malingerers and those who fell. Nelson's work was mainly carrying logs or gravel. A quota was levied: so many logs or cans of gravel per hour. Prisoners who failed their quota were taken to the guardroom and beaten with clubs. Often a log would fall or Nelson would drop it, but weeping and fearful he would lift it again. During his whole time on Coiba, Nelson was in continual despair.

Prisoners sometimes managed to get away into the bush, to rest for a while and perhaps find something to eat. Losing oneself that way was called *vida,* "life," but was dangerous because of poisonous snakes. Nelson heard many stories of needless death, such as supposedly occurred to a pair of prisoners who were made to carry loads across a river and were drowned. Nelson's health was poor for six months after his confinement. Treatment such as he received, and the fear of it, broke the back of resistance to Noriega's tyranny.

Many resistance figures were gone already. Miguel Bernal went into exile in late 1987 after paramilitaries ran him over with a jeep and broke his leg. Aurelio Barría was deported. So was Alberto Conte, though he spent time on Coiba first, and Roberto Brenes, and other crusade leaders. Before the crusade was a year old, its leadership was in exile and its membership cowed. So long as the PDF obeyed Noriega, the people of Panama were no more able to liberate their country from within than the people of occupied Europe had been forty-five years earlier.

The indictments were followed by two other blunders. Puppet President Delvalle was persuaded to fire Noriega. Noriega fired him instead. Then the United States imposed economic sanctions. This was especially stupid, the diplomatic equivalent of bombing the Ho Chi Minh Trail. That is, it was easy to do, made Washington feel it was dealing with the problem, and served to vent U.S. official frustrations, but merely caused destruction without bringing benefit.

The sanctions were urged by Juan Sosa, Delvalle's ambassador to Washington, who defected when Delvalle was fired, and by Gabriel Lewis Galindo. They included retention of payments to Panama from Canal revenue, and some $10 million of these funds were expended, without any leave of the people of Panama, on maintaining Sosa and others in the United States. That may have had something to do with Washington's withholding the funds, a full accounting of which has not yet been rendered. The sanctions damaged the people of Panama horribly but did not harm Noriega or his regime. If anything, they helped the dictatorship by giving it a sense of moral purpose. The thieves could now pretend to be patriots withstanding U.S. economic aggression.

It was a very sad time for American pride. The colossus was being shown up as laughably impotent by a thug who ran a country a hundred times smaller. Every week, it seemed, brought a promise from Elliott Abrams, assistant secretary of state for inter-American affairs, that Noriega would be gone in days or hours, yet each new week found him even more firmly in power. High officials made repeated pilgrimages in fruitless negotiations for Noriega's departure, till one doubted he thought them negotiations at all but merely occasions on which to humiliate gringos.

Saddest of all was Washington's blindness. Noriega was really quite easy to understand if one had the mental toughness to accept what one saw in him. He had spent all his life getting power, had sold his soul for it, and would not give it up just because somebody asked him. What his rule in Panama meant for the United States was not beyond grasping. Yet his friends or pawns hoped the United States could live with him, while the rest were reluctant to face what expelling him required.

"How are we going to get Noriega out of Panama?" Senator Kennedy's aide Gregory Craig asked R. M. Koster in January 1988.

"The same way we got Hitler out of Europe."

Six weeks later, Koster was in the Old Executive Office Building in Washington, saying much the same to staffers of the National Security Council. The indictments made the breach between Noriega and the United States irreparable, no matter what his remaining Washington friends might wish. The United States could not leave Panama for twelve years, until the appointed time for handing over the

Canal to the Panamanians. Noriega would not leave unless he was forced to. The people of Panama couldn't, so the business would end in U.S. military action. The sooner this happened, the fewer people would die.

Koster wasn't advocating a course of action. He was predicting an event, one in which he might lose his life, and suggesting, since it couldn't be avoided, that it be done quickly. The men he spoke to didn't laugh at him, but they didn't really believe him either. Everything he said was perfectly logical, and before the month was out, friction between the United States and Manuel Noriega had begun to express itself in violence.

As early as the summer of 1987, Noriega turned for support to Cuba and Nicaragua, and starting early in 1988, Cuban and perhaps Nicaraguan effectives were present in Panama, supplementing the Defense Forces' counterintelligence and combat capabilities. In late March of that year, units composed of or stiffened with Cuban soldiers began probing U.S. defenses near the aviation fuel tank farm at the western perimeter of Howard Air Force Base, near the town of Veracruz. Firefights occurred almost nightly for some weeks. The United States suffered at least one man killed in these actions, though Southern Command, playing the incidents down to the point of refusing to confirm their existence, described his death as accidental. Noriega took advantage of the situation to needle Southern Command, saying that its troops were shooting at shadows, but there were persistent rumors of Panamanian ambulance's being allowed to take casualties from the area, and according to the *Washington Post,* which cited intelligence sources, U.S. fire killed one Cuban and wounded three others during an action in April 1988.

Neither side would say what was going on, but from March 1988, Panamanian and U.S. forces were engaged in low-intensity warfare. The United States encouraged defection from the Defense Forces and, in effect, stripped their combat air capability when defectors flew Panama's few airworthy helicopters to U.S. bases. The PDF, for their part, intimidated and injured U.S. personnel. On June 16, a soldier was beaten and then locked in the trunk of his car while his wife was beaten and raped. On August 1, a sergeant was detained for "suspicious activity" and questioned at gunpoint and robbed of $300. On November 13, a Navy petty officer was struck in the face, pulled through his car window by the neck, struck again, forced to his knees with a pistol at his temple, and (after having a round fired past his face) made to beg for his life.

Dozens of similar incidents occurred, well over a hundred if one counts petty harassment, and two which though nonviolent were truly unnerving. A colonel assigned to liaison with the PDF had his sons arrested. The boys, aged fourteen and seventeen, were detained just outside the perimeter fence of Fort Clayton one day after school, were handcuffed and put in a patrol truck and taken to La Comandancia, in Panama City, where they were charged with interfering with the Panama Railroad, whose tracks they had been near when they were picked up. They were released later, unharmed but badly frightened, and not before U.S. Southern Command had to petition officially as to their whereabouts. And one morning in March 1989, transit police impounded nine buses full of U.S. military dependent schoolchildren, supposedly because the bus company hadn't paid taxes, and had the buses, with the children aboard, driven into the transit compound, and held them there for about half an hour, until a U.S. Army major arrived to obtain their release. Meanwhile, Southern Command scrambled two Cobra attack helicopters and put them over transit headquarters, action that might seem overreaction only until one learns who was in command there: Colonel Luis Córdoba, Spadafora's chief torturer.

U.S. policy was to pretend nothing was happening, to give the incidents no publicity, and to play them down if news of them came out. A pro-Noriega lobby still existed in Washington, people who thought the answer was patching things up. An interventionist lobby also existed but included mainly State Department officials. The Defense Department didn't want to fight and put forth the argument that if U.S. bases in Panama were used to overthrow Noriega's regime, other countries might evict the United States from other bases—thereby confirming what many had long supposed anyway, that at least a portion of America's military viewed the country's bases as toys for them to play with, not as assets with which to defend the country's interests. After May 1988, when the United States gave up trying to talk Noriega out of power, the United States had no policy toward Panama, unless to duck under the covers and hope it was all a bad dream can be called a policy.

But how does one get on with duty when one's children may be kidnapped, or one's wife raped, or oneself robbed and beaten? Someone ought, of course, to have considered this back when the United States was building an army for Panama. Or if that took too much foresight, someone might have considered it in 1969—or in 1978 or 1987—before that army got nasty with Americans. Then as later, it was a criminal enterprise commanded by sociopaths and degenerates, but the United States gave the latter medals and praised the former's "professionalism." Now the United States was in a predicament, obliged by national interest and treaty commitment to keep forces and personnel on the Isthmus of Panama but unable to guarantee their safety. It had taken decades, but now the monster was bothering its creator.

Meanwhile, Panama was suffering terribly. By June 1988, economic activity was at 55 percent of normal and falling, unemployment above 20 percent and rising, retail sales off 70 percent, construction off 95 percent, industrial production off 60 percent, agricultural output off 30 percent, and planting for the next season almost at zero because of lack of credit for buying seed and fertilizer. Nearly $7 billion had left Panama's banks, and many citizens were leaving also. Panamanians slept in the street outside the U.S. consulate so as not to lose their places in line for visas. Panamanians were streaming out of their country, those fleeing political persecution now joined by those fleeing economic ruin. Every Panamanian's dream was over. Whatever one had hoped for—a new dress or new car, or a college education, or a slab of cement to cover the dirt floor of a shanty—it was not going to happen.

Except for Manuel Noriega and his favorites. Smuggling from the Colón Free Zone was firm. Cocaine reexports were up, so was money laundering. Noriega and his favorites were thriving.

In spirit, Noriega was both buoyant and downcast. The attempt against him in March left him exhilarated. Minutes later, he came out on the steps of La Comandancia, grinning demonically, and called the firing heard before *besitos,* "little kisses." Then he made his enemies pay. Macías was held for a year incommunicado and tearfully begged his first visitor, "Ask General Noriega to forgive me!" More exhilarating still, he was defying El Coloso Yanqui and getting away with it. He seems even to have been successful in imagining that he had support in the country, that people believed (as he himself probably managed to) the United States was to blame for Panama's troubles, and that he, Manuel Noriega, was Panama's champion.

Now and then, however, truth seemed to seep into his mind. In August 1988, Arnulfo Arias died, and hundreds of thousands turned out to pay him tribute—so filled the streets that it took his cortege five hours to go the five miles from the cathedral to the cemetery. A few days later, on the fifth anniversary of his becoming *comandante en jefe,* a lowering Noriega warned his countrymen not to be hasty in wanting him out, as those who would come after were worse than he was.

He drank heavily. Supposedly, he used cocaine as well. He took to changing his sleeping place abruptly, sometimes two or three times in the same night. He refused all food not prepared by Vicky Amado. His behavior, in short, was rationally paranoid. He could not feel safe without power, could not feel powerful without hurting people, and had dispensed so much pain of one sort or another that a great many people earnestly longed for his downfall. For him, paranoia was the sensible course.

As his rule became harsher, as hostility grew, he sought psychic refuge in victimhood. Despite his wealth and power, as if neither existed, or as if he had won them only so as to help others, he identified himself with the disadvantaged, *los de abajo,* saying his mission was to bring them dignity. Dignity, said Noriega, was what he wanted, what his stand against the United States was about. In truth, though, he did not look to the underclass but to the portion of it he had emerged from and had never in spirit left, the segment nothing useful can be done with, called *chusma* in Spanish, *canaille* in French, *Lumpen* in German, and in English riffraff or trash, whose vocation is resentment, violence, and crime. From these Noriega drew his sole firm support, and from them he recruited his shock troops, the armed rabble he called *batallones de la dignidad.*

These were not formations at all, if the word is to be construed with any rigor. They had female as well as male members (though the latter predominated), wore no uniforms (though lounging shorts in loud colors were much seen in their ranks), kept no more order than a tribe of monkeys, and did not (as a rule) carry firearms till near the end. They looked like barbarian nomads of some new dark age, but when it came to a fight, they fought better than the regular PDF units. There were Cubans and Sandinistas attached to them, some Chileans and even Libyans, so rumor has it, but these can't account fully for the battalioneers' willingness, however brief, to risk their lives for the chance to kill a few gringos. They deserved a better leader than Noriega, and he could have done with some of their hardihood.

Their ugliness was on prominent display months before the American invasion. On May 10, 1989, battalioneers assaulted the opposition presidential ticket that had triumphed resoundingly three days before. President-elect Guillermo Endara and Second Vice-President-elect Guillermo Ford were beaten with tire irons. Members of their escort were shot and murdered—all in front of TV crews and reporters so that no one on earth could pretend any longer about the character of Panama's tyranny. There was Señor Ford, splattered with blood from his scalp wounds, trying to fend off a goon's next blow while a *guardia* stood by watching the action. There was Señor Endara, lying in a hospital bed, his head swathed in bandages. What the pictures communicated with great power and economy, to every decent person who saw them, was that the dictatorship had no right to another minute in power. The attack, which must have been sanctioned by Noriega, was one of his most self-destructive acts.

As was having the election to begin with. It had, of course, been scheduled years before, as part of a supposed, regular process. Canceling it would have cost the regime politically. Meanwhile, Noriega claimed Panama was democratic. A fact or two in support would have been useful. Some constitutionality would have been welcome too. When he'd dumped Delvalle he'd had to go outside the supposed succession. His next puppet, Manuel Solís Palma, hadn't even the title "president of the republic," but only that of "minister in charge." But election benefits come only on winning. Neither that nor its illusion could be contrived, and no damage occasioned by canceling the election could have approached that done by what in fact happened.

By May 1989, Panama was in the last stages of economic and social collapse. No one but the rabble of the dignity battalions stood to gain by the dictatorship's continuing. Besides them, the only ones who sincerely supported it were those who might go to prison if it fell. The regime had but a fraction of the country. Still, Noriega and company thought they could win an election, or at least come within stealing range, thereby adding one more, superfluous proof that the main victims of propaganda are its propagators.

Counting duplicate registrations, dead people, and illegal immigrants from China, over one hundred thousand fake voters were stuck onto the rolls. As in 1984, election law allowed PDF personnel to vote at any table they cared to, whether or not their names appeared on the register, and all day long on election day *guardias* were trucked from table to table, so they might vote as often as they pleased. No independent media existed. Opposition offices were bombed and machine-gunned. Opposition candidates were threatened. Opposition supporters were systematically intimidated. Nothing availed. Not even the PDF backed Noriega's candidate, Carlos Duque. The opposition won even at tables where more *guardias* than civilians voted. Conditions in Panama had simply reached the point where *guardias* were less afraid of Manuel Noriega than of their mothers, sisters, wives, and girlfriends.

On the opposition's side, however, there was the temptation not to take part in an election everyone knew would be crooked and dangerous. Happily, courage was found to withstand this temptation. Then there was the problem of unifying the various parties. Here the Christian Democrats and their leader, Ricardo Arias Calderón, did Panama a great service by not holding out for the top spot. They had the best organization and what seemed to many the best candidate, and they could have held that the Panameñistas' larger number of registered voters had ceased to reflect political reality the day Arnulfo Arias died. Instead, like good Christians but all too few democrats, they found the grace to yield. This not only avoided splitting the opposition but also produced a better ticket. Guillermo Endara was not Arias Calderón's intellectual equal—few people were—but he was a man Panamanians could identify with, thus one they felt would represent their interests.

The opposition's main problem, however, was getting the election results reported. No matter how few votes Duque received, Noriega and company would declare him the winner, and would likely get away with it unless the opposition had evidence of its triumph. The solution worked out by John Rendon, an American political consultant hired by the opposition alliance, attacked the weak point (from an election rigger's viewpoint) in Panama's election law. Ballots were counted in public at each voting table before they and the tally sheets were sent to district centers. Fraud might occur at the district or national level. The table count, however, would be straight. Rendon set up a system whereby two counts would be run simultaneously. One, done by the alliance itself, would send the result at each table to a center in the capital, and to backup centers in case the main one should be raided. Meanwhile, the Catholic church would do a "quick count" based on a small number of representative tables. The church's results would be out an hour or so after the polls closed. The alliance count would come some hours later. So, to provide momentum, an exit-poll count would be done as well, whose indications would be available during the voting for Rendon to be released from a press center he set up in Costa Rica. As it turned out, the dictatorship had a set of fake tally sheets, one for each of the country's four thousand voting tables, ready to substitute for the real ones, but the opposition and the church were able to report results before the government. These were strongly persuasive, for the church's count had the opposition winning by a greater margin than that reflected in the opposition's own count.

Another important factor was the presence of prestigious foreign observers. A month before the election, the dictatorship stopped issuing tourist cards and demanded that all entering foreigners have visas. The point was to keep the number of journalists down. Heavyweight observers were even less welcome. But Noriega had been insisting that the U.S. government's antipathy to him had nothing to do with drugs but was, rather, political. He, Noriega, was a nationalist and a patriot. It, the U.S. government, wished to abrogate the Torrijos-Carter treaties and hold on to the Panama Canal. This was about all he could say, and besides it had a certain plausibility, for while the Canal was no longer truly important, the isthmus and who controlled it were. Politics *was* at the heart of the conflict, and Noriega's drug dealings mattered much less in themselves than as an indication of his regard for U.S. interests. But having couched his side of the story in treaty terms, he could hardly object to the presence in Panama as an election observer of their greatest champion, a former president of the United States, Jimmy Carter. Nor could he say no to Gerald Ford, Carter's Republican counterpart and the chief treaty supporter in his party. And there was George Price, former prime minister of Belize. He wanted to come too. And John Spender, the foreign secretary in Australia's shadow cabinet, and Australia had signed the Neutrality Treaty. With these gentlemen welcome, the foreign press could not be excluded. In this way, against all inclination, Noriega and company ended up holding the election in a goldfish bowl, and that made stealing it very difficult.

There were typical abuses before, during, and after the voting. Rigoberto Paredes terrorized the Arrijan district, where he was running for deputy, cruised the Inter-American Highway with an escort of hoodlums who blazed away with machine guns from car windows to intimidate voters. Many citizens were wounded, and when some took refuge in the home of Napoleón Franco, a wealthy and distinguished former diplomat who took no part in politics and lived on a ranch outside the town of La Chorrera, Paredes had Franco put in La Modelo along with his whole family, his wife and children and children's spouses and small grandchildren—a thing without precedent in Panama's history. In Chiriquí, a PDF member named Olmedo Espinosa got annoyed at Padre Nicolas Van Cleef for suggesting that Endara would win the election and shot the priest dead. In the capital, near the Republic of Venezuela School (which was a polling place) a man named Agusto Cajar was murdered by paramilitaries as part of the latters' attempt to disturb the count. Meanwhile, Panamanians came out to vote in record numbers and voted three to one for Endara's ticket. Rich and poor, city and country, black, white, and brown. The margin cut across all the country's divisions.

That night, troops confiscated ballots and tally sheets at gunpoint. Fake tally sheets were substituted for the real ones and delivered to the electoral tribunal in Panama City. On Monday afternoon, the tribunal reported that Duque was running some 60 percent ahead, but by then the opposition's and the church's figures were out, both giving Duque about half that, and Jimmy Carter had been refused entry at the tribunal.

"Fraud!" said Carter and the other observers. "Fraud!" echoed George Bush. Noriega said nothing. He wanted to brazen things out and declare Duque victor, but Duque knew he'd lost badly and wasn't willing. On Wednesday, May 10, unable to win Duque over, Noriega took refuge in violence. As the winning ticket's motorcade wound through the old part of Panama City, drawing crowds behind it chanting, "¡Justicia!" troops broke the procession up with tear gas, others with riot shields blocked the way ahead, and battalioneers surged in from side streets. The president- and vice-presidents-elect were pulled roughly down from their truck. Arias Calderón was saved by a pair of *guardias* who pretended to knock him down, then put their shields over him. Endara had his head laid open but was allowed to go to a hospital for treatment. Ford, though, was not only beaten but arrested, put into a patrol truck with his scalp still bleeding, and taken straight to La Modelo. That night he was brought before a judge, who sentenced him to a year in prison for disorderly conduct. A bit before sunup, he was released on bail, still without having had medical attention.

Ford was luckier, however, than another opposition figure, Olimpo Sáenz, a successful candidate for deputy from a working-class district. Sáenz was arrested that same afternoon and put in a cell with Ford for a few hours. At six, he was taken to the exercise area and hung up in handcuffs from a basketball rim. Coiba Island had come to Panama City! Sáenz was hosed mercilessly by three *guardias,* then left to hang draped in an American flag. He was taken to night court with Ford and assigned the same sentence, then hung up by the wrists again. At midnight or thereabouts, three other *guardias* came to beat him again. While they did so, some gallery prisoners began to sing hymns and others shouted protests of Sáenz's treatment. Sáenz was put back in the cell at four in the morning and kept there until five the next afternoon. Then he was taken back to the basketball court. This time a sign was hung on his back, "Por Diez Millones Vendiste La Patria" ("For Ten Million You Sold Your Country"), and his hands were cuffed with his arms around the backboard post, and he was beaten. At ten that night he was beaten again. Sáenz spent that night cuffed to the post. Friday he was put in a cell.

On Saturday night, May 13, Olimpo Sáenz was released on bail from La Modelo Prison. He could not walk unaided. He was admitted to the Social Security Hospital bleeding internally with a hemoglobin reading of nine grams.

Meanwhile, the electoral tribunal had annulled the election. The vote, it said, was obstructed by foreigners, to the point where many tally sheets were missing and a true count impossible. George Bush ordered more troops to the isthmus. The Organization of American States passed a resolution (by a vote of 20 to 2, with seven abstaining) specifically naming Noriega as the party responsible for election abuses and appointing a commission to "promote measures for reaching a national agreement that will assure, by democratic means and in the shortest possible time, the transference of power, with complete respect for the sovereign will of the Panamanian people." The Panama crisis entered its final stage.

The OAS commission betrayed its charge. That outcome might have been predicted the moment the Ecuadoran foreign minister, Diego Cordovez, was named to head it. His government was in debt to Manuel Noriega in two unsavory particulars: the delivery to Ecuador of the leader of the Alfaro Vive movement so that he might be murdered and the framing of the opposition figure Abdul Buccaram. Cordovez himself was closely related to a business associate of Noriega's and business partner of Noriega's mistress, Vicky Amado, a man in whose home he stayed on his visits to Panama. And Cordovez had the Noriegan cynicism to reveal his bias to Vice-President-elect Guillermo Ford, along with the slavishness to repeat Noriega's lies and relay Noriega's threats:

"I have a message for you from General Noriega. He says, 'The blood you showed off on your shirt was somebody else's. Next time there will be no mistake, it will be yours.' "

This is an aside to Ford before the first session of talks, by which time the commission's treachery was patent. Far from seeking a transfer of power, far from showing respect for the people's sovereign will, the commission had the election's winners sit down to bargain with the men they'd defeated, Carlos Duque, Ramón Sieiro (Noriega's wife's brother), and Aquilino Boyd. And to ensure a total lack of fairness yet another trinity was added, one from the Defense Forces headed by the inimitable Colonel Luis Córdoba.

Thus coddled, the dictatorship made no concessions. Its best offer was to let the people's elected representatives have one spot on a three-man junta which would set a date for new elections. No departure of General Noriega, no withdrawal of the PDF from control of the country, no release of political prisoners, no return of political deportees, no reopening of the independent media. The people's elected representatives had no choice but to decline. Cordovez and company left Panama with the people in worse shape than on their arrival. Then, at least, the people had had the elation of victory, and the hope, however false, that their neighbors might help them make the victory stick. Now the OAS passed a new resolution calling emptily for an interim government and new elections. Noriega, giving it and its authors their full value, paid no attention whatsoever to either.

It was a sad thing for the cause of democracy in the Americas and a very sad showing for El Coloso del Norte. The United States (whose government evidently supposed the battle won when the OAS voted, and lazily failed to follow things up thereafter) found itself again outfoxed by Noriega, this time having might and right on its side. Noriega, for his part, convened a group of timeservers and had them select what proved to be his final puppet president, a man named Francisco Rodríguez, who had proved his loyalty in the post of comptroller. Then he proclaimed something called La Nueva República (The New Republic), though if there was anything new to it besides Rodríguez, neither we nor anyone we know could see it. Perhaps businesses began failing in greater numbers, or Panamanians fled their country at a sharper rate. Maybe the basketball rims of the New Republic were used even less for basketball and more for hanging poor devils up in handcuffs.

This was a low ebb for Sánchez and Koster. When they'd begun work on this book, their worry was getting it finished before the dictatorship fell and the public lost interest in Panama's story. Now, in September 1989, they were done, yet the time of the tyrants continued. Their manuscript needed revision and polishing, but the sort of book that seemed possible was finished, one that began with Hugo

Spadafora's murder—the crucial event of military rule in Panama, the event that at once characterized and unmasked it—and ended with the tyrant at bay but still in power. That had been the situation in August 1987, and that was the situation two years later, and when it might change no one knew.

Koster began making plans to leave Panama. He'd been lucky so far, but not to leave before the book was in press would be foolhardy. He was going to be the first writer to seek political asylum in his own country. The humor of that was small consolation, however, and then, in October, the truly low ebb was reached. A group of PDF officers mounted a putsch, took Noriega prisoner, then bumbled away their chance and their lives with it—and the United States bumbled right along with them!

The attempt, which took place on October 3, was led by a PDF major named Moisés Giroldi. What impresses one most about him and the junior officers who were in the thing with him is their pitiful disconnection from reality. They surprised Noriega on his arrival at La Comandancia early that morning, but did him no harm and allowed him to telephone Vicky Amado. Evidently, the two had a code for such an occasion, for she alerted forces loyal to him. The arrival of these on the scene proved decisive. Meanwhile, the putsch makers issued a proclamation designed, so it seemed, to forswear public support. They described their effort as free of civilian influence, pledged themselves loyal to Torrijos's "revolution," repudiated the failed putsch of nineteen months earlier as having been done by pro–U.S. officers, and justified dumping Noriega, Justine, and others on the ground that these had infringed PDF regulations by not retiring after twenty-five years' service—the equivalent of citing Capone for double-parking, or Hitler for not curbing his dog. Then, having done what they could to ensure failure, they left what hope remained to be smashed by the United States of America.

Despite his proclamation's anti–U.S. tone, Giroldi had revealed his intentions to U.S. Southern Command and had received a promise of support. Once he was in control at La Comandancia, U.S. units closed the Bridge of the Americas over the Canal and the transisthmian highway. This seemed enough to isolate Noriega from relief. The main threat here was the "Machos del Monte" infantry company at Río Hato, eighty miles west of the capital, the PDF's best unit, whose name referred (with virile overtones) to a large, ill-tempered jungle beast, and whose panache included beards and black T-shirts. Closing the bridge seemed to remove them as a factor, but the Machos piled aboard a civilian 727, flew to the capital, and, not knowing who held the airport, landed on the highway near it. There they commandeered private cars and headed for town.

Southern Command did nothing to stop them. All sorts of excuses were produced later: that the government was wary of being set up by Noriega; that the secretary of defense was showing his Soviet counterpart the battlefield at Gettysburg, Pennsylvania, and couldn't be reached to authorize further action; that the Pentagon had no contingency plans for the situation; that the commander in Panama, General Max Thurman, was new on the job and had no advisers familiar with the terrain. Excuses abounded. But to block two access routes and leave a third open spelled bumble, and people died as a direct result—quite a few people indeed, counting those killed in December's invasion.

Giroldi, meanwhile, had vetoed turning Noriega over to U.S. authorities at Fort Clayton. Evidently, his military honor wouldn't allow it. We hope it consoled him that afternoon. Noriega, who had begged not to be handed over, now turned tough and persuasive. Like many who manage to ignore their own guilt feelings, he evidently was adept at playing on those of others. Did Giroldi want Panama to give in to the gringos? Did he want Arias Calderón and the National Civilian Crusade to replace the PDF in power? Is this what he wanted for his country and comrades? Is this how he meant to repay his commander? Well, if he had the balls, why didn't he shoot? Giroldi was already wavering when the Machos arrived. After a brief firefight he surrendered.

By dusk he was dead. Captain Heráclides Sucre dispatched him on Noriega's order. "Kill him," Noriega said. "I'm sick of his whimpering." Stories vary as to exactly how he was tortured. At least nine others were murdered that same day, seven officers and two sergeants. In the following weeks the PDF was purged. Colonels Julio Ow Young, Guillermo Wong, and Armando Palacios were jailed for passive participation, along with a number of majors, but Noriega's fury fell mainly on junior officers. The counterintelligene chief, Captain Nicasio Lorenzo, was strangled. Others died in as yet unknown ways but in such numbers that the capital's undertakers couldn't handle the business without attracting attention and the PDF stopped releasing bodies to the deceaseds' families. In Pacora, a town northeast of the capital, near Fuerte Cimarrón, where interrogations were conducted, there were dawn burials—garbage bags of chopped limbs and torsos. The remains of some sixty men were found in common graves there four months later. And a G-2 agent in the interior defected and took refuge on Fort Clayton after a consignment of eight bodies sent to him for disposal turned out to have no eyes, tongues, or private parts.

Far from showing elation, as he had on weathering the previous putsch, Noriega raged. He asked for and got so-called war laws, which gave the government special powers, though as a practical matter none was required. His and his ministers' power was absolute. Power and more power, though, was what he craved, and since no more was available in substance, he arrogated power's trappings.

He seemed beside himself with contempt and fury. That Southern Command had intruded while he was helpless, yet had been too timorous to do so effectively, probably convinced him once and for all that he need not worry further about the gringos. And, as always, he could not bear being betrayed. He had personally decorated Giroldi for his conduct during Macías's attempt. He and his wife had stood godparents at Giroldi's wedding. Now the refrain had been sung to him again: everything is falsehood, nothing is love. He felt betrayed by the whole PDF, and in fact his real base now was the *batallones.* They knew it, and so did everyone else in the country. More and more they swaggered. They and everyone else knew tomorrow was theirs.

And the rest of the country . . . The rest of the country was numb. What horror was next?

On Friday, December 15, 1989, Noriega had himself declared chief of government, though the title was as superfluous as the "war laws." And while accepting the title, he took refuge in victimhood. A state of war existed between the United States and Panama. So he said, confusing himself with his country, as tyrants are wont to. The words may or may not have led to what happened the next evening. They certainly came to haunt Noriega.

The next day was Loyalty Day, the twentieth anniversary of Omar Torrijos's return from Mexico and of Manuel Noriega's appearance on the Panama scene. By nightfall, the *batallones* were drunk and drunk on power and more or less loose in the capital and Colón. One band tried to loot a supermarket but was turned away by the place's armed watchmen. Another was reveling outside La Comandancia when a private car, whose plate number showed it to be owned by someone connected with U.S. forces, stopped at the checkpoint in front of the building. Four junior U.S. Marine Corps officers had been at dinner at a Panama City restaurant, had taken a wrong turn on their way back, and found themselves at the wrong place at the wrong time. The battalioneers began shouting and rocking the car, tried to pull the doors open and drag the occupants from it. At that, the driver pulled away from the checkpoint, and a *guardia* on duty there aimed and fired his automatic rifle. A number of bullets struck the car. One nicked the ear of the driver. Another entered the head of Lieutenant Robert Paz. He was dead on arrival at Gorgas Hospital.

Another car with similar plates was stopped later. In it were a U.S. Navy lieutenant and his wife. They were taken to the G-2 section and interrogated. Everyone on duty that night at La Comandancia seems to have been terrified by the shooting incident, as if knowing that it might bring fearful retribution. This fear was expressed as rage against the couple. All bullying is grounded in fear, and the thinking in the G-2 seems to have been that if the lieutenant could be made to confess a plot of some sort, an excuse for the shooting might be fabricated. Whatever the case, he was repeatedly kicked in the groin while being shouted at to reveal his unit, what it was doing, and so forth. As for his wife, those present could scarcely have considered themselves soldiers of the Panama Defense Forces and faithful subordinates of its commander had they not abused her also, and duly threatened her with rape. It was this last, more than the murder of Lieutenant Paz, that seems to have caused George Bush to order the invasion.

Time had to be bought, however. An invasion plan had been drawn some months before, but much of Sunday was spent deciding, and nearly two days were needed to get the show mounted. On Sunday, a State Department release characterized Paz's murder as an "isolated incident." No particular attention should be paid to it.

This treatment of the event no doubt fooled Noriega. The same sort of pap had been put out many times before with regard to events almost as serious. It certainly fooled R. M. Koster. He was in Miami to meet with Sánchez and their editor, Starling Lawrence, and spent much of the day calling members of Congress and railing at his government's cowardice. Unlike Noriega and Koster, Sánchez was not fooled. At dinner that night he said this: "What I can never forgive the Defense Forces for is causing an invasion of my country."

It came two nights later, a bit before one in the morning, December 20, 1989. R. M. Koster was at home in the Bella Vista section of Panama City, awake and at work on the manuscript of this book. There'd been word earlier that the Eighty-second Airborne Division had left Fort Bragg. On an exercise, supposedly, but no exercises are scheduled the week before Christmas. Then a journalist friend called Otilia Koster and said that planes were landing every few minutes at Howard Field, and that there was great movement on all U.S. bases. Koster kept working. For two years, he had been predicting U.S. military intervention as the certain denouement of the Panama crisis, yet now, when all signals announced that such was beginning, he found himself hard put to believe it real. Sudden, violent death (he was relearning), however firmly the intellect may grasp it, is hard to accept emotionally when it heads for one's home. The most he could manage was assume that if something was on, whatever it was would happen the next morning.

Noriega and company seem to have felt the same way. Bush had twice sent reinforcements to Panama without ordering them to do anything dramatic. Southern Command had looked wimpish in October. And the U.S. Army's capability for night operations was something no one in Panama expected. But mainly it was a matter of no one's believing war could come to Panama. In retrospect, however, one wonders why not. War was the only twentieth-century demon that military rule still had not conjured.

Anyway, a bit before one, Koster heard the crunch of high explosives off to the southwest. He went downstairs. His wife was on the phone with a friend of theirs. A huge shoot-out was raging, the friend said, in El Chorrillo, a warren of narrow streets and wooden tenements about a mile off. What, exactly, was happening was that Sheridan tanks parked on top of Ancon Hill—up where the Panamanian flag had been flying proudly since October 1, 1979, though the feature itself was still a gringo Gibraltar—were putting artillery fire into La Comandancia (those were the crunches heard in Bella Vista), and armored personnel carriers mounting machine guns were carrying infantry in to take the place.

There it was. U.S. military intervention. In overdue admission of policy failure, Americans were being committed in battle against a force America had invented. The surgeon would now remove a cancerous lung from a patient for whom he'd bought cigarettes during three decades.

Koster and his wife called their children in Boston. Then they called Sánchez in Miami. Then they sat and listened to the crunches, quite loud but clearly distant. Koster thought about how it might be under that bombardment and imagined the poor people of El Chorrillo huddled in dread in their tumbledown dwellings. Then he thought of the Guardia. (He had never accepted their new name.)

How wonderful that those bullies were getting pasted! Twenty-one years of fun, but now, at last, they were getting the bill! Then he thought about hostage taking. He supposed it might already be in progress and reviewed with his wife what they'd do if people came for him.

Taking hostages was Noriega's only hope of countering an American invasion. Had he had the mental courage to think about war, beyond merely talking about it and playing at it, the PDF would have been rounding up American citizens even as American troops moved to their start lines, or at latest when they began firing. To protect them from angry mobs of Panamanian patriots: that would have been Noriega's excuse. George Bush might have found out how it had felt to be Jimmy Carter.

As it happened, a hostage plan existed, though it wasn't well drawn. It was put into execution, though too late and too feebly to be decisive. Raymond Dragseth, a member of the faculty of Panama Canal College, was taken from his home on Punta Paitilla by members of the antiterrorist unit working from a list, and murdered sometime during the next two days. An English-speaking Panamanian suffered the same fate. That was all the play Noriega gave his best card. Other Americans were taken by the PDF and held briefly, but not as part of any plan. Noriega hadn't faced an obvious aspect of his reality, and was soon to prove much less brave than anyone suspected.

Koster had thought the hostage problem out well before the invasion, as part of a personal dilemma. That people might come for him had been on his mind since the publication of the first *Harper's* article, in December 1987. By the time he and Sánchez had done the second, the one about Hugo Spadafora, Koster had decided that if people came, he would not go with them. He had one or two things to do to prepare for that possibility, and when he'd done them, he and his wife settled down to wait through the uneasy night. All over Panama, others were doing likewise in accord with their own situation.

Meanwhile, a number of fights were in progress. The Eighty-second had made a night drop and was seizing Torrijos Airport. Navy SEALS were taking the airfield at Paitilla, where Noriega's personal jet was parked. Beyond Ancon Hill, in Balboa, a U.S. Air Force C-130 gunship was putting pinpoint howitzer fire on the police station, leaving it a smoking ruin without scraping the paint on buildings beside it. And Rangers were teaching the Machos del Monte a lesson, were dropping on them from low level as they were still shuddering from a pair of one-ton bombs and would kill a number before the rest quit. At both ends of the Canal and on the Pacific coast at Río Hato, Americans were showing courage and competence dismantling the army other Americans had showed folly in creating.

That army, for its part, was giving proof that bullying unarmed compatriots is not good preparation for warfare. Colón surrendered almost at once. Chiriquí surrendered without a shot's being fired, and its commander, the hitherto fearsome Luis del Cid, went meekly to stand trial in Miami on the same charge as Manuel Noriega. The main resistance came from the *batallones.* In San Miguelito, they held out for two days, and at Tinajita, which was mined with tunnels, they retreated and reinfiltrated so that the place had to be taken three times. The PDF, however, evaporated.

To the joy of the people, who welcomed the evaporators with a warmth not seen by American soldiers since World War II. Just after sunup, there was a brief fight at the cuartel in Panamá Viejo, where twenty-one years earlier Major Boris Martínez had decided to overthrow Arnulfo Arias. The tide was out, and an American helicopter landed on the mud flat and got stuck. Panamanians came out of their homes to help free it. All over Panama, for as long as the operation lasted, Panamanians welcomed its soldiers as liberators.

And that was how those soldiers felt and acted. What jaunty confidence they showed, patrolling in twos and threes through a foreign city! A dangerous city, too, for till week's end it was also patrolled by armed "dingbats"—the soldiers' slang for dignity battalioneers. How courteous and good-humored they were despite helmets and battle dress and body armor and weapons and boots and gear in Panama's heat! Clearly, they feared no evil. It was partly because they knew their business and could, if occasion warranted, be as evil as, or more than, anyone else in their region. A pair from the Seventh (Light) Infantry set up a fire point across from Koster's house on the evening of the twenty-first and were just about invisible in thirty seconds. It was mainly, however, that their cause was just. Just Cause was the name of the operation, and as far as the troops were concerned it was well named.

George Bush, of course, was different. At about seven-thirty on the morning of the twentieth, he went on television. In justifying Just Cause, he mentioned Manuel Noriega and democracy. He was against the first and for the second—George Bush of the Reagan-Bush administration that moved heaven and earth to help its protégé and accomplice Manuel Noriega steal the 1984 election. George Bush for democracy? Your aunt Eulalia! But when it came to the troops he committed to battle, they were in Panama for the same reasons their grandfathers had been in Europe forty-five years earlier, to put paid to a loathsome despot and bring freedom and democracy to neighbors.

At ten that morning, R. M. Koster went to a friend's penthouse and looked at the city. It was very calm. From off to the northwest came muffled crunches, all one could note of the fight at Tinajita. A helicopter buzzed busily across the bay at very low altitude, past the presidential palace and on to the southeast, over Fort Amador, toward Howard Air Base. Another did lazy wheels over Ancon Hill. That was it. There, to the east, was Punta Paitilla, its high-rise condos floating above the bay, and curving from it in a long crescent was palm-lined Avenida Balboa. But for its emptiness, the absolute absence of vehicles and joggers, it might have been an ordinary morning.

But for that and the smoke. A great pillar of smoke rose from El Chorrillo, from La Comandancia, of course, but also from a wide area behind it that battalioneers had torched the night before. Another column lifted beyond Ancon Hill from what had been Balboa Police Station. A third, of fresh smoke, came from Avenida Central near the Church of Don Bosco. Looters. Looters roamed Panama City all that day and the next, and stopped only when there was nothing left to loot, or where citizens stood guard.

Some of the looted were not much to be mourned for: foreign-born newly rich, the tyrants' chief backers. Some of the looters were simply poor folk doing their Christmas shopping without money. Many ordinary businesses were ruined, however, to the benefit of criminals and members of the *batallones,* yet we do not hold, as some businessmen do, that the U.S. Army ought to have curtailed looting. The army had military targets to deal with. More important, had American troops sought to protect property, they would have ended up shooting people, and Just Cause had already brought enough civilian casualties.

How many civilians were killed is still unclear at this writing. The Endara government, which was sworn in at about the time Just Cause began, accepts Southern Command's figure, 202. The church puts the death toll at about 500. An effort was made, however, and risks run, to keep civilian casualties as low as possible. Twenty minutes before the attack, U.S. personnel flew over El Chorrillo in a helicopter mounting loudspeakers and warned residents to evacuate. Many did and received food and shelter in the Canal area. Others tried and were prevented by battalioneers. And on the evening of the twentieth, R. M. Koster observed an extraordinary and particularly welcome effort to avoid civilian casualties in a neighborhood nearer to him than El Chorrillo.

Very soon after the invasion began, U.S. forces took the Noriega regime off television, but a radio network reaching throughout the country remained functioning all day on the twentieth, broadcasting "news" of phony American atrocities, messages of support from other countries, assurances that General Manuel Noriega was directing defense operations from a secret command post, and exhortations to continued resistance. The hookup, called Radio Nacional, was a most oppressive presence to all those who longed to celebrate tyranny's end. More important, it prolonged the fighting. Its main broadcasting point was in La Contraloría, a twenty-story building facing the bay on Avenida Balboa, the rear of which was across from the Kosters' home.

At 2:00 P.M. on the twentieth, a helicopter came by and made menacing swoops at the building. Those inside were warned to leave. Photographs may have been taken also. About thirty people left. None were in uniform, but most had weapons. Radio Nacional kept broadcasting, however, all afternoon and into the evening. Then, at just about 7:00 P.M., three helicopters showed up, making a terrible din and drawing Koster out to where he could see what they were up to—a gunship to provide cover and two other machines with commandos in them, Delta Force commandos, to be exact.

First one helicopter and then the other inched in to hover above the roof of the building. One by one, in quick succession, men jumped from them, silhouetted in their helmets and battle dress against a sky lit by stars and the glow of the city.

Koster sat down on the front steps of his brother-in-law's house with his brother-in-law, his eighty-six-year-old father-in-law, and two of his nephews. All were rapt by the spectacle. Across the street, others were watching from windows and balconies. Koster had the radio on, held against his ear. "El helicóptero del invasor está en al techo!" the announcer said frantically. "The invader's helicopter is on the roof!" Then the station began broadcasting music.

Between six and eight commandos dropped onto the building. Two did something at the base of the broadcasting tower—cut wires perhaps. Radio Nacional picked up an annoying buzz but was still in business. Meanwhile, other commandos had been going down into the building. They could be heard busting things and breaking glass, the glass, perhaps, of doors between offices. From time to time, flashlight glimmers were visible in windows at the rear of the building, each time on a lower floor. Then, from what seemed to be a floor midway down, there came a crump! then crump! crump!—concussion grenades. Then there were four four- or five-round bursts of gunfire. Then someone with his piece off automatic squeezed off six or eight single rounds. Then silence.

There was silence for what seemed a long time. Radio Nacional kept playing music. Then, from around in front of the building, a voice shouted in pure gringo, "It's me, I'm coming out!"

Silence from the building. Music from Radio Nacional. What was going on? Then a terrific blast sounded. Flames shot out of windows on the fifth or sixth floor. The building bulged visibly. Koster thought it was going to come down on him. Then another blast, much higher up, sent flames into the sky, followed by a sparking, electric sputter that fizzed anticlimactically. The blasts, the noise, the flames, the building's bulging, the sparks, the sputs, the fizz, then silence again—silence from the building and, at Koster's right ear, Radio Nacional was out of business.

In World War II, Patton would have lined his tanks up and blown down the building, killing everyone in the vicinity. In Vietnam, Westmoreland would have called in air to hit it with rockets, and everyone for miles around would have perished. Delta Force did it more cleanly. No one outside the building had a hair mussed. Everyone inside had had a chance to leave it. How much better it would have been for everybody had that courage and competence been present in Washington during the decades it took to botch Panama policy to the point where an invasion was needed!

But where was General Noriega during all this? Directing resistance from a secret command post? Hardly. General Noriega was hiding.

Noriega spent the afternoon of December 19 in Colón, drinking at the Defense Forces post at France Field with Monito Pérez and Tití Sosa. These might be described as professional cronies, though Sosa is a licensed physician. Connoisseurs of what's-in-a-name will enjoy it that their nicknames translate as "Monkey" and "Marmoset," while Noriega, of course, as a military officer, was a "gorilla," according to slang current throughout Latin America. An ape trio.

Toward eventide, Pérez asked Noriega if they could go to La Casa del Recuerdo (The House of Memories). That was how, since Torrijos's death, devotees of *El Proceso* referred to the house on Calle Cincuenta where, in better days, Torrijos hung out with Rory and Toro, where of an afternoon he might have a woman while Chuchú stood guard, where he sweated out the treaty ratification vote in the U.S. Senate, where he told Hamilton Jordan he would shelter the Shah. Pérez had never been inside that shrine of shrines. Noriega was agreeable, so they flew across the isthmus to Panama City.

Noriega was there, at Calle Cincuenta, when reports reached him of the transport planes landing at Howard Air Base and the activity on U.S. installations. He called a knowledgeable foreigner—Harari, perhaps—who said not to worry. The Americans were reinforcing their garrison but would not invade. We don't know whether or not this was said sincerely, but it reassured Noriega. He stayed at Calle Cincuenta with Tití and Monito.

When the invasion began, his first thought was flight. The nearby airfield at Paitilla, where his private jet had landed a few hours earlier, was under attack by Navy SEALS, so he and his pals and his escort headed for Torrijos Airport. The Eighty-second Airborne nearly landed on top of him. Back he sped to the city and went into hiding. There is nothing to show he considered other conduct.

During the five days that followed, Noriega made no attempt to contact his wife or his daughters or any of his girlfriends, not even Vicky Amado. We suppose he didn't want to be scolded or urged to fight. He stayed in the houses of friends—but not of close friends where he might be searched for.

Around noon on the twentieth, for example, he showed up at the home of Jorge Krupnick, with whom he had recently had business differences. His wife went to the door and found a pale, haggard Noriega. Krupnick took one look at him and went and locked himself in his bedroom. His wife, though, asked Noriega to come in. By this time he'd shed Tití and Monito. As the days passed, his bodyguards left him, one by one, but at Krupnick's there were still four or five with him. All came inside. Señora Krupnick offered them beer, but Noriega couldn't drink his; his hand shook too badly. He lay down on a bed in a spare room and went to sleep.

After a time, Ileana Krupnick realized that her home might become a battleground any moment. She prepared to take her children to a friend's home. One of Noriega's bodyguards stopped her. "No one leaves here alive!" the bodyguard told her. She woke

Noriega, and Noriega ordered the bodyguard to let her leave. Very soon he left also, perhaps fearing Ileana Krupnick might disclose his whereabouts.

Noriega moved from one person's home to another. When he tried to return to a place he had been before, he found the doors closed to him. By Sunday the twenty-fourth, Christmas Eve, he was down to one bodyguard, Eliécer Gaitán. Gaitán urged him to seek asylum. At length, Noriega told him to work out the details. That afternoon both took refuge at the *nunciatura.*

Noriega's cowardice was as much a surprise to us as to his admirers. However, not one of his beastlings shamed him by showing courage. Madriñán, who went to the *nunciatura* also, didn't wait for the gate to be opened but scrambled up it like a monkey and flung himself over. Others found temporary haven in this or that embassy or simply surrendered. Luis Córdoba hid out with a pair of prostitutes in their apartment and was one of the last to turn himself in. Southern Command held them for a while, then turned them over to the Endara government. La Modelo survived the assault on El Chorrillo. That's where they are now.

Rigoberto Paredes is there. Luis Córdoba chose exile. As of this writing, the Endara government is showing less energy, perhaps, than we would in their place to bring the tyrants' henchmen and quislings to justice, but some at least are in prison, and that's a comfort.

Mike Harari, Noriega's mentor, got away. He was captured by American forces and then let go. As a courtesy to Israel, or because he knew too much, or in return for something. The U.S. embassy official who announced his capture was made to recant, said it wasn't Harari at all but a man who looked like him. Once back in Israel, Harari said he was only a businessman with no special links to Noriega. He can't tell that to us. We have Noriega's phone logs for October–December 1987, and Harari called Noriega daily from a Panama Defense Forces number.

Noriega left the *nunciatura* on January 3 in the custody of U.S. forces. That same night, he was taken to Miami to stand trial. Calle Cincuenta was packed end to end, all six lanes, with jubilant Panamanians.

Guillermo Sánchez returned to Panama on January 5, 1990, after three years and eight months in exile. He noted the heavy damage done to the airport as a result of the Eighty-second's assault but still found the place improved since he'd last seen it. The huge letters

"GENERAL OMAR TORRIJOS HERRERA" were gone from the façade.

He felt very tired. He thought of spending his last years reading. A few breaths of air in a free Panama revived him. *La Prensa* resumed publication on January 8 with his column in its old place on the last page. By February, he was needling the government for its lack of energy in establishing justice.

One of the first people Sánchez saw was the papal nuncio, Monseñor Laboa. Naturally, they spoke about Noriega. Noriega was green with fear, Laboa said, when he arrived at the *nunciatura.* He had a machine gun, an Uzi perhaps. On no account would he let go of it. Oh, yes—and it was odd, because no one had planned it, during his stay at the *nunciatura,* Noriega had the same room and bed that Sánchez had had when taking refuge there four years before.

"¡No me diga!" Sánchez said. "Isn't that funny!"

"Yes. Oh, and this was odd too. Noriega took the machine gun to bed with him."

Sánchez smiled and shook his head. "It was his teddy bear."

Miami and Panama
September 1987–February 1990

APPENDIX A

THE HAY–BUNAU-VARILLA TREATY OF 1903 HOW IT CAME ABOUT

In December 1898, Rudyard Kipling published a poem in *McClure's Magazine* addressed to the United States of America. "Take up the White Man's burden . . ." is how it went. Uncle Sam, however, had started without him. In July, the United States had annexed Hawaii, and that same December, by virtue of a treaty ending its "splendid little war" with Spain, took title to a number of other islands, all of them suitably nonwhite in population, including the Philippines, Puerto Rico, and Guam. A few months would pass before U.S. troops began civilizing Filipinos with the Krag rifle. A few voices would mutter in dissent. But Kipling's urging to empire was superfluous. No force on earth at that time in its history could likely have restrained the American people from a course that was fashionable in Europe, comfortably (if falsely) altruistic, and compatible with chauvinism, racism, and greed.

The jewel in the crown was the Panama Canal. There American know-how united the oceans and curbed the fever viruses, an authentic American triumph, glorious and utilitarian too, the greatest thing done by the United States outside its borders. But as for getting the rights to build and run it, that was partly rape and partly seduction (though who was seducing whom was not always clear) and blatant enough in the way of extortion to remind careful observers that there was more than one meaning to Teddy Roosevelt's favorite expression, "Bully!" It put a kind of curse on the whole endeavor that haunts the Isthmus of Panama to this day.

The key player was Philippe Bunau-Varilla, one of the great hero-rogues of the imperialist era, the equal of the almost mythical Cecil Rhodes and Conrad's all-too-lifelike Mr. Kurtz. He was born in Paris in 1859, the year French naval units bombarded Saigon and started another chapter in U.S.

imperial history. His mother was a widow with some sort of small income. His father was . . . Nobody knows. His mother's husband died too long before Philippe's birth for the name Varilla to make it onto his birth record. He tacked it on with a hyphen when he was twenty. When he was ten, the inauguration of the Suez Canal made a great impression on him. From then on, he was dedicated to advancing science, world commerce, and French grandeur. So, anyway, he says in an autobiography, and so he may actually have believed, though what he excelled at was advancing himself—a roostery little fellow astrut with chest puffed, in build and bounce (as in bastardy) not unlike Manuel Noriega, and just as tough as Noriega, though nowhere near as mean. Not sinister, not sadistic, albeit Teddy Roosevelt said he had a duelist's eyes. No discernible pathologies, unless boundless faith in himself should be considered one. *His* mother, at least, never abandoned him, but he advanced himself, and he was tough.

He trained as an engineer at the Ecole Polytechnique. While there, he heard Count Ferdinand de Lesseps, conqueror of Suez, lecture on his new project, a canal across the Isthmus of Panama. From then on, the Panama Canal was Bunau-Varilla's personal quest. On completing graduate study, he joined the Corps des Ponts et Chaussées, a branch of the French civil service cognate to the U.S. Army Corps of Engineers, and after a year in North America got himself put on loan to the Compagnie Universelle du Canal Interocéanique. He arrived in Panama—then a province of the Republic of Colombia—in October 1884 and within a year was the company's general manager on the isthmus.

For a man fresh from school, his qualifications were excellent, but they had little to do with his speedy rise. Yellow and blackwater fevers were pandemic to the isthmus. The local population was somewhat immune. Europeans weren't. Thousands of the company's people perished. Whole families were wiped out, sometimes in a few days. A trip to the hospital for any reason was usually fatal, for the nurses knew no more about how fevers spread than anyone else on earth in the 1880s and kept their patients free of crawling insects by placing cups of water under the bed legs. Mosquitoes were bred right in the hospital and spread the diseases without having to leave it. At age twenty-six, by simple attrition, Bunau-Varilla was the senior French engineer in the country, and a year went by before a more experienced man was recruited. The wonder was the company could recruit at all.

According to Bunau-Varilla, something he calls "moral energy" heightened his resistance to fever. It's hard to rule the theory out. Even now, years after he put pen to paper, his utter faith in himself daunts the reader. Might it not have daunted mosquitoes and germs? After two years of exposure, he caught yellow fever, but that was after he'd been relieved of chief responsibility, when presumably his moral energy was less aroused, and he survived the disease, which was almost unique. His account of his experiences in Panama is full of tales of flood and snakes and scorpions, of uprisings survived and obstacles surmounted—full, that is to say, of his own vitality, and to him the canal was "a grand and noble conception which gave [him] many happy years of struggle and danger." He believed himself superior to any challenge. His survival supported the belief, and the belief promoted his survival. This outlook, moreover, remained when youth had left him. In 1916, at age fifty-seven, while on active First World War service as a lieutenant colonel, he was hit by bomb fragments and severely wounded. "Leg cut off above the knee," he wired his children. "Temperature 38 degrees centigrade, pulse 72. Sadness is futility." When he recovered, he had a peg leg fitted and walked a mile a day till he died at eighty.

In Paris on sick leave in 1886, he left the Compagnie Universelle and, with his brother Maurice, set up as a contractor to it. Against his inclination, he maintains; at the entreaty of Charles de Lesseps, the great man's son, since company regulations forbade the revolutionary excavating methods he, Bunau-Varilla, had devised. The contract he got was revolutionary also. Its terms were so generous that the Compagnie Universelle's general secretary resigned in protest when he heard them. In two years of activity, for slightly more than one-fifth of the work allotted it, Bunau-Varilla's firm collected more than 32.5 million francs and turned a profit of almost 11.5 million—6.6 and 2.3 million dollars, respectively, in days when francs were francs and dollars dollars.

Bunau-Varilla took no share of these profits, no salary from the firm either. *Pas un sous!* Members of the Corps des Ponts et Chaussées were required to serve for five years and forbidden to take pay or fees from private sources or to go into business for themselves. It was only by special permission that Bunau-Varilla could, for his government salary, direct the firm's excavations at Culebra. No bothersome rules restrained brother Maurice, though. Brother Maurice was a private citizen. No law of God or man forbade him from being a partner in an earth-moving firm—nay, from being its financial manager! Nor was he so mean and graceless as not to put by a franc here and there for Philippe while Philippe was out there daunting the germs and the insects, for when Philippe's days in the tropics were over, he lived as splendidly as Monte Cristo, and as free of visible means of support. So Philippe returned to Panama while Maurice stayed in Paris, one to send the mud flying, the other to rake the francs in, and which did more to advance science and so forth hardly matters now, after all these years. Both were committed to the Panama project.

So were the life savings of the French middle classes. De Lesseps was a promoter of genius. A man, a plan, a canal equaled profit and glory: that was his Suez venture's lesson. But now he outpromoted a plan that was harebrained, a canal at sea level just like the one at Suez, but this one had to go through jungled hills. And while he infected others with his overconfidence, his associates set standards of fraud and mismanagement not surpassed in connection with Panama until the advent of Omar Torrijos. As when contracts were let to insiders at too generous terms. As when, through bilk or blunder, the company bought several thousand snow shovels, though its many problems with Panama's terrain included neither avalanche nor blizzard. Real problems such as torrential rains and mudslides were scarcely considered until the plan foundered against them. De Lesseps's canal never happened, could never have happened when he attempted it, might not be possible now, a century later.

The failure of the Compagnie Universelle came with terrifying abruptness near the end of 1888 and did France more moral and material damage than defeat by the Prussian army eighteen years earlier. The scandal was huge, the hunt for scapegoats frantic. "Panamiste" was coined as a synonym for "swindler." De Lesseps, *père* and *fils,* were tried and convicted. Charles actually spent time behind bars, and the threat of prison hung over everyone connected with the enterprise. In 1889, a new company was formed, pursuant to a court order, so that the old one's bondholders might recoup something. Certain Compagnie Universelle directors and contractors were "instructed" to subscribe the new company's shares. The alternative was prosecution. Bunau-Varilla's firm bought 22,000 at 100 francs each. That was about 440,000 1889 dollars.

Work on the canal continued in desultory fashion. Extensions of the concession from Colombia gave the Compagnie Nouvelle control of the route until 1904. Bunau-Varilla struggled to keep the project alive, bought the newspaper *Le Matin* so as to have a forum in which to plug it, labored without rest (though without result either) to drum up interest in Britain, in Germany, in Russia. He had over four hundred thousand good reasons, and besides money his ego was invested, yet by the turn of the century, when his obsession was eighteen or twenty years old, its sole hope was that the United States might buy the company's assets, its buildings and equipment and excavations, and finish what the French had started. Otherwise, Bunau-Varilla's shares would be worthless and the Panama Canal only a pipe dream, an empty husk, a burst bubble, a fiasco.

As it happened, the idea of a "path between the seas" had taken on urgency for the United States. The country's most powerful warship, the USS *Oregon,* was in Puget Sound when war with Spain threatened and had to steam around South America to reach Cuban waters and nearly missed the Battle of Santiago Bay. After that, a canal was a certainty, but the U.S. route of preference went through Nicaragua. Two U.S. canal commissions had approved Nicaragua. A canal project there had the backing of a majority in the Senate led by John Tyler Morgan of Alabama. And in 1901 a bill for a Nicaragua canal passed the House by 308 to 2. All Panama signified was disease and disaster. The United States would never build a canal there.

How the case was altered, how Bunau-Varilla lobbied the United States around, cannot concern us in detail. What, essentially, he did was convince George S. Morison, the top man on yet a third canal commission, that the

Panama route was at least feasible. Then he got to the Republican party kingmaker Marcus A. Hanna, and showed him, and through him Theodore Roosevelt, that Panama offered something both wanted: a Republican canal, a canal they needn't share credit for with Morgan and the Democrats. Then, when the Senate was about to debate the issue, after Bunau-Varilla had stressed in books, pamphlets, and speeches that Nicaragua had volcanoes while Panama didn't, Mt. Pelée on Martinique had the decency to erupt and level the capital and cremate 30,000 people. A week later, Momotombo in Nicaragua itself erupted, and in case there were senators who hadn't noticed, or didn't link the explosion to their agenda, Bunau-Varilla found a Nicaraguan stamp that proudly displayed the smoking mountain and sent one to every member three days before the vote. Panama won 42 to 34. The most valuable players were Morison, Hanna, and Momotombo, and Bunau-Varilla was behind all three.

Were his troubles then over? Was his obsession home free and his investment in the Compagnie Nouvelle on its way back to him? Hardly. The bill, as passed by Congress and signed by Roosevelt, called for a canal in Nicaragua should what was needed to build one in Panama not be obtained "within a reasonable time"—title to the Compagnie Nouvelle's property and control of the necessary territory. The key to both was a treaty with Colombia, for the company couldn't sell without Colombia's approval. A pact was finally signed in January 1903—the Hay-Herrán Treaty, after the U.S. secretary of state, John Hay, and the Colombian chargé d'affaires in Washington, Tomás Herrán—but in August the Colombian senate rejected it unanimously.

From 1898 on, for good or ill, a canal between the Atlantic and Pacific oceans meant one built, run, and controlled by the United States. Private companies and other countries need not apply. This meant U.S. control of the land the canal passed through. What "control" meant varied. Outright annexation was rarely contemplated and never seriously proposed (though it might have been a better course of action than the one that in the end was taken). Whatever its scope, however, U.S. control meant greater or lesser adulteration of the sovereignty enjoyed and exercised over the canal territory by the state and nation that had title to it. In return, as counterpoise, there was money—the immediate, massive influx of money such as comes with any vast public works project (and this was the vastest so far in human experience), creating jobs and generating sales and buoying real estate values, followed by the continuing future tide of money connected with the passing flow of travelers and trade, and (tastiest of all to politicians) the lump sums of money put down at the project's start and paid over annually to get and keep the right-of-way. The contrapuntal theme of sovereignty and money are introduced with the Hay-Herrán Treaty and play on through all the long treaty business down to the treaties signed by Torrijos and Carter.

John Hay negotiated Hay-Herrán freely. The U.S. Senate approved it 73 to 5. In other words, the United States was satisfied with it, including what it provided regarding control. What did the Colombians object to?

Selling sovereignty doesn't look patriotic to start with. True patriotism might have meant voting for ratification, but politicians would often rather look than be patriotic. More to the point, selling too cheap is despicable. The money part was Hay-Herrán's main problem. Ten million dollars in gold was a good round sum, but $250,000 was what Colombia was already getting from the Panama Railroad, a fifty-mile line between Colón and Panama City that the Nouvelle Compagnie owned control of. In effect, the Zone was going rent free, five hundred square kilometers for nothing. The chief quibble, however, had nothing to do with what the United States would be paying. Article 1 of Hay-Herrán authorized the Compagnie Nouvelle to sell its assets to the United States, and the price, as all the world knew, was $40 million. Why, the Colombian senators wanted to know, should Colombia give its authorization for nothing? Why shouldn't Colombia get something back from the French? That they had a point seems clear these long years later. The United States, however, couldn't see it, and that circumstance had far-reaching consequences.

The main reason was William Nelson Cromwell, first of the great New York corporation lawyers and a founder of Sullivan & Cromwell, in which the brothers John Foster and Allen Dulles were later partners. Cromwell represented the railroad and the French company, and his fee was coming from funds paid the latter. He didn't want the Colombians getting a cent of them. He got to John Hay and somehow persuaded him, and through him Roosevelt, that the United States of America should share this sentiment, should have it enshrined in the treaty's first article, and then defend it implacably, no matter what. No waif was ever more abjectly Svengalied than was the U.S. government by Mr. Cromwell. When Hay signed the treaty, Cromwell was literally looking over his shoulder, and then Hay turned round and handed him the pen. When, early in June 1903, before debate had begun in Colombia's senate, the U.S. envoy in Bogotá cabled the State Department that Hay-Herrán was in trouble but would likely be ratified if the Compagnie Nouvelle would pay Colombia ten of its forty million, Hay not only rejected the plan but actually let Cromwell write the answering cable! More, after Cromwell had done so, with "an aggressiveness rarely found in friendly diplomatic intercourse," he went to the White House and had a long conference with Roosevelt and then leaked a story to the *New York World,* attributing greed and frenzy to the Colombians while warning that if they rejected the treaty, Panama would secede with American backing. And whether by coincidence or collusion, on the very day of Cromwell's visit with Roosevelt, the day before the *World* published the leak, Philippe Bunau-Varilla cabled Colombia's president and respectfully submitted (no browbeater he!) that if ratification were denied, there still might be a "Panama Canal after secession and declaration of independence of the

Isthmus of Panama under protection of the United States."

What spell did Cromwell use to charm Hay and Roosevelt? No one can say today with full assurance, but the story he leaked on leaving the White House on Saturday, June 13, 1903, asserted, "The citizens of Panama propose, after seceding, to make a treaty with the United States, giving this Government the equivalent of absolute sovereignty over the Canal Zone." This statement and Bunau-Varilla's cable suggest that he and Cromwell were working in concert. For Panama did secede and did make such a treaty, though (regarding the last) not through any "citizens" action. But here is David McCullough on the business, as eloquent a commentator as it is likely to have:

> It was a highly unorthodox arrangement, to say the least, to have the attorney for the corporation most directly in line to benefit from the treaty, a man with no official title, no rightful business to be involved in any official capacity, operating at will at the highest diplomatic level . . . and with full impunity. . . .
>
> That the United States government had no rightful authority in a dispute between a foreign power and a private corporation was lost sight of. A settlement by Colombia and the Compagnie Nouvelle would have cost the United States nothing, and in retrospect it would appear that even a comparatively modest settlement—plus a little tact—could have resolved the whole issue quite swiftly. But to Hay, to Roosevelt, talk of a Colombian lien on the French company was patent extortion, a "holdup." As men of honor they could never be "party to the gouge," as Roosevelt expressed it.

In short, the bearers of the white man's burden were making a common front against the wogs.

It was, anyway, the money they weren't getting, rather than the sovereignty they were asked to give up, that caused the Colombians to reject Hay-Herrán. Roosevelt might then have proceeded in Nicaragua. On September 15, 1903, he mentioned this to Hay as an alternative. That he didn't choose it was due (one feels) partly to the Panama route's technical advantages, partly to its political advantages (providing, as it did, a Republican canal), and mainly to his style and personal feelings. He felt he'd been pushed around by the Colombians (though actually he'd been manipulated by Cromwell), and it was not his style to be pushed around, but rather to ride roughly forward, through and over obstacles instead of around them—a style with which he had certainly done well so far. Here is the second alternative he notes to Hay: "In some way and shape to interfere when it becomes necessary so as to secure the Panama route without further dealing with the foolish and homicidal corruptionists in Bogota." Way and shape was provided by Bunau-Varilla, who now returns to center stage, bringing the Panamanians with him.

First, though, a word on Panama as a nation, for sloppy thought and language on the subject have fostered and spread the misconception that Panama was, somehow, a creation of the United States, or even of Teddy Roosevelt personally.

Panama was always a separate national entity, was never organically integrated into Colombia. The chief reason why was that Panama achieved independence from Spain on its own. The authors of this independence, perhaps frightened by their own audacity, then began to fear a Spanish reconquest of the isthmus, a thing that might have been easily accomplished since Panama was both small and thinly populated, with no troops and few weapons. That is when the idea came up for Panama to join with a larger nation. Joining Mexico was even proposed, certainly by someone who'd never seen a map, for Mexico offered no better protection than Monaco or Moravia. At that point, Panama's leaders opted for Colombia, which at one time had been linked with Panama administratively by the Spanish crown, which was at least closer than Mexico, and which—here was the strongest argument—was then governed by Simón Bolívar in a confederation called Grancolombia. Bolívar was almost a mythological figure, almost a divinity. His prestige drew Panama into a union with Colombia. In no one's mind in Panama, however, was this union intended to be permanent. As soon as the danger of Spanish reconquest was over, Panama would return to independence.

This did not happen, however, and almost at once Panamanian leaders began to repent their overly speedy turning to Colombia and dedicated themselves to breaking the artificial bonds between the two countries—above all when intestine strife broke out between the chieftains of the South American revolution. Nineteenth-century Panamanian history is littered with conspiracies against the central power, besides the three well-known overt attempts at independence. Panamanians were sick of being at once taxed and abandoned by Bogotá. The only things Bogotá sent Panama were its imbecilic and bloody civil wars.

The Thousand Days War (1899–1902) drained Panama's patience. The rejection of Hay-Herrán was the last straw. Panama would now be condemned to eternal penury, eternally at the whim of Colombian politicians. By the time Bunau-Varilla, Cromwell, and Teddy Roosevelt came on the scene, a revolutionary conspiracy was already in progress. But those directing it were realists. They knew Panama's weakness, and the strength of Colombia's veteran army. They seized the moment when a coincidence of interests presented the best chance for independence. Here it is that Panama's national aspirations became bound up with the irresistible expansionism of the United States, the political ambitions of Theodore Roosevelt, and the turbulent intriguing of Bunau-Varilla. But the principal separatist impulse came from within Panama.

American revolutionaries achieved their country's independence with French help. The revolutionaries of South America were helped in their struggle for national independence by Great Britain. The Bolsheviks made their revolution with the help of the Germans, who sent Lenin to St. Petersburg and financed his efforts. All people, it turns out, accept foreign help when they try revolution, but the only ones condemned are Panama's founders. Unfortunate circumstances combined to make the personal participation of these men seem infinitely smaller in the world's eyes than it was in reality. Roosevelt's impulsive joke "I took the Isthmus" (conveniently mocking in tone, though his target was the U.S. Senate, not Panama) gave every superficial commentator the right to trample on Panama, but Panama was not Roosevelt's creation. Much less was it Bunau-Varilla's. And Panama's founding fathers were no less brave, generous, far-seeing, or fallible than those of any other country.

The main conspirators were José Agustín Arango and Manuel Amador Guerrero, a lawyer and a physician, both employed by the Panama Railroad. Dr. Amador, who was seventy that summer, was sent to the United States for money and backing. Six million was the sum the secessionists thought of, to buy a secondhand gunboat or two and to bribe the garrison. Dr. Amador saw Cromwell and found him enthusiastic. He would raise the money. He would get Amador a meeting with Hay. But then, through an indiscretion of Cromwell's, Herrán, the Colombian chargé, got wind of the business and threw such a terrible scare into the lawyer that he refused to deal with Amador further. The latter was about to go home empty-handed when Bunau-Varilla showed up in New York. On September 24, he and Amador had the first of at least five meetings in Room 1162 of the Waldorf Astoria. Bunau-Varilla may be exaggerating when he calls that room "the cradle of the Panama Republic," but a good deal of the country's conceiving was done there.

On October 10, Bunau-Varilla sat down with Roosevelt, who agreed (without actually saying so) to be obstetrician.

"He is a very able fellow," wrote Roosevelt three months later of Bunau-Varilla, "and it was his business to find out what he thought our Government would do. I have no doubt that he was able to make a very accurate guess, and to advise his people accordingly. In fact, he would have been a very dull man had he been unable to make such a guess."

Bunau-Varilla advised Amador to have his revolution on November 3. There was no need to buy gunboats. They would be by courtesy of the U.S. Navy. As for other expenses, $100,000 ought to do. Bunau-Varilla would furnish it from his own pocket. He had, besides, prepared, and would give the doctor when he embarked for the isthmus a cable code, a program of military operations, a declaration of independence, a draft constitution, and a flag. He hoped Amador and his friends could manage the rest. He himself would handle the key front in Washington. All he required was appointment as Panama's minister plenipotentiary to the United States, empowered to obtain recognition and sign a canal treaty.

Amador objected. To have a foreigner serve as their first representative abroad would be a blow to Panamanian pride. If Bunau-Varilla here allowed himself to point out that the foreigner's money and influence seemed welcome, he does not mention it in his account of the meeting. We may, however, imagine his duelist's eyes flashing. No wogs were going to cause him further setbacks in the gratification of his lifelong obsession. He handed Dr. Amador a draft telegram according him, Philippe Bunau-Varilla, the rank and powers he was requesting. When, and only when, he received that message, the money and the warships would be on their way.

Not everything that followed was hitchless. Bunau-Varilla's flag, for instance, pleased no one. It was nothing but a botched clone of Old Glory, with yellow stripes instead of white ones, and a pair of yellow suns in place of the stars. How unlike Bunau-Varilla to be so without imagination! The problem was put straight, however, without trouble. Amador's son designed a flag, and Señorita María de la Ossa sewed it, and it was raised in Cathedral Plaza on November 4 with appropriate jubilation and shouts of "¡Viva!"

Five hundred Colombian soldiers arrived at Colón by steamer on the night of the second, in consequence, perhaps, of Cromwell's blabbing. The USS *Nashville* was there six hours before them, but orders to prevent a Colombian landing didn't reach her master till ten the next morning, by which time the soldiers were already ashore. Amador's wife, however, devised a plan to keep them from disrupting the revolution, and the railroad superintendent, an American named James Shaler (for whom the flagpoled triangle was named), executed it to perfection. The railroad was the sole means of crossing the isthmus (unless one liked jungle hiking, which might take a week) and had the only phone and telegraph systems. Shaler got his rolling stock out of Colón, all but one fancy car and one locomotive, and sent the generals across without their troops. In Panama City the generals were arrested. The Colombian colonel left behind in Colón didn't find out what had happened till noon on the fourth, and after a nervous day and a half, during which his men surrounded the railroad office, and the *Nashville* trained her guns on them, he accepted a bribe from Shaler and reembarked the battalion for Cartagena.

Two Colombian gunboats were off Panama City, and only one of their captains had been bribed, so at dusk on the third, as the provisional government, led by Arango, was being installed, the other, the SS *Bogotá,* began firing shells into the city. One killed a Chinese shopkeeper. Another killed a donkey. Then a shore battery operated by members of the bribed garrison returned the fire. The ship withdrew behind an island in the bay and was heard from no more. In the following days, U.S. warships began arriving. The *Boston, Marblehead, Concord,* and *Wyoming* reached Panama City. The *Dixie, Atlanta, Maine, Mayflower,* and *Prairie* reinforced the *Nashville* at Colón. Their commanding officers had orders to prevent the landing of Colombian troops anywhere in Panama.

In Washington, all went swimmingly. On the fifth, a cable to Hay from the revolutionary government, authenticated by one from the U.S. consul in Panama, asserted that authority had been established, and confirmed the appointment of one Philippe Bunau-Varilla as Panama's envoy. Within the hour, the United States recognized the Republic of Panama. The orders, mentioned above, to protect it against being repossessed by Colombia had gone well in advance of recognition, and the whole affair was looked on as unseemly by prissy legalists and the *New York Times.* Roosevelt, a bit unnerved by the latter, defended himself to his cabinet with much convolution—after which Mr. Elihu Root found the lighthearted tone that characterized the general response of the nation: "You have shown that you were accused of seduction and you have conclusively proved that you were guilty of rape."

Dogs barked, in short, but the caravan moved onward. On November 8, its main mover checked out of the Waldorf in New York and into the Willard in Washington, and the next day sat down to lunch with Mr. John Hay. And found the secretary of state disturbed by a new item: a special commission was about to leave Panama for Washington to negotiate a canal treaty with the United States. Bunau-Varilla was quick to reassure him:

"So long as I am here, Mr. Secretary, you will have to deal exclusively with me."

On the tenth, Dr. Amador and two other commissioners sailed from Colón on board the *City of Washington.* On the fifteenth, Hay sent Bunau-Varilla a copy of Hay-Herrán, requesting his suggestions as soon as possible. The United States, in short, was offering Panama the same deal Colombia had rejected. Bunau-Varilla stayed up all night looking it over and at dawn concluded it wouldn't do. *It was too favorable to the country he was representing!* There was a chance it might not pass the U.S. Senate. The canal might end up being built in Nicaragua. He'd come too far, been striving too long, to risk that. What was needed was a treaty so favorable to the United States that the Senate would have to ratify it.

Immediately after breakfast on Monday, November 16, 1903, Bunau-Varilla, his lawyer, and a public stenographer began crafting an unrejectable canal treaty. They worked all day and on into the night, and while they worked, the *City of Washington* steamed northward. At ten in the evening they finished. Bunau-Varilla delivered the treaty early the next day, the same day the *City of Washington* docked in New York.

What Bunau-Varilla did after that was sweat. He wired Amador to stay in New York and to say nothing to newspaper reporters, but he didn't know for how long his word might be heeded. His august title and full powers would certainly vanish, like Cinderella's coach and four at midnight, as soon as the Panamanians reached Washington, but day dragged into evening with no word from Hay, and when, late at night, the two met at Bunau-Varilla's insistence, the secretary of state still wasn't ready. The wording was fine, mostly cribbed from Hay-Herrán, and the concessions to the United States were sweeping, but Hay wanted Bunau-Varilla's concoction looked over by Philander Knox and Elihu Root and Leslie Shaw, the attorney general and the secretaries of war and the treasury, who would lunch with him the next day for that purpose.

What they ate is nowhere recorded, but the treaty went down smoothly. Late that afternoon, November 18, clerks at the State Department set to work drawing up final drafts, and while they worked, the train from New York steamed southward, bearing Dr. Amador and his party to Washington. At six, Bunau-Varilla arrived at Hay's home. Copies of the treaty were brought over. At seven, the two gentlemen signed them, dipping the pen in an inkwell once owned by Lincoln, in whose White House Hay had worked as a young man. At nine, Bunau-Varilla was at the station to greet the Panamanian commissioners with the news that he had just signed the Canal treaty. As Bunau-Varilla later described it, Dr. Amador "nearly swooned on the platform."

After Amador and the others learned the terms of the treaty, it seemed quite possible that Panama would reject it. The delegation was furious with Bunau-Varilla, and though he pointed out that a special commission from Colombia was on its way to the United States to make whatever canal deal the United States wanted, they were happy to tell Hay in person that they had no authority to act on a treaty that they'd been supposed to negotiate in the first place. All they would do was send it to Panama, where the junta would pass or reject it. The treaty, then, sailed from New York on the *City of Washington* on Tuesday, November 24. The next night, Bunau-Varilla, possibly with Hay's approval and possibly not, cabled the junta that if they failed to ratify it as soon as it arrived in Colón, the United States would withdraw its warships and sign a canal treaty with Colombia. That Colombia would at once land troops in Panama, whose first act would be to string the junta up, wasn't in the cable, because the junta knew it—and knew, too, that Panama wouldn't be independent or prosperous. The next morning, Arango and company cabled back: Tell Washington the treaty will be ratified! And so it was, formally, unanimously, and without modification, on Wednesday, December 2, 1903, the same day the *City of Washington* made harbor.

The U.S. Senate passed it twelve weeks later. Three days after that, Philippe Bunau-Varilla resigned as Panama's envoy extraordinary to the United States, ending his brief diplomatic career with the same chutzpah he displayed before and during it. In lieu of payment for his services, he told the junta, they might raise a monument to de Lesseps.

There is a bust of Count Ferdinand de Lesseps, one and a half times life-size, atop a ten-foot, marble-faced obelisk in the Plaza de Francia in Panama City, in the center of four similar but smaller memorials of Frenchmen prominent in his canal effort. Whether this was paid for with what (his request apart) would have been Bunau-Varilla's fee is impossible to determine but, one thinks, unlikely. What, after all, did Panama owe him? What did he deserve at the hands of Panamanians? A monument of his own of epic dimensions for engineering their independence from Colombia, or a firing squad for betraying their trust, for submitting them to decades of indignity, for pimping in the ravishment of their only valuable natural resource?

The $40 million was paid the Compagnie Nouvelle in May 1904. Bunau-Varilla's firm recouped its forced investment with a profit, and he lived to the age of eighty in wealth and honor.

There it is, then: intrigue and influence, chicanery and extortion. Through the contrivances of this extraordinary envoy and in accord with a contract neither had drawn, the Republic of Panama and the United States began the most intimate relationship ever established between two nations, of which the canal is a celebrated offspring. Its other issue, born, like Bunau-Varilla himself, on the wrong side of the blanket, was the Canal Zone, juridical freak, political monstrosity, within and over which the United States had rights, power, and authority it didn't need and hadn't asked for, didn't want and hadn't even thought of, until Bunau-Varilla dangled them under Hay's nose—as a street fence dangles stolen jewelry to tempt the averagely honest passerby. But once tempted . . . No wonder Hay called in Knox and Root and Shaw! No wonder he dipped the pen in Lincoln's inkwell! He didn't have duelist's eyes like Bunau-Varilla's. He didn't have pirate's gonads either. He was just an averagely honest, temptable fellow. His conscience was giving him nips, and he wanted accomplices. Lincoln especially. If Honest Abe's inkwell didn't shatter, maybe the deal wasn't really that rank. Hay's conscience, however, does not much impress the impartial observer, nor does it make a particle of difference whether or not he colluded in the threatening cable. John Hay, and through him the United States of America, whose foreign relations he had the privilege of directing, knew it was chicanery and extortion, but when the proceeds were dangled, Hay and the United States clutched and kept them, and when you are a knowing beneficiary, you are a party to the offense. "The conquest of the earth," writes Joseph Conrad in *Heart of Darkness,* "which mostly means the taking it away from those who have a different complexion or slightly flatter noses than ourselves, is not a pretty thing when you look into it too much."

APPENDIX B

DEFENSE FORCES

For a biological model of what happened in Panama and (perhaps) other Latin-American countries, where the part whose business it is to defend the whole attacked it instead, we offer the following, from Lewis Thomas, *The Youngest Science: Notes of a Medicine-Watcher* (New York, 1983), 151–52:

Endotoxin is not really much of a toxin, at least in the ordinary sense of being a direct poisoner of living cells. Instead, it seems to be a sort of signal, a piece of misleading news. When injected into the bloodstream, it conveys propaganda, announcing that typhoid bacilli in great numbers (or other related bacteria) are on the scene, and a number of defense mechanisms are automatically switched on, all at once. When the dose of endotoxin is sufficiently high, these defense mechanisms, acting in concert or in sequence, launch a stereotyped set of physiological responses, including fever, malaise, hemorrhage, collapse, shock, coma, and death. It is something like an explosion in a munitions factory.

This is the reason, or one reason anyway, why the problem of endotoxin is so engrossing. It provides a working model for one of the great subversive ideas in medicine: that disease can result from the normal functioning of the body's own mechanisms for protecting itself, when these are turned on simultaneously and too exuberantly, with tissue suicide at the end.

NOTES

1. The Death and Posthumous Vengeance of Hugo Spadafora

P. 22 Noriega's first rape and assault episode and the beginning of his espionage career are reported by Frederick Kempe in "Dirty Tricks," *Wall Street Journal,* October 18, 1989, 1.

Pp. 26ff. Our account of the outrages perpetrated on the person of Dr. Hugo Spadafora on the afternoon and evening of September 13, 1985, was first published in the June 1988 issue of *Harper's* magazine under the name of Guillermo Sánchez Borbón, since R. M. Koster, residing at the time in Noriega's Panama, could not afford to have his name associated with it. We republish it here untouched. It has been questioned in print by a person who is either an apologist for General Noriega or poorly informed or both, but it is entirely consonant with the findings of a panel of physicians retained by Dr. Winston Spadafora to discover exactly what injuries were inflicted. These findings were communicated to Guillermo Sánchez in May 1990 by Dr. Abdiel Juliao of the Centro Médico Bella Vista, Panama City, a panel member.

P. 27 Corozo. Corozo was one of Omar Torrijos's half-baked projects. The word itself means a kind of palm, and the region is called Corozo because palms grow there. In the 1970s, Torrijos encouraged farmers of the region to form a cooperative palm plantation, pledging that his government would put in a plant to process cooking oil from the palm fruit. The government built only one building, what would have been the administrative headquarters had the plant been constructed, but which became a Guardia Nacional outpost. The growers were reduced to shipping the fruit to Costa Rica for processing. The resulting oil was then imported to Panama.

After Hugo Spadafora's body was discovered, when it became clear that Panamanian authorities had no interest in discovering his murderers, much less in bringing them to the bar of justice, Hugo's father, Don Carmelo Spadafora, hired a

Chiriquí lawyer, Rodrigo Miranda, to look into the crime. In the course of his investigation, Miranda encountered one Robledo Miranda (no kin), who owned a farm in the Corozo vicinity and who declared in an affidavit that Hugo Spadafora had been brought to the Corozo outpost in a military vehicle at about 7:30 P.M. on September 13, 1985, in very poor physical condition but alive. On September 26, 1985, Rodrigo Miranda furnished a copy of Robledo Miranda's affidavit to Guillermo Sánchez.

In November 1985, Sánchez received corroboration of Robledo Miranda's declaration from César Pereira, former deputy to the Panamanian National Assembly, currently Panama's ambassador to the United Nations, and at the time of Spadafora's murder counsel to the Corozo palm plantation cooperative. Early that month, cooperative members had requested an interview with Pereira on cooperative business, but in the course of the meeting a number of them informed Pereira that on the evening of September 13, 1985, they had seen a military vehicle draw up at the station. Men in uniform took an incapacitated person from the vehicle. Subsequently terrible screams were heard from the Corozo station.

On November 27, 1985, meanwhile, Mario Obaldia, legislator and sometime *La Prensa* columnist, published a cryptic reference to information he had received from a woman who lived in the Corozo region. The woman's dog, so she declared, had been scuffling at the earth outside the Corozo station and had been shot by soldiers, who later dug up a human head from where her dog had been sniffing.

In February 1990, after the invasion of Panama and the fall of its military government, investigators working under the direction of Rodrigo Miranda (now special prosecutor of the Ministry of Justice charged with discovering the truth about Hugo Spadafora's murder), found a considerable quantity of partially washed human blood in the building, both splattered on the walls and dried up in the station's kitchen.

P. 28 The phrase about the reaction to rabies vaccine is from *The New Encyclopaedia Britannica: Micropaedia,* 15th ed., 8:367.

P. 30 For Yezhof's method, see Henry S. A. Becket, *The Dictionary of Espionage* (New York, 1985), 105.

P. 38 For the two simultaneous meetings, and generally for the twin sets of signals sent Noriega from Washington, see Connie Bruck, "Nabbing Noriega, Letting Him Escape," *Miami Review,* July 12, 1988.

2. The Coup d'Etat

P. 51 The song is "El Tambor de la Alegría." *Tambor* means "drum." An attempt to define *alegría* is made in the text. The song's title might be loosely Englished as "Where the Fun Is." The quoted lines go, "Panamanian, Panamanian, If you still love me, / Take me where the fun is." The rhythm, four heavy beats to the line, pulses powerfully. The chorus, subject to endless repetition by drunken revelers, is:

Que, viva! Viva Panamá!
Que, viva! Viva Panamá!
Que viva viva viva viva Panamá!
Que, viva! Viva Panamá!

P. 52 The historian is Ernesto Castillero Reyes; see his *Historia de Panama* (Panama, 1962), 159. The political scientist is Steve C. Ropp; see his *Panamanian Politics: From Guarded Nation to National Guard* (New York, 1982), 16.

P. 52 For Remón, see Larry LaRae Pippin, *The Remón Era: An Analysis of a Decade of Events in Panama (1947–1957)* (Stanford, 1964).

P. 58 The line about U.S. troops' having to be committed in battle was written in 1988 and proved accurate in December 1989.

P. 58 The quoted phrases are by José Ortega y Gasset.

P. 69 *La Prensa* published an interview with Martínez on October 10, 1980. Guillermo Sánchez Borbón conversed at length with him in March and April 1988.

3. The Brief Time of Boris Martínez

The chief source for the early part of this chapter—that is, the night of the coup and the first days of the Revolution without Dictatorship and of Liberty with Order—is Ms. Britt Jansen de Perez, who graciously made available to the authors the draft of a Ph.D. dissertation she is preparing at the University of New Mexico.

The main sources for the *guerrilla* in Chiriquí were Miguel Batista, who fought on Quijada del Diablo under Ariosto González, and Enrique Moreno, who handled the *guerrilleros'* supplies from Costa Rica until he was shot and kidnapped to Panama and imprisoned. Guillermo Sánchez interviewed him in Miami in 1988.

Gonzalo Menéndez Franco and Licenciate Alejandro Pérez furnished information regarding Torrijos's pact with the communists. They, too, were interviewed by Guillermo Sánchez.

P. 91 The quoted phrase is from Herodotus, 7.135, and concerns the Spartans' willingness to fight for freedom.

P. 93 The phrase "sigh of relief" to characterize the U.S. government's reaction to the coup was used by Jack Hood Vaughn, who at the time of the coup was director of the Peace Corps and who had previously been U.S. ambassador to Panama and assistant secretary of state for inter-American affairs.

P. 102 The spinelessness of Costa Rican authorities needs some explanation. Costa Ricans generally, and the Costa Rican government, instinctively sided with Panamanian democrats and against the Guardia. Costa Rica's exports to Panama, however, constituted the country's main source of foreign exchange. Martínez refused to let Costa Rican goods into Panama until the Costa Rican government changed its tune. This "stick" was supplemented with a "carrot" once Torrijos took over: contrabanding profits for selected Costa Rican politicians—above all, for Diego Trejos, son of Costa Rica's president and minister of the interior.

P. 106 The interviewer was T. D. Allman, whose article appeared in *Vanity Fair,* June 1988.

P. 107 Mother Angelina ran the household of the papal nuncio to Panama when Guillermo Sánchez was refuged there in September 1985.

P. 109 At the time of the attack on the cuartel at Piedra Candela, the Panamanian government put its casualties down as one dead and one wounded, but on the eleventh anniversary of the action a monument to the *guardias* killed in it was dedicated, and it bore fifteen names. See *La República* (Panama), January 13, 1980.

P. 110 Associated Press, in the *Miami Herald,* August 22, 1969.

4. Early in the Time of Omar Torrijos

P. 119 The Rockefeller quotation is from *Quality of Life in the Americas: Report of a Presidential Mission for the Western Hemisphere,* Department of State Bulletin, December 8, 1969, quoted in Penny Lernoux, *The Cry of the People* (New York, 1986), 164. Dodson was interviewed by telephone on October 22, 1988.

P. 120 How Ariosto González died is from an interview with Enrique Moreno in Miami, September 1988.

P. 125 The American visitor was Jack Hood Vaughn, interviewed in Washington in August and October 1988.

P. 132 Information regarding Somoza's help in Torrijos's return to Panama was supplied by Sidar Cisneros Leyva, interviewed in Miami in September 1988. Somoza's participation is confirmed by two other sources. G. Russell Evans, *The Panama Canal Treaties Swindle* (Carrboro, N.C., 1986), 58, has this to say on the subject: " 'The real reason for Torrijos's successful return to Panama,' said [the anti-Torrijos coup maker Colonel Amado] Sanjur, 'was Somoza of Nicaragua' who provided him with an aircraft after his [Torrijos's] party had flown to San Salvador from Mexico in a rented plane." Evans footnotes this text as follows: "César Napoleón Suazo, former Maj. General, Nicaraguan National Guard, interview with the author, August 1, 1984 in Miami, Florida. General Suazo gave details. Somoza had directed him to provide an aircraft to fly Torrijos, [Rubén] Paredes and [Rodrigo] García back to Panama. He used Somoza's Aero Commander (Alfa Sierra Delta) for the flight . . . from Las Mercedes Airport (a Nicaraguan Air Base) to David, Chiriquí province. The plane was piloted by Red Gray, an American." The substantial accuracy of Evans's, Cisneros Leyva's, and our account was further confirmed to Guillermo Sánchez by José Dominador Bazán, second vice-president in the 1968 government of Arnulfo Arias, who conversed at length on the subject with Somoza himself in Managua in 1979.

P. 140 Hugo Torrijos's blackjack system was described to R. M. Koster by a Casinos Nacionales croupier in January 1990.

P. 141 Torrijos's encounter with the surviving González Santizo is mentioned in José de Jesús Martínez, *Mi General Torrijos* (Bogotá, 1987), 241.

P. 147 The quote regarding aid funds is from Robert Howard Miller, Jr., "Military Government and Approaches to National Development: A Comparative Analysis of the Peruvian and Panamanian Experience" (Ph.D. diss., University of Miami, 1975), 157. Miller cites Don Bohning, "Panama Receives Top Per Capita US Aid," *Miami Herald,* January 27, 1974, 20.

5. The Martyrdom of Héctor Gallego

P. 149 Torrijos's motives in seeking to make the campesinos a political base and his attendance at the Fort Gulick course are mentioned by Ropp, *Panamanian Politics,* 48–49.

Pp. 149–50 Vaughn's recollections are from conversations with R. M. Koster in August and October 1988.

P. 150 The Rand quotation is in Lernoux, *Cry of the People,* 157.

P. 151 Information on the *asentamientos* is provided by Ropp, *Panamanian Politics,* 68–69.

P. 153 For Greene's Torrijos see his *Getting to Know the General* (New York, 1984).

P. 154 For "rank" and "hierarchy," see Martínez, *Mi General Torrijos,* 21; for "the Indian" etc., see ibid., 41.

P. 156 Gallego's words on the campesinos' reality are from Yike Fonseca, "Héctor, El Profeta Panameño," *Diálogo Social* (Panama), May–June 1972. *Diálogo Social* devoted a special issue to Gallego on the first anniversary of his disappearance. This issue is referred to below as *DS**.

P. 157 Gallego's statements are from an interview with him conducted shortly before his disappearance and published in *DS**.

P. 158 The bulletin appears in *DS**.

Pp. 158–59 The description of the June 1970 incident is from Lernoux, *Cry of the People,* 131–32. The phrase she quotes is in "Sus Años en Panamá," *DS**.

P. 159 The campesinos' letter to Vásquez Pinto is reproduced in "Héctor para los Santafereños," *DS**.

P. 160 Gallego's description of the situation around Santa Fe on the eve of his death is from a report of the burning of his rancho published in "Así Fueron Sus Ultimas Dias," *DS**.

P. 160 The remark about the joyfulness of infinite play is from James Carse, *Finite and Infinite Games* (New York, 1986). The account of Gallego's abduction is from Peña's declaration, *DS*,* 71. Father Hernández's declarations were reported in numerous Colombian newspapers, among them *El Tiempo* (Bogotá), August 20, 1972.

P. 165 A similar argument, attributed to a "knowledgeable Panamanian source," is mentioned in Miller, "Military Government," 174: "Torrijos' civic-action-style rural efforts . . . provide a good way to make reforms in Panama *without* losing control of the process and allowing it to turn into a self-perpetuating revolutionary flow of reforms beyond the control and interests of the Torrijos clique. The problem of Father Gallegos [*sic*] . . . was that he made reforms *outside* the political control of the government, and thus had to be removed."

P. 165 The source for "my gangster" is Vaughn.

Pp. 165–66 For Noriega and Gallego, see Seymour M. Hersh, "Why the Democrats Can't Make an Issue of Noriega," *New York Times,* May 4, 1988.

6. Trading on Patriotism

P. 170 The labor code was as phony as anything else Torrijos pretended to do for the people of Panama. The World Bank Report No. 5236-PAN, *Panama: Structural Change and Growth Prospects* (Washington, February 28, 1985), says the following about it: "The effects of the [Labor] Code and other Government policies on the functioning of the labor market can be clearly seen in the case of the manufacturing and construction sectors. In manufacturing, during the five years preceding the Code's introduction, the employment elasticity exceeded unity, average real wages were rising sharply and labor increased its share in value added. In the seven years after the Code the employment elasticity fell by nearly 30 percent, real wages declined as unions opted for job security rather than higher financial returns, and the share of labor in real value added diminished. The Code undoubtedly played an important part in discouraging job creation."

P. 182 The leak appeared in the *Times* on September 2, 1969, 20. The phrase "military-type, provisional" is attributed to an unnamed State Department source. For Nixon at Camp David, see the *Times* of October 26, 1970, 1.

P. 182 For Greene and Torrijos, see Martínez, *Mi General Torrijos,* 42.

P. 185 For Richard's capture, see *New York Times,* July 19, 1971, 1. Information about Monchi Torrijos's alleged drug trafficking, and about Panama's claim that the allegation was a fabrication designed to hurt the treaty talks, is reported in the *Times,* March 16, 1972, 14, and in the Spanish review *Somos,* October 21, 1977. A related incident occurred in 1975 when Monchi was returning by ship to Panama from Spain. Passengers were scheduled to debark at Cristobal in what was then the Canal Zone, and Clayburne A. McLelland, redheaded U.S. marshal in and for jurisdiction, was poised to execute the indictment and apprehend Monchi, when the State Department took a hand in events, atwitter (one imagines) with worry over what such use of U.S. sovereign rights might do to brother Omar's disposition. The U.S. ambassador to Panama, Robert Sayre, got in touch with Monchi by ship-to-shore telephone, and the latter left the vessel at Barranquilla, Colombia, and made the last leg of his journey by air, thereby evading capture. R. M. Koster spoke with McLelland in 1977, while on assignment from *Newsweek,* and had his memory of the incident refreshed in January 1990, in conversation with Dwight McKabney, former general counsel to the Panama Canal Company.

7. Snowing the Senate

P. 189 The Carter administration policy of presenting Torrijos and company as good guys was described by Marc Schneider, assistant under secretary of state for human rights during Carter's presidency, in conversation with R. M. Koster in June 1987. Senator Dole's allegation about the forty-four file drawers full of documents was widely reported, including by *Somos,* October 21, 1977.

P. 190 The quotation about Jordan is by Jack Vaughn and comes from an interview with him in October 1988.

P. 193 For the estimate of what the areas turned over to Panama were worth, and for facts on how little use has been made of them, see World Bank, *Panama,* 112–17.

P. 197 Hoyt Purvis, director of the Fulbright Institute of Foreign Relations, at the University of Arkansas, made the first Senate visit as an aide to Robert Byrd. Purvis was interviewed by R. M. Koster in February 1989.

P. 201 The American was Hoyt Purvis.

P. 208 The source for Torrijos's remark is Rómulo Escobar, in conversation with Guillermo Sánchez Borbón.

8. Torrijos the Politician

P. 220 Of Torrijos's hunches, Martínez says this: "It seemed as if he aimed with his eyes closed, but opened wide to intuition, to hunch, what could be called 'steamy reasoning,' as opposed to the pure, cold, solid reasoning we inherited from the Greeks." See *Mi General Torrijos,* 96. And this on his keeping silent: "He knew how to keep quiet very well. One didn't feel the need to say something, anything, to break the silence. With him, silence was valuable, charged with feeling, with ideas forming themselves, with inner peace." The last is a marvelous text, worthy of being memorized by every schoolboy. Keep your mouth shut, it says, and people may think your mind's full of ideas forming, even if you're an oaf like Omar Torrijos!

P. 222 The quoted verse is from W. H. Auden, "September 1, 1939." The quoted words about Panama's constitutional reform are from American University, *Panama: A Country Study,* ed. Richard F. Nyrop (Washington, D.C., 1980), 135.

P. 225 For arms purchases in Europe by Krupnick and Harari, as well as for Noriega's partnership with Echevarria, see U.S. Senate, *Drugs, Law Enforcement and Foreign Policy: A Report of the Subcommittee on Narcotics, Terrorism and International Operations* (Washington, D.C., April 13, 1989), 225.

P. 226 The phrase "Spadafora and his Panamanians" occurs, for example, in Christopher Dickey, *With the Contras: A Reporter in the Wilds of Nicaragua* (New York 1987), 30.

Pp. 227ff. For the Shah's trials, tribulations, and travels, see William Shawcross, *The Shah's Last Ride* (New York, 1988). The Kissinger reference is on p. 13. For the Shah in Panama, see Martínez, *Mi General Torrijos,* 232ff., as well as Shawcross, *Shah's Last Ride,* 232–390.

P. 228 Martínez gives a version of Jordan's visit in his *Mi General Torrijos,* 205–6. Shawcross follows his closely but supplements it with material from Jordan. Neither mention the $12 million. One understands Martínez's reticence to display his revered chief taking a bribe, but Shawcross's is unfathomable. Díaz Herrera's declarations were published frequently in *La Prensa* on and after June 7, 1987, and were repeated copiously in the U.S. and the European press. Why hasn't Shawcross mentioned the money, if only to refute its having been offered and accepted? Jordan's amateurish procedure may be inferred from Martínez's and Shawcross's accounts but was specifically pointed out by Jack Hood Vaughn when the latter was interviewed in Washington in October 1988. Jordan's quoted remark is from his book *Crisis,* quoted in Larry Rohter, "America's Blind Eye," *New York Times Magazine,* May 29, 1988, 27. On attempts to fleece the Shah, see Shawcross, *Shah's Last Ride,* 336.

P. 233 The remark about Farah's sheets is cited in Shawcross, *Shah's Last Ride,* 390.

P. 233 Regarding the anticommunism of the Panamanian lower classes, Guillermo Sánchez remembers a dispute he witnessed in the Panama City slum of El Chorrillo between two persons whom we might call fishwives, except that it might give fishwives a bad name. They cannonaded each other for some time with foul language, until the more vigorous of the two, having exhausted her rich repertoire of blasphemy, scatology, and sexual insult, reached desperately for some yet filthier epithet and at length, with deep contempt, venomed forth, "Communist!" Her adversary could do no better than respond, "More communist you!"

P. 235 Moisés Torrijos's suspicions about his brother Omar's death were reported in the Spanish review *Panorama.*

9. *La Prensa,* the Sack of Panama, and Rubén Paredes

Pp. 250ff. A group calling itself the Movimiento Independiente Democrático (Independent Democratic Movement) published an irregular newspaper called *El Independiente* that criticized regime bungles and swindles. Number 7, dated March 27, 1979, dealt with Cerro Colorado and quoted extensively from a secret World Bank report. A later number, for which no date is available, gave details on twenty bungles and swindles including the Sugar Bungle, the Bus Bungle-cum-Swindle, and the Airport Swindle.

P. 251 For details about the cement plant and mention of the overrun of the Fortuna plant, see World Bank, *Panama,* 45–47.

P. 253 A pleasant touch applied near the end of the airport project exemplifies the thoroughness and gall that characterized swindling in the time of the tyrants, the determination to leave no cent unscammed. A gentleman by the name of Arturo McGowen, a painting contractor and the boss of the tourism institute, got the contract to decorate the terminal's interior. He had no professional background as an artist, or any known artistic talent, but he liked modern art and kept up on new things in the field. Evidently, he liked the work of Martin Schenker, a U.S. painter not really celebrated but well known to connoisseurs—liked it so much that he photographed three Schenker canvases from an art magazine and enlarged the photos and copied the enlargements by silk-screen process and signed the copies "A. McGowen" and sold them to the government as part of the decor he was preparing. Then he had them hung prominently in the new airport, so prominently that an art fancier spotted the forgeries less than a week after the new airport opened, in September 1978. So the mess came out, and the forgeries were taken down, and for all we know the government got back its money, but our hats are off to Señor McGowen for trying, for showing what Panama's swindlers can dream up.

P. 253 The comments about COFINA are from World Bank, *Panama,* 31.

Pp. 258 The prosecutor in the Seguro case, Dr. Carlos H. Cuestas, wrote a book about it, *El Escándalo de la Caja de Seguro Social* (Panama, 1984). It was very useful, although either Cuestas kept quiet about the part played in the swindle by Paredes and Noriega or he was careful not to learn anything too dangerous. People calling themselves Departamento de Empleados Honestos de la Caja del Seguro Social (Department of Honest Employees of the Social Security Fund) published a flier on August 16, 1982, which gives an overview of the swindle and mentions Noriega as the man ultimately behind it. On November 2, 1984, with both Paredes and De la Espriella out of power, Dr. Fábrega swore out an affidavit detailing their part in the swindle.

P. 260 Two Seguro directors who were bribed were Lorenzo Mora Murgas and Phillip Dean Butcher.

P. 261 For Colonel García's and Pons's involvement, see Cuestas, *El Escándalo,* 154. The Restaurante Galaxia meeting is detailed in Fábrega's affidavit.

10. Of the Criminals, by the Criminals, for the Criminals

The principal references for this chapter are the following:

The testimony before the U.S. Senate Subcommittee on Narcotics, Terrorism, and International Operations, Washington, D.C., of José I. Blandón, February 9–10, 1988, and Floyd Carlton Cáceres, February 10, 1988 (cited as Blandón and Carlton, respectively), with Blandón's testimony having three paginations for the morning session of February 9 (A-1), the afternoon session of February 9 (A-2), and the morning session of February 10 (B).

U.S. Senate, *Drugs, Law Enforcement and Foreign Policy: A Report of the Subcommittee on Narcotics, Terrorism and International Operations* (Washington, D.C., April 13, 1989) (cited as U.S. Senate, *Report*);

John Cummings and Ernest Volkman, "Snowblind," *Penthouse* magazine, July 1989, an account of U.S. drug-war blunders structured around the career of the trafficker-informant Barry Seal (cited as "Snow").

A series of articles on General Manuel Noriega published by Seymour M. Hersh in the *New York Times* in June 1986 (cited as Hersh).

Stephen Emerson, *Secret Warriors* (New York, 1988), a look at recent U.S. snoopery in Central America.

David B. Tinnin with Dag Christensen, *The Hit Team* (New York, 1977), which relates a botched operation by an Israeli death squad.

Andrew Cockburn, "A Friend in Need," *Independent* (London), March 19, 1988, a two-page masterpiece of compression detailing many of Noriega's dirty tricks.

Israeli Foreign Affairs: An Independent Monthly Research Report on Israel's Diplomatic and Military Activities World Wide, ISSN 0883-9832, written and published in Sacramento, California, by an indefatigable woman named Jane Hunter, whose quest, it seems, is to restrain the government of Israel from dissipating the spiritual patrimony painfully stored up over two millennia by the Jewish people (cited as *IFA*).

Connie Bruck, "Nabbing Noriega, Letting Him Escape," *Miami Review,* July 12, 1988, a marvelous compilation of Reagan administration blunders by the author of *The Predators' Ball.*

Guy Gugliotta and Jeff Leen, *Kings of Cocaine* (New York, 1989), a very serious and useful account of the rise of the Medellín drug cartel by two *Miami Herald* reporters who, at some personal risk, were the first to expose the cartel's iniquity.

P. 272 The quoted phrase is spoken by Iago (*Othello,* act 1, scene 1, line 62).

P. 273 For Néstor Sánchez's rush trip to Panama, see Jefferson Morley, "The Oddest Couple," *Nation,* April 2, 1988, 450. Noriega's CIA contacts and the allegation that Néstor Sánchez was his business partner appear in Blandón (A-1), 120.

P. 274 The story of Noriega's retreat, or "honey trap," was told to R. M. Koster by Curtin Winsor, Jr., U.S. ambassador to Costa Rica during 1983–84, in Winsor's office in Washington, D.C., in September 1989.

Pp. 274–75 Noriega's CIA expulsion and reinstatement is explained in Stephen Engleberg, "Bush Is Disputed on U.S.–Noriega Tie," *New York Times,* October 2, 1988. Particulars on some of the classified material supplied Noriega by the CIA, mainly background on members of Congress and their aides, appear in Blandón

(A-2), 4. Guillermo Sánchez obtained a portion of the DeFeo report in Miami in June 1989.

P. 275 A précis of Néstor Sánchez's testimony is available in U.S. Senate, *Report,* 239.

P. 277 Kirkpatrick attempted to justify her unjustifiable distinction with the following sophistry: totalitarian (i.e., communist) dictatorships are irreversible, thus worse for those they enslave than authoritarian (i.e., military) dictatorships. As of August 1989, Poland had a noncommunist government, and in some important respects citizens of the Soviet Union enjoyed a greater measure of freedom and dignity than did those of Panama. Seal's earnings are reported in "Snow," 66.

P. 277 The sudden and sickening discovery was mentioned to R. M. Koster by a senior American intelligence professional in March 1988 and is reported by Ambassador John McNeill in his *War and Peace in Central America* (New York, 1989), 284. As for the pooling of intelligence by U.S. and Panamanian agencies, our source was Jack Vaughn, whom McNeil, whose work appeared after our chapter was written, corroborates.

P. 278 For army intelligence and Noriega, see Emerson, *Secret Warriors,* 110–12. The quoted passage regarding the manuals is from Hersh, June 12, 1989.

P. 279 The description of Harari is from Tinnin, *Hit Team,* 67.

P. 279 For Harari as a general, see Cockburn, "Friend"; for his supposed retirement from Mossad, Juan O. Tamayo, "Noriega Supported by Ex-spy," *Miami Herald,* January 19, 1988.

P. 280 Harari's connections with Torrijos are mentioned in *IFA,* February 1988, 5; the end-user certificates, in *IFA,* April 1988.

P. 280 The "my mentor" quotation is reported in David Gardner, "How Israelis Act as Surrogates for US in Central America," *Financial Times,* November 27, 1986.

P. 281 The eavesdropping equipment and the state visit are mentioned in "Israeli Is Power behind Noriega," *New York Post,* July 11, 1988, 1. The control tower is reported by Tamayo in the *Miami Herald,* January 19, 1988; the bodyguard, in Cockburn, "Friend."

P. 281 ISREX is mentioned in *IFA,* May, 1987, 7; and IFMA, in *IFA,* October 1988, 7. The allegation of Harari's extortion appears in Juan O. Tamayo, "Panama's Ambassador to Israel Accuses Noriega Ally of Extortion," *Miami Herald,* April 25, 1988. Our source for Harari at home in Israel is Roberto Eisenmann.

P. 281 U.S. requests for Israel to get Harari out of Panama began early in 1988. A February 1988 request in this vein by Senator Alfonse D'Amato (Republican of New York) was backed up by Morris Abram, chairman of the Conference of Presidents of Major Jewish Organizations, according to the *Washington Post,* February 11, 1988, as reported in *IFA,* March 1988, 5.

P. 282 The help Noriega gave Ecuador's rulers with regard to Buccaram and Alfaro Vive is mentioned in Blandón (B), 63ff.

P. 284 The Torres-Arias affair is in U.S. Senate, *Report,* 197ff.

P. 284 Manuel Piñeiro is mentioned in Blandón (A-1), 69.

P. 285 Noriega's relations with Millán are described in U.S. Senate, *Report,* 216–19, 314–15.

P. 286 Lehder's solution to the transport problem is described in Gugliotta and Leen, *Kings,* and in "Snow."

P. 286 The "piggy-backing" scheme is described in Gugliotta and Leen, *Kings,* 78–79; the communications electronics, ibid., 83.

P. 287 For the formation of MAS, see ibid., 90. For the cited passage, see ibid., 92.

P. 287 For the cartel's consolidation, see ibid., 94. How Noriega helped the cartel is described in "Snow," in Blandón, and in U.S. Senate, *Report.*

P. 288 The material on Noriega's bargaining style and Escobar's comment is from Carlton, 88. The pilots who collaborated with Noriega in the arms and drug traffics are mentioned in Blandón and in Carlton.

P. 290 For the falling-out between Noriega and Rodríguez, see Blandón (A-1), 79ff.

P. 291 For Quiel's double duties, see ibid., 31, 107.

P. 291 The first quotation is from the Miami indictment (Number 88-0079, U.S. District Court for the Southern District of Florida, February 4, 1988), 1. Lawn's statement is from U.S. Senate, *Report,* 248–49.

P. 292 Audemar's being handed over is mentioned in Blandón (A-1), 103; for the circumstances of Millán's arrest, see U.S. Senate, *Report,* appendix.

P. 293 The quotation is from "Snow." The matter of the cartel's $10 million contribution is from Millán's Senate testimony, as reported in (among other places) the *Village Voice,* October 11, 1988.

P. 295 For Mossad's warning to Noriega, see Blandón (A-1), 57.

P. 298 For Millán's payments, see U.S. Senate, *Report,* 314ff.; for Noriega's assets, see Gilles Delafon and Rémi Favret, "La Fortune Qui Attend Noriega en France," *Le Journal du Dimanche,* May 21, 1989, and Panamanian sources who, as of November 1989, preferred not to have their names mentioned.

11. Noriega Tyrannus

Pp. 301ff. The authors witnessed the 1984 campaign at close range but find their memories very usefully refreshed by Raúl Arias de Para, *Asi Fue el Fraude* (Panama, 1986).

P. 311 The one flaw in Shakespeare's great text on tyranny is that he has Macbeth realize that he has given up honor and love for "curses, not loud, but deep" (act 5, scene 3, line 25). That honest realization is untyrantlike.

P. 312 Details of the massacre, according to a denunciation by Major Santiago Fundora of the Panamanian air force, are reported in "Masacre en Coiba," *Critica Libre,* January 30, 1990, 1.

P. 313 Kalish's testimony before the U.S. Senate was reported in James M. Dorsey, "Noriega 'Full-scale Co-conspirator,' Drug Trafficker Testifies," *Washington Times,* 1988.

P. 313 Colonel Seineldin's weirdities are reported in "La Bíblia de los Militares Rebeldes," *Expreso* (Buenos Aires), summer 1988, 46–48. Colonel Herrera talked with Guillermo Sánchez in Miami in June 1989, as did Papito Almanza.

P. 319 "Yira, Yira" is available in Carmencita Delgado de Rizo, *Canzionero* (Bogotá, 1987), 404. The translation is by R. M. Koster. For Malaparte's observation, see his *Tecnica del Colpo di Stato* (Milan, 1983), 247.

P. 321 Peck, *People of the Lie: The Hope for Healing Human Evil* (New York, 1985), 196.

12. The Chancre Bursts

P. 328 Díaz's spiritual crisis is reported in Andrés Oppenheimer, "Blowing the Lid," *Tropic* (Miami), August 13, 1989, 8.

P. 332 PDF riot control training stressed anger and adrenaline production. Persistent rumors have it that dobermans and paramilitaries were systematically given cocaine before operations. Many observers, including trained observers such as journalists and human rights workers, report dobermans and paramilitaries as having bloodshot eyes and dilated pupils. Finally, PDF personnel, like everyone else in Panama during June and July 1987, thought the regime was falling. All the above may account for their universally remarked paranoic fury.

For the experiences of Ricardo L., Katia P., and many others who endured inhumane treatment at the hands of the dictatorship, the authors are indebted to the Centro de Investigaciónes de Derechos Humanos y de Socorro Jurídico de Panamá, and to its coordinator, Otilia Tejeira de Koster. Mrs. Koster's work in the field of human rights, following in her mother's steps, has been recognized by such organizations as Human Rights Watch, Americas Watch, Amnesty International, Physicians for Human Rights, the Committee to Protect Journalists, and the Human Rights Committee of the Organization of American States. The work of the Centro figured prominently in the reports of these and other organizations concerning the sad state of human rights in Panama. Besides their debt of information, the authors are indebted to Mrs. Koster for introducing them to each other a long time ago. R. M. Koster, as may be imagined, is indebted to her for many other things, not least for the example of her serenity in the face of evil.

Coda

P. 357 The source for Nelson's story was the Centro de Investigaciones de Derechos Humanos y Socorro Jurídico de Panama.

P. 360 Incidents of PDF harassment of U.S. personnel are in Steve Ruttel, "Harassment Turns the Sweet Life Sour in the Canal Zone," *Tampa Tribune,* May 1, 1989, 1, and Elaine Sciolino, "Beating in Panama Protested by U.S.," *New York Times,* January 12, 1989, A8.

P. 361 The statistics of Panama's economic decline following U.S. imposition of economic sanctions are from Steven Erlanger, "U.S. Economic Warfare Brings Disaster to Panama," *New York Times,* June 9, 1988, A1.

P. 363 Data regarding inflation of the voting rolls was put out by the opposition alliance in the pamphlet *El Fraude de 1989 del Regimen Norieguista* (Panama City, May 3, 1989).

P. 367 For coverage of the May 1989 election, see James N. Baker et al., "A Test of Wills," *Newsweek,* May 22, 1989, 34–39.

P. 368 For material on the OAS meeting, which took place on May 17, 1989, see "Panama: OAS to the Rescue," *Central America Report,* May 19, 1989, 1–3.

Appendix A

The most authoritative and readable telling of the Panama Canal's story, from the French experience, through the route struggle, and on to construction, is David G. McCullough, *The Path between the Seas: The Creation of the Panama Canal, 1870–1914* (New York, 1977). It is the principal source for the story of Philippe Bunau-Varilla, the Hay–Bunau-Varilla Treaty, and how the Canal Zone came into existence. Gerstle Mack, *The Land Divided* (New York, 1944), and Dwight Carroll Miner, *The Fight for the Panama Route* (New York, 1940), were also useful, the former particularly on money matters regarding Bunau-Varilla's earth-moving firm, the latter for details of political intriguing in the United States. Gustave Anguizola, *Philippe Bunau-Varilla: The Man behind the Panama Canal* (Chicago, 1980), has scraps that others missed—e.g., Bunau-Varilla's threatening cable to the president of Colombia—and also a curious and touching charm, for though a Panamanian by birth, Anguizola fell head over heels in love with his subject. The work by Bunau-Varilla himself referred to in text is *Panama: The Creation, Destruction, and Resurrection* (New York, 1920). Texts of the Hay-Herrán and Hay–Bunau-Varilla treaties may be found in Diogenes A. Arosemena G., *Documentary and Diplomatic History of the Panama Canal* (Panama, 1961).

P. 383 The phrase "splendid little war" was coined by John Hay in a letter to Theodore Roosevelt while the latter was colonel of the Roughriders. The phrase about civilizing Filipinos with the Krag rifle echoes a soldiers' song called "Damn, Damn, Damn the Filipinos," to the tune of "Tramp, Tramp, Tramp the Boys Are Marching":

> *Underneath the starry flag,*
> *Civilize 'em with a Krag*
> *And return us to our own beloved homes.*

P. 385 "Grand and noble conception" is quoted in McCullough, *Path,* 382; "Leg cut off," in Anguizola, *Bunau-Varilla,* 310.

P. 385 Mack, *Land Divided,* 326, gives the income and profits of Bunau-Varilla's firm.

P. 388 Cromwell's language is characterized by Howard Copeland Hill, *Roosevelt and the Caribbean* (Chicago, 1927), 48, quoted in McCullough, *Path,* 334, where the *World* story is also reproduced (pp. 334–35). Bunau-Varilla's cable is mentioned in Anguizola, *Bunau-Varilla,* 223.

P. 389 McCullough's evaluation is from his *Path,* 337–38.

P. 389 Roosevelt's note to Hay is cited in Miner, *Fight,* 351.

P. 391 Roosevelt's remarks about Bunau-Varilla are from a letter to John Bigelow of January 6, 1904, in Elting E. Morison, ed., *The Letters of Theodore Roosevelt* (Cambridge, Mass., 1952), 3:689, quoted in McCullough, *Path,* 351.

P. 393 Root's statement is quoted in McCullough, *Path,* 383. Bunau-Varilla's words to Hay are from Bunau-Varilla, *Panama,* 358.

P. 394 Bunau-Varilla's characterization of Amador's reaction is quoted in Miner, *Fight,* 378.

GLOSSARY

arnulfista A follower or supporter of Dr. Arnulfo Arias (1899–1988), the often elected and often deposed president of Panama.

asentamiento A government-established peasant settlement.

barrio Neighborhood, often a poor or low-class one.

bazuco A cocaine confection, extremely intoxicating and cheap though highly habit forming, hence popular among the youthful poor.

Boinas Negras Literally, Black Berets; a paramilitary force of considerable repute but small effectiveness, organized by Dr. Arnulfo Arias during the early 1940s.

botella Literally, bottle; in slang, a government job where no work is required.

campesinado The peasantry.

campesino A peasant or poor farmer.

¡carajo! A vulgar interjection, sexual in connotation, of about the strength of "Screw it!"

caudillo An authoritarian political leader, often a populist; the Spanish equivalent of the German *Führer* and the Italian *duce.*

cayuco A dugout canoe of Indian design and manufacture.

corregimiento A political subdivision more or less equal to a county.

cuartel A military building or complex; the word usually translates into English as "barracks" or "headquarters," depending on context.

de mierda Shitty.

el pueblo The people.

gorila Literally, gorilla; used colloquially throughout Latin America as a derogatory term for military officers.

gringo A citizen of the United States; strongly pejorative in Mexico, less so in Panama.

guardia A guard; a soldier; a member of the Panamanian Guardia Nacional, the country's armed force, since September 1983 referred to as Las Fuerzas de Defense (Defense Forces).

guayabera The immensely practical, supremely comfortable, loosely tailored, four-pocket, flowing shirt which, in lieu of a jacket, constitutes acceptable dress in most Panamanian social situations.

guerrilla Literally, little war; idiomatically, informal or unconventional hostilities, what is referred to in English as "guerrilla warfare."

guerrillero One who takes part in a *guerrilla;* the person referred to in English as a "guerrilla."

hijo de puta Literally, whoreson; Spanish for "son of a bitch."

interiorano A person or thing from the interior of Panama—that is, from outside Panama City and Colón.

mestizo Literally, of mixed blood, or a person of mixed blood; the mix in question is almost always Amerindian and Iberian.

paila A large metal pot, the banging of which with a serving spoon or similar implement became an antidictatorship signal in the summer of 1987.

pañuelo Handkerchief: when waved, this became the prime antidictatorship emblem in the summer of 1987.

patria Native land; cognate to the French *patrie,* counterpart to the German *Vaterland,* literally "fatherland" but simultaneously maternal also from its feminine gender, hence to be protected as well as revered. Unamuno coined the word *matria.*

pito A car horn, the honking of which became an antidictatorship signal in Panama in the summer of 1987.

preventiva A large holding pen on the ground floor of La Modelo Prison in Panama City.

proceso Literally, process; in Panama in the time of the tyrants the word referred at once to the regime and to the populist program of reform it pretended to establish.

procurador An examining magistrate or prosecutor; *el procurador de la república* is the second-highest law enforcement officer in the country, after the minister of justice, and as such the chief prosecutor.

rabiblancos Literally, white tails; gray songbirds with white tail feathers native to the Isthmus of Panama; the Panamanian upper class, since its members are usually more or less of Caucasian extraction.

rancho A small, rustic dwelling, often with a thatch roof.

sala Living room.

santería An amalgam of Christianity and African voodoo with many adherents in Latin America, especially in Cuba, Santo Domingo, and the Caribbean in general.

sapo Literally, toad; slang for a spy or informer; counterpart in both meaning and tone to American English "rat."

Tío Sam Uncle Sam.

tolete A club, weighted and about two feet long and two inches in diameter, carried by police in Panama and elsewhere.